ST. MARY'S COLLEGE OF MARYLAND
ST. MARY'S CITY, MARYLAND

**IDAHO
OF YESTERDAY**

William H. Wallace, first governor of Idaho Territory, 1863. Photo taken by Charles D. Fredericks, New York City, 1863. This is the only known picture of Governor Wallace.

IDAHO OF YESTERDAY

by
Thomas Donaldson

INTRODUCTION BY
THOMAS B. DONALDSON

Illustrated by photographs

GREENWOOD PRESS, PUBLISHERS
WESTPORT, CONNECTICUT

Copyright 1941 by The Caxton Printers, Ltd., Caldwell, Ohio

Reprinted with the permission
of The Caxton Printers, Ltd.

First Greenwood Reprinting 1970

Library of Congress Catalogue Card Number 70-104218

SBN 8371-3335-1

Printed in the United States of America

THIS BOOK IS DEDICATED TO
CHRISTOPHER W. MOORE
BANKER AND CITIZEN OF BOISE CITY, IDAHO.

I have had the honor of having his friendship
for more than thirty years.

INTRODUCTION

THOMAS (Corwin) Donaldson was born in Columbus, Ohio, December 27, 1843, the son of Luther and Jane Ijams Donaldson. He was educated at local schools and at Capitol University and in 1867 was admitted to the Columbus bar after reading law with Gideon J. Castle, of Columbus. During the Civil War, Mr. Donaldson served with the 19th Ohio and 199th Pennsylvania volunteers.

In 1868 he married Miss Mary J. Gormley, of Columbus, and the following year, 1869, moved to Boise City, Idaho Territory, holding at the time the appointment of register of the Public Land Office. While in the territory, Mr. Donaldson held the following public positions: register of the Land Office, 1869 to 1875; superintendent of construction of the Idaho penitentiary, 1869 and 1870; clerk to the court of the third judicial district of the territory, 1871 to 1873, and clerk to the territory's supreme court. From 1873 to 1876 he was mineral commissioner for the U. S. Centennial commission and in 1876 was Centennial commissioner for Idaho. In 1876 he was also alternate delegate for Idaho in the Republican national convention. From 1876 to 1880 he represented Idaho on the Republican national committee and in 1880 held Col. George L. Shoup's proxy on the Republican national committee. Mr. Donaldson served, in 1885, as Idaho's alternate commissioner to the New Orleans Exposition and was a member of the Art jury of awards. He served on several national assay commissions, was general agent for the Smithsonian and National Museum, 1874 to 1888, and was one of the committee of six appointed by the Government to codify the land laws of the United States. Mr. Donaldson compiled, as a result of the commission's work, *The Public Domain* (1880-84).

In 1890 he was expert special Federal agent in charge

of making a census of North American Indians and was author of five special reports which were afterwards emasculated by authorities in Washington. In the seventies he located remains of the famous collection of Indian costumes, portraits, and equipment collected by George Catlin, famous American artist, traveler, and historian, and compiled for the National Museum *The George Catlin Indian Galley*, a monumental work. He was one of the closest friends of Walt Whitman, poet, and in 1896 wrote *Walt Whitman, the Man*, which ranks high as a tribute to the Good Gray Poet. My father's collection of North American Indian relics was presented to the University of Pennsylvania Museums, Philadelphia, Pa., in 1900, through generosity of the purchaser, John Wanamaker, merchant.

Mr. Donaldson was intimate with Idaho, her people, and her history and, as is told in the chapter of the territorial governors, was offered, but refused, the appointment to the gubernatorial chair of the territory by President R. B. Hayes. He left Idaho in 1875 and made his home in Philadelphia, Pa., where he resided until his death, which occurred November 18, 1898.

For valuable assistance accorded me in revising and completing my father's volume I desire to express my sincere thanks to the following gentlemen: George H. Himes, Esq., of Portland, Oregon; Hon. W. J. McConnell, of Moscow, Idaho; Hon. J. R. McBride, of Spokane; C. B. Bagley, Esq., W. F. Prosser, Esq., and Hon. John P. Hoyt, all of Seattle; Thomas M. Reed, Esq., of Olympia, Washington; Joseph Leggett, Esq., of San Francisco; and W. W. Wallace, of Washington, D. C. Especially thanks are due William A. Goulder, Esq., and C. W. Moore, Esq., of Boise City, Idaho, and Prof. Francis N. Thorpe, of Mt. Holly, New Jersey.

THOMAS B (LAINE) DONALDSON

Philadelphia, Pennsylvania
October, 1903

PREFACE

THIS book is not a history; it contains too much truth. It holds my personal observations of Idaho and pioneers and also much that was told me by reliable people. The historian who attempts to write a history of Idaho will find but little recorded prior to 1875. No history has been written, and I doubt if any Idaho history will ever be written, which will adequately protray the battle for civilization waged by her pioneers, the men and women. Born as she was, a creature of mining excitement, the wild rush of people to her hills and plains in the years of 1860 to 1865 brought to her much of the lawless element of all the states and territories in America. Although disorder, mixed with politics and rebellion, for a time ruled, yet law and order were the inevitable outcome, due above all to the exercise in an American way of the law of self-preservation and the love of home and homemaking. The flood tide in Idaho's territorial history was in 1864 and 1865. She had then within her borders 75,000 white people—miners, prospectors, businessmen, professional men, merchants, packers and freighters, a few ranchers, and a host of adventurers, gamblers, and murderers. The ebb tide was from 1867 to 1869 and due to many causes. Principally the causes were: the opening of the White Pine mines in Nevada, the completion of the railroad on the southern border, the great cost of machinery for quartz mining and the diminishing profit from placer mines, and the incoming Republican administration after President Andrew Johnson's term ended. After 1869 ranching was an industry in the territory. All farming and crop raising were furthered by irrigation. An excessive crop found no market because there was none to consume it, unless the army needed large supplies when an Indian campaign was on. Small markets and high prices prevailed. I heard many predictions while

I resided in Boise to the effect that before 1900 the territory would either be deserted or portioned and attached to adjoining states and territories. In fact, the latter was more than once attempted. In spite of many reverses and a foreboding outlook, brave men and women held on with tenacity and typical American courage until statehood was achieved in 1890.

In my day in Idaho I mixed with all classes. I moved among Indians, camped with packers, hunted with mountaineers, swapped yarns with miners and enjoyed their hospitality, cajoled preachers or churchmen of all denominations, traded with sharpers, sold law (my profession) to many unfortunates, touched elbows with officials and with all grades and conditions of men. I can honestly say that I emerged a better man for the experience. Idaho's battle for existence, like the battle fought in all countries wherein precious metals are mined, belongs to the past and can never come again. The men and women who fought her fight, dead though most of them are, will never be surpassed by any yet to come in this republic. No such conditions as those which surrounded the early settlers in the territory, social or otherwise, will surround another people; and the influence of environment and events produced better results from peculiar natural resources than Idaho's most sanguine partisans ever imagined. The first settlement, the laborious progress, and the final success are epochs. Natural barriers, roving hostile Indians, immense land areas void of transportation facilities—all these were stupendous obstacles. Idaho's battle was a battle royal and was won on its merits. The incessant struggle for civilization evolved and developed a strong line of men and women whose descendants have proved equal to stringent demands of life and duty.

It was my rare good fortune to have camped on the trail with the true old-timers. Glory enough for one life! I was honored by a handclasp from men whose strong manhood and indomitable pluck and earnest purpose builded a commonwealth in a desert. The grave holds many of them; their names may not all be on history's pages, but they deserve fame for the work they did.

I write the last pages of this book, and this preface, touched with emotions which I can not describe. Old friends and others look upon me and pass in review along the milestones of more than a quarter of a century. In the review march the strong and the weak, the brave and cowardly, the good and bad; but now, in the gratitude and affection of a man beyond the sunset peak, they come to me as men and women. There are no blurs, no dark spots on them. No memories are with me but those soft and sweet. Injuries are forgotten and scars so healed that not even the surface is marked. All are "old pards" and comrades of the time when manhood's colors were mentally nailed high upon the mountaintop of any possible effort and when the goal seemed easily within reach. I look back upon my years spent in Idaho, and my after association with her, as an education; and her people on the whole I recall as the best I ever knew. Her barren plains were gardens of delight, her mountain peaks were diamonds standing above a reluctant earth. Her men were the bravest, her women the best, and her children the sweetest that blessed life and made it holy and tender. My purpose is a tribute; the humor herein is for illustration; my effort is to be truthful and just.

THOMAS DONALDSON

Philadelphia, Pennsylvania
October 24, 1897

TABLE OF CONTENTS

	Page
INTRODUCTION	7
PREFACE	9

Chapter
- I. IDAHO'S POPULATION, HOME AND DAILY LIFE OF THE PEOPLE ___ 19
- II. STAGE-LINE OWNERS, TRAVEL AND DISCOMFORTS, FIRST RAILROADS AND TELEGRAPH ___ 72
- III. SOCIAL LIFE AND AMUSEMENTS AT THE CAPITAL ___ 102
- IV. NOTABLE CHARACTERS IN SOUTHERN IDAHO ___ 125
- V. VIGILANTES AND CRIMINALS ___ 162
- VI. COURTS, JUDGES, AND ATTORNEYS ___ 185
- VII. IDAHO'S TERRITORIAL GOVERNORS ___ 223
- VIII. IDAHO INDIANS ___ 276
- IX. A CHAPTER OF WESTERN MISCELLANY ___ 336
- X. HOW IDAHO RECEIVED ITS NAME ___ 368

LIST OF ILLUSTRATIONS

William H. Wallace, first governor of Idaho _____ *Frontispiece*

                                                                                 FACING PAGE

Main Street, Boise, Idaho, 1864 _____ 32

Boise, Idaho, 1866 _____ 33

Business establishments in Silver City, Idaho Territory _____ 38

Pinkney Lugenbeel, the army officer who established Fort Boise _____ 39

Idaho City, Idaho Territory _____ 60

The Rev. Toussaint Mesplie _____ 61

Old Overland Hotel, 1885 _____ 68

Central Hotel _____ 69

The Overland Stage _____ 72

Concord coach _____ 73

Old-time Rocky Mountain mail coach _____ 73

A. H. Boomer, representative of the Northwestern Stage Company _____ 76

George Ingram, stage driver for Ben Holladay _____ 77

Homes of prominent Boise City residents _____ 102

Homes of prominent Boise City residents _____ 102

Residence of General L. F. Cartee _____ 103

Boise City business establishments _____ 103

Handbill used by traveling entertainer _____ 114

Group dressed for festive occasion _____ 115

"Pony" Young, whose race track furnished pioneer Boiseans with many thrills _____ 120

Front page of leading newspaper of Idaho Territory _____ 126

Stage office, Silver City, Idaho Territory _____ 132

LIST OF ILLUSTRATIONS

FACING PAGE

Shoenbar Mill in the Owyhee mining district — 132

Poor Man Mine near Silver City, Idaho Territory — 133

Silver City, Idaho Territory — 133

Group of Idaho pioneers — 144

Idaho Territorial Penitentiary — 182

Milton Kelly — 196

William Bryon, early-day sheriff of Ada County — 212

A. W. Flournoy, famous Boise jurist — 213

Judge H. E. Prickett — 213

J. Waldo Huston — 213

Caleb Lyon, Idaho's second territorial governor — 232

Governor David Ballard — 242

Edward I. Curtis — 274

Marry Hallock Foote's cottage — 360

Christopher W. Moore — 361

Title page from *Laws of the Territory of Idaho* — 384

IDAHO
OF YESTERDAY

CHAPTER 1

IDAHO'S POPULATION, HOME AND DAILY LIFE OF THE PEOPLE

SCAN your map and find the mouth of the Columbia River, between the states of Oregon and Washington. Follow the river toward its headwaters until you reach a state line running north and south and at a distance about 250 miles from the Columbia's mouth. That state line is the eastern limit of Idaho, a territory created in 1863 and a state by erection in 1890. Neighboring Oregon became a state in 1859. Her lands and the territory of Washington, to the north, were familiar, in name at least, long prior to 1859. But Idaho—she not only lacked definition in 1859; she was unnamed until 1863, and she was practically unknown ten years after she was created a territory. When I speak of "yesterday with our pioneers," I do so because "yesterday" expresses the truth; because the tent towns on the frontier in 1870 are the cities of today; less than thirty years lapse. The average Eastern man of the present time knows continental Europe far better than he knows his interior Northwest. He knows something about Washington and Oregon because they are coast states; but as for the land area two hundred miles from tidewater and bounded on the north by Canada—of that he is sadly ignorant. In relative extent of time, it is nearer than yesterday when Idaho—an area almost twice as large as the state of New York—was in her stagecoach days. Not a railroad touched Idaho until 1874 when the Utah Northern built just one mile to Franklin from Utah.

When I first took residence in the territory, July, 1869, she was almost as untraveled and as unknown as ten years before when her lands were included in that vast and vague limit, "Eastern Washington." Army officers' reports and indefinite guides for immigrants, compiled and distributed by transportation lines, alone described her. National land surveys began there no earlier than 1865, and the area surveyed was small. People east of Salt Lake were willing to remain in ignorance of the territory because there were, in 1870, few if any inducements for settlers. The precious metal mines, the cause of the vast influx of prospectors and squatters after 1860, had failed to pan out well, and in the late sixties Idaho was on the decline.

To recall a timely incident, while I held the position of register of the Public Land Office of Boise, I made a business trip to Washington, D. C., and while there called upon Mr. Dallas, chief of the survey division of public lands. During our chat I soon ascertained that the surveyors had not done justice to at least one feature of Idaho. Upon looking at the survey maps, I was astounded to see that the wonderful Shoshone Falls had been omitted, or were unmarked. Mr. Dallas was at first much inclined to doubt the existence of falls of such grandeur as I described them; he could not reconcile himself to the belief that his subordinates had overlooked them. It took some persuasion on my part, but finally Mr. Dallas placed "Shoshone Falls" where I indicated, and the Government map of 1873 for the first time contained the marked location of the cataracts. The amusing part of this comes to me now, for Shoshone Falls are among the most famous in America.

The population of Idaho in 1869 was about 20,600. That total included: 5,600 Indians, 4,274 Chinamen, and 68 negroes. The white population of 10,618 steadily decreased until 1874. An average made in the census of 1870 gave 17 people to each square mile of territory. Idaho, Ada, and Owyhee counties contained in 1869 more than half of the entire white population. Boise City was the metropolis in all that the word comprehends.

A country situated as was Idaho, open to sudden invasion by fortune seekers who were prepared to leave just

IDAHO'S POPULATION

the minute fortune—or misfortune—overtook them, was in an unenviable position. Her population centered in small towns, and in any one of them the greatest variety of people could be seen. In the courtyard of the Overland Hotel I saw, the morning of my arrival in Boise, an Irishman, a Spaniard, a Frenchman, two Chinamen, a Canadian, an Englishman—and not an American. This was chance, of course, but it gave me a queer impression of the Northwest.

In main, the Idaho citizens were as orderly as were the citizens of any other frontier territory. Road agents and murderers were not as numerous as they were dangerous; the "scum" of the trade had been driven out and thoroughbreds only survived. All wage earners, the producers, merchants, tradesmen, miners, farmers—called ranchers—mechanics, and professional men were progressive and honest. Idaho people offered a commendable trait not found in more thickly populated lands. They were unsuspicious; they took men for what they were and not because of a long line of ancestors, believing no doubt in the old saying that when a man boasts ancestors, the best part of him is underground. Idaho people dispensed hospitalities, real and sterling hospitalities. I learned from the pioneers that it is not the thinking which makes men and women good or bad. It is the doing! Sect or belief has never since affected me in the slightest in forming my opinion of men and women and their virtues or failings.

IDAHO A TRI-TERRITORY

Owing to its immense area, lack of internal transportation lines, and the immense natural barriers, Idaho territory was divided into three distinct portions with separate interests. As she was primarily a mining country, the inhabitants were consequently restless; prospectors had to hunt new ground, for it never hunted them. Northern Idaho—north of a line drawn between Idaho City and Salmon City—was identified with Lewiston and paid tribute to Oregon and Washington. The completion of the Northern Pacific Railroad, crossing northern Idaho east and west, rather served to ally trade interests of that section with Oregon and Washington, instead of with southern Idaho. Eastern Idaho, from a line drawn north and south through Salmon City, paid tribute to both Montana and Utah because it was greatly influenced by the Mormon settlements at Franklin and Malad and those in the Cache Valley. Ogden and Salt Lake were nearer this section than was Boise, and supplies and goods mainly came from the East. Central Idaho, south of Salmon River and southwest from Salmon City, received its supplies mainly from California and paid tribute there. Kelton, Utah, the shipping point for south-central Idaho, began to receive many supplies from the East about 1872, and trade had both an east and west direction rather than, as formerly, a westward direction. South-central Idaho contained, in 1869, about three fourths of the white population of the country. The completion of the Oregon Short Line, in 1884, from Granger, Wyoming, on the Union Pacific, almost entirely changed the old trade of both eastern and south-central Idaho to Chicago, St. Louis, and the East. This railroad also enabled the individual cattle ranchers to market beef in Omaha and Chicago. Prior to this date, the capitalists or wealthy ranchers, bought up small bunches of cattle, placed them in immense herds, and drove them to the nearest shipping points: viz., Winnemucca, Nevada, or Kelton, Utah, for the San Francisco market; or to Ogden, Utah, for the Eastern market. A cattle drive was expensive not alone because herders and horses were scarce, but also because the scarcity of water made it hazardous to trail range-fattened stock through a desert.

NORTHERN IDAHO

In the few trips that I took to northern Idaho, I saw little that was interesting. The country was massively mountainous, with the exception of the district about Kootenai and Pend d'Oreille lakes. Singularly enough, there was a belt of mild temperature stretching across northern Idaho which enabled that region to grow small fruits in abundance. Altitude did this.

L. P. Brown was, in 1870, the most prominent man in northern Idaho. He kept a hotel at Mount Idaho and was several times in the territorial legislature. He was a tall, well-conditioned man, intelligent and companionable, an old-school Republican in politics.

Three other interesting men were Jason, Lawyer, and Timothy, leaders of the Nez Perce tribe and well known to the whites. Old Lawyer, tall and dignified, clad in broadcloth and an eternal silk top hat, always attended the opening of each term of the territorial district court at Lewiston. It was quite interesting to see Lawyer walk gravely in after court was opened, bow to the bar, and extend his right hand to the judge. Then the judge would politely wave Lawyer to a seat of prominence. Lawyer's entrance, and the courtesy always accorded him by the court, had good influence, or effect, among his tribesmen; they considered him a part of the ceremonies and a man of authority with the palefaces. This old Indian was a son of the Nez Perce with whom Lewis and Clark left their horses when they started toward the coast.

Because of the dissimilarity of interests in the natural divisions of Idaho, there were recurring attempts from 1863 to 1890 to annex the best portion of northern Idaho to the state of Washington, and several times the plan almost succeeded. The residents of northern Idaho talked not of their own state, but of Portland, Walla Walla, Vancouver, and Olympia, and seemed to imbibe much of the spirit and progress of these places. Seattle, Tacoma, and railroad cities outstripped Vancouver and Olympia and captured many of northern Idaho's first citizens.

North Idaho's scenery was superb though somewhat awesome; scenery alone isn't a good inducement for immigrants. People can not exist on scenery, so the apparently barren lands of southern Idaho caught the drift. Barren as the lands appeared, a slight touch of water made them blossom and yield like the arable lands of the East. As a matter of history, northern Idaho was explored long before its southern portion. Canadian trappers, woodsmen of the Northwest Company and the Hudson's Bay Company, were established in northern Idaho shortly after Lewis and Clark journeyed through there in 1804. The admission of Idaho to statehood effectually squelched the possibility of future changes in her boundaries.

NAVIGATING THE SNAKE RIVER

Practically all of central and southern Idaho was an unknown country as late as 1862. Snake River, or the Lewis fork of the Columbia, was then a subject for navigation possibilities. The Oregon Steam Navigation Company, operated by Captain J. C. Ainsworth, Sam Reed, and others, was a progressive corporation, and as early as 1860 ran steamboats to Lewiston, on the Clearwater. Snake River, from Wallula to its head, along Oregon's eastern boundary and across Idaho, nearly to Wyoming and Shoshone Lake, was known solely in spots, and these spots were where immigrants forded or ferried. The Oregon company was of the opinion that as a result of the Lugenbeel expedition of March, 1863, which built Fort Boise, immigration would follow. So this company decided to build a steamboat to run on Snake River east from Olds Ferry, where freight teams from Umatilla, on the Columbia, could have access to the steamer. The steamer would then ply eastward until opposite Boise City, and from there goods could be freighted again to the city and fort and interior. They felt certain that the Snake would be found navigable from opposite the head of Great Salt Lake and, if so, the company could then control all freight traffic from Salt Lake City and adjacent points. The scheme was well planned but it failed entirely to work out, because Snake River was navigable only from Olds Ferry to a point beyond the mouth of the Bruneau, a distance not exceeding two hundred miles. Bruneau River was a small tributary that ran northward through Owyhee County and entered the Snake near 43 degrees North, 116 degrees West.

At all events, the steamboat was a reality. She was built inland, the first steamer on the Snake River. Her machinery, fittings, and hardware were hauled overland from the Columbia, and the boat was joined at a place on the Snake above Mundays Ferry. The mechanics were imported from Oregon for the occasion. Work began upon her in the winter of 1865-66 and she was christened *Shoshone*. She was 120 feet long, 25 feet in beam, and was, of course, a stern-wheeler and of light draught. The lumber for her was cut in the Owyhee hills, and, if I'm not mistaken, A. H. Robie supplied it. She cost at least $80,000, an immense sum for a venture, and she never earned one cent! Her trial trip took place May 16, 1866, but here she experienced another difficulty. Even had she been able to navigate, there was an entire absence of fuel along the Snake River. The result was that from 1866 until April, 1870, the *Shoshone* lay tied up at an island below Mundays Ferry; Mundays was thirty miles below Boise. I saw her make steam in April, 1870, under Captain Miller, preparatory to chancing a run through the grand canyon of the Snake. The *Shoshone* started off bravely despite her years of waterlogging and reached The Dalles, Oregon, in five days. She was a sight! Her bow was crushed out of all semblance and her hull looked as if cannonballs had been shot through her, fore and aft and broadside. I saw her at The Dalles, where she lay in her battered condition, eliciting much sympathy. She was used several years on the upper Columbia and then was run on the Willamette by the Willamette Transportation Company. She was wrecked on the Columbia in November, 1874. I remember reading at the time that her cabin floated downstream and was rescued by a farmer, who used it for a chicken house. The end of the *Shoshone* was both tragic and prosaic.

THE RECURRENCE OF NAMES AND CUSTOMS

It was curious to see how the names of San Francisco music halls, theaters, hotels, gambling places, and saloons spread through frontier towns. In every mining camp or town there was a "Bella Union" saloon, a "What Cheer" hotel, or a "California" theater. Another favorite name for a saloon was "The Bank." Customs as well as names were imitated and perpetuated. A Boise custom was an imitation of "steamer day," which fell on Mondays as it did in Frisco, where most of the departing steamers left on Mondays. Prior to the completion of the transcontinental railroad, California merchants made it a rule to collect money early on Mondays so that remittances could be forwarded on the outgoing steamers. As late as 1872 it was the habit of Boise merchants to seek their debtors on Monday and ask them to "fork up." It may have been an excuse to demand payment or it may have arisen from allegiance to sacred customs of California. At any rate, when a creditor would spy his Boise victim and come abreast of him on the street, he would flaunt bills and cry, "Come, come, it's steamer day! Walk up to the purser's desk and settle!"

One of my old friends, honest though he was and a good

payer when cash was plentiful, was worried to death by his creditors on each steamer day. Finally, he made it a rule to disappear entirely on steamer day, and all that his pursuers saw was a sign on his office door, *"Gone to the ranch!"* Just where the "ranch" was, it took some time to ascertain. We finally located him in the southwestern portion of the town on a lot which he had rented to a pious and aged Methodist. The saintly churchman was engaged in chicken ranching. He was in the habit of purchasing, or hauling away, a dead horse, which he cut into tender morsels and fed to his chickens. I mention this because I recall the excitement in Boise when it was found that his birds—formerly prized and highly paid for because of their wonderful flavor—were so fed. The godly gentleman sold no more in Boise; Silver City purchased thereafter.

THE RESTLESS POPULATION

The restlessness of the citizens of Idaho was always in evidence; it was in their very conversation. The Isaac brothers, H. P. and J. C. (Josh), millers and merchants of high standing in Boise, both of whom I knew well and often chatted with, had lived at Walla Walla prior to going to Idaho. They were natives of Lewiston, Pennsylvania; both were intelligent men, decidedly above the average in education. At Boise they did a splendid business, but their entire aim in life was to get away from Idaho. Their conversation was constantly turning to the Shenandoah Valley, Virginia, and these men daydreamed and nightdreamed of the joy that was to come into their lives when, someday, they would pull stakes and build their homes in the Old Dominion. In fancy, they had already dug the foundations; Boise was but a stopping place. Neither brother had ever seen Virginia, but from reading of it they were wonderfully familiar with the entire state. Time after time did the Isaacs weave for me word pictures of the beauties of Virginia, of her climate and people—but it was a true air castle they builded. They moved to Walla Walla soon after I left Idaho and both brothers died there without ever having seen or dwelt in their fair Virginia. Chats with the Isaacs were typical of chats with scores of other "squatters" anxious to get rich quickly.

A rap on my door one morning in June, 1870, was followed by the thrusting inward of the shape of a healthy-looking man of fifty years. He was almost winded and seemed much out of mental composure.

"What is it?" I asked.

"You're Mr. Donaldson, register of the Land Office, aren't you?" he said. "Well, I want to change the date of my homestead filing. My name is Jennings. I've located a homestead over on Catherine Creek, Owyhee County. That's sixty miles southeast of Boise. I want to draw my filing and have it dated tomorrow, for I'm going to Arizona." I soon guessed that the man was Colonel Isaac Jennings, one of Idaho's pioneer Indian fighters and first settlers.

"What's the matter, Colonel Jennings?" I inquired. "What's your great hurry to reach Arizona?"

"Well," said he, irritably, "I'm off, that's all. I've rounded up my cattle, got pack animals in line, and I'll pull south ten minutes after I get back to Catherine Creek."

"Smallpox or fever down there?" I persisted.

"Naw!" snorted Jennings. "It's neighbors! Day before yesterday, a Piker with a bunch of cattle, a redhead wife, and a harem of towheaded kids moved in adjoining me. Can't stand neighbors and I won't. They're too damned close to be healthy!"

"Living next door, Colonel?" I asked.

"Certainly. Ain't more than nine miles from my house to theirs, and that's too intimate for me."

A MINING RUSH

The meaning of the phrase "transient population" struck me forcibly one day in 1870 when the Loon Creek "strike" was announced. Loon Creek was a point fifty miles northeast of Idaho City. An honest (?) miner had come into Boise one night with a ten-pound sack of nuggets which, he said, had been panned out on Loon Creek. "Ten dollars a day easy," said this honest miner, "plenty of ground, and they ain't two people out there." He further stated that he had entered Boise from the east and the news had not reached Idaho City. Well, in an hour's time Boise was bustle and confusion. New diggings at Loon Creek! Great news! Millions in it! Volunteers came forward who knew, so they said, every speck of dust out there. Before daylight came, one hundred men were riding or trailing northward.

At nine o'clock in the morning I heard a kick at my door and in walked one of the Idaho supreme bench judges. His appearance was quite startling. He wore black clothes, a tall silk hat, low shoes, a white kerchief about his neck, and odd gloves. His trousers had crept waveringly up to his knees, and firmly grasped in his right hand was a vicious-looking club. I gasped, "What's the matter?"

"Matter? Nothing!" said the judge. "Haven't you heard? Big strike at Loon Creek. Whole town's alive and everybody's riding, walking, or creeping. Barney Kelley came in last night with a ton of nuggets and brought the news. Get something and come along. I borrowed a horse and I'll be on the trail in ten minutes. I called to ask you to get for me a continuance of a couple of cases on the trial docket, district court. You'll do it? All right. Thanks! Can't wait! Lord knows I'm losing time." I accompanied him to the door, trying to smuggle my grins. "Look at the horse!" he said. I looked and then I grabbed the doorframe for support and yelled with laughter.

"Judge," I asked weakly, "do you think that horse will reach Loon Creek?"

"With the help of Providence and this club!" said the judge savagely. "Good-by. I'm off." He scrambled to his charger, a forlorn, spavined white horse the size of an elephant, and disappeared in a cloud of dust, belaboring the animal, coattails flying, harness flapping and jigging like mad.

Boise was deserted. "On to Loon Creek" was the slogan, and the town emptied itself. Not fivescore able-bodied men were left in town, but the stragglers soon returned, footsore and weary, with the news that the "boom" had busted. The diggings proved to be ordinary diggings for Chinamen, four dollars a day at most.

The only pay streak struck by the pilgrims was that made by a Frenchwoman who kept a restaurant at Idaho City. She was a mere child, a sylphlike thing beaming at 220 pounds. The boys had dubbed her "Gentle Annie." At the first cry of Loon Creek, Gentle Annie packed pots and kettles and followed the rush. She rode a horse and trailed two pack mules. She met a stage coming south, and at a narrow point in the trail the stage crowded her downhill and she fell and broke her arm. She sued the company and obtained damages to the amount of several thousand dollars. The defense was that Annie knew the diggings were no good and, finding that she was a loser, she persisted in obstructing the stage in midroad and her mount frightened and carried her off the trail. As in the Emma Cox case, the jury were with the little (?) girl, and Gentle Annie struck a rich pocket—but not on Loon Creek.

NEWSPAPERS

At that time we were far remote from the states and the coast, compared to their accessibility fifteen years later, when we got railroads and the telegraph. Packing and freighting was costly. We did, however, receive newspapers regularly, barring blizzards and muddy roads, but those from foreign points reached us about a week after issue. Newspapers played an important role in Idaho's home and public life; Hill and Reynolds, with the *Avalanche* and *Statesman* were powers, and so were the outside papers.

Our most popular journals were Mark M. Pomeroy's *Democrat*, the San Francisco *Chronicle* and *Examiner*, the Sacramento *News*, the Salt Lake *Tribune*, and the Oregon papers; the last-named circulated mostly through northern Idaho. As our population was transient, the settlers who were able to read naturally procured papers from home.

Mark M. Pomeroy, "Brick" Pomeroy, was fairly worshiped by a certain class in Idaho. Pomeroy published his sheet at Oshkosh, Wisconsin, and until 1870 his paper was a bible for ex-Rebels, Democrats, and Copperheads among us. Groups of ranchers and miners would cluster about the post office at mail time and anxiously query, "Hain't Brick Pomeroy's paper got in yit?" Ah, the zeal with which they followed and swallowed his word-fire! To a recipient perusing his paper in silence, less privileged bystanders would feverishly ask, "What's old Brick say this week? Do he give the Rads hell, as usual?" Copies of Brick's paper were reverentially filed and placed in conspicuous places in the home. Rumor had it that when an old Democrat was passing in his chips, out on Rattlesnake Creek, he made a last request of the doctor attending. "Doc," he implored, "mebbe I'll be cold when I goes. See that Brick Pomeroy's last issue is put in the box with me. Brick kin write things so red hot."

A neighbor of mine, the wife of a Mr. G., of Boise, was such an enthusiastic admirer of Pomeroy that she made a special trip to Oshkosh, Wisconsin, to bow at his feet. On her return, she succumbed to a stroke of paralysis. She was a good woman, raised by a Christian mother, and how she ever grew that Pomeroy bee in her bonnet, we could never understand. Probably the poison of Brick's paper had crept into her system and it needed but a personal interview to bring on fatal results.

THE BOISE FIRE DEPARTMENT

From 1869 to 1875 we had no fire engines of any kind in Boise. Our fire department was a volunteer bucket brigade of all available people. Men, women, and children stood in double lines and passed water buckets from stream, well, or ditch, and it was quite astonishing to see with what skill the buckets were passed. In mining towns, built as a rule in gulches or ravines, the greatest destroyer is water, especially in spring floods. Towns built like Boise on the open plain were subject to fire. In all Idaho, during the time I was resident, I am sure that there were fewer than one hundred brick buildings used for private dwellings. When structures were erected of brick, they were designed for opera houses, stores, or warehouses and I feel safe in saying that two hundred and fifty brick buildings were the total in the entire territory, for homes or for other purposes. Conflagrations were frequent and often overwhelming, but fire usually ravaged public places, not dwellings.

Boise fires resulted mostly because sheet-iron chimneys were in constant touch with the framework of buildings. Brick chimneys were costly; sheet iron, or the ordinary stovepipes, were more convenient. Oil lamps, exploding or upsetting, also caused much damage. Fires of incendiary origin were few and far between because the insurance rates were so high that few people insured. There was no reason for incendiarism when temptation did not exist! Almost all our buildings were built of one-inch hemlock or pine. After the interior had been lined with tar paper or muslin,

From an oil painting by Arm Hincelin, courtesy Henry L. Tucker, Boise.
Main street, Boise, Idaho, 1864.

Picture given to Mrs. M. A. Calder, Matron State Soldiers' Home, Boise, Idaho, by Col. Judson Spofford.
Boise, Idaho, 1866.

IDAHO'S POPULATION 33

ordinary wallpaper was applied. As you may imagine, the structures were tinderboxes awaiting a spark.

When an alarm of fire was yelled, occasionally aided by a town bell, the entire population hurried to the scene of trouble. Men and women grabbed convenient buckets, and a few procured axes and ropes. Once at the fire, a volunteer captain took charge; a water line, or bucket line, was drawn up, and the fun commenced. If the building were an ordinary frame structure, standing alone, the strong men of the gang at once lassoed it and with a "Heave, lads!" the entire structure was unceremoniously yanked out of contact with its neighbors. Out of harm's way, the fire burned itself out or was doused with water. At times, powder was used to separate the burning timbers. A few of the Idaho towns had annual fires that practically wiped out everything. Idaho City had a series of fires in 1865 and 1866 that were the worst the territory had known.

Judge Curtis told me an amusing incident of the frequent fires in early days at Idaho City. A Hebrew merchant had been repeatedly burned out and he finally camped in a tent on Mores Creek. He had saved his trade sign, an immense affair supported by two uprights, and this he placed before his tent. His entire stock of clothing, spread out on boards along the creek, was open to inspection by the citizens—and the weather. The Hebrew was zealously guarding a new importation of goods from Frisco and was on pins and needles for its safety. A mischievous boy ran past the tent one morning yelling "Fire!" The Hebrew turned livid, rushed out, placed his shoulder under a heavy board containing the best of his goods, and sagged and scrambled to high ground, calling at the top of his lungs, "Vere is dot fiah? Vere is idt?"

Fighting fire in our early days was largely a matter of strength, judgment, and courage. Today mechanisms do for us what hard work did then.

MONEY AND ITS FLUCTUATION

By a decision of the supreme court in 1868, a change designed to be beneficial had been made in the monetary system of the territory. In spite of it, greenbacks, or national currency, were unstable; they were apt to have varying values six days a week. In 1870 San Francisco fixed the price of money for Idaho, just as she fixed it for Oregon, Washington, Arizona, and Nevada. The fourth session of the Idaho legislature ordered that the revenue paid to officials should be in gold coin, or in currency 2 per cent above San Francisco quotations. The California papers reached us five days after publication, so greenbacks fluctuated often during a week.

Gold and silver were called "coin." Gold dust was also a legal tender and was receivable at $10 and $16 the ounce. The Owyhee dust, owing to its debasement with silver, was receivable at the lower price. Bullion was taken at par. Currency was taken at 80, 78, 76, or 75 cents on the dollar as against gold coin. After the passage of the Resumption Act in 1879, gold and silver reached par in Idaho. From 1863 to 1868, taxes were collectible only in gold coin or its equivalent. At the January, 1868, term, the case of *Misener & Lamkin* vs. *A. Haas*, tax collector and assessor of Ada County, was argued, and the supreme court sustained the contention of the plaintiffs that United States currency should be received in payment; gold coin was thus deprived of its status as sole legal tender for taxes.

Our bankers, merchants, hotelkeepers, and traders always kept at hand a pair of small brass balances, or scales, with necessary weights and brass or copper pans; the pans were shaped something like crumb trays. These balances were known as dust scales and were for weighing gold dust, the gleanings of placer mining. The scales usually rested upon a piece of carpet. I saw one carpet strip, not more than fifteen inches square, yield nearly one hundred dollars from dust which had fallen or been blown from the pans in the course of a year. Customers usually presented their dust in buckskin sacks six or eight inches long by two in diameter, with a drawstring at one end. These sacks were made in California and sold as a regular commodity. The buyer or weigher turned the dust into the pans of the scales and then blew smartly on the mass to weed out all valueless light stuff. At the same time, he juggled the pans so as to free all parts of the mass. Dishonest buyers were very apt to blow much harder than was warranted in order to scatter bits of gold into the waste heap and so cheat the seller. With the scales was a horseshoe magnet which was run through the dust to extract the iron, black sand, or minerals always allied with the dust. Black sand, under a microscope, showed iron, rubies, garnets, quartz, iridium, platinum, emeralds, and sometimes diamonds—all infinitesimal in size.

Chinamen were very ingenious in preparing nuggets for sale. They had a neat way of tossing bits of lead into a pan filled with amalgam; the amalgam coated the lead, under heat action, and a fair imitation of gold was soon presented. To protect themselves, buyers would have at hand a pair of heavy nippers, and each nugget handed them was assiduously clipped into halves and quarters. Once in a while, a clever scamp would slyly insert his long fingernails into a pile of dust that had been weighed and purchased and be the winner by a dollar or two.

In remote parts of Idaho, gold dust and amalgam were the sole mediums of exchange. Amalgam was a mixture of quicksilver and gold, formed when the miners ran "quick" through a pan of earth and gold to extract the fine gold grains lying among earth particles. To separate the gold from the quicksilver, the miner would place the mass in a pan and roast it over a slow fire. In a short time, the quicksilver would evaporate, leaving pure gold in the pan. When this was done on a large scale, and the quicksilver was needed, the fumes were led through an iron pipe covered with wet cloth and terminating in a bucket of water. The quicksilver vapor condensed on the cool pipe surface and dropped into the water in its original state. This is the principle of resolving amalgam, no matter how large the amount or the machinery employed.

Blowing, weighing, and buying dust was an art. The buyer could cheat in several ways, and the seller had a good chance to defraud the purchaser. Amalgam's color indicated its value; a white tinge indicated silver, which increased the bulk but decreased the value. A man with a good eye for color for various grades of dust fineness, was indeed a jewel. Sometime in 1869, metal teeth, or combs, on a ring, were brought into the territory. The teeth were tinted to represent the different finenesses of gold, and their value per pennyweight was indicated. They were a great help.

We had in circulation a few pieces of money, curious objects called "slugs." They were fifty-dollar gold pieces of California, hand-minted, swedged, and octagonal—no doubt imitations of the old Spanish pieces of eight. They were mostly retained by former Californians as mementos of early days and rapidly disappeared from circulation. They were the result of private coinage in California after the discovery of gold and before a mint was established there. Now and then a person would produce a five- or ten-dollar gold piece of Oregon mintage. Soon after gold was found in California, the Oregon legislature passed a law authorizing coinage of gold dust from California or coinage of any gold washed in Oregon. Some $38,000 of gold money was coined to pay the state troops for services in the Oregon Indian wars prior to 1860.

W. P. Thompson, an Englishman by birth and a queer old genius, was draughtsman in the office of L. F. Cartee, surveyor general of the territory. Mr. Thompson had resided for many years on the coast and had dropped his "pile" in copper at Copperopolis, California. I recall that he imported a particular brand of Scotch whisky into Idaho and brewed warm potions that sent our local connoisseurs into dreamland. In the fall of 1869, Thompson blossomed out as a financier, and his ingenuity deserves mention. We had no coin in the territory smaller than two bits, a quarter dollar. Thompson sent one hundred dollars to a friend in San Francisco—the "Bay" as we called it—and requested 1,000 ten-cent pieces. When they arrived, Mr. Thompson distributed them at the rate of two for a quarter, that is, as "bit" pieces. He consequently made $20 without the slightest difficulty. Loud and lasting were the curses of merchants against the unknown who had done the trick!

THE ASSAY OFFICE

Until 1871 Idaho had no assay office under the Government's control. Private assay offices melted gold into bars and shipped it to Frisco for coinage. All the mining towns of any size had small assay places but only in the larger towns were they reputable. The best known were the First National Bank, at Boise, the same bank's branch at Idaho City, and Blake's office at Silver City. C. W. Moore, of the First National Bank, was his own assayer. Quartz and ditch mine owners who were engaged in large operations melted their own gold and shipped it, thereby saving the usual assay charges. Wells, Fargo express handled the outgoing bullion save that carried by passengers.

A chance occurrence gave Boise a Government assay office. In 1864, Oregon's congressional representative secured an appropriation to build a mint at The Dalles for the purpose of coining the bullion product of Oregon, Washington, Montana, and Idaho, assuming of course that the flow would follow the building of the mint. Portland wanted the mint as badly as The Dalles wanted it, but neither place succeeded in obtaining it. The Union Pacific Railroad was built in the meantime, and the $100,000 appropriation act was revoked because it was patent that gold could easily be shipped by the Union Pacific either to San Francisco or to Philadelphia. Subsequently, an appropriation was secured at Washington for the building of an assay office at Boise, for the purpose of saving miners, or bullion producers, the freight charges to coinage centers outside the territory. In spite of the fact that the appropriation act was passed, the money was withheld, because George S. Boutwell, secretary of the Treasury Department, doubting that the Boise assay office could be built for the amount appropriated, $81,000, refused to sanction the operation. Judge John R. McBride, of Boise, was then in Washington and he called upon Mr. Boutwell, chatted about the needs of the territory for an assay office, and closed by offering to erect the building, as specified, for the sum of $81,000. Mr. Boutwell said that if Judge McBride would pledge himself personally to erect the office for not more than $81,000, he would appoint him treasury agent and superintendent of construction. The pledge was taken, and kept, and Idahoans may thank Judge McBride entirely for at least one useful creation in the territory.

WAGES AND PRICES

Wages, and their complement, prices, were high. Miners at Silver City received five dollars a day; their wages were controlled by a miners' union. Carpenters received four dollars, at least; brick layers, five and eight dollars; laboring men, three to five dollars; farm hands, fifty to sixty dollars a month and "found"; stage drivers sixty dollars a month and found; good clerks and bookkeepers, one hundred dollars a month; schoolteachers, male or female, seventy-five to one hundred dollars a month. The stone masons who worked for me while we built the Boise

Business establishments in Silver City, Idaho Territory.

Pinkney (*not* Purckney) Lugenbeel, the army officer who established Fort Boise and helped lay out the townsite of Boise on July 7, 1863.

penitentiary made from four to six dollars a day. When Major Lugenbeel built Fort Boise, in 1863, his stone masons were paid eight dollars a day in gold. House servants, mostly Chinamen, received forty dollars a month; if the servants were white, the wages were sixty dollars a month. Doctors charged from three to five dollars a visit, although many people paid them yearly sums for attendance.

There was, perhaps as a result of high wages and prices, an independence about our Idaho people such as I have never seen elsewhere. One man considered himself quite as good as another simply because the poorest man of Monday might be a millionaire on Tuesday through striking a pay streak. With scarcely ten minutes' warning, men could, and did, change their vocations. In the blink of an eye, churchmen, merchants, laborers, lawyers, would turn miners. The term "miner" included anything from a bishop to a gambler, a child of six to a man of eighty; it meant any person capable of handling a pick and shovel. The education of 90 per cent of miners begins after they have made a location, or staked a claim.

Food, with the exception of meat, was very dear. Vegetables sold by the pound; potatoes brought from one dollar and twenty cents to four dollars a short bushel, and apples were often eight dollars a bushel. California fruits were fifty cents a pound, with oranges at fifty cents each and lemons as high as a dollar in price. Flour was comparatively cheap, for mills were in operation in Boise, and wheat was grown within easy hauling distance. Green corn, pumpkins, and squash were plentiful, but watermelons and cantaloupes, now so plentiful in Idaho, were luxuries. Dry goods and groceries brought from the coast were quite expensive. Anything for building was costly, because most of it was imported. Bar iron was worth twenty-five cents a pound. In 1870 I paid twenty-seven dollars for a barrel of cement worth one tenth that in the states. Nails were twenty and twenty-five cents a pound. The absolute dearth of hardwood in the territory necessitated the importation of ax handles, spokes, and good furniture. Much of our furniture, necessarily, was homemade. I built the table, beds, and chairs in my own home. The one furniture shop in Boise, run by Captain Munson and one Slocum, contained the weirdest collection of furniture ever designed. The wood was common pine stained forty different colors, and the shapes and finish beggared description. We paid well for the necessities, but we were consoled when we compared our tariffs with the prices of 1862, when the mines about Florence, Idaho, were in full swing. The following modest prices were then asked and obtained: flour, one dollar a pound; butter, three dollars; coffee, two dollars; tea, two dollars and fifty cents; gum boots for miners, thirty dollars a pair; shovels, sixteen dollars each. As late as 1865, sugar brought fifty cents a pound and ordinary sirup four dollars a gallon. Ordinary ginghams, check, or striped goods ran as high as fifty dollars a yard in boom times.

While I write, I have at hand a bill from Falk's merchandise store for purchases made in 1870. The phrase, "terms: gold coin" leads into a few high-priced articles. One pair of trousers is slated at eleven dollars; I remember those trousers very distinctly. They were ordinary apparel worth about one third the price in the states. A box of candy is charged at two dollars and a box of apples at eight dollars and fifty cents. The apples were probably a bushel in measure.

It may be interesting to give an idea of local taxation. For the year ending May 1, 1871, I paid nine dollars and seven cents to the internal revenue collector for the privilege of practicing law. My personal property tax (I owned no real estate) was eighteen dollars and forty cents, levied upon a total assessment of four hundred and seventy-five dollars—two watches, seventy-five dollars; library, two hundred dollars, and furniture, two hundred dollars. The

IDAHO'S POPULATION 41

city tax on the same total for this year was two dollars and eighty-eight cents. The Ada County poll tax was five dollars in 1871.

Ready money was always able to command high interest rates. I have a note, dated 1873, that reminds me that I agreed to pay the First National Bank, of Boise, 2 per cent a month. It may have been that my collateral wasn't of the best. At all events, the rate was alarmingly near the usual pawnbroker's extortionate demands. The home I occupied in Boise was a one-story adobe house, about forty by twenty-five feet. The one room was partitioned so that my office adjoined the bedroom and the bedroom adjoined the kitchen. Everything was awesomely plain. The house cost us twenty-five dollars a month.

SPORTS AND GAMBLERS

Three things are requisite for mining—fuel, water, and pay dirt. Four things indicate prosperity in a mining town—Hebrews, gamblers, common women, and fleas. Hebrews, gamblers, and common women are accurate thermometers of ready money and prosperity. When Jews and gamblers pull stakes for another town, it is a safe guess that prosperity is also going.

Gambling was done openly and under license in Boise. In the early seventies we classed gamblers as gentlemen or loafers. The cheap sports, the "tin-horn" gamblers, were driven out by vigilantes prior to 1868. Our regular faro or poker player was considered as respectable as a reputable merchant, for they were honest in all things but their occupation; and the majority of them pursued straighter courses in gambling than our businessmen did in their lines under the guise of respectability. Many of our licensed gamblers moved in polite society and were very popular. Eastern people find it difficult to reconcile gambling with respectability, but when custom permits a thing—when, in fact, gambling takes the rank of an industry—the social crime disappears. The high class of our gamblers, generally designated "sports," seldom drank, never cheated at cards, never lied to or swore at man or woman. Their credit was the highest everywhere. Among our solid resident class, we claimed many keen and hungry sports who would have rebelled against the appellation "gambler" but who nevertheless took an occasional chance with the deck. They were "back-room" gamblers and played only for high stakes. I recall that several of our people refused to gamble with home talent, so they were obliged by traveling sports who journeyed to Boise once or twice a year from Salt Lake or the coast cities.

One day in the fall of 1872, I was, with Mr. A. P. Minear, brother-in-law of C. W. Moore, of Boise, en route by stage to Silver City. Another passenger was Vince Harbison, a traveling sport, of whom we saw much but knew little. Mr. Minear had with him two sacks, each containing $5,000 in gold, with which to pay his employees at Silver. Soon after we started on our trip, Mr. Minear confided to me the extent of his burden; he was plainly nervous. Harbison sat opposite us, and something in Minear's appearance must have attracted his attention, for he stared very hard at Minear for several minutes. Thereupon Minear slyly and nervously kicked me on the foot, intimating no doubt, "Watch him. He's getting ready to take my wad." This "eye contest" continued until we reached Snake River.

I am now disposed to think that Harbison considered Mr. Minear a lunatic. We drove on the ferryboat, manned by Perry Munday, and as we were thirsty, jumped down from the stage—Harbison first, I next, and Minear last. Just as Minear alighted, he whispered to me shakily, "Grab a coin sack and put it under your coat." I did as requested, and we stood at the rear of the boat while Harbison went forward. Minear placed his coin sack on the deck, knelt, and took a drink of water; he fairly gulped it, expecting no doubt to have his throat cut while prostrate. The minute Mr. Minear had quenched his thirst he jumped to his feet and scrambled into the stagecoach and sat beside me. Astonishing as it may seem, he had left his treasure bag where he knelt. His nervousness caused an entire mental lapse. Harbison started to mount the coach, but just as his foot touched the brake bar, he looked back and said, "Say, Minear, get out and pick up your coin sack. You left it on the deck."

I promised Mr. Minear that I wouldn't tell—and I haven't done so until now. What Harbison did was what others of his thoroughbred class would have done, and there is, and was, reason for the respect shown gamblers. The money could easily have been stolen, and Harbison could have been beyond the law's clutches in twelve hours.

Joel B. Oldham kept an immense gambling house and saloon on Main Street, Boise, in a building one story high and about a hundred feet long. The door stood wide open, and passers could note the extent of the bar and see the games of chance in full operation. My wife and I walked past one evening when the place was so crowded that tobacco fumes made it difficult to see past the door. Suddenly, oaths and shots rang out, and a fight was on! More shots came, and instantly the crowd in the saloon fell on their faces and crawled out the door. It was one of the most ludicrous sights I ever saw: miners, great hulking brutes, scrambled through the dust until protected by the adobe walls and then stood up and looked about for better cover. The banker had quickly grabbed all coin in sight and crawled out behind the first rush. When the confusion quieted, we looked in and saw the bartenders lying prostrate beside the huge timber that ran about the bar for a fortification. The shots had been fired by a drunken man who was intent on shooting at all the lights in the place.

He snuffed lamp after lamp but as he suddenly chanced to get near the door, one of the floor-huggers promptly knocked him down and disarmed him. He was carried out, the lamps were repaired, and the games went on as before. It wasn't cowardice that made the gamblers drop and crawl; it was a proper exposition of the law of self-preservation. They knew that when a drunken man shot at lamps, he was quite as likely to hit a man.

With all the intermingled good and bad in the early days of Idaho, the average of social life was good. Divorces were not frequent, although the marital tie was once in a while stretched by people who wanted to be free. Some of our men and women did not care to have their former marriage conditions touched upon. I have been in mining towns where the ten or twelve respectable women were far outnumbered by common women. But all women were given respect and consideration by Idaho men.

Men were not suffered to abuse common women any more than they were suffered to abuse respectable women; any and all acts of cruelty to females met with prompt retaliation, within or without the provisions of the law. Eastern people, raised in the midst of what are termed—often erroneously—moral surroundings, where external piety is in vogue at least one day in the week, cannot comprehend the gallantry, yes, the chivalry, with which men of the frontier, removed from the customs and restraint of older communities, treat women of all classes. Men thus situated see in every woman the image of perhaps a mother, a sister, or a betrothed; they see this image even in the worn features of those poor women who, as much sinned against as sinning, must at one time have been gentle and innocent. This reverence—and it existed in the largest and smallest town of the territory—was not an encouragement for vice: it was the form and name of the object which begot this veneration.

MASONIC ORDERS

I was not and have never been a Mason, but the great order had a strong foothold in Idaho. There were not many lodges but those established furnished much club life for our people and filled in with dances and entertainments many tedious hours in long winters. Many of my close friends were prominent in the order. General L. F. Cartee was a Mason of high standing, and I recall his well-timed efforts to rid the order of gamblers and saloonkeepers of bad character. His crusade made him very unpopular at first, but chiefly through his efforts the order was, in our vicinity, kept to a high standard. The majority of our early-day Masons, were, like General Cartee, worthy and exemplary citizens, but a clique of them in questionable occupations and dealings, and who were involved in vicious murders, used every obligation of the brotherhood to hinder and evade the process of law. From Thomas M. Reed, later grand secretary of the Grand Lodge of Masons in Washington, and formerly a representative from Nez Perce County in the Idaho legislature of 1864, I have received a few facts relating to the establishment of the lodges in Idaho.

Masonry was first introduced into Idaho on December 23, 1862, when a dispensation was granted William Kaufman, Frederick G. Schwatka, Frederick H. Simmons, and nine others to establish a lodge at Lewiston; of course, this was then in Washington, but Idaho's boundaries claimed it a few months afterward. November 26, 1863, the lodge was chartered, with twenty-one master Masons and one entered apprentice. Difficulties were met with, and some bitter dissension arose among the members, with the result that on December 1, 1865, the lodge surrendered its charter. A. Rossi, Robert Newell, David Isaacs, and Joseph Livingston were among the lodge members taken in after 1863.

The second lodge organized in the territory was chartered June 22, 1864. Dispensation had been granted July 7, 1863, by the Oregon Grand Lodge for this lodge at Bannock; Bannock afterward changed its name to Idaho City. The principal officers were J. A. Raymond, Henry Allen, and H. C. Hubble and there were forty-three master Masons in the lodge at the inauguration.

Pioneer lodge No. 12 was the third to be established, at Pioneerville. Dispensation was granted June 7, 1867, to L. N. Brown, S. B. Connelly, N. C. Roatman; the date of charter was September 21, 1867. S. B. Connelly, Michael McCormick, and John Merrill were the officers, ranking in the order named. The membership was sixteen master Masons and six apprentices. This lodge and three others, all of which had been chartered under Oregon jurisdiction, joined in the organization of the Grand Lodge of Idaho, December 16, 1867. In Ada County we had two lodges, Boise No. 2 and Shoshone No. 7. The two lodges were well organized and had strong influence in the territory.

The first Masonic funeral probably ever held in Idaho took place at Centerville, Boise County, in the winter of 1862-63. In a volume, *Reminiscences of an Old Timer*, by Colonel George Hunter, of Oregon, there is a most interesting description of a Masonic funeral at Centerville, when William Slade, an editor from Yreka, Siskiyou County, California, was buried. Colonel Hunter states that Slade's wife and the wife of a Dr. Owsley were the only respectable women in the town, but all the women in Centerville assisted in making clothes for the dead man and his family. Colonel Hunter and Dr. Owsley toured the saloons and stores, asking assistance for the burial of the dead Mason and for his family. Joel Oldham, brother of famous Sam Oldham, of California, was present. The description follows:

> There were eighty odd Brothers, dressed in woolen shirts and patched pants. After making the necessary examination, we "clothed" ourselves in white pocket handkerchiefs in lieu of the proper aprons and prepared

to bury Slade. We had prepared as good a coffin as could be gotten in such a place, and the family were dressed in appropriate mourning. Forming in a procession, we repaired to an adjacent mound and there gave our Brother the usual Masonic burial, with all rites, etc. Then we returned to our improvised hall, placed a table in the center of the room with gold scales, a blower and a purse on it, stating that all Brothers had been made aware of the destitute circumstances of the widow and orphans, and asked that all would perform their duty. We then formed in line and marched around the hall; as a Brother came up to the table he would select a weight and balance it with gold dust, put the dust in the purse and move on, giving place to another. Oldham marched immediately in front of me, and as he came to the table, he pulled out a purse of some hundreds of dollars; carefully untied it, then poured the contents into the blower, shook the purse and dropped it on the dust, turned and said to me as he shook my hand—the tears trickling off his long mustache, "Brother George, we can do something to atone for our cussedness, can't we?"

This settled it; I did not take time to untie my purse; my eyes being rather dim at the time; I suppose caused by a bad cold that I had contracted a short time before. I just dropped what I had and passed on, as many others did. Suffice it to say, that on all being weighed, we found after paying all the expenses, we had a purse that we presented to the widow of nearly three thousand dollars. This purse, Owsley, Oldham, and myself were delegated to carry to the widow, which we did, and upon our presenting it to her she utterly refused to take it as she said it was too much to accept from strangers. But after we had explained that if she did not take and use the money for herself and children we would be forced to appoint guardians for the children, who would take and care for them and that which was donated to and for them, their use and benefit; our arguments prevailed and she accepted the generous aid and within a few days started in the care of a Brother for her distant home and friends.

I have offered the above not only to illustrate the benevolent spirit of the pioneers, the generosity of men of early days irrespective of their calling, but because the funeral was historical, in that it was the first Masonic burial held in Idaho.

CHINAMEN

From 1869 to 1875 there were about four thousand Chinamen in the territory; the majority of them were in or near Ada County boundaries. Probably seventy-five Chinese women were residents, of whom the great majority were making a living by immoral ways; the distinction should be made, however, that they were for the convenience of their own countrymen. Idaho City had a cheap joss house where Chinese women burned incense sticks as freely as if they were spotless angels.

The Chinamen were mostly employed as miners, laundrymen, cooks, house servants, and gardeners. In mining, the Celestials always worked placers; they carefully washed claims which the white men had abandoned as paid out, and were satisfied with profits of two or three dollars a day. They worked more hours than any miners I ever saw and, poor souls, were often the victims of Christian (?) extortion and discriminations. Mr. John paid four dollars for his license to work a claim, but he was forced to pay this more than once during a year because white loafers, hard up for cash, would procure blank licenses, visit the diggings under the guise of license collectors, and poor John would be threatened and bullied until he handed over four dollars—perhaps for the fourth time in a year.

Resistance to white men was the last thing a Chinaman dared. They were the only laundrymen in the territory, in my time, and when a God-fearing white man chose to run up a bill and refused to pay, the Celestial was practically helpless. I never knew a case when a Chinaman in reputable business refused to pay a debt; I have known hundreds of cases when white men among us took every possible opportunity to cheat the Chinaman. John feared our Idaho courts; he preferred to be pillaged outside the halls of justice. In a suit to recover money—I speak from experience—not one Idaho justice of the peace or one juryman in a hundred would have given judgment in favor of a Chinaman! Poor John was the crushed worm, treated like a pirate!

The Chinese cook and house servant was our mainstay in the territory. They were worth every bit of the forty dollars a month paid them. Splendid cooks they were, ideal servants, neat and tidy, thoroughly reliable, and attending to children with fidelity and delicacy. Apparently ignoring everything that occurred in a home, they never peddled scandal and came and went quietly. When they departed, it was without the slightest show of affection or regret for their former employers. Our Chinese would not sleep in the house wherein they labored; they preferred the houses of their own people where they congregated, drank tea, smoked, and gambled. "Me go to my clousin's home," they would answer to our inquiry. Cousins must have been legion, for every pigtail was always "my clousin." For people who desired and could afford servants, the Chinese were Idaho's sole hope. Did you but send to the states, hire a girl, and pay her passage westward, she was very likely to marry within a few weeks after arriving; in many cases, the girls were married en route to an amorous miner or settler and failed to finish their journey. To my mind, the strongest recommendation for Chinese servants is the fact that they are not only intelligent but educated. I have yet to see one who is unable to read and write.

Truck gardens owned by Chinamen were plentiful in Boise Valley where, on account of the climatic conditions, warm days and nights, splendid yields were obtained. The altitude of Silver City and Idaho City made it impossible in these places to vie with the Boise truck gardens. John Chinamen grew his beans, melons, and pumpkins on upright racks and, by his marvelous skill and unwearied attention, obtained as much from one acre as a white man could from two. While light showed in the garden, they were ever at work, and their vegetables grew as sprightly as flowers in a conservatory. Their favorite carryalls were two baskets swung from a yoke, curving about the neck and balanced across the shoulders. I have seen Chinamen tramping across the plains with complete mining kits on their yokes, a weight of at least 150 pounds. They moved along with a shuffling gait so as to ease the carry and avoid tilting the baskets. Fifteen to twenty miles a day was their ordinary journey by foot; they were too poor to pay the stage rates. Their heavy straw hats were used for seats when they camped along the trail for the night.

When our noble red men caught John Chinaman, they made a swift and violent kill. John's long hair was indeed a prize. Among their own people the Chinese fought like devils incarnate, although, as I have said, they seldom resisted the whites. Long Malay knives were their favorite fighting weapons, and in early days it was no unusual sight to find, after trouble in Chinatown, a Chinaman pinned to the floor with a knife thrust through his entire body. Where they were numerous, they enforced their own laws and ruled with a rigid hand, and some of their punishments were fearful to think of. All our Idaho Chinamen belonged to one or another of seven companies which had headquarters in San Francisco. Our Chinese were mostly of the "See Up." A yearly fee was paid to the company, and in consideration of this an agent looked out for them if arrested, cared for them if ill, and gave them a Chinese burial; that is, transported their bones to China. Parties of exhumers toured once each year or two, dug up the Celestials' bones, packed them in small linen bags, and forwarded them, carefully labeled, to the agencies on the coast, from where they were shipped home. The companies were really insurance companies.

I saw a Chinaman show fight on one occasion in Boise. I was chatting with Peter Sonna at his store one night in 1871, when a fearful hubbub arose in a Chinese laundry opposite. We rushed over and found a white man in peril of his life. The man was a prominent stage agent who had run up with poor John a very fat laundry bill, nearly a hundred dollars. John had failed to deliver the last batch of laundry, and the white man traveled down to force John to hand it over. The next day was Sunday and the white man needed clean linen to attend divine service! Irate as he was, and the crowd of loafers applauding him, the Chinaman was cool and easy. "No monee, no clothes!" said John. The white man cut loose with profanity and made a show of violence. The laundryman and his colleagues promptly drew long knives, and in the twinkling of an eye the stage agent and his satellites were gone. I never saw men more scared.

In Boise there were a number of young blackguards, young Irish toughs, who amused themselves by unmercifully beating every lonely Chinaman found on the roads. I recall that one Sunday morning, while St. Michael's church bell was calling the people to worship, a youthful tough named Coffin almost killed a Chinaman in front of my door. The Celestial was minding his own business but he was set upon by Coffin and others, knocked down, cut, and kicked, and would no doubt have been brained by Coffin, who had a revolver in his hand, when Mrs. Donaldson heard the disturbance, ran out, and drove the crowd away. She hid the man in our woodshed until nightfall.

I remember a ludicrous thing that occurred when the first tricycle, or velocipede, came to Boise. The same valiant Coffin rode it along Main Street at full speed and ran directly through the level floor of a Chinese laundry. He went through with a yell, and disappeared through the back doors; both ends of the shop were open because of the heat. With screams of terror, the Chinamen jumped to the shelves along the walls and hung on like apes. After Coffin disappeared, they locked the doors, huddled together, and burned incense to ward off another attack of the strange foreign devil on wheels. In 1872 a velocipede was certainly a novelty in the Northwest. Barbarous treatment to Chinamen was very common in the entire frontier district, and the chief actors in the persecution were always hoodlum Irish, many of whom, escaping from persecution in Ireland, were the meanest exponents of it in America.

Idaho Chinamen were hard-working and peaceable and they contributed thousands of dollars a day to the material wealth of the territory by working claims abandoned by white men. They were human beasts of burden for the whites but they were good livers. Their imports gave millions a year to our national treasury in customs duties, and their freight bills, on tea and goods, swelled the financial statements of the railroads and express companies. When they had money, they lived high; when poor, they were modest but in no way approached the slovenliness of our cheap immigrants from European countries. At Boise and Silver City and Idaho City, several Chinamen attained prominence in mercantile affairs. Idaho City had a Celestial goldsmith who was most clever, especially in engraving and making finger rings.

In important law cases, it frequently happened that Chinamen would insist that Chinese witnesses be sworn in by the native method. Judge Lewis granted this concession one day in 1871 when sitting at Silver City; the case was that of murder, charged against a Chinaman. The interpreter, beginning his preparations to adminster oath, explained that a Chinaman devoutly believed that if he violated the truth under oath, he would meet with dire punishment, continual decapitation, in the other world. Rube Springer, sheriff of Owyhee County, brought into court a live chicken and a tin platter. The Chinese witness cut off the chicken's head, and the blood was let drop on the platter. The witness then took several squares of red paper and with a Chinese brush dipped in ink, wrote on the papers his oath to tell the truth. The bits of paper were then rolled into pellets, soaked in the chicken blood, sprinkled with incense, and burned with a taper. The smoke, slowly curling upward, was silently watched by the Celestials present. Judge Lewis, much interested, leaned across the bench and asked the interpreter, "What does that all mean?"

Said Hop Wo, in reply, "Well, Chinaman, he write out that he won't lie. The blood means danger if he do. When he burns papers, they go to heaven and take oath along. When Chinaman die, if he lie he find the oath showing he lie, in heaven. Then he hab mooch trouble. They chop, chop, chop he head off, allee time!"

"Well," smiled Judge Lewis, "does that make all Chinamen tell the truth, that way of placing them on oath?"

"Can't say, Mis'r Lewis," said Hop Wo gloomily. "Chinaman he allee samee Melican man! Sometimes he lie like hellee." On this occasion, the Chinamen were much annoyed because they learned that Sheriff Springer had taken the dead chicken home and eaten it for dinner.

THE MORMONS

When the Latter-day Saints had dissension within their own ranks, a body of them, followers of Joseph Morris, called "Morrisites," settled at Soda Springs, Idaho, in 1863. The following year, Oneida County was organized by cutting a strip from Alturas and Owyhee counties. The second settlement in Oneida County was made at Malad Valley, in 1864, by five Mormons, Benjamin, W. H., and Thomas Thomas, Henry Peck, and Lewis Gaulter. In 1870 the population of Oneida County was equally divided between Mormons and Gentiles. Bear Lake County, the little slice of southeast Idaho which directly adjoins Utah, organized in 1875, took its name from Bear Lake, which is half within Utah and half within Idaho. A body of Mormons under General C. C. Rich organized a Mormon settlement there when the country was within Utah's boundaries, and the county was known as Rich County. After the national survey of 1872, Rich County was divided so that Idaho obtained the larger part of it and Utah the smaller. General Rich, with Amasa M. Lyman, had successfully founded a Mormon colony near San Bernardino, California. The Mormons knew good agricultural ground when they saw it; southeast Idaho was beautiful as well as fertile, and a visit to Oneida and Bear Lake counties well repaid the visitor. Stock raising and agriculture were the main industries, and finer farms one would not ask to see. "One for all" was the Mormon rule. Co-operation was attempted in utopian rigidity.

In 1869, Brigham Young, for reasons best known to himself—although it was patent that he desired to drive Gentiles out of business and also desired to share personally in the mercantile pursuits of his own Saints—devised the "Zion's Cooperative Mercantile Institution," headed by himself as president, and assisted by Apostles Hooper, George A. Smith, George Q. Cannon, Horace Eldredge, William Jennings, and Henry W. Lawrence. Brigham planned to have one big store that would supply commodities on the co-operative plan, to branch stores in every ward in Salt Lake and the entire Mormon country. In the Bear Lake country roads were built, ditches dug, mills erected and worked, all on the co-operative plan. In 1876 the Idaho Mormons inaugurated the "Paris Co-Operative Institute," which was capitalized, and the Paris Mormons did a successful merchandise business. The capitalization was five dollars a share, and no man could own more than four hundred dollars worth of stock.

There seemed to be an article of Mormon faith which demanded the planting of trees. Gentile towns, for the first few years after their founding, are usually marked by environments of squalor and filth. The outskirts of the towns are indicated by heaps of refuse, giving the impression that the town isn't a town but an abode of campers. When the Mormons located they planted trees, not solely for beauty and shade, but also for windbreaks and future fuel use. Cottonwood, a hardy, quick-growing tree, seemed to be their favorite.

Brigham Young, in accordance with the administrative demands of the church, was the head of Zion. The Zion was divided into stakes; the Bear Lake Stake of Zion comprised all Bear Lake County, Idaho, all of Rich County, Utah, and part of Oneida County, Idaho. The stakes were subdivided into wards, over which presided bishops and assistants, or counselors, who had the right to demand help at any time from constituents. This vast system comprehended that the bishops and assistants should keep careful watch upon the individual members and teach them and counsel them in their homes. C. C. Rich was a Mormon bishop at Malad, and the main Mormon factor in Idaho. The Mormon question was ever a serious matter in Idaho, especially in the matter of suffrage. Politicians, under the belief that Brigham Young, chief of Zion, was actual dictator, were wont to pull wires so that Salt Lake would favor their ticket. Bishop Rich was naturally catered to on all occasions. Our Idaho Mormons were lawabiding, frugal, and good citizens. I feel safe in saying that polygamy among them was far in the minority. At any rate, it was quite astounding to hear Idaho men denounce polygamy, especially when many of the denouncing Gentiles were masses of personal corruption. I knew several women who had been burdened with two or three husbands, and who were never able to make clear why they were "detached," declaim loudly against the evils of polygamy! It was quite amusing.

The prejudice against the Saints was mostly occasioned among our people by the apparently unswerving obedience and loyalty to the Mormon church. The Gentiles considered this devotion to be anti-American and anti-

Republican. But there was another reason. The lands occupied by Mormons were attractively fertile, and thus arose a jealousy. It was thought that expulsion of Mormons would result in a nice "whack-up" of lands among Gentiles. Extending the national survey lines over their territory had brought Mormons and Gentiles in active competition, and perhaps greed rather than religious intolerance really lay at the foot of most Gentile opposition. Mormons, in their home life, were modest and conventional. Every social event began and ended with a dance. I was at Malad in the fall of 1874 and while there attended a Mormon reception. A bishop was in attendance and participated in everything. The people were dressed in homespun, and their countenances were those of contented and cheerful people. Young and old danced vigorously from eight until eleven o'clock in the evening. Refreshments for the occasion consisted of large sticks of candy and a three-gallon bucket filled with whisky, from which the dancers drank with a tin dipper. Not a person showed the slightest effect of drink; the whisky was produced at a local still and was known as "Valley Tan" and "Bust Head."

Prior to 1875 many schemes were proposed by public men for the suppression of polygamy in Idaho. Judge J. R. Lewis proposed that evidence of cohabitation with a female other than the common-law, or first-sealed, wife, should be considered adultery. That looked well in print, but when the operation of the law was considered, it was seen that many people not Mormons would have been seriously implicated. It made such a stringent, broad, and new rule of evidence in such matters that, while it did away with, or extended, the ordinary evidence as to adultery by giving a "sealed" wife a standing in court ("sealed" meant married in Mormon lore), it would have bastardized a large number of children by other Mormon wives. These children would then have become a public charge. J. H. Beadle, author of *Life in Utah*, a genial, clever newspaperman who edited a Corinne paper (probably the *Reporter*) wrote to me in 1876 upon the subject, and we had a voluminous correspondence. Soon afterward he printed a series of editorials against polygamy. The result was that a delegation of Mormons waited upon him, told him a few things, and then beat him so severely with clubs and pistol butts that in fear of death he soon left the territory.

The Mormon question in Idaho was settled by Congress during Governor Bunn's administration. The Edmunds Confiscation Act, the most rigorous and indefensible act of confiscation ever passed by a lawmaking power, settled the Mormon question in Arizona and Utah, as well as in Idaho.

CHURCHES AND CHURCH DIGNATARIES

Churches were not numerous in Idaho from 1869 to 1875. The loss of population retarded the establishing of many houses of worship, for though it is true that mining districts attract the clergy, small congregations seldom thrive. The death of boom times and the departure of many squatters put churches on the decline. The Catholic Church was in Idaho at a very early date; the first church established in central Idaho was Catholic. The first Protestant establishment was at Lapwai, founded by colleagues of Dr. Marcus Whitman, among the Nez Perce Indians. The Mormons were earliest in southeast Idaho, about the settlements of Malad and Franklin.

When a temporary or incipient diocese is formed, the Catholic Church frequently erects a space, or area, of territory into a vicariate apostolic, under a bishop. This temporary organization is usually transformed into a diocese when the population warrants it, and the diocese is then given the name of the county or chief city in which, or about which, it has been erected.

The Right Reverend Louis Lootens was the first vicar apostolic in Idaho; he was consecrated Bishop of Castabala,

August 9, 1868, but he had been assigned as vicar apostolic of Idaho on the creation of the vicariate, March 3, 1868. Bishop Lootens failed in health, and his resignation was accepted July 16, 1876. His successor for a time was the Right Reverend F. N. Blanchet, D.D., archbishop of Oregon.

When organized in 1868, and until 1875, the Idaho vicariate included within its boundaries that part of Montana west of the Rockies, including Deer Lodge and the St. Ignatius Mission, as well as work among the upper Pend d'Oreille Indians and others. In 1875 the church was supposed to have had about 1,000 white and 700 Indian communicants, eight priests, seven churches, and about twenty-five stations, or missions. The Indian communicants were composed of 300 Nez Perces and 400 Pend d'Oreilles. In 1869 the Catholics had seven churches in Idaho: St. Thomas', at Placerville; St. Dominic's, at Centerville; St. Joseph's, at Idaho City; a small chapel at Boise; St. Andrew's, at Silver City; Lawai (Lapwai) Mission Church, at Lapwai; and Coeur d'Alene Mission, at Coeur d'Alene. The eight priests were kept constantly on the move to administer to the missions and stations.

The men who did the most effective work for the Catholics were men who not only worked unceasingly but who also mixed with the people and won their respect. Father A. Z. Poulin, of Silver City, I knew quite well. At Idaho City he built the first Catholic church in Idaho proper. This church was dedicated by Father Toussaint Mesplie. Poulin was a homely, pockmarked man, a Frenchman by birth and enormously large—he weighed nearly three hundred pounds. Always wearing a large sombrero and carrying an immense cane, he was a noted figure in the territory. Poulin could rough it with the best of the boys. In camp he was a useful and generous liver, and his popularity was pronounced.

Father Toussaint Mesplie, also French by birth, I knew

well for several years. He was stationed at Idaho City when I first met him, but frequently he visited his church people at Boise, most of whom were soldiers at Fort Boise. Many were the delightful chats we had at my home. Mesplie had had a long and interesting career among the Indians in the service of the church. John G. Shea's *Catholic Missions Among the Indian Tribes of the United States* mentions Father Mesplie in connection with the Northwest coast Indians and those along the Columbia. The St. Anne mission was to have been founded in December, 1847, by the Reverend John B. Brouillet; it was destined to be among the Cayuse Indians near the present site of Pendleton, Oregon. An Indian outbreak occurred about this time, and the mission was not erected. Shea's book says: "A war ensued and the Cayuse Mission was deferred; but the Reverend Louis Rousseau and Toussaint Mesplie began another among the Waskosin (Wascoes) in June, 1848, which (in 1854) still exists."

In November, 1852, Father Mesplie was the priest in charge of a mission at The Dalles, Oregon. He was unable at that time to speak a word of English but was known for his hospitality and charity, especially toward distressed immigrants. In the latter part of 1852, a young Irishman named John Haligan came across the plains with an ox team to Oregon, and he resided with Father Mesplie. Haligan had been educated for the priesthood and about 1854 he was ordained. It was he who taught Father Mesplie to speak English.

Father Mesplie was a priest at Walla Walla in 1862, but in the fall of the same year he removed to Idaho City. At the time I first met him he was a man of forty-five years, short and stout, with keen black eyes and closely cropped hair. He was a genial little man, smart and cunning, and a general favorite. His life among the Indians had covered a dangerous period of twenty years; he kept accurate diaries of all he saw and heard. These diaries were in his study at Idaho City when, in 1871, a fire raged and the good priest's literary work of many years was consumed. He was heartbroken over the loss and said to me: "Zey is all gone, all burned up! My love's, my life's labor! All, all, all! But, oh, why?"

The policy of the Catholic Church is to keep its priests from too much contact with the people; a policy, probably to conceal from its constituents in the lower classes the amount of the human there is in a priest. Mesplie's conduct, though jovial, never permitted familiarity, and his dignity was never for a moment lowered despite the fact that he mixed with all classes.

He was in Washington in 1876, and while there I saw him often. On one occasion he performed the marriage ceremony for two of my friends, and at the reception the priest was the most entertaining man in the assembly. He became a general favorite at the capital, and Mrs. W. T. Sherman, a rigorous Catholic, obtained for him an appointment as chaplain in the regular army. I am under the impression that this was a special concession to Mrs. Sherman because I recall but one other Catholic chaplain in the army at that time. Whatever was the true reason, Father Mesplie at length fell from grace. He was accused of duplicating his pay accounts, but I trust that charges less severe than that were laid against him. He was court-martialed and dropped from the army in 1884. He went to France and remained away for years. Meanwhile Generals Sherman and Sheridan took up his case and recommended that he be reinstated and retired on half pay. The plucky priest would have none of this. In 1889 he returned to America, went to live at Grass Valley, California, and died there in 1894. He was a jolly little soul, appreciating and loving his fellow men. His mistake in the service was that he showed himself too human; I always felt that an injustice had been done him by his associates in the army.

The Catholics whom I knew in Idaho were like the

Idaho City, Idaho Territory.

The Rev. Toussaint Mesplie, who came to Boise in 1863 as the first Catholic priest of the valley.

average of the population—some good and some bad. In the professions, the Irish portion of them were especially bright. The turbulent characters among them were well held in check by the priests. An able priest is worth more than a company of militia in a turbulent community. But as a sect there was absolutely no discrimination against Catholics. Free life and pure mountain air were antidotes for bigotry!

An event to which we looked forward was the annual visit of Daniel Sylvester Tuttle, bishop of the Episcopal Church. Everyone who had ever heard him traveled miles to hear him speak again; those who had never heard him was as eager to meet him. He came unostentatiously, performed his duties with remarkable energy and thoroughness, and departed as quietly as he had come. He had a surprising hold upon our people but he obtained it apparently without effort; in the pulpit or in the home he was entirely devoid of sensationalism. He was a Connecticut man by birth; in 1868 he had been consecrated missionary bishop of Utah, Idaho, and Montana, in Trinity Church, New York. If I remember rightly, there were but three Episcopal churches in our territory in 1870: those at Boise, Silver City, and Idaho City. Possibly there was one at Lewiston.

My first meeting with Bishop Tuttle was in the autumn of 1869. I heard of his arrival in Boise and at once went to the home of his brother-in-law, the Rev. G. D. B. Miller, rector of St. Michael's. Mr. Miller was not there, so I walked toward his church. I met Miller, and he led me to the rear of the building and called to a man busily digging in a cellar—a cellar, evidently, for an addition to the church was to be made. The digger was a man of six feet in height and with whiskers of the style the English call "Piccadilly Weepers." A tam-o'-shanter hat lolled on his head. With shovel in hand, he leaped from the hole and smiled at me.

"Bishop Tuttle," said Mr. Miller, "this is Mr. Donaldson, who has come to pay his respects."

"Glad to meet you, Mr. Donaldson," smiled the bishop. It was a hearty handshake he gave me, and then he chatted briskly for fifteen minutes. I said good-by, and Bishop Tuttle jumped into the hole and commenced digging again. I formed my opinion of him right then and there and never had reason to change it. I reasoned that if a bishop of a silk-stocking church could, and was willing, to handle a shovel in a public place he would certainly be able to touch the hearts of his people; sincerity and common sense made him outrank any churchman in the territory.

William Flannigan, an Irish laborer, was working in the same cellar, and he said to me afterward, "Whin he come an the jab, Oi tought as he were a tinderfut jist arrove. But whin Oi seen him trow mud wid his shovel, Oi knowed he were an auld hand! Whin Oi were told he were a bishop, Oi trowed up me hands an' says Oi, 'What a waste fer to make a bishop out av a foine shoveler loike thot! He cud boss a hundred shovelers!' Yez kin git foine preachers ivery day in the wake, but foine shovelers is few an' far bechune. It's a great waste av flesh!"

I saw Bishop Tuttle at Salt Lake and heard him preach often. He almost converted me; he might have done so, but that I remembered how disgracefully Copperhead the Episcopal Church was in the North during the Rebellion. Bishop Tuttle was the best and most convincing pulpit preacher I have ever heard. One Sunday in 1871 at Boise I heard him receive a class into membership in St. Michael's, and he fairly lifted me into space above earth by his eloquence and affectionate reception of the applicants. He was by all odds the strangest pulpit preacher or bishop, from 1870 to 1895, within the Episcopal ranks.

It was early in the nineties, I believe, that he became bishop of St. Louis. His strength lay in his evident manhood and love of his fellow men. Humanity beamed from his free and honest countenance; he was dignified and courteous to every man, woman, and child with whom he came in contact. His credit embraced at least two thousand miles of desert, plains, and mountains, and with the stage drivers he was immensely popular. They knew him as the "Star Weno" man ("weno" being doggerel Spanish for "bueno"). The gamblers swore allegiance to him and always attended his services; the "hat" contained something substantial when the sports were present. With the gamblers he was the "Star Gospel Sharp." All his circuit required pioneer exertions as this was long before the railroads were built, and he did his work thoroughly because he combined the traits of businessman and churchman. These two traits are seldom combined in any but Methodist ministers, where at times we find an ability to swap horses and to trade in patent rights coupled with that of labors for the Lord.

The bishop of the Moravian Church was the Rev. Weaver, who came to Boise from Oregon on a visit. He had lived in Pennsylvania prior to 1870 and when he came to Boise he searched for me and presented a letter of introduction from friends in the East. Weaver was a man of forty-five years, mainly conspicuous because of his height. He was six feet and four inches. "Just the same height as Abraham Lincoln," he was wont to explain. Bony and gaunt in build, yet with striking, if not handsome, features, he indicated the strong mental forces within him. He was intelligent and kindly, and spoke English with a slight German accent. The first time he preached in Boise was in the Methodist church. Bishop Weaver walked unattended into the building, proceeded to the pulpit, dropped on his knees and prayed silently for five minutes, and then arose and faced the assembly. There was neither music nor singing. The bishop read a chapter from the Bible and then, without reference to notes, preached an eloquent and forceful sermon on "Faith and hope." At the conclusion he again knelt in prayer, and the services were concluded. Its strict seriousness and simplicity made it very impressive.

After service, Governor Ballard and I drove the bishop to the hot springs above Boise. Several ramshackle buildings made the place quite unsightly. I called the attention of the bishop to the extraordinary heat of the water and mentioned that there were scores of such warm springs in the territory, some hotter than the Boise springs. He asked some questions about the temperature, and I told him that John Gray, an old friend of ours, had had his leg parboiled by accidentally stepping into the water at the Idaho City springs. "Um-m!" said the bishop. We had brought a few fresh eggs with us. These we dropped into the water, and in five minutes they were boiled hard. The bishop was very much interested but withdrew hurriedly when we requested that he enter one of the bathhouses and feel the heat. However, he poked the tip of his nose in and then emerged instantly, streaming with perspiration.

"What do you think of it, Bishop Weaver?" we laughingly asked him.

"Think of it, my sons?" said he, from behind his handkerchief. "Think of it? P-h-e-w! I think that Hell is very near this place!"

As far as I was able to learn, the oldest church in Boise was St. Michael's Episcopal. Several people claimed that the First Baptist was entitled to priority. St. Michael's was, however, erected in September, 1866, by the Rev. St. Michael Fackler, and I feel sure that his church takes precedence. I have heard it stated that the Catholics built Boise's first church. It is true that they built at Idaho City, in 1863, the first church in the central part of the territory, and that their missions were established in the north before that date, but they were not the first builders in Boise.

Until 1870, when the Rev. Robert M. Gwinn, a Methodist, came to Boise and built a church, St. Michael's

Episcopal was our only church building. Even that solitary structure lacked a bell. To remedy the condition, we took up a subscription and purchased a bell. John Hailey "chalked" it over from Kelton. Its arrival was an important event. It was hung with ceremony in the belfry, and I recall vividly the feeling which came over us on Sunday morning, February 27, 1870, when we heard it chime through the town. It was the first church bell ever heard in Boise Valley. The Catholics finally built a church; most of the work was done by Catholic soldiers at Fort Boise. Father Mesplie, as I have said before, took charge.

We had no town bell in Boise, none that I recall, prior to the arrival of St. Michael's bell. When a man or woman died in Boise, the church bell or school bell was rung to indicate sex and age—one stroke, a male; two strokes, a female. After a pause, the bell was tolled once for each year of the dead person. I was standing on the Overland House porch one morning when the bell began to enumerate the years of a man who had died. Every sport in the vicinity at once made a bet on the age of the dead man! Ah, we had true sports in those days!

NORTHWEST LIARS AND THEIR LIES

Idaho claimed for her own a variegated and redolent assortment of fiction narrators who were marvels in their line! These worthies were in many instances first settlers of more than one territory who had begun a backward march from the Pacific eastward by way of Idaho. I have never seen or heard their equals! Old and young alike were finished and great on the tuneful lyre of fictitious description—almost equal, in fact, to the North American Indian when coaxed along by firewater and tobacco. Many of our Munchausens had served with the troops against the Indians in early wars; others had lived near the army posts and had, in various capacities, become familiar with men and officers.

An incident in the life of one of the pioneers completely captivated me. This man said that General Winfield Scott had spoken to him in Vancouver in the fifties, while he was there in the matter of the San Juan boundary claim. General W. S. Harvey was also there. The pioneer told me that General Harvey demanded, "Why in hell is whisky so hot in these parts?" and General Scott contributed, "Why is good whisky so scarce in these parts?" The yarn was told over and over again and never varied; not even to the description of the military clothing, habits, deportment, and gestures of the two distinguished soldiers.

Not one man of national importance was spared. Captain (General) Grant, Captain (General) Joe Hooker, Lieutenant (General) Sheridan, Captain (General) William T. Sherman, and many of the Army officers who had served on the coast prior to winning laurels in the East, were referred to in such places as, "Dear ole pard! In kourse I knowed him—knowed him better as any man on the coast." Why, from what I heard—had I believed it— Sheridan, Grant, and Sherman must have been intimate with every male resident of the Pacific Coast! The men who knew Grant and who had crossed on his boat at Knights Ferry and those who had been with Sheridan at The Dalles blockhouse, or who saw him capture Rogue River John, down in Oregon, seemed to be numbered by the thousands. The men who had coddled Joe Hooker and who had loaned him two bits for a drink at the "What Cheer House to Frisco, when he were dead busted and out of the army" numbered as many as crickets in an Idaho raid. Captain (General) Pickett and others who had gone into the Rebel ranks and and suffered defeat, were not so cordially remembered. General Rufus Ingalls, quartermaster general of the Army of the Potomac, was dubbed "Rufey." And it was: "Old Rufey? You bet we knowed him, at The Dalles and at Wancouver, whar he war post quartermaster."

When I first visited the Columbia River country, in 1870, in addition to its wonderful scenery, then unadvertised, the country was overrun by an unchoice assortment of half-breed Indians whose parentage was laid at the door of noted Army officers who had been on the coast. It was—outrageous as it seemed—a matter for cordial and common gossip; people with whom you were chatting were apt to break off an interesting conversation in order to call attention to a red man and perpetuate a libel.

A man was describing Mount Rainier to me one day and as we saw its natural beauty miles and miles before us, he waxed eloquent, employing a hyperbole something like this:

"Rainier's grand peak, sir! There it is! (sweeping gesture) Beautiful in its prodigious grandeur; sublime in restfulness. Superb in storm when lightning and fire wrestle for mastery (he said "m-a-as-tery") on its cloud-tipped summit. In winter, when snow-capped, 'tis refulgent on summit and it reaches upward, opes into the promised vision of that sweet by-and-by, where angel choristers (he beamed sweetly) sing lullabies. There will sin and misery find no foothold, and liars, vilifiers, and scandalizers of their fellow beings will be debarred the entrance. Ah, would that I——"

In a trice he had stopped, gasped for breath, and yelled to me, "Look! Quick! See that Indian!" I looked, a trifle startled, to where he pointed. On the ground squatted a bow-legged, miserable, half-breed Indian, feet bound in gunnysack, and enveloped by a stench that thwarted the mosquitoes. "What about him?" I asked.

"What about him?" said the orator fiercely. "Why, don't you know who he is? Why, he's a son of General Grant! No nonsense about it! Sure thing! He's a catch-colt! The thing occurred in the fifties, over in the Siskiyou range, north California. Straight as a die, it is."

I have heard and seen enough of so-called sons of Grant,

Sheridan, and others almost as prominent, to win for these men, had the children been theirs, the literal meaning of the title "fathers of their country." I would be ashamed not to acknowledge—after telling the above—that I could never see or conjure up any resemblance between these miserable, diseased, crippled Indians and our splendid generals. Foolish as the yarns were, they were heard everywhere.

On the porches of the Luna Hotel at Lewiston, the Eastman at Silver, and the Overland at Boise, I met quaint specimens of old-timers and from them heard much local history, a part of which was truth and a large part of which was not. These men had toured most of the Western states and territories and were encyclopedias of gossip relative to the men and women of the West. It was a singular thing that none of them—none that I heard—spun yarns in each other's presence. There was no sewing-circle chat, no free-for-all and may the best man win! If one patriarch started to turn reminiscent, the others quietly slunk away. Each had his separate stamping ground; no two were happy in the same camp. Whether they feared the truth or contradiction, I could not determine, but individuality and priority were supreme. It was king or nothing!

One of our Boise characters was a bewhiskered globe-trotter who always carried with him a large manuscript balance sheet. He was in the habit of drawing this sheet from his pocket, tenderly spreading it before his victim, methodically marking the debit and credit sides, with the debit side as large as it may have been years before, and then saying dramatically, "By God, read that—and reflect! See what I was worth! Now, don't you wonder, like me, where in hell it all went?" He had worried so long about this balance sheet that it had become a part of him and his apparel. His hard-luck story would be repeated time and time again, day after day, with precisely the same emphasis and the same dramatic readings.

Old Overland Hotel, 1885.

Central Hotel, located at corner of Idaho and 7th Streets, Boise City. J. H. Bush, proprietor.

IDAHO'S POPULATION

At Boise, one evening in 1874, I heard a party of men relating experiences. The chat—for they were traveling men just in from the stage—turned upon the origin of names. One of the bystanders, Thomas Davis, who owned much land along the river to the south of Boise, chipped in when one of the strangers mentioned Illinois and stated that he, Davis, had lived in Knox County, Illinois, and while there was an intimate of old General Knox, a celebrated character. It chanced that in Knox County, near the general's home, four children had been born at once to a poor family. General Knox offered the parents, a Mr. and Mrs. Phillips, one hundred dollars for the privilege of naming the "kids." The people were very poor and eagerly accepted the offer. Old Knox took a crowd of satellites down to the christening and told the family to trot out the four. The husband and wife, a child in each arm, swept into the room all smiles, and General Knox surveyed the squallers. Then, beginning with the one which yelled the most, he said soberly, "Your names shall be Awful, Wonderful, Circumstance, and Fact." And the four Phillips babies couldn't yell "Stop!" This sounds almost like the truth; perhaps I owe Tom Davis an apology for classifying this under the heading of "Northwest Lies."

Rumor had it that in the days of strikes and high prices at Florence, an embryo financier named Blevins hauled a wagonload of riffraff cats from the Willamette Valley, Oregon, appreciating the fact that miners wanted a reminder of home. He was quite right in his assumption; Dick Whittington had ne'er a more lucrative feline tour. Blevins trailed for Bannock, now Idaho City, and retailed the cats at ten dollars a head, payable in good dust. As you may imagine, an incident like that gave the patriarchs the chance of many seasons. Why, when retailing it, they went into minutest details of how pussy yowled or how one's eyes weren't mates. Said one of Boise's best:

"Ad Collins, he ups and buys a fourteen pounder, built

like a burro and with one eye out and half a tail. He fit and fit and near mauled three other toms wile Ad was pickin' him out. Says Ad to Blevins, 'Are he a tom?' Says Blevins to Ad, 'He's a him, all right!' Well, Ad totes it home, and the tom near chawed Ad's shirt off, pullin' to git out for exercise in the alkali dust. Dod swat me, Ad hadn't owned him ten days afore that tomcat give birth to a litter of rabbits, an' Ad made nigh onto three ounces sellin' them kittens."

GRASSHOPPERS AND CRICKETS

On three occasions while I was in Idaho we received visitations which were neither expected nor welcomed, despite the eagerness with which we looked forward to novelties. Grasshoppers and crickets! An Idaho farmer quailed at the names—and so did every man who owned a garden or truck patch. I recall that on August 2, 1869, a swarm of grasshoppers descended on Boise and entirely obscured the sun in their flight. They numbered by millions! Mile after mile of them came and passed, and every green thing in sight, save the hardy potato vine, succumbed to their ravages. Every garden in the path of their flight was seared as if by fire. Worst of all, they dropped eggs in their flight, which had every chance of hatching. Owners of gardens armed themselves for forcible resistance by taking poles or switches, building fires, and "fanning" the grasshoppers from the vines. Exhausting work it was, too, fanning all day. The miscreants not only covered fences and hid the earth from sight but they also invaded our homes, closets, and bed linen.

When crickets would drop in for a call, the damage was as great as by the former, but the sight was far more disgusting. Idaho crickets are two or three times as large as the ordinary Eastern cricket and are brown, black, and yellow in color. Unlike the grasshopper, they could not fly; their advance was a hopping, loping, crawling, a vast undulating field that wavered like the surface of a dank and oozy swamp. Just as surely as their winged neighbors, the crickets "got there all the same." They were so thick that water wheels along the irrigating ditches were clogged and stopped. A smooth rock surface, a river, or lack of green food were the only things to check their advance.

BOISE CLIMATE

As for climate, Boise had her extremes: I have seen the thermometer as far as 108° above and as low as 15° below zero. But the extremes were not insufferable. The best thing about Idaho climate is that its crisp, dry air makes a zero day quite bearable in comparison with the bone-chilling, penetrating cold of moist atmosphere in other localities. In looking over my old diaries and summing up from a home thermometer, I find that in 1871 the average temperature for January was about 27°; for July, about 76°. Boise's elevation is 2800 feet above sea level and, all things considered, no other portion of the territory surpasses her in comfortable climate. It was in Boise that the fact was made plain to me that altitude, not latitude, makes climate. The health of a community is always influenced by its climate, and Idaho usually offered a lower mortality rate than any of the territories. In the mortality census returns of 1870, Idaho's death rate was far below that of any state or territory in the Union. The influence of the warm currents in the Pacific was felt, with moderating effect, in the north. When the warm chinook winds wafted in from the Pacific, they were caught on the crags of the Bitterroot and Rocky mountains and deflected southward. Idaho's topography is a great factor in her climate.

CHAPTER 2

STAGE-LINE OWNERS—TRAVEL AND DISCOMFORTS—FIRST
RAILROADS AND TELEGRAPH

WHEN, by order of Congress, Isaac Ingalls Stevens made his first trip to survey a route from the headwaters of the Mississippi to the inlet of the Pacific, in his party was John Mullan, lieutenant of the 1st Artillery. Stevens, a man of remarkable personality and energy, became noted in the annals of the Northwest. Mullan, a much younger man, was a worthy follower, and the frontier has had few men more useful in her history and progress. Stevens aimed to aid commerce and provide against Indian attacks in the vast extent of new country by connecting the headwaters of the Mississippi and the navigable waters of the Columbia by means of a wagon road. In 1853-54 John Mullan and a few companions were detailed to survey, and did so, the route from Fort Benton across the Rocky Mountains to Coeur d'Alene. In February, 1855, when Stevens' survey was favorably reported, Congress appropriated thirty thousand dollars to construct a military road from the Missouri's great falls to Fort Walla Walla, a distance of seven hundred miles. John Mullan built the road, and it was always known as "Mullan's Road." In 1855 a town was built where the road crosses the Coeur d'Alene Mountains in Idaho, and the town was also named after Mullan.

John Mullan was born in Virginia. He was graduated from West Point in 1852. From 1853 to 1855 he was on the survey for the Northern Pacific Railroad. He served in the Florida Seminole Indian War and then, in 1857, was detailed to frontier duty. At Four Lakes and Spokane Plains he was conspicuous. Mullan was appointed captain

The Overland Stage.

Concord coach in which Thomas Donaldson rode from Salt Lake City to Desert Station.

Old-time Rocky Mountain mail coach.

of the 2nd Artillery in 1862; the following year he resigned from the army.

Captain Mullan was the first man who projected and ran a stage line carrying mails in Idaho. I knew him for many years in Idaho and elsewhere. In 1870 he was a man of forty years, short in stature, agreeable, and interesting in conversation. He practiced law in San Francisco after leaving Idaho and was also at Washington, D. C., representing several Western commonwealths as stage agent. I saw him frequently in Washington.

The Greathouse brothers, George and Henry, resided at Boise City in my time and were stage-line proprietors and mail carriers in central and southern Idaho. The brothers were in the banking business at Boise and were men of high character and cultivation. They were Kentuckians who had settled in California before going to Idaho and were connections of Lloyd Tevis, of Tevis & Hagin, the California bankers, and Mr. Tevis, with money and influence, was always at the support of the Greathouse brothers. Ben Holladay, who once owned the Overland Line, I knew intimately from 1869 until his death.

Hill Beachy was a man famous and respected on the Pacific Coast. I had the pleasure of knowing Mr. Beachy. In 1869 he was a thickset man of fifty years with brown hair and blue eyes, and much resembled General Grant in appearance. Beachy was a man of intense energy and when aroused was indomitable. For many years he ran a stage line from Boise to Winnemucca, Nevada, but gradually relinquished it until his brother-in-law, John Early, saved all that was left of the "Hill Beachy Line"—that was the short line from Boise to Silver City. Mr. Beachy became famous through his pursuit and capture of the murderers of Lloyd Magruder and party in 1863. His pursuit led him as far as California, and when he caught the criminals he took them back to Lewiston, where they were tried and executed. Beachy and Lloyd Magruder were close friends, and this lent interest to his efforts to catch the murderers. The expense of their capture, six thousand dollars and more, was borne by the Idaho territorial legislature. Mr. Beachy fell dead on a street in San Francisco in 1875. I remember him as one of the pioneers of Idaho who was of great use to her and her citizens.

John Hailey was the main stage-line proprietor in 1869 and held this title for several years. Hailey was then a man of thirty-eight years, a trifle above medium height, with brown hair, blue eyes, and a modest, unassuming manner. He was kindly and charitable and just to everyone— kind to everyone but John Hailey! He made money and as promptly gave it away. He had a host of friends and relatives whom he aided without stint. His purse was always open, his latchstring out. His house was Liberty Hall. His charity knew neither sect nor condition; it was as broad as his manhood. He hauled as many free passengers as those who paid. Hailey was charity personified and the most popular man in Idaho. The Idaho people elected him as a delegate to Congress in 1885.

Mr. Hailey was a Missourian by birth and, like Beachy, somewhat resembled General Grant in appearances. In manner and speech he was far above the main body of "Pikers," or Pike County, Missouri, people, who prevailed among us. Until his advent to politics he was reticent, but in public notice he soon became a fluent and capable orator. Mr. Hailey seldom became angry but when he did, something was bound to break! His favorite oath, delivered under great excitement, was "By Goney," accompanied by an amusing snap of his eyes. He was known to us as "Uncle John," and if Idaho had any better men I failed to find them. He finally retired to a ranch near Hailey, Idaho, a town named after him.

If I remember rightly, in 1870 Mr. Hailey was running the stage line from Kelton, Utah, to Umatilla, Oregon, on the Columbia River, a distance of about seven hundred miles. That same year the entire stage lines, or mail routes, of Idaho, went under the general control and management of the Northwestern Stage Company by reason of security, by bidding, the mail contracts from the Post Office Department at Washington. This great corporation was chiefly composed of Bradley Barlow, of St. Albans, Vermont; J. W. Parker, of Atchison, Kansas; a Mr. Sanderson, of Kansas City, Mo.; and C. C. Huntley, originally from Illinois.

Mr. Barlow was president of a bank at St. Albans which came into prominence during the Civil War when it was robbed of a vast sum by Rebels who swooped down from Canada. He was a pleasant and agreeable man and was once in Congress.

C. C. Huntley was the general manager. He was a large, handsome man, popular with the fair sex and completely wrapped up in himself and in pursuits of pleasure. He died comparatively young after a long battle against paralysis. While an invalid, he rode about Washington, D. C., in a phaeton accompanied by an attendant and he was a living example of the results of too much society life.

The Northwestern Stage Company continued to hold the mail contracts for many years. Mr. Hailey's livestock and coaches were bought at a nominal price, and then the company brought into the country, as managers, two remarkable men.

A. H. Boomer was the chief reliance man in the practical management of the entire stage lines. He was from Missouri, where he had been for many years in stage service and gained an experience which made him the embodiment of good judgment and energy. Whatever success the Northwestern Stage Company met in Idaho was entirely due to Mr. Boomer's good sense and ability. After the general company retired from the field, Mr. Boomer became a contractor for carrying the mails and ran many stage lines on his own responsibility and acquired wealth and station through his energy and integrity. He was an ordinary man in appearance but intelligent, agreeable, and about as taciturn as Beachy or Hailey. When aroused in coping with emergencies—which frequently arose in connection with the routine of the stage company—he was a mass of energy and prudence, and his level head overcame all obstacles. His wife was a delightful woman whom everyone admired.

The other remarkable man brought into the territory by the Northwestern Stage Company was William B. Morris, an antique specimen of human nature encased in a body which was just a trifle larger than his soul and conscience. He was a mass of prejudices and sinuous vindictiveness, and all questionable work of the company—there is always one man in a corporation who is paid to do the underhand work—was carefully and conscientiously attended to by Mr. Morris. The reason I mention him, although he deserves to be forgotten, is that his character should go on record for what it was and, in addition, the names of the decent men connected with that corporation should be made more brilliant by comparison with his name.

BIDDING FOR MAIL CONTRACTS

There were some queer incidents connected with the bidding of the contract to carry the mails into Idaho at the time the Northwestern Company was successful. There were several expectant, and several actual, bidders. C. W. and Silas Huntley, first cousins, were bidders—but under the name of William De Lacy. After the letting was made to De Lacy for the Idaho line, the Northwestern Stage Company became the actual contractors under De Lacy's bid; De Lacy was merely acting for the Huntleys. General De Lacy came to Boise City to start his newly acquired line, and with him came Boomer and Morris.

General De Lacy was an Irishman and had formerly resided in Brooklyn, New York. He had served with dis-

A. H. Boomer, quixotical representative of the Northwestern Stage Company in Boise.

George Ingram, stage driver for Ben Holladay in the early sixties.

tinction on the Union side in the Rebellion; in fact, he was a colonel of one of the Irish Brigade regiments of New York. He had a printing office in New York—I think it was on Ann Street—and I met him there in 1884 and took an opportunity to do him a favor in a business way. He was about fifty years of age when he came to Idaho, a quiet and dignified man. I traveled a great deal with him and remember that he had a splendid voice and sang ballads with good effect. After he left Idaho, in 1874, the Northwestern Company had full possession of his contracts for carrying the mails.

Concerning De Lacy's bid for the mail contracts, there was some speculation in Idaho. The bidder was under suspicion. The *Owyhee Avalanche* of February 28, 1874, made an interesting comment, which I here insert because it also gives the amount of the bids for carrying the mails:

> A Washington dispatch announces that Wm. De Lacy is awarded contracts for carrying mails, as follows: Dalles to Boise City, at $9,500; Boise City to Winnemucca, $13,500; Kelton to Dalles, $67,900; Boise City to Placerville, $33,000—this last is evidently a mistake. We'll wager our old boots that Mr. De Lacy will not carry a daily mail from Winnemucca to Boise City for $13,500 per year. There is some kind of chicanery mixed up with the entire arrangement—something rotten in Denmark, sure.

STAR ROUTE INCIDENTS

Laws passed by Congress later in the seventies very much abridged the early speculation in mail biddings at Washington. There was some "star route" mail service in Idaho, especially in the northern part. The game of the star routers was first to get a weekly line established from point to point. Next, a large number of names were taken from Ayer's almanac, Webster's dictionary, or directories of cities in remote parts of the Union and attached to petitions which were filed at the Post Office Department at

Washington. With local and Congressional influence the weekly service, previously established, was raised to three times a week or possibly daily. It was done by alleging a great incoming of settlers and the need of opening up new sections of the country. C. W. Huntley owned one of these star routes which ran from Helena, Montana, through Hell Gate, across northern Idaho to Lewiston, or perhaps to Walla Walla. Most glowing accounts of the richness of this section of the country had been filed in the office of the postmaster general, together with many certificates as to the great influx of immigrants, all advocating in strong terms the need of efficient mail service. Mr. Huntley enjoyed the modest revenue of $72,000 a year from this, and for some time he managed to live comfortably, but a business enemy, or competitor, whispered slyly in the ear of the postmaster general that there was no need of a mail route in this country. Colonel John H. Wickizer was chief inspector for the postal service at that time for Idaho, Utah, and Montana. The colonel was advised of the report and ordered to go by stage and inspect this vast and, to the government, costly, mail line. Colonel "Wick," as we knew him, was offered every courtesy by the Huntley stage lines, but the colonel promptly declined favors. He went over this "well-established and essential mail line," operated under a general clause in the appropriation law, by way of Helena, out at Walla Walla, and back to Boise, where he visited us several days before returning to his headquarters at Salt Lake. Colonel "Wick" found that the mail route ran through a wild expanse uninhabited save by the residents who were in old, established towns. The average cost of carrying letters over this route in a mail sack under the personal escort of one man and a plug horse was $27.00 each! As immigration had really begun in that region and it was not advisable to abolish the route, the colonel simply recommended that the appropriation be cut down one half. It was done.

PACK TRAINS

Trains of mules burdened with packsaddles were most frequently used for freighting in the early days, 1862 to 1865, on the narrow trails leading to the mining camps. With the advent of stage roads, about 1865, hauling wagons became the custom. James and William Francis had a pack train of fifty Mexican mules, in my time, and a pretty sight they were on the trail or when camped in the timber. In the vernacular "timber" meant the forest; it was designated timber because the trees were for use and not ornament. The usual load for a pack mule was 300 pounds. In addition to the stage roads, good roads were also built, after 1865, to the mining camps, and the wagon entirely supplanted the pack-mule trains. Freighting by wagon was a costly thing in early Idaho, to both the freighter and the owner of the teams. Twelve to twenty cents a pound was the tariff for freight from Winnemucca, Nevada, or Kelton, Utah, or Umatilla, Oregon, to Boise City. Return freight was taken cheaply, but then outgoing freight from points in Idaho did not average one pound to a thousand that came in. Loads of rich ore going to a smelter at Salt Lake or some other Eastern point constituted most of the outgoing freight. The only smelter in Idaho from 1869 to 1875 was at South Mountain, where the mines gave out in 1874.

Great rivalry existed among the freighters to get to the railroad, usually at Kelton, Utah, on the Central Pacific, early in the spring. Merchandise and freight for towns in Idaho was shipped by merchants so as to reach Kelton, Utah, or Winnemucca, Nevada, by the first of April. Horses and mules were used mainly; oxen were used in a few instances. In the fall or winter months, when the roads were usually impassable, the horses and mules were turned loose on the range to grub for themselves. In March a roundup was made, and the animals, mere skeletons, unless they had been given grain—which was scarce and expensive, were made ready for a trip to the railroad. The freighter who was the first to deliver goods at Boise or Silver City reaped a rich reward, for the people then procured from him new goods and the latest styles. The freighter worked his way laboriously, depending upon grass growing along the road to feed his stock. When he arrived with his wagon, it was a fine sight and of eager curiosity for the towns. The teams were sometimes ten or sixteen horses, or mules, attached to a lead wagon and driven by a single line. The driver bestrode the near wheel animal of the team. A huge wagon called a "trail" was hooked to the wagon drawn by the team. Ten to sixteen tons of freight could be handled this way in one trip. When the freighter unpacked, it was no uncommon sight to see scores of mice and perhaps a stray rat hop from the boxes and bundles.

THE STAGECOACHES

The stagecoaches used in Idaho from 1862 to 1875 were "mud" wagons and Concord coaches. The Concord coaches were "baits"; that is, they were advertisements! The Concord coaches were imposing affairs which held sixteen to eighteen people, counting both inside and outside. Swung on leather springs called "thorough braces," they rode as steadily as a ship. Fine horses were kept for them and when the passengers left main ports they were started off in a superb Concord. Once on the road away from the town or city, the passengers were unceremoniously hustled into a "mud" wagon and put through to their destination. One of these Concord coaches ran out of Corinne, Utah, to Franklin, Idaho, in 1873, and another was driven by John Early out of Boise and toward Silver City in 1869-73. The Concords were brought to the Pacific Coast by the Wells, Fargo Company and by Ben Holladay in the early sixties. They must have weighed three tons each and for this reason were unfit for rough staging. On pikes or well-kept hard roads they were the best vehicle on wheels. I used to see many of them at Columbus, Ohio, when I was a boy, on the Old National Road, which was before railroads were built from Washington to St. Louis. These coaches were built at Concord, New Hampshire, by the Abbott-Downing Company and the harness was made by Hill, of Concord. The mud wagons were also made by the same company. Mud wagons were compact, low, well-built vehicles swung on thorough braces and with substantial running gear. They were technically known as six- and nine-passenger coaches, but the six-passenger coach usually did duty for eight people and the nine-passenger coach accommodated twelve.

Along in 1869 many of the mud wagons came from Chicago, where they were made, I think, by Ten Eyck or Ten Broeck. They were in use on the plains but never gave the service nor rode as easily as did the Concord make. After 1869, all the coaches were equipped with the "Sarvin" wheel, an outgrowth of the transportation service of the Civil War. In the Sarvin wheel, a spoke could be taken out or inserted at pleasure without taking off the tire, and this wheel was also supplied with an iron hub. The felloe of the wheel could be expanded so as to hold the tire in place along with the tire bolts. The old-fashioned wagon wheel was a source of constant trouble, for the spokes worked loose in the wooden hub and and the tires dropped off through shrinkage in the wooden fellies, or, as we called them, felloes. We had another form of vehicle used when roads were bad or travel was light. They were four-seated affairs called "jerkies." We also had buckboards or even dead-axle wagons.

DISCOMFORTS OF TRAVEL

The amount of physical suffering consequent upon a long trip on a stagecoach can never be adequately described.

I have ridden continually for days and nights sitting upright with my knees jammed against the knees of another unfortunate and both of us suffering the agonies of the damned! Try to realize what it meant when you are told of the overland stage journey from St. Joseph, Missouri, to Sacramento, California! Twenty-four days and nights of ceaseless travel and the passengers unable to recline; nothing to do but maintain a sitting position. If a passenger was ill or tired and chose to lay over at a station, the chances were that the following coach would be crowded, and he might remain for days awaiting a coach with a vacant seat. Ten days was no unusual wait.

The coaches, rigged for two, four, or six horses, were built for hard usage and stood the wear and tear remarkably well. Curious accidents occurred. I was on a coach in December, 1874, ten miles south of Silver City on the way to Winnemucca when an axle broke off short at the wheel and the team bolted. Joe Tuttle was driving. (Tuttle was afterwards hanged in Arizona in the seventies and according to the statement made to me by my friend, G. W. Grayson, of Oakland, California, he was executed for a crime which he—Tuttle—never committed.) We inspected the break and found that continued knocking against the stones of the road had crystallized the axle in clear cubes. [Actually, a flaw in the steel when made.——T.B.D.]

In the severe winters at Silver City and Rocky Bar, I have seen the mail dragged out to the valley below, wrapped in the skin or hide of a beef, for roads were impassable. The mountain grade on the stage road from Boise to Silver City began at a point near Gardner's Station. I have crossed the Owyhee Mountains on a road beaten down on snow that was thirty feet deep in places. On the stage road of the mountains near Silver City you could see piles of young pines or poles which lay undisturbed during the summer months. When the snow began to fall, the stage managers would place these poles on end in the snow to serve as guides for the drivers, and along this pole-marked road the coaches passed. If the snow became deeper, the poles were raised.

The stages were not used during the heavy winter from ten miles north or southwest of Silver City. Passengers and the mails were transferred to sleighs, usually drawn by two horses. The horses used for the snow traffic were splendid beasts. Their good-weather shoes were removed so that in stumbling or falling the animals would not cut their legs. The beaten road, or grade, for sleighs or wagons over the snow was as hard as a floor, but one inch to the wrong side and horses and man would disappear in the soft snow. I have frequently seen a horse drop off the grade, and it was a circus to get the beast back to the surface! Every male passenger would get out, tug, pull, swear, and yell at the poor brute, which eventually scrambled to its feet. It was always amusing to see the patient air of submission of the fallen horse as he lay in the snow. He knew he would be helped back to safety and seldom made a move for himself. The legs of the animals were often badly swollen and cut from the snow service.

IDAHO SNOWSHOES (SKIS)

All through the Idaho mountains one could see, lying on the ground near the roads or trails, rough snowshoes made of split tamarack or pine logs. These shoes were about six feet long, half an inch thick, five or six inches wide and bent at one end and were split and tied on the end with strings or thongs. A man could make a pair in a very short time and invariably dropped them at the spot on the road where he had no further need of them. The next man who came along was entitled to their use as well. When I saw these made and used I recalled the pictures in books of beautiful bent-wood and skin-crossed snowshoes. Experience is a sad teacher! I never saw anything in the snowshoe line in Idaho fancier than these.

KELTON, UTAH, IN 1869

Kelton, Utah, was where we left the Central Pacific road and took the stage line for Boise or points farther northwest. My first view of Kelton was July 5, 1869, when our train pulled in there at seven o'clock in the evening. The town consisted of not more than a hundred people; the entire population lived in tents, and there was but one frame house, a hotel. All that remained of the great Overland stage road was this branch which ran from Kelton, via Boise City, and Baker City and La Grande, Oregon, to the Columbia River at Umatilla, Oregon. The distance to Umatilla was about seven hundred miles, and after that the journey was continued by water to Portland. From Kelton to Boise was three hundred miles of rough, wearisome riding. The equipment, horses, mules, wagons, and stages were mostly from old Wells, Fargo and Ben Holladay outfits. Ben Holladay bought the best animals that money could secure, and as late as 1879 I rode behind some horses which had formerly belonged to him and which were in active service despite eighteen or twenty years of wear and tear. Kelton died as a stage point when the Oregon Short Line Railroad was completed.

Upon our arrival at Kelton, the town was participating in the burial of a section boss named Smith, who had been killed three hours before by a train. There was no ice in the town, and Smith's burial, like every other interment, was within three hours of his death. In that short three hours, a few good-hearted people had stolen everything that belonged to the man, and there was nothing to identify him or to tell from where he had come; his papers, money, and clothes had been purloined. As we left the train and were in search of food, I recall that our party stopped before a tent and willingly paid a woman $2.50 in gold for three cups of tea. The woman, to make change for us, pulled a wooden box from beneath a bed and we saw that the box was well filled with gold and silver. The recent completion of the railroad made flush times in Kelton. While we drank the tea, we heard the woman say to a Chinaman out in the kitchen, "Hurry, you son of a gun or I'll kick the stuffin' out of you! I want to git out of this rotten country!" Next day she had folded her tent like an Arab and departed.

The frame hotel at Kelton was the Kelton House. When a traveler left a warm, comfortable train at Kelton and was forced to stay at the only hotel in Kelton—well, no description could ever do justice to the complete change from clean environment and comforts. To say that the Kelton House was the dirtiest house in the West, and its vermin the largest and the best fed, might offer too much opportunity for comparison. The people in charge were kind and attentive, but no artist could have painted dirt so realistically as that which was daubed on everything. The stage from Umatilla, via Boise, started at daylight, so that, arriving at Kelton from east or west about 11 P. M., you would have four or five hours—not to sleep, but only to lie down on a couch in the Kelton House. The minute a weary traveler placed his form upon a bed or couch, a fierce battle began with the crawling and prior occupants. After my first experience I always reclined in my clothes and kept a light burning at the side of the couch. Bedbugs will seldom parade under inspection! About four o'clock in the morning we would be aroused by a cry of "All up! Break'ust on table and ther stage is ready!" The breakfast was bacon, mustard, hot lard biscuits, canned butter, condensed milk, and coffee with brown sugar. It didn't take long to dispatch it, and after that we bundled into the coach. The driver would settle himself on the box, call out, "All set?" which means "Are you all in?" and the coach would start.

The following three days and nights on the stage before reaching Boise was, to the tenderfoot, a pilgrimage of agony and bitter misery. Ruts, stones, holes, breaks, all combined to make this journey distinctly one to be remembered. The alkali dust bit into the eyes, and one's lips, cracked and irritated, hurt for weeks afterward. In case there was but one passenger, or perhaps two, the stage company filled the bottom of the coach with sacks of barley to store at the stations during the coming winter or grain-feeding season. The company saved money by doing its own freighting in this manner. One could recline comfortably upon these sacks of grain. It was not unusual that a woman would be ill on the coach, and the drivers, usually the most kindhearted of men, would then fill the coach bottom with hay and make a couch for the invalid.

STAGE STATIONS AND "HOME" STATIONS

The stage stations, relay places, were twelve to fifteen miles apart. The "home" stations, where the drivers, and, frequently the stages, were changed and where meals were served, were fifty to sixty miles apart. The driver's daily work averaged this fifty or sixty miles, at a rate of about five miles an hour. The stages kept on day and night, and so of course the drivers had both daylight and darkness. The stage stations were one-story log houses with dirt or mud roofs, the men and horses sleeping under one shelter. These stations were miniature forts by which frequent attacks of the Indians were withstood. Stage fare was twenty cents a mile. Often the stage stations, by reason of water supply, were but six or seven miles apart. In such localities one team of horses hauled a coach both directions, back and forward, on the road the same day. These teams were called "swings"; they were driven by two different drivers on the respective trips. As a rule, the horses made but one trip a day between stations.

The "home" stations were houses built of logs and usually occupied by families. They were rich in little save dirt. The meals were uniformly bad and one dollar each. Bacon and "white-lead" bread were the staple articles of food. These meals were always prepared after the stage arrived because it was not possible to know beforehand how many passengers would be aboard and how much food to cook. The stage company's employees were boarded at these home stations. The coaches stopped forty minutes at the home stations and about five minutes at the other stations, time enough to change horses or teams. I have eaten dinner at a home station when the meat was never more ambitious than bacon. This seemed ridiculous to me, for on entering the house I was often compelled to drive away scores of chickens in order to pass through the door. Pie was another staple article, and such pie! It consisted of a sole-leather, lard-soaked lower crust, half baked, with a thin veneer of dried apples daubed with brown sugar. A large pot of mustard containing an iron spoon which had partially succumbed to the attack of the vinegar always decorated the center of the table. Ten times each meal you knew it was a standby because ten times arose the call, "Pass the mustard, Jedge." The butter was canned, and the milk was condensed. Cows in plenty were browsing about in the brush, but milk was kept for the calves. It was, moreover, rather troublesome to milk the animals. The inventors of canned foods and bottled products deserve a place of honor in the annals of our country, for without their products the settlement of the West would have been a far worse task. The dining room of a home station was the main room of the house, and it held an open fireplace which burned sagebrush or logs in cold weather. The table was of rough pine boards and the benches or chairs were equally rough. The table furniture was of ironstone ware and tin, with iron spoons and heavy knives. No ice was ever seen on the table. The bread was the result of "self-raisin' " flour, nearly white lead in consistency, and about as indigestible for one's stomach. The coffee and the tea were peculiar to the country. I never tasted anything quite so bad in any other part of the world.

With all this dirt and neglect, it must be said that as a rule the people who kept the home stations were good, decent people, charitable and attentive to the travelers. They were ordinary "Pikers" who had never known any better living in former days. The prices they received, the profits accruing, were but meager compensation for the hermit existence forced upon them and for the many comforts denied them by living so far from communities of their fellow men. When the home-station people chanced to be educated and had known good living in the states, you could see it in every feature of the station. The food, service, and the cooking showed it, and the walls of the houses were decorated with chromos. Books were lying about, and in a corner one could perhaps see a parlor organ, one of those sobbing melodeons.

The names of the stage stations, like the names of many homes in the East, bore not the slightest relation to scenery, position, or the country's resources. "Paradise Valley" hadn't a living thing about it but snakes! There wasn't a tree for miles! There were favorite names, among them "Dry Creek," "Canyon Creek," "Mountain Home," "Sand Springs," and "Rock Creek." Many stations were named after the man who owned the ranch where they were located. "Corder's" and "Black's" were named after the owners. Charley Black was noted and known as the owner of the famous horse, Rocky Mountain Chief, and he also boasted two of the prettiest daughters in Idaho. They were Hattie and Mary Black, and after the long drag from Kelton it was a comfort to see their pretty, bright faces. City of Rocks was not a city at all but a log cabin and stables built amid hundreds of tall, toothlike granite rocks on which were inscribed the names of many of the emigrants who had passed through to Oregon in the earlier days. This place was a noted point on the old Overland road that went down into the Humboldt Valley. The stations were of course laid out with an eye to the grass and water supply.

City of Rocks I remember as the one home station between Kelton and Boise which offered anything out of the ordinary; in fact, it was delightful. Mr. and Mrs. William Trotter were in charge. William Trotter, a brother of Charles Trotter, had served his time as a stager under Ben Holladay on the old Overland route from St. Joseph, Missouri, west to Denver. If I remember rightly, he had been the division superintendent under Ike Bromley who, in 1869, had a ranch and public house below Webers Canyon, Utah. The Trotter brothers were both worthy men and capable stage managers. Mrs. Trotter was a quiet, motherly woman of forty years and she supplied meals that were excellent. She also had clean, comfortable beds for those compelled to remain at City of Rocks when the roads were impassable. She employed, as did everyone else in Idaho's early days, a Chinaman to do the cooking. On her table were napkins—clean, red ones at that! Napkins in those days were suggestive of everything cultured and luxurious. In September, 1878, I was passing by stage from Red Canyon, Idaho, to Helena, Montana, and we pulled up at midnight in a station for supper. As soon as I saw the table I recognized the red napkins and cried out, "Mrs. Trotter is here and I know it!" I was not very much surprised when Mrs. Trotter came with her husband from the kitchen and gave me a hearty welcome.

The Overland stage going north usually reached, about dark, the foot of King Hill, Idaho, on the north side of Snake River. This was below Paynes Ferry. The grade was a teriffic uphill pull of five miles. A large station called King Hill was near the foot of the hill. It was not a home station but a regular stage station frequented by teamsters, packers, and freighters who camped there and "doubled the hill"; that is, they drew the wagon up first and then returned and hauled the trail wagon.

The first time I visited King Hill Station was a hot night in July, 1869. I jumped from the coach and asked for a drink of water. The water was hot and impregnated with alkali. It occurred to me that I might get a drink of milk, for many cattle were about. I walked to the door of the station house and rapped. No answer, so I walked in. A man was lolling on a bunk and when he saw me he said, "What do you want, pardner?" I told him, and he said, "There's some milk on the window ledge." I found a teacup full of milk and swallowed it at a gulp. The man on the bunk said, "I've got the ague! Don't bother me! How much for the milk? Four bits! Lay it on the windowsill." I placed fifty cents in silver on the spot indicated and fled. I was certain that he was about to charge me for looking at him. I saw him frequently afterward and always involuntarily grabbed my wallet. The ague may have done it, but I trust that if he has crossed the Great Divide he is not now in the milk business.

A FAST MULE TEAM

Over on the Goose Creek Range, beyond City of Rocks, was a mountain station which I think was called Goose Creek Station. From this station to the next was a distance of seven or eight miles. The road was a natural gravel road, hard surfaced, and solid in winter and summer. It ran on even grade along the mountainside, below the ridge. The stage team that made this trip always challenged my admiration. It was a mule team, a "swing" team, composed of four mules. The leaders were white mules; "Crazy" was the lead and "Coyote" the off lead. The wheelers were bay animals known as "Jim" and "Beauty." They were small bunchy animals with the longest and sharpest pointed ears I ever saw on mules. They were well bred and particularly well groomed. The first time I rode behind them was in July, 1869. Jimmy Adams, a daredevil driver but a kindly fellow, held the ribbons. The wheel mules were brought out and hitched, and then Jimmy told us to "git aboard." Next, the lead mules were placed in position, but the traces were not hooked. The four mules stood like the most peaceful-looking animals one would care to see. Jimmy was in position, a hostler handed him the ribbons, and Jimmy addressed his passengers, "Gents and likewise lady! I want youse to hol' on like blazes and don't let nothin' drop out—not even yerselves, fer ef ye do ye won't be picked up, and th' coyotes will browse on yer bones before mornin'. When these here mules goes, they goes, and they doesn't stop till they reins themselves up at th' next station. So hol' on tight an' watch yerselves, fer in a minute, hell will pop! Now, Jeems [to the hostler] hook in them leaders! Gee, whoa, scat, youse hellions!" At the crack of Jimmy Adams' whip, the four mules struck a short gait peculiar to themselves, and we never stopped once until the eight miles had been covered. It took a few minutes less than an hour. The ride in the crisp mountain air was an invigorator, and the view of the mountains and valleys was superb. We rattled along at a bumping pace, and Jimmy told me about the animals. No matter what happened, whether or not a wheel broke and stranded the coach, the mules kept right on. Jimmy also said that no matter if the weather was hot or cold the mules never turned a hair from perspiration. As we rattled along I saw a mail sack full of letters, lying on the road. I was surprised when we whirled past it without stopping, but Adams said, "I can't stop! The upstage lost it out of the boot and couldn't stop neither! The division agent will be along soon in a buggy and he'll fetch it. Then we'll put her on the stage for Boise." I rode often behind these animals and marveled at their speed and endurance. Jimmy Rodgers was another of their drivers. Rodgers was a tall, handsome Oregon boy whom John Hailey had adopted.

MONEY TRANSPORTATION

The stagecoaches carried money in considerable amounts, and they were prey for the road agents of earlier days. The road agents would rob passengers and the express box, but they were careful to avoid robbing the mails. This was because they feared pursuit and capture by the United States marshal, who invariably made short work of the men who robbed the mails. From 1869 to 1872 I saw fortunes in gold dust sent by mail from Boise to San Francisco. The gold was in tin cans which weighed, with the dust, four pounds. I have seen four ten-thousand-dollar packages of greenbacks, or national notes, come in a single mail from San Francisco to the First National Bank of Idaho. The bank paid letter postage on it. I shipped my law library from Columbus, Ohio, to Boise in 1869. The books were in four mail sacks, and the postage was sixty dollars. The cost of expressing them at that time would have been at least two hundred and fifty dollars.

CARRYING THE MAILS

In another volume which I have compiled, I have endeavored to pay a well-earned tribute to the splendid men who drove the stages; not solely the Idaho stages but the stage lines throughout the great West. These drivers were, many of them, rough in their exterior, slaughtered the King's English, and ofttimes indulged in the prevailing form of entertainment the country afforded, whisky. But —as if conscious that they were the real factors in opening up the interior, the connecting links between civilization and barbaric life—no set of men, considered generally, ever were truer to their duties than were these stage drivers of the early West. They were real "Knights of the Ribbon" in every sense of the phrase and true knights in their region.

In addition to passengers and expressage, the stage carried mail. Not solely the mail from the railroad to the interior and vice versa, but between intermediate points. Each stage driver was a sworn officer of the United States, a United States mail carrier. For the accommodation of the people along the line, between post offices, the drivers were provided with a leathern receptacle called a "way pocket" in which the settlers deposited letters. The driver of course noticed the address and was sure to deliver his mail at the right place. Newspapers were deposited in bundles in the "boot" of the stage, and all along the route, for hundreds of miles, Idaho people received their mail or their papers, and not once in a year was there cause for complaint. Barring severe storms or an aftermath of mud, the Idaho settlers looked for their communications as regularly—but not as often, to be sure—as do those in the great cities.

Mention might be made here of the important part played by the Wells, Fargo Company, not only in the delivery of the express but in the delivering of letters throughout the frontier. The Wells, Fargo Company anticipated the national postal service in the prompt collection and delivery of mails throughout the West; that is, west of Kansas City. In 1852 the Government granted to express companies the right to carry letters in Government stamped envelopes. The Wells, Fargo Company paid the regular postage rate, usually three cents, and then fixed their stamp at the top of the envelope and sold the double stamped envelope at five cents or perhaps more. The company had its own delivery and collection routes not only in the towns but scattered throughout the border. In the days of the first Pony Express it cost two dollars and fifty cents for each letter carried from the East to the Pacific slope, a nine days' journey. The Wells, Fargo Company did not abandon their mail express service until April, 1895. The old express stamp reads: "Paid. Wells, Fargo & Co. Over our California and Coast Routes."

With all the discomforts attached to Western stage-coaches, I have always cherished a warm affection for them. They were true pioneers! When I visited Boise City in 1890, I asked for my old friend John Hailey and the other stage men I had known in central Idaho. Mr. Hailey was away on a trip; Alexander Boomer was living in San Francisco. In strolling about Boise City, I came across a "bone yard" of my old friends, the Idaho mud wagons. Crawford Moore, son of C. W. Moore, of Boise, clambered upon one of the coaches, and my son, who was with me, snapped some photographs. The recollections of old times and the old drivers came back to me all too distinctly as I saw the decaying relics of the former days when the stage was the link which bound us to "the States."

FIRST RAILROADS AND TELEGRAPH LINES

The Union Pacific Railroad pushed its lines, early in 1869, westward to Promontory Point at the head of Great Salt Lake, ninety miles west of Ogden, Utah. The Central Pacific laid its lines east to Ogden; the two roads overlapped. The two roads were seeking the Congressional mileage subsidy. The Union Pacific had built the dump west of Ogden but laid very little, if any, rail. The difference between these roads, in regard to the overlapping portion, was afterward settled by arbitration and possibly Congressional action, and the Central Pacific ran its rails to Ogden. The former road intended to construct lateral roads after 1869, under its grant and charter. It contemplated running a line from Corinne, Utah, to Umatilla, on the Columbia, via the Snake River Valley and Boise. In 1868 Colonel Hudnutt made an instrumental survey of the proposed route for the Union Pacific. One year later, I made, at the request of the road's vice-president, John Huff, a report of my personal observations on the materials for construction and alteration in the country through which the branch road would pass, were it built.

From 1869 to 1875 there was much agitation over the question of railroads to pass through central Idaho. Colonel W. W. Chapman, of Portland, Oregon, then a tall, intelligent, and energetic man of sixty years, wanted a road built from Corinne, Utah, to Portland, via the Snake River Valley. A company was chartered for the purpose in 1872, and ground was broken at Corinne for the new road. Chapman was in Boise in 1872 applying to the legislature for permission to do this work, and I met him on my return from the East at City of Rocks station on the Overland stage road and had a long chat with him. He and Colonel A. B. Meacham were riding up front with the driver. I told him what I had done in the East with reference to the new road and advised him to call upon Oakes Ames. Chapman's head was bound in a bloody cloth, and he told me that a brutal driver had driven his coach full speed down King Hill. The jolting had thrown him from the seat of the coach against the top, cutting his head. He was convinced that the driver was intoxicated and said that he would have him discharged. That was the last time I had the pleasure of meeting Colonel Chapman.

The incident filled me with some anxiety because I knew that the driver could be no other than my old friend, James Tutwiler. At King Hill, "Tut" hailed me from his box. I returned his greeting and asked, "Tutwiler, what induced you to give Colonel Chapman and Colonel Meacham that 'Hank Monk' drive down King Hill yesterday?"

"Was that venerable person in the fur cap, Colonel Chapman and that gold-headed-cane party, Colonel Meacham?" queried Tutwiler. "Well, I heard just as I took them up to the station that they were coming here to build a railroad from Salt Lake to Portland, Oregon. Now,

Judge, what are stage drivers to do when staging is done with? Staging is done when a railroad comes in. I am sorry for that venerable Colonel Chapman because he hurt his head against the top of the coach when I took two ruts at full gait. Colonel Meacham didn't give me a chance to square up; he sat outside. Sorry, Judge, very sorry, but I've got my business and profession to protect!"

Both of Tutwiler's victims reported him, but he pleaded in extenuation that his stock was particularly well cared for and, feeling their oats, had become unmanageable. He was let off with a slight reprimand.

Three years later, we were again together on the box and after leaving Silver City for Winnemucca, Tutwiler turned and said to me, "Judge, do you remember the ride I gave Chapman and Meacham down King Hill and how you scolded me? Well, sir, both of those colonels reported me, sir, both of them! Colonel Meacham has since met retribution for his discourtesy. He was, as you probably know, shot in the belly by an Indian in a Modoc war. And Colonel Chapman has gone out of sight—but he will be overtaken, overtaken, sir! Better keep hands and mouth off old Tut! He has avengers. The Lord cares for His own."

During the winter of 1871-72, a small squad of men used to meet in the office of the First National Bank of Idaho at Boise City to discuss the hope of ultimately getting a railroad through Idaho from any quarter. These men were C. W. Moore, L. F. Cartee, surveyor general in the territory, John Hailey, afterwards delegate in Congress, then chief stage owner in Idaho, and myself. My appointment as Centennial commissioner from Idaho had just been made, and it was patent that much of my time in the coming years was to be spent in the East. Mr. Moore thought that with proper figures and statements it would be possible for me to interest the right people to extend a branch road from the Union Pacific through Idaho. General Cartee drew maps of the proposed route from Corinne, or from Ogden, along Snake River to the Columbia River, at or near Umatilla. Cartee, an excellent man, was a practical engineer with a thorough knowledge of Idaho and Oregon. His maps detailed the proposed routes, with profiles and estimated elevations, and offered notes regarding the mountain passes. Hailey and Moore made tables of resources and the possibilities of new developments with an incoming railroad. I wrote the general physical description of Idaho and eastern Oregon and detailed the sources and possible income of a railroad along Snake River from Utah to Oregon. We worked constantly on these documents for many months. In November, 1872, all were prepared and I carried them, a great roll, East.

The Honorable James G. Blaine was the first person whom I saw, and I sought his aid to get a personal interview with Oakes Ames. The next day at the House of Representatives, Mr. Blaine called me into the cloakroom. Oakes Ames was there and greeted me cordially. He said, after our conversation had lasted half an hour with details, "My brother Oliver must see you at once. You have just the data he desires. You must remain in Washington until he returns. I think that this matter is decidedly feasible, and we can best begin the Oregon branch from a point east of Ogden on the Union Pacific. Then we can cross the Blue Mountains to Pendleton, Oregon, by a pass back of Baker City. We think we are entitled to some subsidy under law of Congress for branch lines if constructed within a given time just as we are entitled to subsidies for additions to the main line. We have been recently considering this matter, and you know we have Colonel Hudnutt's instrumental survey from Corinne, or Ogden, to Baker City and Burnt River via Boise. At all events, send your data to our chief engineer, Theophilus E. Sickles, and let him have the benefit of it."

I replied that Mr. Sickles and I were old acquaintances

and the data should be sent him. Mr. Ames then bade me a cordial good day.

Just then a curious thing occurred. Mr. Ames was resting in characteristic attitude upon a sofa when Mr. Blaine excused himself and passed into the House. He relinquished the speaker's chair to Cox, the New York Democrat, and just as I took a seat in the gallery, Blaine opened the famous investigation which has gone down into history—the "Credit Mobilier," which almost wrecked Oakes Ames politically and otherwise. Mr. Blaine had been stung to the attack through a personal matter—a bitter criticism hurled at him that morning in the New York *Tribune*.

The panic of 1873 followed, and all railroad building throughout the West was suspended for a long time. Sickles, the engineer, I saw frequently, and he invariably told me that our branch line through Boise was sure to be built. Not until 1882, however, did direct knowledge of the building reach me. I was in the office of Stephen B. Elkins, in New York, when Sickles entered. He expressed gratification at seeing me and stated that he was about to write to me. The Union Pacific had again taken up the matter of running a branch line, but this time it was to be from Granger, Wyoming, through Idaho along and across the Snake River. The object in building was to head off C. P. Huntington. Sickles said that the data which I had given to him in 1872 was the best in the possession of the Union Pacific and, now that the Gould-Vanderbilt-Tilden interests were united, he thought that my services were valuable, or would be, and he offered me compensation. I refused any compensation by saying that although I was not then a resident of Idaho, I cherished my friendship for the territory and her people and would aid her whenever possible without compensation.

The Oregon Short Line was built chiefly on the data in the maps, elevations, contours, statements of resources, and the ideas of Moore, Cartee, Hailey, and myself which I had carried East and given to Oakes Ames in 1872. Samuel J. Tilden ventured a million dollars in the construction of the Oregon Short Line. Mr. Sickles came to me and asked me what the company could do for me.

"Name a locomotive after me," I said.

"We'll beat that," laughed Sickles, "for we will name a town after you." He didn't, probably for the reason that there were not enough towns to carry the names of those directly interested. Our original data and plans of 1872 are now in the office of the Union Pacific's chief engineer.

The fact that Boise City is at the present day on a branch line and not on the main track of the Oregon Short Line is due entirely to the shortsightedness of Boise citizens. When it was practically assured that the Oregon Short Line was to be constructed, I did all within my power to impress upon my Boise friends the importance of inducing the Union Pacific to run the branch line through Boise. The customary and infallible argument, money, was the sole requisite. One man urged the question, but no general subscriptions were made. For thirty thousand dollars Boise could have been located to great advantage. As it resulted, the capital of the territory was forced to be content with a branch railroad extending twenty miles west to join the Oregon Short Line.*

The first telegraph line of any length constructed in Idaho ran from Winnemucca, Nevada, to Silver City, Idaho. A. P. Minear, John Catlow, and I were responsible for its building. Minear was a mass of energy and specula-

---

* Through the courtesy of President W. M. Jeffers, of the Union Pacific Railroad, the following summary of the origin of railroads in Idaho is extracted from original Union Pacific records:
(1) Idaho's first railroad was begun in 1874, when a narrow-gauge line of the Utah Northern was constructed from Brigham, Utah, about a mile of track being laid from the Utah border to Franklin, Idaho.
(2) In 1878 the Utah and Northern Railroad extended the above narrow-gauge line from Franklin to Pocatello, and then north into Montana, as far as Garrison.
(3) The third line was that of the Northern Pacific. Construction began at Wallula, Washington, where connection was made with the line of the Oregon Railroad and Navigation Company in 1880. In the summer of 1882 the road was extended across the northern tip of Idaho into Montana.
(4) Construction of the Oregon Short Line in Idaho began late in the summer of 1881 at two points—Pocatello and Border.

tion and was interested in the reopening of some old mines at Silver City and was the head of the boom at South Mountain, near Silver City. In 1874, while Minear, Catlow, and I were together in San Francisco, I impressed upon Minear the necessity for a telegraph line in a mining operation for the proper handling and conducting of affairs. Catlow voiced similar sentiments, and Minear was convinced. Catlow, who was a freighter on a large scale, said that he would cut and haul poles for compensation of half cash and half stock. This was no inconsiderable offer, for poles usually had to be hauled twenty-five or more miles from the timber regions. The Northwestern Stage Company agreed to haul the wire at odd times, free of charge. The conversation referred to took place in the Russ House, San Francisco.

A company was organized with Minear as president. Minear, Catlow, and others had but recently placed new machinery in the old Oro Fino mine at Silver City and were expecting big developments. In 1875 I sold the control of the Oro Fino, on behalf of Minear, Catlow, and their partners, to a number of speculators in San Francisco headed by John D. Fry. Fry placed Cunningham, his own superintendent, in charge of the Oro Fino. Now, a singular fact. The telegraph line was built from Winnemucca to Silver City and opened in August, 1874. In December of the same year, it was extended twenty-five miles to South Mountain. In the fall of 1875, it was built northward to Boise City, sixty miles. The South Mountain mines played out in 1875 and the boom "busted." Catlow had 750 of the 1,000 shares of the telegraph line from Winnemucca to Silver City. The line was a failure. Catlow transferred the stock to me, so that I practically owned the line for several months, a line that was kept in repair by the assistance of the stage drivers, who were instructed to advise the office of fallen poles and of breaks in the wire.

James Gamble was then manager of the Western Union

Telegraph Company on the Pacific Coast. I called upon him personally with the hope of disposing of our line. Mr. Gamble thought favorably of purchasing and told me to call again. The sheriff was continually threatening to seize the line, and as seldom more than three messages crossed the wires each day, we were highly anxious to sell. The last call I made upon Mr. Gamble ended the matter. One of his agents had personally inspected the line, reported that it was illy constructed, the wire was thin, and the poles small. He said that the line began nowhere and ended nowhere in the light of business and it was a poor investment. The agent also said that since the mines at South Mountain were played out, and the sheriff would sell the line within a short time, the Western Union would be able to buy cheapest by waiting.

Mr. Gamble bade me good day. I went out and saw Catlow and transferred the stock and line back to him. The Western Union finally secured the line for almost nothing. It was ultimately extended to Baker City, from Boise, in 1875 or 1876, and then to Portland, Oregon.

CHAPTER III

SOCIAL LIFE AND AMUSEMENTS AT THE CAPITAL

BOISE'S population was, as one may realize, dependent upon itself for entertainment or amusement. Church fairs, singing by church choirs—the same music, by the way, was charged for on weekdays that we heard free on Sundays—private dances, reading parties, observance of national holidays, amateur theatricals, lectures, and horse races, all helped round out the year. The winters were usually open, so that the officers at Fort Boise did much to contribute to Boise's enjoyment by giving dances and music or minstrel shows by the men in the service. I recall that the army band obliged us at Slocum Hall one evening when a subscription dance was given to raise a fund sufficient to place a fence about the graveyard! Awaiting the mail or entertaining visitors, two very successful time killers, were practically the only reliable chances for diversion.

One of the worst social calamities that ever fell upon Boise was during a fair held at Slocum Hall for the benefit of the Episcopal Church. In the midst of festivities, a loud crash startled the multitude. Then came a rush toward the corner from which the sound had reverberated. Four dozen china plates had fallen to the floor and smashed to atoms! The fragments were carefully gathered, and the owners of the loaned goods stood about as solemn mourners and heard sympathy expressed. The plates were ordinary china but the freight rate made them worth a dollar each. Some of Boise's leading families did not possess two dozen. The success of the fair was blighted by the calamity of broken plates.

I recall another shock given the community, though of different nature. In 1871, a number of us made up a purse and purchased a stereopticon from McAllister, of Phila-

RESIDENCE OF MILTON KELLY, BOISE CITY, I. T.

RESIDENCE OF C. W. MOORE, GROVE ST. BOISE CITY, IDAHO.

Homes of prominent Boise City residents.

RESIDENCE OF JONAS W. BROWN, GROVE ST., BETWEEN 10TH & 11TH, BOISE CITY, IDAHO TER.

RESIDENCE OF H. E. PRICKETT, COR. MAIN & 3RD STS. BOISE CITY, I. T.

Homes of prominent Boise City residents.

Residence of General L. F. Cartee in Boise City, Idaho Territory. Cartee is responsible for the many trees which grace the present city of Boise.

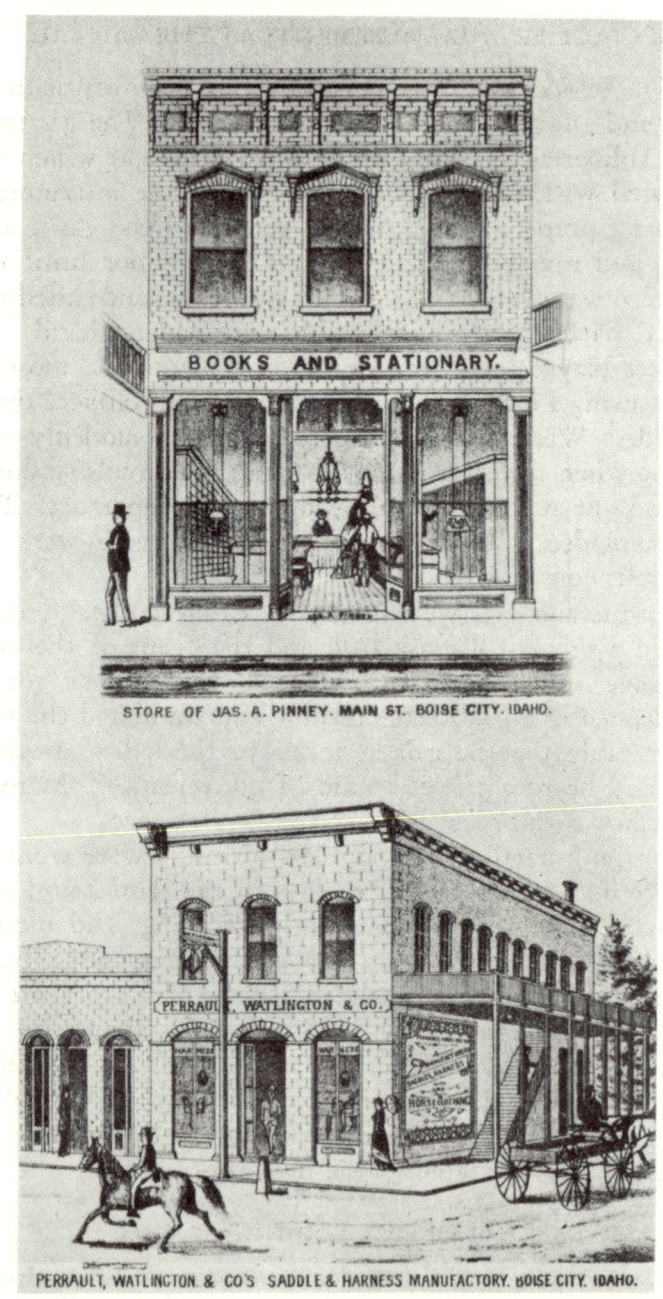

Boise City business establishments.

delphia. It was the "proudest" and only stereopticon in Idaho and afforded us much entertainment. The gas tank was a rubber bag, a huge affair filled with gas which we generated with chemicals accompanying the instrument. When we prepared for a show I generated the gas in my house, and my wife usually visited a neighbor until the operation was over. We gave public lectures and suited the subject matter to the views which we had on hand. Ed Hollister played incidental music on a piano, and most of the lecturing I did: the subjects ranged from biblical times to wildest West. The lecture series ended suddenly one evening when the gas tank gave a series of convulsive shudders and our audience was moved to rapid departure. The tank exploded, but, barring excitement, there were no dangerous consequences.

Masquerade balls were in vogue. In December of 1871 we held a successful mask ball, and the event of the evening gave much food for discussion. One of our young men dressed in a soubrette costume and simulated the role so admirably that he gained access to the ladies' dressing room and heard a choice round of conversation. Many a sly wink was tipped in Boise for days afterward.

Camping parties were popular. Families were wont to "bundle up" for two or three days in the mountains, and delightful days were passed hunting, fishing, and mountain climbing. The Masons gave frequent lodge balls, which were always well attended. I have here as I write an invitation to a dance given at Silver City on October 4, 1871, by the Owyhee County Masons. Tickets, including supper, were ten dollars. J. H. Hall, W. H. Van Slyf, F. E. Ensign, and other prominent men of Silver were on the committee, as stated in the invitation.

BARTHOLOMEW'S EQUINE PARADOX

In the small list of regular professional entertainers, was George Bartholomew with his wonderful troupe of horses. Bartholomew carried a tent with him, and his remarkable circus—which he called the Equine Paradox—was always in favor. I first met him at Boise in 1870, and at that time he was a young, dark-haired man and a ready and interesting talker. I saw him in Philadelphia at late as 1891 and though he had aged considerably, his skill as a horse trainer had by no means deteriorated. Bartholomew usually had dogs in his troupe, but the cleverest part of his show was his command of the horses. He used the most ordinary animals on the coast, those known as cayuses, raised in Oregon by the Cayuse Indians. Except for saddle purposes they were looked upon as useless and sold for about five dollars each. People on the coast could not realize or understand how he taught the animals.

THE PIXLEY SISTERS

Annie and Minnie Pixley visited Boise in the winter of 1870 and as usual took the town by storm. The sisters brought a small company with them and produced light comedies and farces in Slocum Hall. The Pixleys were clever in songs and dances, and, exemplary in conduct, established themselves as favorites throughout the territory. They were devotees of outdoor sports and horseback riding. The little Annie Pixley of 1870 I had the pleasure of seeing in star roles years afterward in the East. She became Mrs. Robert Fulford. In 1894, she died in England under distressing circumstances.

BILLY WILKERSON AND THE CARTERS

One of the old reliables with every wandering stock company that came to Boise was Billy Wilkerson, or Wilkinson. Billy was as unconscious a comedian as he was an unnatural tragedian; in either role, tragedy or comedy, he was positively extreme. Billy was small in size and his voice was shrill, but in ambition and earnestness he had no superior. It seemed to us that whether he portrayed duke or serf, clown or tragedian, neither grease paint nor clothes ever concealed from us the lines of our one and only Billy Wilkerson.

A dramatic company came to Boise in 1872 headed by Mr. and Mrs. J. C. Carter. Carter was a capital actor: his wife, Carrie Carter, was intelligent but too masculine in her readings. Mr. Carter died in Salt Lake a few months after he appeared in Boise and his sorrowing widow soon joined in wedlock with a Mormon bishop; it was the bishop's seventh offense. I saw Mrs. Carter at Salt Lake in 1873 and five years later saw her at Philadelphia with a stock company. She had "unsealed" herself from the bishop in the meantime.

Billy Wilkerson was with the Carters in Boise and one evening played the role of an injured and outraged husband. Carter was the bold bad villain, and the third act offered a fine chance for climax when Carter was due to rush on and encounter Wilkerson, whereupon Wilkerson was to stab him. Carter's dying scenes were thrillingly realistic, and naturally Wilkerson needed to be emphatic in his rule of injured husband. Boise's audience was awaiting the finale with bated breath. On rushed Wilkerson, downstage toward Carter, and stormed, "Ho, ho! Base betrayer of me sacred home, ruiner of me fair name, have I caught you at last?" Then Wilkerson struggled toward Carter, who awaited him with dagger in hand, pulled out a property sword, made a feeble swipe at Carter which missed by two feet, and in a shrill, piping voice cried, "Die, villain, die!" The audience went into hysterics! Carter remained standing and sadly eyed Wilkerson until order was restored in the theater. Then he calmly walked front, gave a most appealing look at the audience, and said, "Ladies and gentlemen! I have been in the business twenty years. You'll excuse me I know, but that was the damnedest weakest 'die' I ever heard." The curtain came down amid yells of delight, and that was Billy Wilkerson's last appearance in Boise for two years.

When Billy returned to us, his own, he fooled the people. We awoke one morning and found that during the night, Boise had been plastered with flaming sheets which announced, "Engagement Extraordinary! The One Great & Potent Magician, The Fakir of Stromboli!" The posters attracted attention. Prospectors wanted to know if Stromboli was "one of Brig Young's wards." At any rate, the posters enticed many a victim, at one dollar each, to Slocum Hall the night that the Fakir was to perform.

The performance opened with a display of red fire, and then through a black curtain appeared the Fakir of Stromboli. The Fakir was quite small and clad in red with a sugar-loaf hat. He did a clever invocation with his hands and then chanted a podrida of words. Not twenty words had he spoken when Bob Gillespie jumped from his chair and yelled, "So help me God, it's Billy Wilkerson!" And it was Billy! A few guns were drawn, a few chairs were poised on high, but the peace-loving spectators quieted the tumult, and Billy, much embarrassed, proceeded with legerdemain that was exceedingly good. Still, the stench of imposition rankled within the breast of Boise! Daniel Cram auditor for the territory, was in his accustomed place on the front row and kept the audience in control for a while. At last one of our dignified citizens arose and addressed the Fakir.

"Mr. Wilkerson, sir, your attention! The good people of Boise have tolerated you in the past in many theatrical companies and have been courteous to you under many discouragements. Off the stage, you were, sir, handled tenderly and often were you irrigated. You were known to us as plain, very plain, Billy Wilkerson. How in hell, sir, are you the Fakir of Stromboli?"

Billy realized his danger and he proved a true diplomat. He stepped forward, doffed his hat and wig, and said,

"Gents, especially the gent who has just spoken, and ladies—such as are here—I owe you an apology. I was raised a magician, a kind of trick clown. I knew that before I went into the legit. I was with a company three weeks ago, over to La Grande. We had a dub for a star, the ghost didn't walk for six weeks, we bucked agin a travelin' sport with a poker game which interested all the intellectual element in La Grande, the leadin' man he totes off with a pack train to Umatilla, leadin' lady makes eyes and floats off with a Walla Walla dude. The rest of us just moseyed out of town. Billy Wilkerson was poor as the rest but he had friends. Along comes a trick clown with his cards, 'The Fakir of Stromboli.' He was clean bill, sure thing, the only and original! Tries it one night and then he busted—jumped and left his outfit. I gets them. Uncle John Hailey's man, Joe Reemy, he chalks me over the line, and I've been doing the small towns. Gents and ladies, I throw myself on your mercy. I'm heading for Salt Lake. Sit peaceful and I'll give you a good show and tote out for Utah tomorrow. If you want your money back, I'll hand it out. But, remember, if I do, I'm here for all winter and I'll anchor with you all for grubstake." The appeal touched manly bosoms, and Billy gave a fine performance.

GEORGE PAUNCEFOOT

The American stage has had no more unique character than George Pauncefoot. In experiences and wanderings on his theatrical tours, he occupied a class entirely his own. He was an English actor of prominence and achieved considerable reputation in early stock companies in America. In September, 1854, he appeared at the Boston Theater as Captain Absolute in *The Rivals;* the playbill now hanging in the Boston Theater states that Mr. Pauncefoot had just come from the "Theatre Royal, Dublin." In the cast with Pauncefoot at Boston were John Gilbert, Julia Bennett Barrow, and others of prominence. Pauncefoot played the leads for two seasons and on several occasions supported Edwin Forrest. For several years following he had a company of his own and toured the smaller of our Eastern cities. About 1863 he appeared at Maguire's Opera House, San Francisco, and supplanted Charles Thorne, Jr., as leading man. Charles Wheatleigh then engaged him to open with the first California production of *Arrah Na Pogue*. In this company, as his support, were Mrs. Sol Smith, Mrs. Annie Yeamans, J. H. Warwick, afterwards of the California legislature, and Belle Devine, whom Pauncefoot married in 1865 or 1866. A son, George Pauncefoot, who also took to the stage, was born to them. A few years afterward it was discovered that Pauncefoot was a bigamist; he had a wife and family in England. In the course of time, his American wife, Miss Devine, died in the East. Pauncefoot then went to Japan. He played in Yokohama and other places and saved enough money to purchase a hotel. He located the "Shakespeare Inn," near the Yokohama race track, married again à la Japanese—marrying was a habit with him—and died there about 1896.

One day in the spring of 1870 a two-wheeled gig rattled into Boise. In it, the sole occupant, was George Pauncefoot. The gig was drawn by a strong American horse; a leather top to the gig provided against stormy weather and beneath the seat of the vehicle was a cooking outfit, fodder, a tent fly, and guns. The shooting outfit was valuable. Pauncefoot had come overland from St. Paul by way of the Targhee Pass, near Henrys Lake, over the Stinking Water Divide and to Boise on a road of his own making until he struck the Snake River. In spite of weather, accidents, mountains, deserts, sickness, drouth, or the possibilities of famine, Pauncefoot forged through the Northwest. How he ever escaped being robbed and murdered mystified us. Evidently he wanted to hide his tracks when he came to Idaho; he was entirely successful.

At that time Pauncefoot was a handsome man of forty-five years, stout, above middle height, with black curly hair, high color, a mustache, and good teeth. He spent two days in billing the town with the announcement, "George Pauncefoot, the Eminent English Actor, will read, etc." His personality was his best card, for in his stay of two days he became very popular, and the best audience Boise could muster greeted him when his performance began. The officers at Boise liked him and gave him two large flags to decorate his stage. Before Pauncefoot appeared, the lights in the hall were turned down, and when he appeared in full evening clothes, handsome and gentlemanly-looking, the sight was so rare that an irrepressible youth in the hall cried, "Gee, look at the spike coat!" Mr. Pauncefoot read from Shakespeare and also from Tennyson. His rendition of "Eugene Aram" was most effective and dramatic. It was a tribute, a compliment for him, that his classical repertoire met with such favor in Boise, for the usual traveling shows engendered a taste for performances of lighter vein. Pauncefoot realized large sums from his readings not alone because of his talents but because he was a good advertiser of his own wares. The morning after his reading at Boise, he drove westward in his gig.

Henry Irving, the English actor, was at my house in Philadelphia in 1893, and I chanced to mention the tour of Pauncefoot. Mr. Irving asked me the man's name. I told him, and thereupon he said, "Why, Mrs. Pauncefoot is now with my company. She is playing old-lady roles and a charming woman she is. Tell her about George. She often speaks of him and his sudden disappearance." Of course, this was Pauncefoot's English wife. One of her daughters came to America in 1890 with Mr. and Mrs. Kendall. Mr. Irving, with customary liberality, pensioned Mrs. Pauncefoot after she left his company.

PROFESSOR PLUMMER

About once a year handbills were scattered in Boise announcing the coming of "Professor" C. B. Plummer, an entertainer who toured the territorial cities and gave humorous readings. Plummer, like Pauncefoot, earned many a deserved dollar, for he was a clever man in his line. His handbills were a laugh in themselves. His leaders were frequently his own; many times they were quotations from popular comics, such as "Fare Ye Well, Brother Watkins" or "Cap'n Rice, he Gin A-huskin'." Plummer caught Boise with an announcement which read, "A highly colored, distinguished, and talented Mississippi River Fireman will, at intervals during the afternoon and evening, perform 'Wood Up' on the Caloric Organ and assist in making it 'mighty warm' for the audiences. The beautiful, unique, and high-priced Cast-iron Caloric Organ, used on this occasion, is [such and such a distance] from the Stove and Hardware House of F. R. Coffin & Co. A voluntary donation of an American Dollar will be cheerfully extorted from each of the audience on entering the hall." The note which particularly appealed to us was, "Parties inviting friends between the ages of Three Weeks and Four Months will be required to make a deposit of $11.00 per cherub as a guarantee that they will not applaud where the applause does not properly come in."

MUSICAL DIRECTOR CHAPMAN

The always-on-hand musical director in chief of Boise was one Mason Chapman. I am not competent to pass upon Chapman's musical ability but I remember that he was a muscular performer upon violin or piano and ripped out melodies until the instruments fairly shrieked. He was the central figure at all dances and was conspicuous at all times because of his florid complexion, his enormous mouth full of white teeth, and a never-varying style of brown suit. After the success of P. A. Gilmore's famous jubilee, held at Boston in 1868, similar concerts on a smaller scale were given throughout the Northwest. When the jubilee craze struck Boise, Chapman was the chief perpetrator, assisted by Boise's brass band, a backwoods affair led by Peffly, a local barber. Chapman advertised the jubilee far and wide and prepared to make it a social and musical success. He procured from Fort Boise a cannon and placed it in the lot to the rear of the dance hall. Chapman tied a rope to the cannon fuse and at times he would tug this and thereby punctuate the music of the orchestra with a roar that kept all Boise awake until the early hours. The gun made as much racket as the orchestra: the orchestra was a wonderful creation. Barring the roars from the bass drum and Chapman's cannon, the feature of the orchestra was a Mexican greaser named Señor Baker. Baker sat on a large coal-oil can, beat time with his left hand, and wheezed the melodies through a hair comb covered with paper. As the excitement grew and the "boys" yelled, Señor Baker beat time with his legs and elbows and succeeded in giving a fair imitation of a large hairy spider, a tarantula, mesmerizing a victim. The editor of the local newspaper stated next day that Baker's work was the feature of the jubilee. The editor's enemies retorted that he, the editor, wasn't competent to judge music for his early education in harmony was gained solely through yelling "Gee-haw" at mules and oxen while persuading them on a pedestrian tour across the continent. After the jubilee, Chapman was created a professor and used the title unstintedly.

LOCAL CELEBRITIES

Mose Lyon, city marshal for some years, was a local character who had blown into Boise from his natural element, the sea. Mose tried to reconcile himself to life ashore, but whenever the wind howled and his mariner's bump began to itch, Mose would roll along Main Street, cast an eye to leeward, sniff, and then treat bystanders to a dissertation upon cloud shapes, wind storms, and other sights he had seen in foreign ports.

Boise claimed a poet, Captain H. Houghton, the "Rocky Mountain Poet," so styled by himself. He was an indigent, half-witted old fellow who wrote harmless and almost rhymeless doggerel which none ever heard unless Houghton grabbed him in an unsuspecting moment, dragged him to a retreat, and read bursts of poetic fancy. The poor captain was found dead in a cellarway one morning where a hoodlum or drunken passer-by had hurled him.

There were but four colored men in Boise and of these John West and Joe Allen were the aristocracy. One of the cheerful sights in Boise was Joe Allen and his one-horse dray. Allen had procured the vehicle in Frisco, and it was an echo of the style of vehicle used in Eastern cities about 1830. The dray had long projections at the rear and was held together by massive iron drawpins. Allen was a native of Newburyport, Massachusetts, and was a bright, industrious man. He was conspicuous because of his red hair and freckles. Allen left Boise in 1869 for the reason that he was unable to obtain permission to place his children in the public school.

John West had been raised in Philadelphia and claimed to be a Quaker by training. He told me that much of his life had been spent with the Dundas family in the old mansion at Broad and Walnut streets, Philadelphia. He had mechanical ability and also did chores about Boise. West belied his Quaker instincts by often indulging in whisky, and when he did, the effect of the intoxicant was unusual; the negro's legs would dance a jig, but even when he was full-seas over, his head remained clear. There was a fellow negro in Boise at one time, a man of vicious character, with whom West had an altercation in a card game. Pistols were drawn, and West killed his man. Because of the bad reputation of the other, West was acquitted. One morning in 1872 West was standing at my home, chatting about work to be done, when a negro woman passed by. West spoke to her, but the woman passed by and scowled at him. "My, my!" said he, not at all abashed. "How ungrateful women can be! I did a great favor for that woman —I freed her from the meanest coon in Idaho." I did not know what he meant, so West very casually remarked, "That's the wife of Nigger Bob. I killed him in that card game, you know."

Old Bill, another negro, was town crier. He walked Boise streets, rang a large auction bell, and announced fairs, auctions, and amusements, and also hunted for stray children. He was a typical Southern darky in looks, manners, and originality. When the Carters produced *Don Caesar de Bazan,* Bill roamed the streets shouting, "All come! Et's a most int'restin' play by er pritty young gal. Ah seen huh mahself! She's got a pahty wid her named Don Kiser the Baboon. All come!" I lectured one night at Slocum Hall and Bill volunteered to announce because the lecture was for the benefit of the Episcopal Church. Someone told me that Bill's announcement was, "Oh, yas, oh, yas! Jes' you come to heah him! Ah doan know de subjec' but Ah knows him, Ah knows de man! He is good stuff, good stuff, an' de lekshuh is foh de glory o' Gawd an' de benefit uf de chu'ch." A bystander asked him why he yelled so loudly, and Bill snorted, "Didn't de gemmen pay me an' say to yell like de debil?"

Boise's chief funmakers were four men: James D. Agnew, proprietor of a livery stable; George Stilts, a blacksmith; George Englehard, a carpenter; and Billy Flannigan, a brickyard laborer. Wherever they were, fun and mischief predominated, and of all the natural comedians I have seen, those men were the best. To recount their pranks would take a separate volume. Men who make people laugh are just as much a part of a country's history as are those who direct the serious affairs of life, and Boise should remember in her history the four men who so superbly acted for years a comedy that was clever and enjoyable.

Soon after Judge Hollister took his seat on the bench George Stilts was summoned into court to serve on a jury. When court opened, I called Stilts's name but there was no response. I again called very loud, "George Washington Stilts!" Thereupon, the marshal pushed Stilts from a rear seat toward the jury box. Stilts walked down the main aisle until he stood directly before Judge Hollister. His face was innocent and blandly questioning. Judge Hollister looked sharply at him and then said, "Mr. Stilts, take a seat in the jury box." As if he had seen the judge's lips move, Stilts placed his hand to his ear and smiled and said, "Eh?" The judge said louder, "Take your seat in the jury box!" Stilts bowed and said "Thanks," and then made a flying exit down the aisle. The marshal grabbed Stilts and pushed him forward and by this time Judge Hollister had become somewhat excited. "I did not tell you to go," cried Hollister. "I told you to take your place in the jury box." Of the two hundred people present, at least one hundred and ninety-nine knew that Stilts was no more deaf than was Judge Hollister. They were speechless at the impudence of the action. Judge Hollister never suspected the imposition, so he said, "Mr. Clerk, discharge that man from the jury. He could not hear evidence. You may go, sir!" he said to Stilts. Stilts again walked very innocently toward the judge, but Hollister wildly waved him off, and Stilts walked calmly out, leaving the spectators in roars of delight. When court had adjourned, I explained to Judge Hollister that Stilts was not a deaf man, and then Hollister laughed loud and long. Next day Hollister walked past Stilts's blacksmith shop, and George was busy rapping shoes on a horse. The judge touched him upon the shoulder,

A LIVE ENTERTAINMENT!

PROFESSOR
C. B. PLUMMER

Respectfully invites all those who appreciate the Pure, Beautiful, Vigorous and Elevated in POETRY and LITERATURE, and all who enjoy a GOOD HEARTY LAUGH at genuine HUMOR without coarseness, to a

SELECT PARLOR ENTERTAINMENT
AT
TEMPLAR HALL,
TUESDAY EVEN'G NOV. 25.

PROGRAMME.

```
HAMLET TO THE PLAYERS..................SHAKSPEARE.
KING DAVID'S LAMENT FOR ABSALOM.......N. P. WILLIS.
BARBARA FRIETCHIE,................................WHITTIER.
THE SKINN'D MAN (Imitation of Author),......MARK TWAIN.
THE LITTLE HERO (A gem of simple pathos),........MATHISON.
HEZAKIAH BEDOTT (In costume),............MRS. WHITCHER.
THE HAYTHEN CHINASE,.............MRS. MULROONY.
NO SECT IN HEAVEN,........................MACKAY.
SOME LEEDLE SHDORIES........PY DEEVEREND BEOPLES.
THE GHOST,......................................SAUNDERS.
"HARP OF A TH A O U' SAN' STER RINGS—AH!".....ANON.
```

The Exercises will Commence at 7:30 o'clock Precisely.
N. B. To protect the audience ...... during the rendering of each Selection. Persons coming in will be admitted only during the short interim between the pieces.

A Voluntary Donation of an **AMERICAN DOLLAR** will be cheerfully extorted from *each* of the audience on entering the Hall.

Parties inviting friends between the ages of THREE WEEKS and FOUR MONTHS will be required to make a deposit of $11.00 per cherub, as a guaranty that they will not *appland* where the applause does not properly come in.

[*Alta California, San Francisco.*]
Plummer has fairly earned the reputation of giving the best monologue entertainments of any performer, and has literally succeeded in capturing the critics.

[*Morning Call, San Francisco.*]
Mr. Plummer possesses powers of mimicry and facial expression, combined with graceful modulation of voice, and that rarest of accomplishments, the power to read a good thing well without overdoing it, to a much greater extent than many who .... and largely puffed.

Handbill used by traveling entertainer in Boise City, Idaho Territory, in 1870.

This group is dressed for some early Boise festivity—perhaps a Fourth of July celebration. On extreme right is Orlando ("Rube") Robbins, famous Indian fighter and officer of the law. The others are, left to right: Lt.Col. John Green, who was for twelve years commandant of Boise barracks; Mr. Cold (?); and Jim Griffin.

and, half laughing and half frightened, George looked at him.

"That was very funny, George," said Hollister, "but don't do it again."

"I won't, Judge," said Stilts, sighing his relief. "The reason I did it was because there were ten animals here to be shod when the marshal took me to court. Oh, I needed the money, Judge, I certainly did!" Hollister laughed again and walked down the street.

Billy Flannigan had his own way of expressing his views. Until he talked, we could imagine that we were talking to his brother James, for James was Billy's counterpart. I was walking on Main Street one day when I met Flannigan and chanced to say to him, "Were you born in Missouri?"

Billy gave me a reproachful look and then shouted, "No, thank God, I was not!" He leaned against a fence and appeared to be in so much distress that I was alarmed and asked him whether or not he was ill. With a vague gesture, indicative of suffering, he waved me back and gasped, "Sick? Not me. I was busy saying one hundred and six short prayers of thanks to Heaven for not lettin' me be born in Missouri."

James D. Agnew, clever soul that he was, owned the chief livery stable in Boise. Jim had the best equipment procurable and boasted the one hearse in Boise; he drew to funerals and hauled to weddings. The pride of Jim's stock was a pair of claybank, or yellow, horses with white manes and tails, and when a sport desired to blow himself, the acme of extravagance and real devilishness was reached by hiring Jim's yellow horses and trotting down Main Street. Agnew was also the possessor of a wonderful dog, a pet Newfoundland named Tige. General Cartee's dog was the only one in Boise spoken of in the same breath with Tige. Once in a while, kind and loving neighbors were wont to feed poisoned meat to Cartee's dog, Watch, and then poor Watch would crawl home, whine like a child, and yowl for help until the Cartee household rallied to the rescue with liberal doses of sweet oil. Jim Agnew's claybank horses held a warm spot in his heart, but Jim held Tige above home and country in his estimations. The dog deserved his popularity, too, for he was the town pet and a doggy dog of the true Newfoundland type.

George Stilts and Tige were bosom friends; their meetings were daily and their greetings were warm and sympathetic, for whenever business was slack, Stilts would stroll to Agnew's stable and fool with Tige, if Jim chanced to be absent. One day in 1871, Stilts went to call on Agnew and found no one home save Tige, who offered hospitalities. Stilts played with Tige for a short time and then returned to his shop. The dog then decided to return Stilts's call and in a few minutes he sauntered about to the blacksmith shop and greeted George with a wag of tail which meant, "Little lonely round there so I thought I'd drop in for a chat." That day was Tige's Waterloo! Stilts conceived a brilliant scheme. He closed the door of his shop and coaxed Tige into the wagon shop, or repair building, at the rear. With a pair of horse clippers, or shears, Stilts dug into Tige's thick wool. As the hair succumbed to the assault, George became enthusiastic, and his artistic gifts came to the surface. He clipped Tige bare with the exception of a large neck ring of hair, a fluffy fetlock, and a luxuriant bunch on the tip of Tige's tail. Then Stilts seized paintbrushes and painted the dog's head white. The ring about his neck he painted flaming red, each leg a different color, the body variegated white and yellow, and the tail a pale blue with a yellow tip. Fixing the back door of his shop so that Tige could escape, Stilts sauntered carelessly around to Agnew's stable. By this time Jim had returned and was in his favorite attitude of rest, leaning against the door and puffing a large meerschaum pipe. Agnew had procured an East Indian helmet without which, day or night, he never was seen. "Ah, James," said Stilts, "on duty, I see!" Then Jim and Stilts passed the time of day and chatted about new deviltries to be tried on unsuspecting citizens. Ten minutes passed by, and then, from around the corner, came sounds of men and boys in pursuit of something. The next instant, around the corner came Tige, and at his heels was a pack of Chinamen, boys, and hoodlums. Never had such a creature been seen in Idaho! Stilts gasped, "Jim, for God's sake, what is it?" Jim was startled and disposed to take flight, but the fun came when Tige ran into the stable and whined and barked and rubbed paint all over his master. Then Stilts yelled, "Jim, so help me, it's Tige!" Agnew fell gasping against the stable door and was unable to speak for five minutes. The crowd hooted and jeered, and then Stilts drove them away. When Agnew could speak, he said impressively,

"I'll kill the man who did it. George, will you help me?"

"Will I, Jim?" said George. "You bet! Hand in hand, we'll hunt the villain down!"

At that, Agnew reached for guns. He had a rack of firearms at hand, articles which were very useful in persuading drunken sports to return teams; sometimes the guns were of use about the first of each month when Agnew desired to collect money due. Jim armed himself to the teeth, and while he buckled on a cartridge belt Stilts had another inspiration.

"Jim," he said, "let's take Tige with us. Maybe he'll recognize the measly sneak that done this!"

"Good idea, George!" said Agnew savagely. "And when Tige points him out, I'll feed his heart to that ruined animal!"

The unsuspecting Agnew tied a rope to the dog's collar and throughout all Boise went the two. At intervals Stilts forced a sob and cried, "Jim, ain't it a damned shame? Look at Tige." The ovations tendered them were many and varied. Men who wanted to laugh, went behind doors and did so and those who caught an inkling of what had really happened to Tige offered Agnew a handshake of sympathy. In every saloon liquid consolation flowed for the two men; the dog was the only one that seemed not to enjoy the parade. At four o'clock in the afternoon Stilts and Agnew were carried home on shutters, and Tige led the funeral cortege. Half of Boise's population followed, concealing their grins. I am quite sure that Agnew never learned who had painted his pet. Certainly Tige didn't peach!

On July 4 of each year, Stilts, Agnew, Englehard, and Flannigan paraded the "Hornique Brindles" or "Horribles." A band of forty men, clad grotesquely and speaking a fearful jargon, would assemble in front of Green's "Missouri House," and Corporal Engelhard addressed them in his annual oratorical outburst. A mock court-martial would be organized and on frivolous charges preferred, a member of the band was condemned to be shot in the public square. Preparations for the "Brindles" parade commenced about three days prior to the holiday. The quartette met and talked over "recruiting" plans; their draft list comprised the name of every man, woman, and child in Boise. A very full program, lengthy and meaningless, was drawn up, and then a motion was offered to change a trivial matter on the schedule. This would be firmly resisted, no matter what it was, and then pipes and drinks came on and for two or three days the quartette stayed in executive session and drank themselves blind. On the night of July 3 a motion "slapped the thing on the table," and immediately after sundown the four men started out and walked all night in order to be awake when the glorious Fourth dawned.

Stilts led his comrades to the public square and as he stood beside the wooden statue of George Washington—an equestrian statue that will be referred to later—he would, with much dignity and feigned solemnity, apostrophize the great George. Knew him well, so he did, Stilts always said, and the George Washington he knew was a man of color—waited on tables at the What Cheer House down in Frisco! When Stilts finished, the others roared the national anthem in voices that beggared description. When their braying sounded on the night, a crowd rushed to the square. At their arrival, Stilts and his funmakers strolled from behind the statue and asked in innocent bewilderment, "Say, what's all the noise about, eh?" When the sun reached high noon on July 4, the leaders of the Brindles quietly passed into unconsciousness, and John Henry Thomas Green, hostelry proprietor, helped carry them to the cots which had been awaiting them for three days.

Some time in February, 1871, a Boise genius planned a "fireball" night, and the idea was so new that many of us contributed money. A barrel of turpentine, numerous cotton-wick balls, and some twine were purchased, and when darkness came the public square was crowded with people who had been attracted by the announcement of the novelty. Fifty men were placed on a side and were armed with wick balls sewed with twine and soaked in the turpentine. Through the night flashed the blazing balls, roaring and hissing as the air fanned the blazing spirits, and a beautiful sight it was. At times a ball unraveled and wrapped about a tosser and set his clothes blazing. The crowd then rushed at him, threw him down, and rolled him in the dirt to extinguish the flames; it looked to us, the spectators, as if death by burning were preferable to death by trampling.

At ten o'clock the fun was fast and furious, and to climax matters, the "big four" of funmakers began to assert themselves. Shrieks, yells, curses, and groans suddenly arose in the ranks of fire tossers. A man would pick up a ball, drop it, jump into the air and shriek, "Hell and blazes! Wow! I'm cooked!" In five minutes' time every ball was lying on the ground idly burning; there was not one in the air. Investigation showed that someone had wrapped a few dozen balls with wire and tossed them into the arena. The turpentine soon heated the metal and the result was that for days and days men walked about Boise with hands wrapped in bandages and on a still hunt for "them fiends." It was but natural to attribute the brilliant climax to the busy brains of George Stilts and his pals.

In connection with the Brindles, I recall another Boise man, a German who worked as a sign painter and paperhanger. He would express rapture, or grief, on the slightest provocation, and in matters with which he was not in the remotest way connected. I saw him working in a room one day, stretching wallpaper, when a passer-by looked in and said, "Dutchy, Bill Jones died this morning!" The German cried, "Mein Gott, is dot so!" He didn't know this Bill Jones from Adam but down he came from the ladder, left buckets, paper, and paste, and went into mourning for three days in a secluded spot. The German applied for admittance to the Brindles, but Corporal Engelhard wouldn't hear of it. Englehard said that the man would be a constant menace to the corps. Should armed enemies attack the city, the German would, said Englehard, consider it a great event and desert in the enemies' face to sneak off and enthuse.

HORSE RACING

Horse racing was a constant and popular sport. The Boise track was a half-mile course north of the town, toward the fort. John ("Pony") Young owned it, and each year we had good races and much excitement. Neither at Idaho City nor Silver City was there level ground in or near the town limits. The Silver City track was at Wagontown, and the Idaho City track was a stretch, a straightaway, on Mores Creek flats. The heats were short heats; as a rule, six hundred yards. Our race-track sports of early days were legion; to name them means the naming of the

"Pony" Young, whose race track furnished pioneer Boiseans with many thrills.

SOCIAL LIFE AND AMUSEMENTS AT THE CAPITAL

entire male portion of the town's population. Racing season was not solely a season for gambling; rather, it was an opportunity to meet friends in an open-air picnic, and greetings and gossip were as popular as bookmaking. There was really the best of sportsmanship shown in making bets, and very large sums of money frequently changed hands. A man's word was his book; if a sport said, "Bet you a thousand that Medoc wins," and he was accepted, no money was put up then. Very seldom was a written acknowledgment recorded, but the verbal bond was as good as gold.

I recall a race at Boise in 1871 where the entries were absurdly named. Three of the horses were down respectively as "John the Baptist, "Crooked Back Bill," and "Gambler's Ghost." We had with us a negro barber, from Silver, named Walker; he was usually dubbed "Silver" Walker. He owned a string of half-breed racers with which he circuited the territory and played for second money. I frequently met him on the road between Boise and Silver, leading his racers. Walker rode a gaily caparisoned animal and was ever neatly dressed. Trailing behind him, with a lariat, trotted his animals, and on the back of each was a racing outfit and sacks of barley. Walker owned his string for years, and many a dollar did he win throughout the Idaho circuit, for he watched the entries carefully and knew his ground. He was genteel in manner and equal in intelligence to the whites. The sports, most of them Southerners, never drew the color line against Walker; they dubbed him "Silver" and admitted him without objection to the sporting fraternity. Walker was a Republican and always occupied a front seat at all political meetings in Silver.

GENERAL W. T. SHERMAN AT BOISE

Excluding political seasons, when statesmen from the coast visited Boise, we saw very few Eastern men of prominence because there was little in the territory to attract them. I recall, however, that we enjoyed on September 25, 1870, a visit by General William T. Sherman and his daughter; Major General John M. Schofield; and Colonels William M. Wherry and Joseph C. Audenried. The Army men were on a tour of inspection of the Department of the Columbia and with them were two civilians, Dr. A. B. Linderman, afterwards director of the United States Mint, who was then reporting for the Treasury Department on mineral resources, and Alvinza Heyward, the California capitalist. Sherman and Schofield were inspecting for the purpose of determining which Army garrisons could best be abandoned. Our Boise people were anxious to have the Boise garrison retained, so the town turned out to welcome General Sherman.

The visitors stayed at the Overland, and proprietor Griffin did the honors to make them comfortable prior to their hard journey to Kelton by stage. A reception was held at the Overland, and General Sherman addressed the citizens from the hotel balcony. Governor Curtis introduced him, and Sherman spoke on the Indian question, saying that the raids were practically over and that there was little necessity for many Army posts in the Northwest. The future, he said, the near future, would see all Indians gathered upon one reservation. In this Sherman was a poor prophet, for Idaho suffered from three Indian raids within the succeeding nine years. After the crowd had dispersed, Sherman sat with us on the hotel balcony and for two hours he chatted on a wide range of subjects—stars, the great aurora he had just witnessed, Indians, the Civil War, and various officers. During the course of his chat, he said that his brother, John Sherman, was not a great man but that he won recognition because he was industrious. He also said that Grant had told him that he preferred to remain in the Army as its general rather than be president. Sherman discussed the effect of the late war upon the South and expressed his belief that the South had nothing promising before it, and that there was no hope for it until new generations had come.

About eleven o'clock the travelers retired. I chanced to go upstairs toward midnight, and I saw the general sitting in his doorway tugging at his boots. I assisted him to "strip" and then mentioned that I was a friend of General Walcutt, of Ohio. "Oh," said Sherman, "is that so? Charles Walcutt was a good soldier—one of the best." He further said that it was at his suggestion to Grant that Walcutt had been appointed internal revenue collector for the seventh district of Ohio. Walcutt, by the way, held the position for thirteen years and amassed a snug fortune. Years afterward when I met Sherman in Washington, I reminded him that at one time we had been on intimate terms and mentioned the boot incident. He laughed heartily and said that he remembered the Overland House very well.

Sherman was always in action both in body and in mind. He talked as constantly as he smoked and he was one of the best and most versatile conversationalists of his time. He jumped from one subject to another in flashing and brilliant style, but whatever he said was meaty and compact. Sherman was a man of extraordinary ability; under a loose and easy manner he concealed good judgment, caution, and the faculty of unerringly judging the character of men. When he smoked he had a quaint habit of flipping the small finger of his hand against the tip of the cigar, and the habit was so pronounced that he invariably flipped at a weed whether it was lighted or not. If anything, he was a more devout smoker than was Grant. Sherman was a great social favorite because he enjoyed public life far more than most men of station. In Washington, St. Louis, and New York, up to 1891, he was always at theaters or receptions; in fact, he haunted places of amusement. Of young people, especially children, he was noticeably fond, and though it seemed at times that he gushed, he was honest at heart and his strong nature was above meanness.

I saw him chatting with a group of young people one night in Washington, and he was the busiest talker of the group. One of the young women said, "General Sherman, you certainly are a great talker!"

The general replied instantly, "I grant you that, my dear. But you see, I have earned the right to talk. I have done something."

General B. F. Potts, who commanded a division under Sherman, told me that while in Atlanta, Sherman explained why he did not assign Joe Hooker the command of the Army of the Potomac after McPherson's death. Sherman had known Hooker in California when Hooker was so far in the depths that he asked Sherman for a small sum of money, evidently purchase money for drink. Hooker wasn't denied the loan, but the incident stuck in Sherman's memory, and he never had much respect for Hooker.

CHAPTER IV

NOTABLE CHARACTERS IN SOUTHERN IDAHO

JAMES S. REYNOLDS and William J. Hill! These two men, the former of Boise, the other of Silver, guided public opinion in the territory more than any other of the Idaho leaders from 1869 to 1875. In my acquaintance with them I learned their true character: they were men of the highest and most unselfish aims, of the true altruistic spirit that alone promotes the welfare of a community. In their public-spirited desire for Idaho's future, both lost sight of individual gain of money or position, and the matchless energy of the two, through their powerful newspapers, dug the channel for law and order, and the directing they did was an epoch in the history of the territory.

A history of Idaho will fail in its purpose unless it pays proper tribute to the memory of James S. Reynolds, his personal traits, and public services. When I met Reynolds in 1869, he was a man of perhaps forty years. He was a New Yorker by birth but had lived in Ohio and Wisconsin, crossed the plains to live successively in California, Oregon, and Washington, where he worked as printer, attorney, and schoolteacher, and then journeyed to Boise. He was six feet four inches in height, had enormous hands and feet, a long head with a thatch of sandy hair, and kindly blue eyes that never deceived. A thick husky voice and a scraggy beard completed the physical make-up of a machine of energy and industry. He was absolutely devoid of fear and when angered was a fiend, but Reynolds' heart was as soft as a woman's.

He came to Boise in 1864 with two companions, R. W. and T. B. Reynolds—no relation to him, however. The brothers soon left the territory, but Jim remained as editor and proprietor of the *Statesman*.* The paper was started as a triweekly on July 26, 1864, at one dollar a week, or twenty dollars a year. The office and printing materials were purchased by the joint owners at The Dalles, Oregon, where the brothers published The Dalles *Journal*. Except for two months of the time, the *Statesman* has always been a Republican paper. During those two months it was temporarily disposed of to Democrats, but after that it was reclaimed to the fold of Republicanism.

As editor of the *Statesman*, Reynolds wielded more power than any twenty men in the territory; he was a terror of evildoers, for his paper stood ever for law and order. He edited a Republican paper in a rank Democratic community and he not only made money, but his paper was respected. He dethroned political bosses and accomplished the removal of incompetent Federal officials. When Idaho was overrun by gamblers, thieves, and murderers, from 1864 to 1866, the power and skill of Reynolds, in his editorials and in his personal conduct, did much to drive them from the country. His paper led public sentiment, honest sentiment, on all occasions, for Jim was vigorous, exact, trenchant, and penetrating in his style. We usually called him "Judge" or "Old Jim."

Jim had a small encounter in 1865 with Judge A. Heed, then temporarily serving as district attorney in Ada County, and the outcome nicely illustrates Reynolds' lack of fear. Reynolds had commented adversely upon Judge Heed's action in a matter, and although Heed was an excellent man, his bad temper cropped out occasionally. The day that the criticism appeared, Heed met Reynolds on Main Street, in front of Riggs's saloon. In a flash Heed

---

* James Reynolds had strong views on political matters and did not hesitate to express them. His first editorial said, "Politically, it may as well be understood, once for all, that we are opposed to this rebellion [the Civil War] in every phase of its causes, or its results, and to everybody who is not opposed to it." On August 25, 1864, the triweekly was supplemented by a weekly edition. About 1869, when the paper was sold, its name was changed to the Boise *Statesman* but soon after it was repurchased by Reynolds and it resumed its old title. Throughout its history, the name *Statesman* never left it, and the paper has always been the foremost journal in the territory.
—T.B.D.

Idaho Tri-Weekly Statesman.

VOL. 1.   BOISE CITY, SATURDAY, APRIL 27, 1865.   NO. 120.

Idaho Statesman.

PUBLISHED EVERY
Tuesday, Thursday and Saturday Mornings,
BY
JAMES S. REYNOLDS & CO.
T. B. REYNOLDS, JAS. S. REYNOLDS, S. W. REYNOLDS
Proprietors.

Terms of Subscription:
One copy one week, payable to Carrier..$0 25
One copy one month by mail or express.. 3 00
One copy three months by mail or express 6 00
One copy six months by mail or express..10 00
One copy one year by mail................20 00
Agents supplied on liberal terms.
Terms—Invariably in Advance.

Rates of Advertising:
One square (10 lines or less) 1 insertion $ 2 00
One square two insertions............... 4 00
One square one week................... 5 00
One square one month.................. 10 00
One square two months................. 15 00
One square three months............... 20 00
One square six months.................. 30 00
One fourth column one insertion........ 5 00
One fourth column one week............ 10 00
One fourth column one month........... 15 00
One fourth column three months........ 20 00
One fourth column six months.......... 30 00
One half column one insertion.......... 10 00
One half column one week.............. 15 00
One half column one month............. 25 00
One half column three months.......... 40 00
One half column six months............ 60 00
One column one insertion............... 15 00
One column one week................... 20 00
One column one month.................. 30 00
One column three months............... 40 00
One column six months................. 90 00
One column six months................ 150 00

Transient Advertisements to insure insertion must be paid for in advance.

Special Notices charged for at the rate of one dollar a line each insertion.

Office—Corner of Idaho and Seventh Streets.

AGENTS FOR THE STATESMAN.

The following is a list of the authorized Agents for the STATESMAN, to whom all dues for subscription are payable:
B. M. SWINNERTON—Idaho City.
P. W. JOHNSON—Centreville.
D. M. MARTIN—Pioneer City.
B. M. MOORE—Placerville.
J. C. HOLGATE—General Agent Owyhee County.
JOHN CUMMINS—Ruby City.
KELLY & JOHNSON—Walla Walla, W. T.
OLIVER WHITE—Dalles City, Oregon.
L. P. FISHER—San Francisco, California.

FRANK MILLER,   CHAS. C. DUDLEY.
MILLER & DUDLEY,
Attorneys and Counsellors at Law.
Office south west corner Wall and Montgomery streets, next door to Frontz & Co.'s Packer's Joint, Idaho City, I. T.   n1tf

M. KELLY,
Counsellor at Law
BOISE CITY, I. T.   n1tf

A. G. COOK,
Attorney at Law and
Notary Public,
BOISE CITY, I. T.   no1tf

L. P. HIGBEE,
Attorney & Counselor at Law
Ruby City, Owyhee County, I. T. au18tf

Daniel McLaughlin,
Attorney at Law,
Idaho City, I. T.

W. R. KEITHLY,
Attorney at Law and Notary Public,
IDAHO CITY, I. T.
Office—Montgomery Street near Wall. no1-tf

B. MARTIN,   J. W. MURPHY
MARTIN & MURPHY,
Attorneys at Law.
Offices at Ruby City, and Idaho City. oc4tf

E. F. GRAY,
Attorney at Law.
Office at Law's Art Gallery Building, Boise City, I. T. Will attend the Districts Courts of Idaho City, Owyhee, and South Boise.   m4tf

JOHN CUMMINS,
Attorney and Counselor at Law,
Office—Court House, Ruby City, Owyhee County, I. T.   oc18tf

NEW STORE! NEW GOODS

CRAWFORD, SLOCUM & CO.,
THE OLDEST AND FIRST ESTABLISHED firm in Boise City, take this method of informing their friends, and the public generally, that they have just removed into their new and commodious building

Corner of Sixth and Main streets,
where they offer for sale the largest and best selected stock of General Merchandise, this side of Portland. Our stock consists in part of

Groceries and Provisions.
GAITERS, BOOTS AND SHOES,
DRY GOODS AND CLOTHING,
CROCKERY AND GLASSWARE,
SHELF AND HEAVY HARDWARE,
WINES AND LIQUORS,
CIGARS AND TOBACCO,
IRON AND STEEL,
NUTS AND CANDIES,
Paints, Oils, Glass, Brushes,
LAMPS;
Lamp Fixtures, & Kerosene,
HATS AND CAPS,

**All of which we offer
AT THE VERY
LOWEST MARKET PRICES.
Wholesale and Retail.**

Having our own transportation enables us to offer customers superior inducements to purchase of us. Persons from a distance may rely upon having their

Orders Promptly Attended to.
de15   CRAWFORD, SLOCUM & CO.

**DRIDE'S
Livery Stable & Corral,**
Montgomery Street, Idaho City,
(Between Commercial & Wallula sts.)

BUGGY, SADDLE AND CARRIAGE HORSES.
NEW AND FASHIONABLE BUGGIES and CARRIAGES, always ready, day or night, at a minute's notice.
N. B.—Horses received on board per day or month, at a reduced value.
DRIDEN McCLINTOCK,
au25 3m   SAM STEWART.

**DR. F. C. CLARK,
DENTIST,**
HAS REMOVED HIS LOcation from Placerville to Boise City, where he intends to make his home for coming years. He is confident that his old friends and patrons, having had the experience of his Dental Surgery, will call on him again if requiring his services. For reference inquire, as there are many in the Territory who know him. Office on Main street, one door above Stage House.   up stairs.   oc1tf

**DR. J. B. ISBAIL,
DENTIST.**
HAS REMOVED HIS Office, and late rooms over the International, up stairs, on Main street, Idaho City. All operations guaranteed to give the best satisfaction. I shall visit Boise City, and the outer Camps at stated periods, of which I shall give notice.   oc13tf

M. A. CARTER,
Attorney and Counselor at Law,
BOISE CITY, IDAHO,
WILL ATTEND the District Courts in the different counties in this District. Particular attention paid to collections. May be found at the Overland House.

D. G. HIMROD,
Physician and Surgeon,
Office at the City Drug Store, Boise City, I. T.   n1 tf

D. G. CAMPBELL.
Physician and Surgeon.
Office on Main Street, opposite Stateman office, Boise city.   oc13tf

GEO. I. GILBERT,
Attorney and Counsellor at Law,
Idaho City.   fe14

B. M. DuRell & Co.,
DEALERS IN
Exchange and Gold Dust,
Will pay the highest rates for
Gold Dust, Legal Tenders,
QUARTERMASTER'S VOUCHERS,
Ass't Treasurer's U.S. Checks.
WILL SELL
Sight Drafts on Idaho City, Ruby City, and Silver City, Idaho,
GREAT SALT LAKE CITY, UTAH.
ALSO ON
Portland, Oregon,
AND
San Francisco, California.
Collections Made in all the above Named Places.

REVENUE STAMPS for SALE.
Money Received on Deposit.
B. M. DuRELL & Co.,
Fire Proof Brick Buildings,
a21f   Boise and Idaho Cities, I. T.

IDAHO HOTEL,
BOISE CITY, I. T.
THE Proprietors of this well known and POPULAR HOTEL, take this method of informing their patrons and friends that they will continue to furnish the best accommodations to be had in this City. Having renovated and refitted their building throughout, it is now one of the most comfortable and convenient Hotels in the Territory.
The Best the Market Affords
will be used to supply the tables, and no pains spared in its preparation.
GRIFFIN & HUGGINS,
ca23tf   Proprietors.

Pioneer Livery & Feed Stable.
RIGGS & AGNEW,
Corner Main and Seventh sts., Boise City, I. T.
NOTICE TO ALL, THAT THE undersigned have reduced their prices to suit the times, and are prepared to take care of stock in a manner unsurpassed in Idaho Territory. A good supply of
Buggies, Carriages, & Gentle Horses,
always on hand, and can be had at a moment's notice. Also, SADDLE HORSES, and in fact everything pertaining to the Livery and Feed business. Our ranch is in good condition, and we have plenty of room for more Horses and Mules.
n1tf   RIGGS & AGNEW.

QUICKSILVER!
THE UNDERSIGNED HAVE BEEN appointed Agents for the sale of the
New Almaden Quicksilver,
And are prepared to furnish it in quantities to suit at
San Francisco Prices!
Terms—STRICTLY CASH.
SMITH & DAVIS,
m14 6m   71 Front Street,
Portland, Oregon.

FROM THE
NEW MILL!
THE UNDERSIGNED are now prepared to furnish
Lumber in Quantities
to suit, both clear and common, in Boise City and Valley, 9c at the Mill, on Stewart's Gulch, ten miles from town. Bills promptly filled. Office at Jacob's & Co's store from 9 A. M. to 3 P. M.
Hand in your Orders.
PURVINE BROTHERS,
W. B. Purvine, Agent.   fe28tf

THE ELEPHANT
AUCTION & COMMISSION HOUSE,
(Corner Montgomery & Wall Sts.,)
Idaho City, I. T.
THE UNDERSIGNED HAVING PURchased the above establishment, is now prepared to attend to any business entrusted to his care.
Commissions Solicited
He also keeps on hand the best assortment of GROCERIES and PROVISIONS.
E. E. CHEENT.
February 27th, 1865.   fe94tf

SEEDS! SEEDS!
A LARGE LOT OF FRESH GARDEN Seeds of every variety in bulk. Just received and for sale, by cash by
a1tf   B. M. DuRell & Co.

JAS. M. BLOSSOM,
North East corner Main and Eighth streets,
BOISE CITY, I. T.,
WHOLESALE AND RETAIL DEALER IN
BOOTS, SHOES, HATS,
CLOTHING,
Dry Goods, Groceries, Shelf
AND HEAVY HARDWARE,
PROVISIONS.
Farmer's, Mechanic's, and Miner's
TOOLS,
Cigars, Tobacco & Pipes,
POWDER, SHOT, LEAD,
Caps, Nails, Blankets,
GRIND STONES, STATIONERY, &c.
For sale at the
LOWEST MARKET RATES FOR CASH.
w24tf   JAMES M. BLOSSOM.

Overland House!
Corner of Main and Eighth Streets.
BOISE CITY, I. T.
GEO. A. YOUNG & CO. - - - Proprietors.
THIS NEW AND SPLENDID HOTEL is entirely completed, with a large number of rooms neatly finished and handsomely furnished now ready for the reception of guests. The Restaurant connected with the Hotel is under the immediate supervision of Mr. Young, whose long experience in the business, and well known reputation as a caterer to the public wants, is a sufficient recommendation. The BAR is always supplied with the finest LIQUORS and CIGARS. Attached to this Hotel are a first class BARBER SHOP and BATHING ROOMS.
General Stage Office for the Overland, Walla Walla, Umatilla, Salt Lake, Owyhee, Idaho City, and South Boise lines.   oc1tf

ROBERTSON & CO.,
Watchmakers & Jewelers,
Opposite Jacobs & Co's corner Main and Seventh streets, Boise City.
HAVE FOR SALE A GOOD assortment of GOLD and SILVER WATCHES of all kinds.
Also a well selected stock of Jewelry, Diamond Pins and Rings.
Clocks, Silver & Plated
WARE, GOLD PENS, TOYS, &c.
Solid gold Jewelry made to order, of the latest styles. Particular attention given to the repairing of Watches. All work warranted.   feb4 tf

RE-OPENING
OF THE
STAGE HOUSE.
(Boise City, opposite Geo. Chick's.)
Monday, March 27th, 1865.
Myers & Lee, - Proprietors.
Board per Week..................$14 00
Board and Lodging per Week.......$18 00
Boise City, March 25, 1865.   m25tf

J. R. WILKINSON,
LA GRANDE,
WHOLESALE AND RETAIL DEALER IN
MINERS' OUTFITS, PROVISIONS, AND
GROCERIES,
Orders from Idaho promptly attended to.   fe14tf

FOR SALE.
ONE BUILDING AND LOT, situated on Washington Street, CENTERVILLE, will be sold at a bargain. For particulars inquire of the undersigned, Main Street, Idaho City; or, Main Street, Boise City.   ja28tf   G. H. CHICK.

NOTICE!!
THE IDAHO HOTEL
CHARGES ONLY
**Fourteen Dollars per Week
FOR BOARD!**
SQUARE MEAL, - - $1 00
GRIFFIN & HUGGINS,
Boise City, March 21st, 1865.

LONG HANDLE SHOVELS.
40 DOZ. Round Pointed, Stiff and Spring Blades, for sale for cash, by
B. M. DuRELL & Co.,
Boise and Idaho Cities.

Front page of the leading newspaper of Idaho Territory.

drew his gun, placed it against Reynolds' heart, and yet hesitated a moment because he knew that Reynolds was never armed. Old Jim never moved a muscle; he kept his eye on Heed's face, and when the judge hesitated, Jim yelled, "Shoot, you coward, shoot!" The next instant, Jim grabbed Heed's gun, beat the judge over the head until he fainted, kicked him into the street, and leisurely continued his walk down Main Street. His nerve was so superb that not a bystander interfered. It is true that Jim carried no firearms, but in his office he kept within easy reach a choice assortment of iron bars, wagon spokes, ax handles, and one or two ancient horse pistols. Jim had a knack of using anything handy for a weapon. One day in 1870 an old friend of mine walked into Jim's office and intimated that Jim and the truth were strangers. Jim made a back-arm swipe, knocked the speaker down, and carried away a few teeth in the melee!

Reynolds especially disliked Judge David Noggle, chief justice of the territory, and continually waged a crusade against him in the *Statesman*. Reynolds journeyed to Washington in 1870, partly on business, but mainly in an endeavor to remove Noggle from the bench. He afterwards dramatically related to me his interviews on the subject with President Grant and Attorney General E. R. Hoar. Judge Hoar was exceedingly irritable, as the Senate could testify; the Senate paid him for small courtesies by rejecting his appointment in 1871 as an associate justice of the U. S. Supreme Court. Reynolds haunted Judge Hoar's office in Washington until Hoar became tired of hearing and seeing him. But Jim didn't despair. Hoar was fully aware of the reason Grant retained Noggle on the bench, so when Reynolds voiced his request, Hoar opened up the vials of his wrath against Reynolds and his mission. Jim sat calmly down and in a short time Judge Hoar concluded a tirade that was worthy of him. Then Jim took his turn. It was a Payette roof lifter, a Winnemucca gale! Jim told me that it was the ablest effort of his life; Hoar evidently was of the same opinion, for he sat spellbound long after Reynolds had finished. Then Hoar leaned toward Jim, grabbed his hand, and said, "Permit me to shake hands with you, sir! You have such a pointed way of saying things. Your language and manner are those of the West, but, sir, your courage savors of the early Puritans. Sit down, and we shall discuss your business." Reynolds completely captured Hoar, and before Jim concluded with his statement of the Noggle case, Hoar and he were old friends.

From 1869 to 1872 the *Statesman* office was a two-story frame building opposite the City Hotel, at Seventh and Idaho streets. Reynolds slept in the front room of the upper floor. The room opened on to the small porch, which was supported by posts running to the ground. One night as Jim lay awake in his bed, with both windows of the room open, a man's head appeared at the window, showing plainly in the moonlight. In a few minutes the burglar lighted a lantern and slipped into Jim's room. Armed with a short club, he poked about in a heap of papers and trash.

Jim sat up in bed and asked, "Excuse me, pardy, but who are you?" Jim's tone was quite natural, so natural that the man was surprised.

"I'm a robber!" said the other. "Ain't you skeered?"

"Nope!" said Jim, stealthily reaching for his gun. "On the contrary, I'm enjoying myself. But say, what are you hunting for in that pile?"

"Money!" said the thief, vigorously thrusting about.

"Money?" queried Jim, as if puzzled. "Think you'll find any? You do? Well, I'll get up and help you hunt. I've been here for six years without finding any." Then Jim covered the thief with his gun as the man made a dash for the window. "You get!" yelled Jim.

"You bet!" yelled the man, as he rapidly slid down the porch post and disappeared in the night.

Reynolds' assistant on the *Statesman*, an assistant who was foreman, manager, assistant editor, and all, was Judson A. Boyakin, or, as we knew him, "Jud." No more manly or no quainter fellow ever breathed than he. Boyakin was as fierce a Democrat as Reynolds was a Republican, and the arguments which the two had over editorials for the *Statesman* surpassed anything ever heard in Boise. People who chanced to pass the thinly boarded walls of the office must have thought that a debating society, or a real battle, was in action. The discussions were always mixed with humorous sallies and bright wit.

Boyakin set up the editorials and often when he read a line which hurled invectives against the Democratic Party, he would say to Reynolds, "Does this thing go in?"

"Yep!" Reynolds would retort.

"Well, it's a damned lie!"

"Indeed?" Jim would remark. "Well, she goes in all the same."

"All right, Jim, you're boss," Jud would say, "only you know it's a damned lie! Democrats ain't built this way." It was Boyakin who placed in the *Statesman* the advertisement which read:

STOLEN—from this office. A revolver. The person returning it will be given its contents and no questions asked.

Reynolds had an unfortunate matrimonial experience which resulted in his voluntary withdrawal from the territory. He was a widower when he came to Boise, but while there, through his efforts to procure a teacher for the public school, in which he was much interested, he met a young woman and her mother, two Californians. Against the advice of friends, Jim married the girl. The outcome was bad—too much mother-in-law and too much hidden past in the girl's case. After a few months of married life, his wife ran away and took with her everything portable. This was in 1872, when Jim sold the *Statesman*. For three years he hunted through California for his wife, and when I saw him in San Francisco in 1875, he described to me how he found the girl and her mother in an out-of-the-way place, one winter night. Certainly a tragic scene was enacted there. Jim considered himself fortunate in escaping with his life; two of his predecessors in the woman's affections were not as fortunate. The unfortunate alliance blotted out a useful life from Idaho. Had Reynolds remained until the territory became a state, he would undoubtedly have represented her in an important public role.

His California career, until the time of his death on September 14, 1897, was typical and remarkable. He began to manufacture barrels at Vallejo, in association with the late General John F. Frisbie. That failed, and so did his next venture, the manufacture of brass butts in Frisco. He then opened a law office in 1877, and entered politics as the nominee of the Workingmen's Party. He was nominated in 1879 for county attorney but refused, declaring it unconstitutional to pledge to return part of his salary. He then ventured in mining in Calaveras County, and when this failed, he undertook farming in San Luis Obispo County but was cleaned out by drouth. Finally, he took a desk in the law office of Judge Henry C. Dibble, of Frisco, and from that time until his death was best known as a single-tax man.

Edward C. Marshall, while he was attorney general of California, in 1883 or 1884, had advised Reynolds to read Henry George's *Progress and Poverty*. Reynolds sat up all night and read the treatise and was from that time an ardent disciple. George's *Protection or Free Trade* made him, a former Republican, an ardent Free Trader. After 1891, Jim was president of the Single Tax Society in Frisco and wrote more literature on the subject than any ten men in California. In 1897 Reynolds personally presented to the legislature, and succeeded in getting passed through the assembly, a resolution to submit to the vote of the people a

NOTABLE CHARACTERS IN SOUTHERN IDAHO

constitutional amendment providing for local option in taxation. Adolph Sutro, then mayor of Frisco, defeated the motion: Sutro declared himself to be the "largest owner of unimproved land in the state." By copious writings, Reynolds advertised the blessings which had come to New Zealand through the single tax, and one of his letters, in the San Miguel *Courier*, was a forerunner of the famous report by Senator Bucklin, of Colorado. Mr. Joseph Leggett, of San Francisco, writes to me: "In all vocations, Reynolds taught more men to think straight, than any man I have ever known."

WILLIAM J. HILL

He was "Old Hill," to us, and the sound of his name always aroused admiration. Six feet in height, of swarthy complexion, with brown eyes, smooth face, and a bearing that showed brains and strength, this was the editor of the *Owyhee Avalanche*. Hill, like Reynolds, never knew the meaning of fear. He revelled in things of force and power; even the name of his paper had a tinge of fight in it. He was a younger man than Reynolds and lacked a trifle of his ability, but he ruled southern Idaho with a rod of iron, and his touch and his opinions were felt in all portions of the territory. He was king of the foothills and monarch of the valleys; we compared him to an Idaho windstorm that swept desolation through the Snake Valley. Hill was admiringly dubbed "a holy terror." In 1875 Hill told me that he had spent ten years, one third of his life, in Idaho; consequently, I placed his age at thirty. He was as a rule, a reticent man, and common sense and nerve were his salient points. He had Reynolds' temperament—as gentle as a woman until honestly aroused and then—flight was his opponent's hope. Hill despised Rebels and Democrats, and so did Reynolds: Hill despised mean men and actions, and so did Reynolds.

At the time I first met Hill he was proprietor and editor

of the *Owyhee Avalanche* at Silver City; the paper was published weekly. His paper and job-printing office produced a living, little more. Hill was a compositor by trade and had worked on the *Avalanche* under its former proprietors, J. L. Hardin and Joseph Wasson, who had established the sheet in August, 1865. On August 17, 1867, Hill and H. W. Millard purchased the *Avalanche* and managed it for a year or so until it was sold to John McGonigle. February 19, 1870, McGonigle again sold the paper, and Hill became sole proprietor, for he had purchased Millard's interest in 1869. Sometime in 1868 the Butler brothers, T. J. and J. T., had established a modest paper called the *Tidal Wave* in Silver City. In 1869 or 1870 the *Tidal Wave* was purchased and incorporated with the *Avalanche*. When the telegraph line was constructed from Silver City to Winnemucca, Hill became ambitious and began issuing the *Avalanche* as a daily, but two years later, in 1876, the paper gave up the ghost. Hill sold out to C. S. Hays, who had been an editor for some time, and Hays re-established the *Avalanche* as a weekly. Under Hill's management, the sheet saw its best days, and it was, like the *Statesman*, respected because law and order was Hill's text, and at no time did he aid speculative mining booms by the printing of false information. Hill's purpose was to make Silver City the metropolis of Idaho and to establish Silver as the center of Owyhee County's mining interests; in the mineral resources of the county he had, like very few others, sublime faith. Owyhee's ups and downs, her spasmodic periods of booms and "busts," never disheartened Hill. In October, 1873, his faith was so pronounced that he established a monthly magazine, *Old Hill's Monthly Souvenir*, a sixteen-page quarto, with glazed blue-paper cover. It contained reprints of standard fiction and general reading for home circles. How long the *Souvenir* lived, I do not know, but I feel confident in saying that it was the first magazine published in the territory.

Shoenbar Mill in the Owyhee mining district.

Stage office, Silver City, Idaho Territory.

Poor Man Mine near Silver City, Idaho Territory.

Silver City, Idaho Territory.

NOTABLE CHARACTERS IN SOUTHERN IDAHO 133

As a newspaper writer of vigor and terseness, I knew none equal to Hill. When the wrath of his pen was turned upon a person through the columns of the *Avalanche,* the editorial was a thing to be read and never forgotten. Hill was a bitter enemy of Judge Milton Kelly, of Boise, who purchased and edited the *Statesman* after Reynolds withdrew from the territory in 1872. One of Hill's best-known efforts was an editorial turned against Kelly. Hill wrote six hundred words of vituperation that were classic and when he had vented his spleen and used, as we thought, about all the terrifying words known to man, he closed his editorial with a "You, Kelly!" in the manner of a man shouting "ho-o-e-y" at a dog and hurling bricks. But for the fact that Judge Kelly is dead, I would reproduce the article, because it has probably never been excelled in its line and would best give an idea of Hill's ability with language.

Hill was a Canadian by birth but a devout lover of America, the land of his adoption. He had literally fought his way through life, in all that the phrase means. I saw him in swimming one day and noticed that scars, most of them from Indian arrowheads, covered his body from head to foot. Hill described to me how he and companions were caught in an adobe ferry house by Snake Indians, at the crossing of the Nevada stage road on the Owyhee River. The Indians rushed an attack and jumped upon the roof of the building. With pieces of sod, they covered the chimney, and the men were almost suffocated in the room below by smoke from the fire. Instead of running out to certain death, Hill and his comrades lay on the floor and gasped for breath, and when a party of settlers chanced along, the men in the cabin were unconscious—though not scalped.

Hill married Miss Belle Peck, daughter of an early settler and famous miner. If I am not mistaken, the "Belle Peck" mine was named in her honor. In 1876 Hill moved to California where, at one time, he was state senator.

After he left Idaho, I lost trace of him, but wherever he now is, there will be found a man worthy of the name and one to be sought.

STAMPS V. ANDERSON

Stamps Volney Anderson was his full name, but "Volney" didn't suit the West, so Anderson was dubbed, "Stamps." In 1869 he was a probate judge in Alturas County and leader of the Democratic hosts in Rocky Bar as well as an attorney and member of the territorial council. Anderson was six feet in height and of portly build. His genial disposition and melodious Southern dialect made him a general favorite. I recall that when I visited him at Rocky Bar, in 1869, his office furniture was decidedly primitive. The legs of a bed on one side of the room were placed in cans filled with oil to thwart the progress of marauding denizens peculiar to beds, and on a rough table was an oilcloth cover which gave unmistakable signs of home cooking. Judge Anderson was graduated from Yale in 1858 and from the Albany (N. Y.) Law School in 1860. Like all Yale men, he announced the fact of his graduation when he first met people. Anderson, at home, would draw from a large trunk, which contained nothing else, a morocco-bound classbook of his own class at Yale. Upon his lap he would spread the book—it was superbly printed —and talk proudly of the men with whom he was graduated. "Nice fellow that!" he would say, touching a portrait, or, "Damned uncommon cuss, Jim was!" and again, "This book cost me fifty dollars."

The judge told me that his Uncle Stamps sent him to Yale and when he graduated he had great expectations, but his uncle's niggers in Missouri and Mississippi disappeared at the coming of Union soldiers. Said he, "The wah—you Yankees—cleaned out Uncle Stamps and Nephew Stamps at the same fell swoop." After he left the Albany Law

School, he practiced for a time in St. Louis; he had been born at Keytsville, Missouri, in 1835.

In 1862 Anderson reached Idaho with a stream of argonauts moving into Florence, after he had served as clerk of the city council in Portland, Oregon. As an attorney he was not pecuniarily successful but he dabbled in mining claims all his life and ever expected riches. Honest and chivalric to the highest degree, he represented his county creditably in politics and civil life. Poor old fellow, he was in sore financial straits one winter, and we suspected that his long-tailed coat was buttoned tightly at the neck to conceal the lack of shirt front.

At a private dance given in Boise, Anderson was particularly impressed by a rich and handsome widow, and when we twitted him and urged him to propose, he stormed, "Don't you know, sahs, thet I am a gentleman! How, in the name of Heaven, could I offah myself to that lady when I am impecunious!"

However, Judge Anderson ventured into matrimony twice; first in 1878 and again in 1882, for his first wife died a year after marriage. The judge's dignity was perfectly natural; it was cultivated and on the right side as well. He was a daydreamer who lived in air castles built by the to-be-limitless wealth from all his schemes. He was a consistent and faithful rainbow chaser, and I hope that at length he found the rainbow's end with its pot of gold.

Typical of Anderson was the enthusiasm which cropped out one day when he and I were journeying along the Snake River in a coach. He called my attention to the miles of bunch grass free to anyone who might use it. With a majestic wave of his arm, he said, "Look, my friend! See that superb growth of bunch grass? Ah, I am losing ten thousand dollars a day. How, you ask? Why, by not owning herds of cattle and having them live and fatten for the market on that grass!" That was his happy philosophy, which I hope he carried to his grave and which in life soothed him in troublesome times. Memory of him and his delightful disposition came back to me all too plainly when I heard years later that Judge Anderson died in London on March 21, 1894.

We had a rule in the district court at Boise that when a criminal was docked who was too poor to employ counsel, the court could assign an attorney to defend. Of course, the duty was performed gratuitously, unless the attorney could prevail upon the imprisoned man to collect fee money from acquaintances, which happened in rare instances.

On one occasion, in 1870, a Chinaman had chanced to be near Peter Sonna's store when robbers were detected forcing an entrance. The Chinaman had nothing to do with the robbery but he had now been in jail six months. The grand jury remanded him, though the court entered the plea of not guilty for him. The Celestial apparently could not speak a word of English. Judge Anderson saw a chance to make money and he hurried to my house one night and requested that I ask Judge Lewis to assign him for the defense of Hop Wo. Judge Lewis answered me by saying, "Certainly, I shall be glad to assign Anderson to defend. I've seen the record, and that Chinaman is no more guilty than am I. Six months in the terrors of the Boise jail is punishment enough for a criminal, let alone an innocent man." When court opened next morning, and the case of *Territory* v. *Hop Wo* was called, Sam Upop, Chinese court interpreter, said that Hop Wo had no counsel, and thereupon Judge Lewis requested Judge Anderson to defend the Chinaman.

"Suttinly, youah honah!" said Stamps and he stepped forward smiling and complacent. At once Judge Lewis whispered to me, "If that Chinaman goes before a jury, he'll be convicted. Tell Stamps to motion to quash the indictment. I will sustain the motion and discharge the prisoner. He'd better plead guilty than to have Stamps or anyone else defend him!"

I did as Judge Lewis requested but Stamps was wild. "No, sah!" said he. "There's no evidence against this man, and I can acquit him. I have been, sah, up all night preparing a speech, and it's a good one which I must delivah. If I do well, I'll get the trade of all these Chinamen in court. This Chinaman knows no English—it is my duty to defend him."

Judge Lewis was a trifle annoyed when I whispered Anderson's ultimatum but the case was started. The prosecution finished, and the territory's side of the case was concluded in thirty minutes. When Judge Anderson stepped forward to address the court, he was the personification of dignity. That morning he wore the tallest collar I ever saw on a man; it served to hold up his head so far that he spoke mostly to the ceiling. He spoke:

"Gentlemen of the jury, put yourselves in that man's place, sahs! Helpless would you be, sahs, in far-off China were you American-born and knowing no Chinese: helpless is he in America, speaking no English. The prosecution has no case against this man. Judge Prickett did not demand conviction, sahs, because he knew my client was and is innocent. Gaze at him, sahs, look at his sad face, the drooping eyelids. I call you, sahs, to witness that his color is gone. What did it? Ah, we know! Six months' incarceration in the Boise jail. Were any of you ever in that jail? I hope not, although you may yet be. It is an ulcer on the body social. When the grand jury inspected that jail, sahs, last summer, they stood across the street and used a telescope. Take thither, if you go there, your own blankets and a box of bug powder. My client—look at him, sahs—is apparently bloodless, for in six months he has not been bugless! He sits calmly before you awaiting predestined exoneration; 'tis the calm, sahs, the quiescence, which anticipates assured success. Although Hell has no terrors for him since he has been incarcerated in our jail, his future would be sullied by any but fair treatment from this august and honorable body of jurors. In China, gentlemen, it is a stigma when a member of the family is convicted of crime—a stigma upon all the family. Think, sahs, that perhaps where the wavelets flow down the Yellow River of the Celestial Kingdom, a poor, old, and worn mother possibly sits and weeps and wishes for her lost boy, her Hop Wo! Send her, gentlemen, glad tidings that her boy is free. Why should Hop Wo try to force entrance into Peter Sonna's store? Why should he seek to wrench off Peter Sonna's back door? What, sahs, could he do with that back door?"

For twenty minutes this continued in Stamps's dialect, which I have but faintly reproduced, and in his inimitable style. Many of us were convulsed, but scores of spectators thought that Anderson was a marvelous orator. The Chinese spectators were much interested, but puzzled. When Stamps had concluded, he was as bright as a new dollar and smiling and agreeable. Judge Lewis charged the jurymen to agree on acquittal, and then the sheriff started to take them out, but the foreman of the jury—it was the best panel I had seen in Boise for many a day—arose and stated that a verdict had been agreed upon and it was unnecessary for them to adjourn. At the statement, Judge Anderson beamed kindly. I asked them formally if they had agreed, and on affirmative answer, Judge Lewis asked, "How say you? Is the prisoner guilty or not guilty?"

"Guilty!" said the foreman like a shot, and down in his chair with a thud sat orator Anderson. Judge Lewis was equal to the emergency.

"Mr. Clerk," said he, "set aside that verdict and enter an order quashing that indictment and also one discharging the prisoner. Gentlemen of the jury, you may go, but I want to say that I'm ashamed of you! No Chinaman in

Idaho can get a fair jury trial, and that man, Hop Wo, is not guilty. Sheriff, adjourn court!"

Poor Hop Wo apparently understood nothing, until Sam Upop told him to go, and then he walked quickly toward the door. Judge Anderson gave chase and so did I, because I knew something was about to happen. The Chinaman was halfway downstairs when Stamps grabbed him by the coat and pinned him to the wall.

"You," said Anderson, "chase round among your friends and get fifty dollars for me. You would have been jailed only for me. I got you off!"

Thereupon, the unintelligent Celestial, who knew no word of English, shook his fist under Anderson's nose and said, "You no gettee me off! Judge, he say I go! You go to hellee!"

J. H. T. GREEN

John Henry Thomas Green was for many years proprietor of the Missouri House, a frame hotel opposite the "Stone Jug" in Boise. In 1869 Green was a man of sixty years, tall and heavy and partially gray, with a face hidden behind a bushy and unkempt beard. John Henry Thomas was slow in actions and speech and marked in mannerisms. He seldom wore a coat, whether indoors or out, and I never saw him but that he wore a black, low-crowned slouch hat. Mr. Green's hat may have been tacked on or glued on, or he was perhaps born with it on; the last is a feasible explanation. Green was a primitive type of Missourian, a relic of the advance guard of civilization in the great valley. From 1830 to 1861 he dwelt along the Missouri River and he was a walking encyclopedia of its boats, captains, and fatalities. Green had entered Idaho with the "left wing of Price's army," and was naturally a rabid Rebel. At the Missouri House he did a fairly good business and was looked upon as a useful citizen and ornament in Boise. He was interestingly reminiscent and attracted large audiences of gaping-mouthed settlers who applauded and urged the colonel to recount deeds done in Missouri "befoah de wah, an' befoah them damned Yanks upsot the glorious South, suhs!"

The chief furniture of the porch and office at the hostelry maintained by Colonel Green consisted of tall split-seat hickory chairs and a vast number of deep wooden boxes filled with sawdust, in which the guests were wont to "pflug" their tobacco juice (the proper word is "ambeer"). The comfort of the guests demanded deposit boxes to the right, left, middle, and below. About the hotel were numerous satellites who had known, or who claimed to have known, the proprietor in halcyon days, and these men were his patrons, for newcomers seldom visited the Missouri; it was at the other end of town from the stage station. Once in a while I dropped in to chat with Colonel Green—not to eat—and to see him preside at his banquet board. His hotel was Liberty Hall; in it John Henry Thomas dispensed his viands with the air of a manor lord. He was the embodiment of hospitality when he headed his table, in shirtsleeves and with knife and fork in hand, smiling at hungry guests. To permit a guest to depart with appetite unappeased would have been a crime in Colonel Green's eyes; the guest who swallowed the most was accorded the place of honor. From the head of the table Green would call, "Gents, nominate yer fud! We have beef, ham, and mutton!" The colonel had a trait not unpeculiar to Pikers. When his hands became a trifle soiled in carving, he used the seat of his trousers for a napkin. Again, he suffered from a constant cold, and his index finger of either right or left hand—the colonel was truly ambidextrous—would swipe east or west with a caressing motion and the wherewithal was snapped from his proboscis with a sudden gesture. These two characteristics made Colonel Green a most interesting carver! But he was the idol of his people, and his army defended him and his habits, and when a guest chanced to utter words of disapproval, that guest was squelched and labeled "stuck-up" or "tenderfut." For, said his admirers, the "kunnel" was an old settler, a square man, and he could up and do as he good and damned pleased, for his heart was right, and them wot criticized cud up an' git!"

Some years before I went to Boise, Green had served a term as treasurer of Ada County, and when his resignation took place his accounts were somewhat muddled. Ed Sterling was one of the investigating committee, and Ed told me that the examination was a treat. Colonel Green possessed an iron safe, a "salamander," which he had brought across the plains and which served as the county treasurer's strongbox. When the investigating committee asked for a key, Green said, "She hain't got no key. Git in her without a key. I'll show you, gents. Lay her on her back!" The committee heaved and succeeded in turning it. "Now," said the colonel, with arms akimbo, "put coal ile in the hole and limber her up." A quart of oil was squirted, and then Green said, "Wobble her a leetle an' she'll open all right." The committee wobbled a little and cussed a little more, and in five minutes the salamander's bolt shot back with a thud. Inside was an aged and torn daybook, a large comb with but few teeth, and a dozen bleached corncobs. "Them cobs is fer stoppers fer jugs!" explained the colonel. "I brung 'em from Pike. They is skeerce in these parts." Then the committee asked for an explanation of his bookkeeping method. Green started on a column of figures in this way: "Seven frum seven you kaint come down, and three and three makes six, carry one!" The committee was too busy concealing grins to audit then and there, but investigation showed later that nothing was at fault save Colonel Green's bookkeeping.

There was great excitement in Boise, one day in 1871, when it was heralded far and near that John Henry Thomas Green had been robbed of a valuable heirloom, a silver watch. Until the thief, a drunken roustabout, was captured, Boise held its breath. Judge Hollister sat as a committing magistrate and held the man for grand larceny for stealing an article worth more than sixty dollars. A great crowd gathered in the court, and it did seem that the penitentiary was yawning for the poor wretch for his sacrilege in annoying a man of territorial distinction. When Colonel Green testified as to the watch's value, Major Huston, for the defense, asked him where he had purchased it and for how much money.

"Suh," snorted the colonel proudly, "I riz up sixty-five dullahs fo' thet watch. Bought huh forty yeahs ago from a pusuh on a Missouri Rivah boat." Then Huston asked him how long he had worn it. "All me life," said Green, "an' I will weah huh until me death."

In the meantime, John G. Broadbent, Boise's only jeweler and a very honest man, came on summons to look at the watch. Being sworn in and put on the stand, he subjected the watch to the closest scrutiny. While he made examination, Green alternated between smiling at his friends and glaring at the culprit. Broadbent, who was an Englishman, held the watch so that all of us had a look. The timepiece was an old-fashioned "turnip" in a bull's-eye case. It had been made by Tobias, of Liverpool, about 1825, and was heavy enough to drag down a healthy man.

"If the court pleases," smiled Broadbent, "I have seen many watches like that discarded in England. It would be dear at three dollars and a half."

Judge Hollister broke in with, "Do you mean, Mr. Broadbent, that three dollars and a half is the total value—the entire value?"

"Yes," answered Broadbent, "for the works are almost useless, and the case is of no value except for the silver in it!" When Broadbent finished, I confess that I feared to look at Colonel Green. His eyes bulged out of his head and he gasped for breath.

"What!" yelled he. "Does that bloody Englishman dare to take thet stand an' impugn my veracity? Why——"

"Mr. Broadbent does not impugn your veracity, Colonel Green," interposed Judge Hollister, "for he simply stated that your watch was worn out. You have carried it forty years and it is very apt to be worn out."

Colonel Green blinked and gasped, marshaled his thoughts, and then roared, "Suh, my fathah told me in 1828 that the longah a man woah a watch, the bettah she got. By the livin' gods, I believe my fathah, and no bloody Englishman can belie him!"

Trouble was imminent until Hollister said, "The prisoner will furnish bail to await the action of a justice of the peace. It is, at its worst, a case of petty larceny. Court is adjourned!"

Colonel Green, escorted by hosts of friends, walked away as if dazed. The blow was exceedingly severe, and he was joined at the hotel by many mourners. Day after day did John Henry Thomas hold impromptu mass meetings with sympathizers. He would assume a tragic pose, place the famous watch in his hand, and explain the outrage done him by the court. The history of the watch would be told, and at the conclusion of the recital John Henry Thomas would swing the ticker into his pocket and conclude with, "Gents, let's licker!"

E. D. HOLBROOK

Holbrook was Idaho's delegate to the U. S. Congress from 1864 to 1869. He was a well-built man of medium height with black hair and whiskers, and, in 1869, appeared to be about thirty-five years of age. Holbrook was a noticeable figure, and his manner, though somewhat stylish, indicated the genteel rough. He had a swaggering walk and always dressed in black broadcloth, with a low vest of buff color, and a broad slouch hat, black in color. To everyone he was "Ned" Holbrook.

When a gentleman in Idaho aspired to political prominence and failed to be accorded the title of "Colonel," or "Judge," it was certain that the gentleman had a screw loose. It is true that these titles in Idaho, as in all other sections, were mental creations, and usually signified prior service neither at bench nor war. But the very fact of their inapplicability to a politician made him conspicuous. When I first met Holbrook he had entered into his final stage in politics—his decadent stage—and yet he was a young man. Judge J. K. Shafer, of Idaho City, had defeated him in 1868 for the nomination to Congress and had been elected to Congress, much to everyone's surprise.

Holbrook was born in Ohio, and his chief regret was that he had not been born in South Carolina. He served Southerners and their interests with so much fidelity in Idaho that it was patent he did his best to repair the error that permitted him to be born north of Mason and Dixon's line. Holbrook was a poor lawyer in culture and extremely verbose as a speaker. His Southern satellites, with whom he was always surrounded, referred to him as "a great oratah, suh." Perhaps he had been, at one time, but his environments had gradually deteriorated him.

Holbrook's birthplace was Elyria, Ohio, and, after an education received at local public schools, he went to California and practiced law at Weaverville. In the mining rush of 1861, he went to Oregon, then to the Nez Perce mines in Idaho, and eventually he reached Idaho City in 1863. At once he became the god of "the boys" and was elected on the Democratic ticket to the 39th and 40th Congresses. Certainly Holbrook's nerve and courage were unquestioned, and he possessed remarkable energy. He stood by his friends with unswerving loyalty, "lushed" freely, and ever held up his end with his clientele. He possessed education above that of the ordinary man, in

The two men at extreme right are: standing, (4) E. D. Holbrook, territorial delegate to Congress, who was shot to death in front of his law office, and sitting, (8) Marion More, central figure of the bloody Silver City mining dispute. The others in the group are: standing, left to right, (1) Ben White, (2) Lav Lindsay, and (3) N. B. Wood; sitting, (5) Sank Owens, (6) John B. Wheeler, ex-governor of California, and (7) G. White.

fact, was above the average, else he never would have obtained the prominence he did. He masked himself in a dignity that was specious, though well acted, and made it a rule to be reticent, though when he warmed up to a subject, his vocabulary was unusually vigorous.

Territorial delegates had no vote in Congress, and Holbrook, as Idaho's representative in Congress, was also handicapped by conflict with an enormous Republican majority. He was more useful to his constituents, however, than most men would have been under the circumstances. Astute politician that he was, Holbrook overcame serious obstacles more than once, and the Senate confirmed many of his requested appointments that seemed almost sure of rejection.

One piece of strategy executed by him was the most ingenious ever brought to my notice. A friend of his, one Carroll, was receiver of the United States Land Office at Boise. Holbrook watched his opportunity and inserted in a general appropriation bill of March 3, 1869, an item which gave to Carroll three thousand dollars for the year 1869. The trick of inserting a clause for a private claim in a bill of the kind had never before been done in our legislative annals. The insertion of the item, which passed slightly changed, was not a result of chance; it was the result of Holbrook's ability to grasp, to see and grasp, an unusual opportunity. General Benjamin F. Butler, of the committee on appropriations of the House of Representatives, favored the item or clause—for a reason strictly personal: Some weeks before the bill was put before Congress, General Butler was interested in a private social function. To assist in decorating rooms he had borrowed from the Treasury Department several large mirrors. One of the mirrors was returned badly damaged, and through employees in the department Holbrook learned of the incident. He promptly laid a snare for General Butler, who was forced to the conviction that unless John C. Carroll and Tubman Ayres, respectively register and receiver of the Boise Land Office, were provided for by a little "wad" in an appropriation bill, the mirror incident would be brought before the House and the newspapers of America. At any rate, the item passed with the bill, and Holbrook's friends received three thousand dollars each for the year ending June 30, 1869, for *fees not received!* Truly, it was a great feat in legislation.

The assay office and the penitentiary were the result of acts passed while Holbrook served his last term as delegate, although Holbrook had little to do with the passing of the bills. Similar places were erected at the same time in other parts of the West. When Holbrook retired from Congress he settled down to practice law at Idaho City and lost much of the picturesqueness and glamour surrounding him when he was the political idol of "the boys." He retained his popularity, however, in local fields, and his tragic death was much regretted in the territory. Charles Douglass, a gambler, shot and killed Holbrook in front of the latter's office on June 18, 1870. Douglass was tried for the murder but was acquitted. He immediately left Idaho; it was safest for him to do so. Judge Noggle presided at the trial, and Noggle's unpopularity was so pronounced that the jury was firm in its belief that Noggle was persecuting Douglass: hence the verdict for acquittal. Had Douglass been tried before Judge Lewis he certainly would have been convicted. The respectable element in the territory considered that Holbrook had been assassinated, and when tidings of the fatality reached Boise there was talk of a vigilance committee being organized. On all sides could be heard, "Charley got the drop on him." I recall now that Holbrook had a peculiar manner of turning and peering behind him whenever he walked. He told me once that he always had a horror of being shot from behind. Douglass killed him from behind! Between the two men there had been bad blood, feud blood, and the climax had to come. Remarkably, the killing of Holbrook was about the last incident of its kind in southern Idaho.

AUSTIN SAVAGE

One of the most peculiar men it has been my lot to meet, to meet and to know intimately, was Austin Savage, a resident in Idaho from 1863 to 1881 and for several years collector of internal revenues. Mr. Savage, one of several brothers, was born in Skowhegan, Maine, in 1820 and received his education at local schools. He engaged in the lumber business—until a slight disagreement over the possession of logs cost him a little of his reputation. In 1849 Mr. Savage sailed for California on the ship, *Rob Roy*, from Boston around the Horn. For some months I had possession of his logbook, a private book of passengers and events which read like a romance. Mr. Savage engaged in California for several years in mining ventures, then moved to Nevada and then to Idaho. Mr. Savage was a man of intelligence and fair education. If I am not mistaken, he attended Waterville College, now Colby, and was in General Benjamin F. Butler's class, 1838, for two years. Savage was never popular in Idaho, principally because of his bluntness and his dislike of Rebels; he incurred the dislike of every Southerner in the territory. He was a clever judge of men and distrusted most of them. Somewhat of a recluse in his way, he lived in a house of his own building, in company with animal pets. I have never known a man in private life who possessed more power with animals. His horses, cats, and dogs were trained to circus pitch!

Mr. Savage was frugal; in fact, he was out-and-out stingy! One of his sisters was "sealed" to Brother Angell, to whom is given the credit of designing the Mormon Tabernacle, the huge inverted soup tureen at Salt Lake. Stenhouse's history of the Latter-day Saints states that

Brothers Angell and Folsom wanted the major share of the glory—after Brigham Young took what he thought was due him for the designing of the Tabernacle.

The transitory nature of Idaho's population made rents very high for modest buildings. A property which cost one thousand dollars to erect would usually bring six or seven hundred dollars rent, that is, if it were advantageously located. Mr. Savage occupied, while he was revenue officer, an office that was a feature of Boise. It was a frame building, one story high, lined with tar paper, seven feet wide by twelve feet long, and it contained a door, two windows, and one partition. The foundation was a large wagon truck with wheels—which were kept well greased. The shanty stood on the cross streets opposite the Overland Hotel and adjoining Judge Prickett's office. Mr. Savage received nine hundred dollars each year as rental from the Government on the assurance that the place was fireproof. Late in the sixties, the Treasury Department sent an inspector through the Northwest to inspect all revenue offices, and a good yarn went the rounds on Mr. Savage. The inspector came to Boise and at once expressed his astonishment when he saw nothing but squat buildings, most of them frame. Mr. Savage effusively greeted the inspector, and when he escorted him to the office on wheels, the visitor gasped, "Is this your office? Is this the place that the Government gives you nine hundred a year for? Great Heavens, man, this isn't fireproof! I'll have to report this."

"Be seated, sir!" smiled Mr. Savage. "Take a cigar."

The inspector sat down and lighted a cigar. Mr. Savage closed the door and then tugged on a rope which hung overhead. "I want to say," continued Mr. Savage, "that this is the only fireproof building in the territory. In fact, it is the only hygienic structure in all Idaho. You will agree with me in five minutes." The inspector grunted his disbelief. Outside there was considerable commotion caused by passing teams and shouts of teamsters. All of a sudden, the building began to rock from side to side and then came a wild gallop. The inspector grabbed Mr. Savage, but Savage held him down in his chair. For two minutes everything was riot and confusion. Then came a jolt, and the shanty lay in calm. Mr. Savage laughed in the inspector's white face, opened the door, and said, "Step outside, sir!"

The inspector fairly leaped out. To his surprise, he found himself at the public square, facing a statue of George Washington carved in wood. He looked at Mr. Savage, who calmly puffed his cigar. "Look at the other end of the ship!" grinned Savage. Two of his horses were hitched at the front end of the building.

"Why, what is all this?" asked the inspector.

"It's this way," said Mr. Savage. "I get nine hundred for a fireproof building. And it's little enough. I keep this shanty in the middle of town but I've got my teams around the corner in Jim Agnew's stable. If a fire breaks out, I jerk a rope and a bell rings—you didn't hear it because of the noise in the streets. Jim gets my horses, gallops them around, and hitches them to this building, and papers, records, men, building, and everything are dragged away from any burning buildings in the vicinity. There is nothing in here to catch fire, and this house is dragged away from anything that may be burning!"

"Good God!" snorted the inspector. "Couldn't you have said so without giving me heart trouble? I wouldn't take that ride again for a million. Oh, you're fireproof, all right, and I'll mark you O.K. I guess people think hell has broken loose somewhere when they see a young house rollicking down Main Street with a scared team in front."

Mr. Savage had much practical knowledge of mining and served well as a juror in the department of mining at the Philadelphia Centennial in 1876. He had a placer mine on Feather River, California, and had worked with his brother on the Comstock Lode; the Savage mine was named after them. As a Government official in Idaho, he rigorously administered the revenue laws, even to causing the arrest of prominent men who tried to evade the laws. His zealousness and anti-Rebel traits incurred so much unpopularity that in 1877 a petition asking for his removal was signed and forwarded to the Treasury Department. As soon as Mr. Savage notified me of the action taken against him, I called on President Hayes, and action was delayed until Mr. Savage could file papers in refutation. Two years later Savage forwarded his resignation and told me to present it. I did not do so. President Hayes refused to accept it because he had received from worthy friends in Idaho letters testifying to Mr. Savage's character. The Idaho petitioners could not understand how and why Savage was retained; they did not appreciate the fact that President Hayes echoed Lincoln's policy——that of believing no charges brought against officials through personal bias. President Hayes forwarded me all the papers filed, and I still have them. Not until Garfield assumed office did Savage resign, and then it was entirely voluntary on his part. Family matters interfered—a stepson wanted the position—and although James G. Blaine desired to retain Mr. Savage, he refused another appointment.

After 1882 Savage sold everything he had and invested in Government bonds. During the remainder of his life he occupied himself by traveling to and from Europe. He visited me often in Philadelphia until 1892. Sometime in 1894 the first news for two years reached me about Mr. Savage. A Mrs. Edwards, of London, who was unknown to me, wrote and explained that Mr. Savage had once boarded with her, and after he left, in 1893, she learned that he was confined in a madhouse at St. Luke's, England. She had found a scrap of paper containing my name and address in a bureau drawer and had forwarded it to me, so she said, hoping that I would notify Mr. Savage's friends. At once I took up the case and found that Mr. Savage had been snared by criminals. His mind was somewhat impaired in his old age, and on one of his trips to England he lodged at Shearing, in Essex, with a woman who passed as a Mrs. Williams. She was in reality Caroline Shrimpton, who carried with her an aged father, a stalking horse for his energetic daughter. The Shrimpton woman fastened her clutches on Mr. Savage, took all he owned, made him sign a will giving everything to her, and then placed him in an asylum without medical examination or due process of law. He was ill at the time, and she used his illness as a subterfuge. She changed his name so that it read, "Jacob A. Savage." Had it not been for the scrap of paper found by Mrs. Edwards, I doubt that Savage's friends would ever have learned of his sad death in the asylum.

GILMORE HAYS

One of the most interesting men in the pioneer ranks of the territory was Judge Gilmore Hays, of Silver City. He was a Kentuckian by birth, but most of his early life had been spent in Missouri. Hays told me that he was intimately acquainted with the famous colonel, John Doniphan, and that he had sat as judge more than once before Doniphan in Missouri. Doniphan told Hays on one occasion that he attributed his success at the bar to the fact that he had never read a law textbook.

In 1850 Judge Hays crossed the plains to California and took up residence there, but two years later returned to Missouri and captained a train of emigrants bound for the Northwest. When Snake River was reached, the train followed the north-bank wagon road which ran through Boise country. Hays's wife and two children succumbed to cholera during the march, and their bodies were buried under a cairn of stones near Salmon Falls, in July, 1852. Hays pushed west and settled in Olympia, Washington, where his ability was soon recognized. In 1854 he was Whig candidate for Congress but he was not elected. In the

Washington Territory Indian War of 1855, he took active part and was captain of the first company organized—Company A, in Olympia, which, with Company B, was mustered into the national service. The companies were cavalry, and the members supplied their own horses. Captain Hays, by election, was promoted to major of the 2nd Washington and had separate command of a large number of troops. In 1861 the Washington legislature—for Idaho was not then organized—granted Judge Hays a franchise for a ferry across Snake River within one mile of its junction with the Clearwater; this was within a short distance of the present site of Lewiston, Idaho. This crossing was afterward known as Hays Ferry and was on the trail leading north to the newly discovered mines now within Idaho's boarders. When, in 1863, the Owyhee mines were opened, Judge Hays drifted down with the advance guard of prospectors. In the summer of 1865, Hays and a companion named Ray discovered the richest silver mine in the Owyhee country; in fact, the richest silver mine, the richest ore, on record. The claim was first named the Hays and Ray Ledge, but while the two men, both of them poor, were prospecting, a man named Peck dropped in and offered to purchase. The two men refused to sell and then, with Peck, foolishly left the ground for a few days. Another party of miners jumped the claim and held possession despite all that Hays and his companion did to prove prior occupancy. The original finders were so poor that they lacked even sufficient money with which to buy food and tools. The new company, or stakers, named the streak "Poorman." The ore was natural chloride of silver, "horn silver," impregnated with gold, and was readily salable at an enormous price as it came from the mines.

Judge Hays often visited Boise, where he was well known and liked. His son Charles was Wells, Fargo's agent at Silver City from 1869 to 1875. In the late seventies, Charles bought the *Owyhee Avalanche* and published it successfully for several years. Judge Hays represented Owyhee County in the territorial councils of 1870 and 1872. When he came to attend the 1870 session at Boise, he was dressed in a suit of clothes strikingly new, and, when good-natured banter was hurled at him, he laughingly replied, "Don't laugh at my clothes! I'm poor, you know. My son Charley's wife gave me this suit, for she said that I needed to 'spruce up' when with the lawmakers! Bless her heart, I was very comfortable in my old clothes. You all know me, at any rate, so what's the difference what I wear?"

He was a capable legislator, able and evenminded. When I first met him he was a man of sixty years and of cheerful disposition, notwithstanding all that he had passed through. Most entertaining were his chats of early days on the coast, especially his reminiscences of Grant, Pickett, and Sheridan of the regular army. He was a mine of information, especially on the Indian question, and the Indian Office at Washington often availed itself of his services as consultant. The honest old fellow had passed through too active a life; broken in health, he left Idaho about 1876 and returned to Olympia. He died there on October 10, 1880.

JOHN CATLOW

The name of John Catlow is indissolubly linked with the history and development of Silver City and Owyhee County from 1864 on. Slow in action and speech, above medium in height, with dark hair, pug nose, and blue eyes, with a laugh and bearing that betokened honesty and determination, this was the industrious, patient wheel horse in the boom days and the dull days of Owyhee.

Catlow was an Englishman by birth and, in 1869, was about forty years of age. He was older in bitter experiences than in years. He was freighter, miner, mill and mining supply furnisher, and general man of affairs. He owned an immense cattle range at the foot of Steens Mountain, Oregon, and he also bought John Farnum's ranch ten miles below Silver City. Catlow's great ore teams were always seen hauling ore about Silver and South Mountain; his freighting was the quickest and most reliable. He was never tired, never seemed to sleep, was ever plodding along, and in his generous, manly way he moved in a vast circle of industry, himself at the center, liked by women and respected by men. To us, he was plain and frank "Uncle John."

Mr. Catlow was the victim of mining operations. Had he been dealt with as he dealt with others, or had fortune favored him, millions would have been his share. Like "Old Hill," he stood with Silver City when the bottom was declared to be "clean out of her," and yet, with all his faith in the prophesied someday riches of Owyhee, he never saw prosperity return.

From 1869 to 1875 Silver City and environments presented to visitors the usual features of Idaho and Nevada mining towns; mining towns that were dead. War Eagle, Florida, and the lesser and unnamed hills and mountains of the whole Owyhee Range were ribbed and seared with lines of prospect holes and piles of dump dirt which, in the distance, as they sparkled and whitened in the sun, looked like piles of oyster shells or the refuse of limekilns. Here and there were wooden walks and dirt trails, and abortive houses constructed of scrap lumber, logs and boards which had once stood sentinel at the mouths of shafts—shafts which delved into the bowels of the hills and concealed perhaps millions in pay dirt. Hoisting apparatus, which cost many thousands, lay idle and open and weather-beaten, to be casually sniffed at by tourists. A dead mining town is like the arm of an ocean after a great storm has passed. The storm has gone but behind it is a desolate track. Millions in wealth have been swept away, hearts broken, lives wrecked and blasted, but over all the sun again shines brightly, and Mother Nature looks on unruffled. As I recall the decline of Owyhee, recall the hopes and fears of those who labored and grew old hoping ever for the revival of old times about her hills, the figure of John Catlow looms up as if it were that he combined the strength and purpose of the many who worked with him against bitter discouragements.

JAMES STOUT

My colleague in the land office at Boise was James Stout, of Pontiac, Illinois. Stout was born at Cadiz, Ohio, in 1819, and after an education at local schools moved to Springfield, Ohio, and read law with General Charles Anthony. He pursued courses for a time at Miami University. About 1845 he moved to Ottawa, Illinois, and five years later went to Pontiac, where he was farmer, lawyer, and editor. He joined issues with the Owen Lovejoy school of Abolitionists, those fearless men who fought against all odds in late antislavery days. Stout must have been a terror with his editorial pen, if his writings reflected his violent, though sincere, partisan views such as we heard from him in Idaho. A former resident of Pontiac told me that when Stout, as editor of the *Sentinel*, turned loose against Copperheads and slavery partisans, there was a sudden scattering to the woods! Stout's father and mother, Charles and Margaret, ran a branch of the famous "Underground Road" and, while they lived in Springfield, Ohio, helped scores of slaves to escape to Canada. James and his brother, Dr. Joseph Stout, quite naturally imbibed antislavery views and they, like their parents, helped many a slave to freedom.

In 1869 Stout was a man of fifty years, a free lance in creed but correct in morals. He was kindly, earnest, and able, but when he undertook a task and was convinced of his point, he was equal to Oliver Cromwell and had about as much consideration for opponents as Oliver had. When

Stout expressed his cordial hatred for Rebels, his command of English was wonderful and lasting. Soon after we met, I ascertained that we were distant relatives, for an uncle of mine married one of Stout's nieces; Stout was, interesting to note, a brother-in-law of my old friends General J. Warren Kiefer and Judge William White, both of Springfield, Ohio. When Stout came to Boise, he listened attentively to all that was told him, and the loungers about town stuffed him plentifully with yarns of rich men and riches. Stout was in my office one day when a man named Crouch drove a wagon to my door and began to move dirt from the adjoining alley.

"There," said Stout impressively, "is a man who is said to be worth a million. He's hidden it somewhere."

"Who, Crouch?" I queried. "Who told you so?"

"Some of the boys at the Overland told me so. Said he had money in bags!"

"Oh, yes!" I laughed. "He's hauling dirt at two dollars a ton just to save millions, isn't he?" Stout laughed then and was afterward wary of fables.

A ludicrous thing happened to him while he occupied a small building in the rear of General Cartee's residence. A night or two after Stout moved into the premises he hung his silver watch upon a nail in the wall. In the morning he was astounded to find that the watch was beautiful gold. He rushed to me in delight and said, "It's a wonderful country! Gold everywhere. Just hang up anything silver, and before morning it turns to gold." The explanation was that prior to Stout's occupancy the house had been cleared of much vermin by boiling kettles of sulphur. The walls were saturated and during the night sulphur fumes had attacked Stout's silver watch and tinted it yellow.

Stout acted upon impulse, often to the astonishment of people about him. Life was a wonderful problem for him, and he pondered and reasoned and tried to get at the root of matters in his unusual and impulsive manner. A fine specimen of Bannack Indian stopped at my office one day, in quest of tobacco, when Stout wandered along. He admired the Indian for a minute and then spoke out with, "Donaldson, what splendid hair and teeth these Indians have! They wear no hats, and that keeps hair natural in color and healthy. They eat no sugar, and their teeth do not decay. Look, see the fine teeth this man has!" He shoved the red man against the wall, grabbed his throat and choked him until the Indian opened his mouth and then rubbed his fingers over teeth and gums. The Indian gave me an appealing look and was so startled that he failed to interpret my signal to close down on Stout's fingers. Once released, he stalked down the street, casting timorous glances backward. He spread the report that Stout was locoed, or crazy. With all his eccentricities, Stout was a faithful Government official and was respected by Boise people.

I have at hand an account of one of the most remarkable antebellum slave cases on record. It is in the handwriting of James Stout, for he and his brother Joseph were principals. The case was that of "Negro Jim," rescued and kidnaped at Ottawa, Illinois, on October 11, 1859. The negro's owners had chased the escaping man and caught him, but Stout and the Ottawa Abolitionists determined to rescue him in spite of judge, jury, and court. They actually tore the negro from the grasp of the United States marshal, ran him out of the Ottawa court room, and galloped with him to a place of safety. The Stout brothers and a Mr. Joseph Hassack were held and tried at Chicago in November, 1859, for aiding the escape of a negro, and Hassack and Joseph Stout were imprisoned five months. The ablest attorneys in the state vied against each other to secure the case, but James Stout employed no counsel. He was his own attorney. He secured an acquittal for himself through an unparalleled exhibition of brains, nerve, and violent temper. He scared the presiding judge, made the jury roar with laughter, and gave the prosecuting attorneys the shock of their lives. The case is on record in the Illinois decisions. I regret that there is no space here to give in detail a most vivid description from the pen of James Stout.

AH KEE—FAKIR

The locally famous Chinese doctor, Ah Kee, was in vogue when I arrived in Boise. Ah Kee was uncrowned king with his Mongolians and a "to-be-plucked" in the eyes of Gentiles. His shop and surroundings indicated vast wealth, for he was physician, soothsayer, and a man of mystery. The white people eventually expected a heavy yield from the treasure chest which was, so rumor avowed, secluded within the shelter of the Chinaman's guarded house. Ah Kee was a portly Mongolian with a huge flowing mustache; from across the counter of his establishment, a combination of drugstore and money-lending shop, he greeted everyone with a smile.

Boise was in the wildest excitement one evening in 1869. Men were yelling and running to and fro, horses were being saddled, and through the darkness galloped night riders bound for Oregon. Main Street looked like war, but not until daylight did I find out the cause of the trouble. A solitary horseman tore past my home but pulled up at my hail. I asked if an Indian outbreak had occurred, and he snorted, "Naw! Ah Kee has skipped! Took French leave! I got a writ fer him and I'll land him yet!" Into his nag went cruel spurs, and he disappeared westward. Everything was heading for Olds Ferry, a spot eighty miles from Weiser where travelers crossed the river and entered Oregon. Ah Kee had a flying start on his pursuers and he meant to keep it, for behind him was an army of angry men. All of them were armed with writs, and the first writ served was preferred mortgage; they intended to throttle the great doctor and relieve him of valuables. Ah Kee had indiscriminately "tapped" Chinese, Germans, and Irish in profusion; he was distinctly cosmopolitan, sparing none because of color, creed, or previous condition.

He reached Olds Ferry one hour before the advance guard. Across the river he was ferried in the usual way, and then Ah Kee commenced operations. The ferry was worked with a block and elevated cable which, being geared longer at one end, allowed the boat to be pushed across by force of current. Ah Kee asked the ferryman what the cable was worth. The man told him, and just as soon as the boat touched Oregon shore, Ah Kee paid for both cable and passage, drew an ax from his bag, and cut the rope. Then he took the ferryman prisoner and calmly waited until his pursuers reached the opposite shore. He was in Oregon and safe from writs, but Ah Kee took no chances with personal contacts; pursuers armed with writs and firearms administered law, as he knew, irrespective of time and place. Within an hour the advance line of writ servers pulled up at the opposite bank. They at once realized the situation, but the sole satisfaction they had was to stand and hurl across the river loud and lasting curses. Ah Kee blossomed out as a real comedian. He pulled a rifle from beneath his coat and walked to the water's edge. He delivered an oratorical outburst, lengthy and personal, gesticulated in a manner that was far from polite, threw a few rocks in the direction of his pursuers, and, while they jumped and cursed in wrath—not one of them was armed with a weapon larger than a pistol—he threw a kiss and yelled, "You all go to hellee!" Ah Kee commanded the ferryman to go down the riverbank for half a mile, and the terrified man did so. Within a half hour a pack train came along. Ah Kee offered a good price for a horse and when he paid, two packers lifted him upon the animal. Along the Burnt River trail he thundered and waved a few last "day-days" to the howling mob on the Idaho shore. The packers afterward stated that Dr. Ah Kee weighed at least five hundred pounds when they lifted him to his horse. They were right, for Ah Kee was loaded with dust and nuggets. He was never again recognized in Idaho, for by shaving his mustache and acting a part he mingled with other Chinamen without fear of detection. The morning after his departure I passed his old shop, and on the door was the usual sign which designated exits similar to his, "*Gone to the Springs.*"

THE BUTLER BROTHERS

Interesting men in early Idaho were Thomas J. and J. S. Butler, who published the first newspaper in Boise County, the *Boise News*. This paper first made its appearance as a weekly on September 29, 1863, and was the second paper published in Idaho territory. The Butlers were from Red Bluff, California, where they had edited and published the Red Bluff *Beacon*. Throughout Boise Basin the *News* was popular though it was not partisan. Tom Butler told me that he saw single copies of the paper bring three dollars in flush times. About a year after the *News* appeared, the Butlers sold it to I. H. Bowman, and Bowman, with Henry C. Street as editor, changed the name to *Idaho World*, and launched the sheet on strongly Democratic lines.

Thomas Butler I knew very well, for he frequently came to Boise and resided there for some months in 1870, during which time Reynolds employed him on the *Statesman*. Butler was a very tall and swarthy man who dwelt, so to speak, within himself, and by his outward demeanor gave the impression that he was suffering either from chronic dyspepsia or embitterment from constant and grievous disappointments. He was extremely caustic and held many grudges against his former colleagues. In 1868 Butler was nominated for delegate to Congress and in 1870 again demanded the nomination, contrary to the advice of his friends. The preceding year had brought into Idaho several Federal officials who were bright men; Butler no doubt thought that they desired the nomination, and, typical of him, brooded within himself, "bucked" against odds, and was badly beaten at election time. He contributed nothing to the campaign fund and made no speeches, probably deeming his popularity sufficient to carry him through. I recall that I presided at the Slocum Hall convention in 1870 when we nominated him and I also wrote the entire platform. Butler left for Arizona before the election took place.

At times he was very companionable, but the best elements in his address were dwarfed by disappointments, and his popularity in Idaho waned rapidly. Through all he was of high character, and he is remembered in Idaho as one of the pioneers. How he and his brother established their newspaper, the disadvantages under which they labored to equip their establishment at Idaho City, how they printed the *News*, is a most interesting chapter in Idaho's annals. Knocking about as he did, Butler saw much of the humorous side of pioneer life, and once in a while he would resort to quaint expressions and recollections that were decidedly original. He gave me one of the best "pointers" of my youthful days. I was perplexed, on one occasion, to find the name of the author of a poetical quotation which I placed at the head of an editorial. Butler looked over my shoulder, rubbed his hand slowly across his chin and drawled, "Sonny, don't let things like that bother you in life. Do as I do when I'm in your fix. Simply write down, 'Old Poet.'"

CHAPTER V

VIGILANTES AND CRIMINALS

A VIGILANTE, or vigilance committee, is a terrific power in a new country. When well directed it invariably aids and supplements the law. In my own personal recollection I never knew but one man hanged unjustly by the vigilantes, and he, Joe Tuttle, was hanged in Arizona for a crime which he never committed. A noticeable fact about all central Idaho vigilante matters was that the participants on the law-and-order side were particularly reluctant to talk about any proceedings. From 1869 to 1875 I "pumped" every man I met in Idaho who was supposed to have had relations with the vigilantes, but only at odd times was it possible to ascertain anything definite. I frequently chatted with several of the men who hanged David Updyke and James Dixon. Hill Beachy I knew well and frequently talked with, but he was extremely averse to mentioning the Lloyd Magruder murder and the capture of the murderers. Rapid change of administration and Idaho's transient population probably occasioned this secrecy. The vigilantes of 1869 to 1875 did not care to discuss the events of earlier times because many of those who sympathized with the murderers and robbers of 1865-66 were still in Idaho and held their particular grudges. Some of the worthies who escaped the rope in the early days were public men in the territory during my time, 1869 to 1875.

The vigilantes moved in a mysterious but certain way. A member of the Boise City committee told me that when the vigilance executive committee had voted to hang a man, one of the committee was detailed to notify twenty or thirty members to be at a place at a certain time and to come armed. At the meeting either the member of the executive committee or another man was selected to lead, and the assembly was for the first time informed as to procedure and the name of the victim. The sign of the vigilantes was a triangle, and the executive committee kept the list of members. When the executive committee voted to notify a man to leave the country, one man was entrusted with the matter. The person so notified usually went at once—sometimes within the hour. The number of ex-Rebels, murderers, gamblers, robbers, and dangerous loafers driven out of central Idaho by vigilante notices from 1865 to 1870 was enormous, and a list of their names published at the present time would cause surprise as well as consternation. Some of the worthy gentlemen are now back in Idaho. I recall that one or two men who bore fairly good reputations on the surface made sudden departures for parts unknown and offered the excuse that large fortunes had been left them, or that "business" called them elsewhere. Theodore Burmester, who killed Russell B. Morford, and Charles Douglass, who killed E. D. Holbrook, were both marked for hanging, but the latter left the country very suddenly in the night and the former escaped through the intercession of his wife.

One day early in 1869, in Columbus, Ohio, two pretty women came into my office. One was named Mrs. William H. Parks; the women were sisters and their maiden name was either Genoise or Jervoise. Mrs. Parks asked me to aid her in recovering certain mining property of her late husband at Silver City, Idaho. A legal correspondence was begun, but later that same year I went to Idaho to reside. Mrs. Parks had surrendered to me all her late husband's papers, and when I arrived in Idaho I began to investigate. William H. Parks was originally from Columbus, Ohio; he had died near Boise City in 1864. A brother, James Parks, was in the dry-goods firm of John Greenleaf & Co., of Columbus. William Parks crossed the plains into Oregon in 1862 and settled at Baker City. He was successful in starting a livery stable and, being a popular man, was elected sheriff of Baker County. During the Owyhee (Idaho) quartz-mining excitement in 1863, Parks moved to Flint, near Silver City, and became a mine owner. Not having sufficient capital to develop his property, he decided to go East and try to enlist the services of his friends. Parks arranged his business, went to Boise for a few days, and in June, 1864, took the Overland stage for the East. He had with him a few hundred dollars in coin and a large valise of gold and silver specimens from his Flint locations. The valise attracted attention from its shape and weight. Parks ranked as a money-maker in Oregon and Idaho, and it was taken for granted, by those who made it their business to keep watch on such things, that the valise contained either gold dust or bars.

Boise City contained at that time a splendid assortment of murderers, robbers, and tin-horn gamblers. They were the offscourings of all the abandoned and worn-out mining camps in the territory. Boise's isolation from the railroad made it desirable for such men to locate there. The law-and-order element did not assert itself until after 1865, when in three or four years it succeeded in clearing out the undesirable characters. The notorious Dave Updyke and Dixon gangs were in full power at Boise in 1864 when Parks began his trip East. Parks left the Overland Hotel, Boise, just before daybreak. The coach rattled along for six miles until it reached Boise River, a short distance beyond Warm Springs. At this juncture, several masked road agents made their appearance. They evidently were awaiting the traveler with the treasure. Parks, excited at the attack, drew his revolver and in so doing shot himself in the hip. The robbers then looted the express box and took Parks's valise. The stage was turned back to Boise, and the wounded man at once put under the care of the Overland Hotel landlord, Captain James Griffin, and the brotherly care of the Masons. Griffin told me of the intense suffering of Parks while he lingered four days. The Masons buried him in the Soldiers' Cemetery.

Mrs. Parks was notified at Columbus of her husband's death; Judge L. F. Higbee, of Silver City, was appointed administrator. In the letters from Idaho which Mrs. Parks gave me—personal correspondence—one letter was a proposal of marriage from the postmaster at Flint who had seen her photograph and was smitten at long range by her charms. She was much shocked, and so was I, but a few months' residence in Idaho showed me that marrying on photographic sample was not unusual. When I arrived in Boise, Judge Higbee came to see me about Parks's estate. He came to my office, and we had a very agreeable chat. Higbee was a clever gentleman of sixty and, if I remember rightly, was married to Lyle Lester, a literary woman of fame on the Pacific Coast. After some correspondence the estate was settled.

Parks's robbery and murder was credited to David Updyke, Charley Marcus, Dixon, and their gang, but the Boise citizens lacked positive evidence. In the summer of 1865 came the attack upon a stage in the Portneuf canyon where murder and robbery resulted. These murders and many others were correctly attributed to Updyke's gang, working in conjunction with other criminals to the north of Boise City. In March, 1865, the Updyke gang controlled the Democratic legislature of Idaho, and it was not a difficult matter to "persuade" the legislature to nominate Updyke for sheriff of Ada County. Ada County had just been organized. Updyke was elected and at once abused his official position. The Payette Vigilance had been organized in 1864-65 (details are given later), and through its influence many of Updyke's old pals had been killed or had been driven from the country. Updyke determined to squelch this vigilance and formed his plans for an effectual wiping out of its leaders. He had, with usual effrontery, sworn out warrants of arrest for members of the Payette Vigilance, but news of Updyke's purpose and his departure from Boise City was sent in advance by a messenger to the Payette region. He was fairly checkmated by the Payette men, who met him on the prairie with an armed force and stated that they would submit to arrest provided that they be permitted to carry their arms to Boise and be placed in custody there. There was no alternative; Updyke's gang were outnumbered and thwarted, and the warrants were never served. This wholesale attempt at murder—for the Payette men would never have survived had they surrendered their guns—cost Updyke many of his admirers, who were somewhat above an expedient of the sort.

Matters grew worse. In the spring of 1866 John C. Clark, an Updyke satellite, murdered Reuben Raymond, a boy of nineteen, because Raymond had testified unfavorably in a lawsuit against Updyke's gang. Raymond served as an important witness against Clark's interests and he was naturally a marked man. The murder took place on April 3, 1866. That same night Clark was taken from the Fort Boise guardhouse and hanged. The Boise vigilantes had begun their work! Updyke saw trouble imminent. He was about to pay the penalty for all his crimes—the Portneuf affair, the shooting of Parks, and a score of outrages as violent. He fled from Boise on April 12 and was followed by another ruffian, John Dixon. On the Rocky Bar road at either Stirrup or Syrup Creek the Boise vigilantes, about fifteen in number, overtook the thieves at a cabin thirty miles from Boise the following day and carried them ten miles further. Updyke was strung up in a shed. He made no protestations of innocence but went quietly to his fate. When passing prospectors found him the next day hanging from a rafter, pinned on his coat was a pencil-written note which read, "Dave Updyke, the aider of murderers and horse thieves. X.X.X."

James Dixon was hanged on the same day by the same men at a point four miles down the creek. He tried to escape and was captured outdoors. His names and crimes were also written on paper and pinned to his body; both men were later buried where they were hanged. The vigilantes returned to Boise late on the night of April 13, 1866, and on Saturday and Sunday the news of the hanging of Updyke and Dixon was told through Ada County. Many hurried departures took place. On Monday, April 16, 1866, there was posted on Updyke's stable, on Main Street between Seventh and Eighth the following:

DAVE UPDYKE

Accessory after the fact to the Portneuf stage robbery.
Accessory and accomplice to the robbery of the stage near Boise City.
Chief conspirator in burning property on the Overland stage route.
Guilty of aiding and assisting West Jenkins, the murderer, and other criminals to escape, while you were sheriff of Ada County.
Threatening the lives and property of an already outraged and suffering community.
Justice has overtaken you.

X.X.X.

JAKE DIXON

Horse thief, counterfeiter and road agent generally.
A dupe and tool of Dave Updyke.

X.X.X.

All the living accomplices in the above crimes are known through Updyke's confession, and will surely be attended to.
The roll is being called.

X.X.X.

The handwriting of the notice pinned on the pole on which John C. Clark had been hanged a few days before and the handwriting of the notices on the bodies of Updyke and Dixon were identical. The notices were written by one person and by one who had a legal education. I knew him in 1869 at Boise.

The executive committee of the Boise City vigilantes, 1865-66, was controlled, so one of the active members told me, by three men. They were James S. Reynolds, D. N. Hyde, a merchant of long standing and father-in-law of John Huntoon, and one McKee. McKee moved to Virginia City, Nevada, in 1870; he was a Scotchman. These three were men of strong character, integrity, and ability. They had the casting vote in all capital cases and cases of "hurried departure." It may be said of them that they never wrongly advised the hanging of innocent parties but frequently passed over men who should have been hung.

One member of the committee told me of a curious instance occurring in 1869-70 which figured in the history of the Boise vigilantes. About the time of the murder of Reuben Raymond by Clark, a resident of Boise Valley was under suspicion. He had, if I remember rightly, poisoned a neighbor's cattle well. This man I knew from 1869 until my departure from Idaho. He was a swarthy, glib-tongued Missourian and ex-Rebel. He rather courted the reputation of "bad man," and his face and manner were against him. When his case was taken up, a short time after the hanging of Clark, a report reached the vigilance committee that the suspect had vowed vengeance against Clark's punishers and also wore about his neck a triangle and rope in derision and defiance of the vigilantes. The committee was about to vote for hanging when D. N. Hyde, of the committee, began an earnest plea for the suspect and said that he would vouch for his good behavior in the future or would personally see that he left the country.

The man under suspicion had one of the prettiest and truest of women for a wife, so the amazement of Hyde's companions on the committee was assuaged when they were told that the woman had suspected—at whose suggestion was never known—that the vigilantes were about to hang her husband and had sought Hyde in his office. Her tearful pleadings influenced Hyde so that he in turn swung the balance of the committee in favor of acquittal. The pleadings of a tearful woman had an effect even upon the stern body of men who through the most violent measures were alone able to rid Idaho of her criminals. This was told me in 1870, during the contest between Bryon and Lindsay for the position of sheriff of Ada County. The suspected man was a warm adherent of Lindsay, and it was reported that he had made threats against Judge J. R. Lewis, who decided the case in favor of William Bryon, the Republican candidate for sheriff. Another consultation was held by the vigilantes. The absence of an overt act, not the pleadings of a tearful woman, saved him the second time.

Vigilantes had meted out such severe punishment that when I arrived in Idaho, Boise was, comparatively speaking, passing through an era of peace. There were, however, moments when my wife and I realized that the territory was very wild. The day that we arrived in Boise and alighted from the stage, just as we touched ground, there at our feet lay a man shot through the mouth. Another stood above him glaring down and preparing to finish the fallen man. A lady who came with us jumped quickly at the man with the pistol and held his arm. She cried, "You brute!" This brought him to his senses, and he lowered his gun. The man who had been shot was a drunken hostler who had vowed to kill the other, a respectable citizen. The respectable citizen took no chances and shot first! This little incident gave us quite a warm welcome into the territory. Chats with stage drivers and ranchers brought about many interesting reminiscences of Lewiston and Florence in 1862 to 1865. Many a yarn did I hear spun of Henry Plummer and his murderous gang; tales of George Ives and Dutch John, Plummer's associates, in their many raids and murders through Idaho and Montana.

Not one murder alone but a succession of murders and outrages brought about the vigilante organizations in Idaho. It is quite natural, however, to attribute the origin of lynch law by the respectable element to a particular event, and the vigilance movement's origin in the Boise country has positive dates and events.

Public excitement in Boise Basin was at its highest as the result of a murder which occurred in July, 1865, at Idaho City, Boise County. Ferdinand J. Patterson, a gambler, killed Sumner Pinkham, the United States marshal. Until that time no vigilance group had existed in Idaho City or Boise, but when Patterson gained his liberty, freed by strong influence upon the jurors, citizens took action. Rev. G. S. Kingsley, formerly of Portland, Oregon, and one-time editor of the *Pacific Christian Advocate,* had gone to Idaho City in the winter of 1863-64. He at once started to build a Methodist Episcopal church by public subscription. The first timbers erected in the church Mr. Kingsley cut by his own labor. He was a man of remarkable integrity and energy. The existing outlawry struck him forcibly as a menace to Idaho's progress. Through his efforts the second vigilance group in Boise Basin was organized. He was assisted by about forty men, who represented the best element of Idaho City and Boise, and although this new organization did not, as it desired, hang Ferdinand Patterson, at least it used its power to good purpose with Updyke and his associates.

In connection with the trial of Patterson for the murder of Pinkham, Judge John R. McBride later related to me many interesting events connected with the killing of Pinkham. Judge McBride had been on the bench about one month when the murder occurred. He told me that he did not have any recollection that a grand jury indicted Patterson. Patterson was held for murder on a general charge, and in a few days Judge McBride was approached with an application for bail for Patterson. A preliminary hearing was held and McBride, believing that Patterson was a dangerous character, refused to release him or take bail. In October or November, Patterson was indicted and had his trial, but capable counsel, aided by powerful influences, brought about an acquittal. The feeling against the murderer was very bitter. Patterson at once withdrew to Rocky Bar, eighty miles distant, but soon afterward left the territory; public opinion was too warm for him. He met a violent death a few months after the murder of Pinkham. He was killed in Walla Walla by a man named Donohue; he was shot, it was said, while in a hotel corridor. Judge McBride told me that Donohue fled the country, and an effort to extradite him from San Francisco failed. He enlisted on a man-of-war, and all trace of him was lost.

Judge McBride knew nothing of the organization of the vigilance committee at Boise because knowledge of the formation of that body was concealed from him. He was known to be particularly opposed to lynch law, and, besides, he was an officer of justice which placed him in a position to punish lynchers. Judge McBride told me that he was intimately acquainted with G. S. Kingsley and said that Kingsley was a man of great force and ability and did much to preserve law and order in Idaho. A son, G. S. Kingsley, Jr., was afterwards in the Boise Land Office.

I have referred to Mr. Kingsley as the originator of the second vigilance committee in Boise Basin. The first vigilance committee in southern Idaho was formed in the winter of 1864-65 through the efforts of W. J. McConnell, a farmer over on the Payette River. The Boise vigilance committee was directly occasioned by the Pinkham-Patterson affair; the Payette Vigilance resulted rather because of election riots and theft of horses and property from farmers. Both were created for the same end—the riddance of toughs from the territory. Certainly the Payette Vigilance thwarted David Updyke's gang. Mr. McConnell is now living to enjoy honors accorded him by an appreciative people. When Idaho received statehood, Mr. McConnell was chosen as the short-term senator. He is now (1897) governor of the state of Idaho. His vigilance group in the Payette country served as a model for the formation and action of the Boise Vigilance. Upon request, Governor McConnell has forwarded to me a brief description of his efforts to effect law and order, and the description is here given with his permission. So many years have elapsed since Idaho had her reign of terror that the following is additionally interesting if but for comparison with Idaho of the present day:

The territory of Idaho was created during the spring of 1863. The placer-mines in Boise Basin were discovered the fall previous. During the spring and summer months of 1863 a large population of miners and adventurers were attracted to that region, many being refugees from the War of the Rebellion then in progress, while a large per cent of gamblers, horse thieves, stage robbers, and all-around toughs added their quota to Idaho's disturbing element. Murder and robbery were rife. The laws of the country which were adopted when the territory was created were practically those of the state of New York, while the judges appointed by the administration were men of character and legal attainments. It might be thought that under those circumstances no trouble would have been experienced in enforcing law and order in the protection of life and property and it is perhaps difficult for the student of history today to understand why it was necessary for the people to organize courts and officers of their own through the medium of what was termed a vigilance committee. That it was so, is doubtless due to the fact that a large majority of the residents of that country located there for the purpose of making money quickly and would not accept any political office nor did they care to participate in politics. Hence, the conventions were manipulated largely by the element which laws are designed to suppress. Delegates to the nominating conventions went there armed with proxies, navy six-shooters, and bowie knives. As may be presumed, the nominations for the leading offices, including the sheriff's, were made with a view of protecting, rather than punishing, crime. The result was the selection of juries which would acquit rather than punish offenders.

I was perhaps the first promoter of a vigilance organization in Idaho territory although in the outset I started to protect myself personally with no idea of perfecting an organization for that purpose. I went to the Boise country in April, 1863, for the purpose of gardening. I immediately commenced operations and was successful beyond my most sanguine expectations, but at once the horse thieves commenced preying upon my stock and for nearly two years practically everything I made was stolen from me. There was no protection to be had under the law and the expense of pursuing horse thieves, including the neglect of my business, was so great that it was better to submit to what seemed to be the inevitable. Finally, however, I followed two men who had stolen a horse during the night previous, hoping to intercept them in Boise City. I failed to intercept them but during my search of the stables and corrals I found a mare which had been stolen from me some time before. She was stabled in a barn which belonged to the sheriff. The man claimed the mare and refused to give her up. I resorted to the courts to gain possession, the cost of which procedure was $70.00. Everyone knew that the animal was mine! As may be surmised, I was not in a very amiable frame of mind. I led the horse out in front of the stable where were assembled at least half a dozen horse thieves and stage robbers and I told them that I desired to make them a speech before taking my departure. One of them said, "Fire in!" I said to them that I was one of the fools who did not recognize any "chief"; that I could catch any tough who ever marked those prairies and the next one who stole a horse from me would be my "Injun." There would be no lawsuit about it! Apparently not fully realizing how thoroughly worked up I was they took no immediate exception to this remark but determined to "teach me how to take a joke." I did not have long to wait! They stole from me nine head of stock, five horses and four large American mules. The four mules at that time were worth two thousand dollars. I meant what I told them at Boise City, fully realizing that I had to make an example for the future or that it would be better for me to leave that country and seek other fields.

I experienced a good deal of difficulty in getting track of my animals but finally did so and with one man, took the trail after them. There were five in the robbers' party and after a ride and adventures which seem today incredible we came upon their camp nearly two weeks after we had started the pursuit. We saw four men in the camp. The leader had gone to the town of La Grande, Oregon, to buy supplies. We had ridden nearly all night, aiming to make the attack at daylight. Our approach, however, was announced by a dog they had with them, and without bidding us "good morning" or making any inquiry as to our business they raised out of their blankets and commenced firing at us. How we ever won that battle has always seemed a miracle! We followed the leader to La Grande and found him in the custody of the sheriff. The history of our meeting, the release and capture of this man, would read like a novel. He was at the time under death sentence at Fort Union, New Mexico.

I arrived at my ranch with the recovered property on a Saturday afternoon and on the following day was visited by all the adjoining gardeners and neighbors. They informed me that they had held a meeting during my absence and resolved that if I came back alive they would stand in share and share alike on my expenses and that thereafter they would make joint cause against all horse thieves and stage robbers. We there and then entered into a solemn and binding contract to that effect, and although our original number was only fifteen we boldly announced our determination to pursue, capture and punish all offenders.

That we had taken this action was heralded throughout the land and the citizens in the lower Payette Valley called a meeting at which a committee was appointed to visit us with the purpose of uniting and extending our organization. This was accordingly done, and from beginning an organization was perfected which extended from Walla Walla, Washington, to the eastern boundary of the territory of Idaho, and there united hands with the Vigilance committee in Montana. To relate the actions and methods of this organization would require chapters. For the present it must suffice to say that we accomplished our purpose; compelled the lawless bands to disorganize and leave the country, and made it possible for even the most timid to take part in the nominating conventions (which occurred bi-annually) until life and property were as safe under the protection of the laws and courts as in any state in the Union. I removed from the territory of Idaho, returning some years later to engage in the mercantile business. Taking a retrospect view of the nearly half a century which has elapsed since the first settlement of that country, in memory casting my eye upon the sodless mounds I have helped erect over the forms of those I loved and whose lives went out in battle with the savage foe or by the still more dastardly hand of a white renegade and then contemplating that country as it is today, with its railroads, its waving grain and orchards, its beautiful homes, its church spires and schoolhouses, I can not but think that the early pioneers were but instruments in the hands of Him "Who doeth all things well."

CRIMINALS AND FELONS

Prisoners sentenced under territorial laws were as a rule confined in the jails of the counties wherein they had been convicted, and the territory bore the expense of keeping the prisoners. Until 1872 the prisoners sentenced for crimes against the United States were confined in the county jails of the counties where conviction had been made, and the United States paid the counties for the keeping of the criminals. For several years, however, those committing crimes against the U. S. Government were held in custody at the Idaho City jail. The penitentiary at Boise was built in 1870-71 under my supervision, and after 1872 the United States marshal, or warden, held the United States prisoners in this penitentiary.

In my time some criminals and felons were pardoned in gross cases, and the public marveled much. Prior to 1875, one convicted and imprisoned murderer was pardoned by the use of a large sum of money. I could readily state the amount and name the officials who received it. Legal executions were very few; the execution of Sim Walters in 1869 was, I think, only the fifth legal execution in Idaho. Three of the men hanged earlier were Howard, Romaine, and Lowery for the murder of Lloyd Magruder, William Phillips, Charles Allen, and Horace and Robert Chalmers near the Clearwater River, 1863. These three men were hanged at Lewiston, March 4, 1864. In 1867, Anthony McBride, an Irishman, was hanged near Boise for killing a Chinaman on the Weiser River. McBride was hanged in Crane's Gulch, a spot one and one-half miles north of Boise. From 1863 to 1896 eleven men have been legally hanged in Idaho for murder, and yet the number of murders in the same period probably exceeds two hundred and fifty. Many men convicted of murder in the second degree and of manslaughter should certainly have been convicted and hanged for murder in the first degree. Many of the convicted murderers went to prison for a short time and were pardoned; others escaped from detention. In some cases the grand jurors were tampered with, so that no indictment could be found.

Governor D. W. Ballard did not look with much favor on pardons or pardonings for convicted felons. No tainted money ever touched his palm. In January, 1870, Governor

Ballard, having been urgently pled with, commuted the death sentence of James W. Wood, convicted of the murder of Thomas Duffey at Lewiston. Ballard commuted Wood's sentence to life imprisonment, and the citizens of Lewiston, hearing of it, took Wood from the jail on January 13, 1870, and hanged him. This made Governor Ballard cautious. Vigorous efforts to save the life of Sim Walters, who killed Joe Bacon in 1869, had no effect upon the Governor. Reverend Father T. Mesplie, the French Catholic priest, had been in attendance upon Walters at Idaho City and received him into the Catholic Church, or in any event, he had assisted in pinning wings to this frightful criminal so that when the drop fell at the earthly expiation for the foul crime he had committed, Walters could float gently into Heaven. Father Mesplie came down from Idaho City to plead with Governor Ballard; he prayed and strove with the Governor half the entire night before the day set for Walters' execution, begging that reprieve, pardon, or commutation of the death sentence be granted. Governor Ballard was firmly polite; he excused himself and came to my house shortly after midnight and waited until the priest had gone away from his home. He showed no mental distress at having refused the priest—whom all of us respected—but said that Walters was a guilty man and should be hanged. Walters was hanged that same day in 1869 at Idaho City, and he died like a braggart. It was acertained that he had murdered many other people besides Joe Bacon. He was a bold type of degenerate criminal.

The murder which Walters committed was never fully or properly reported. E. J. Curtis gave me a full account of it soon after Walters was hanged. I asked Curtis to write it up and print it, but he never did, and this is the first printed account of it. Joe Bacon's daughter was Sallie Jackson, wife of Commodore Jackson, who had a farm and stage station at Rattlesnake Station south of Boise on the

Overland road. Joe Bacon had a ranch, in 1868, a few miles south of Boise on Eight Mile Creek, near the Owyhee stage road. Walters hired out to Bacon as a rancher. He knew that Bacon had considerable sums of money about the house and undoubtedly hired himself out to Bacon for the purpose of murder and robbery. Bacon had but one eye, a right one, and one day while he and Walters were riding in a brace wagon, Walters fired a pistol on Bacon's "off side." Bacon was startled, but Walters said that he was shooting at a snake under the sagebrush. The truth was that he was testing the horses to see whether or not they would scare and bolt at the sound of a gun. He was contemplating the murder of Bacon in the wagon and feared that the team might run away. Upon arriving home Bacon chanced to tell of Walters' pistol shot and its effect upon the team. A few days afterward Bacon drove away with a large sum of money to pay bills and he was never again seen alive. Walters was with him, and the two had driven toward Boise in the brace wagon.

When they with the team were well upon their journey, Walters, on Bacon's blind side, placed a pistol to Bacon's head and blew his brains out; the team did not break. Walters caught Bacon's body as it fell over the dashboard and then placed the murdered man under the buggy seat and drove for Snake River. Blood from Bacon's body saturated the wooden bottom of the vehicle and left a clue which eventually caught Walters. Once at the river, Walters stripped and swam with Bacon's body to the middle of the stream and set it adrift. Dressing, he drove to Boise and did an errand as if for Bacon, meanwhile quartering the horses in the livery stable where Bacon usually stopped. One of the employees noticed the blood on the wagon bottom and made comment, but Walters allayed suspicion by saying that he had shot a rabbit, placed it under the seat while it was bleeding and afterward gave it to an Indian. Walters also said that Bacon had stayed home on the ranch and sent him to do his errands. That night Walters enjoyed himself in town and drove home next day telling the Bacon family upon arriving that Joe was still in Boise on business. The following day Walters took a horse, ostensibly to search for stray cattle, and rode to the Snake River where he had placed Bacon's body. The body was floating in an eddy in some driftwood near the end of a small island. Walters again undressed, swam out to the body, grabbed it by the hair, and swam with it a half mile down the river to free it from the currents. Returning to the ranch, he told Bacon's children pleasant stories until bedtime. Bacon didn't return from Boise nor could anyone find him there, and in a short time matters became so suspicious that Walters was arrested. Everything pointed to Walters as the murderer, and yet men believed him guiltless and wanted him pardoned. Walters told the details of the murder the morning before the execution when he was sure that Governor Ballard would not pardon him. He also recited the pleasing details of a few other murders he had committed in other states. He was indicted in Ada County but, owing to prejudice, got a change of venue to Idaho County and was hanged at Idaho City. I confess I am circumspectly suspicious of a murderer's innocence when clergymen are earnest in requests for pardons!

From 1869 to 1875 the United States Army paymaster used to visit Boise about once in three months. Officers and men were paid off at Fort Boise and leave granted many of the men to visit town. Once there, money went in drinking, gambling, and visits to houses of low repute. At that time gambling was carried on openly as a legitimate business, and saloons and brothels were necessities in the eye of the law. One day, early in 1870, the soldiers at Fort Boise were paid off and soon became troublesome in town. Captain James Sinclair, 21st Infantry, most gallant officer on the Union side during the Civil War, was in command at Fort Boise. When word reached him that his men were drunk and disorderly in town, he dispatched Peter Vogel, a trusty sergeant, with twelve men to arrest the disturbers and take them back to the fort. Vogel marched his men into town and immediately went to an improper house on a thoroughfare back of Main Street where, he had been told, were two of his men. Vogel knocked at the door, opened it, and walked in. In the room was William Tracy, a gambler and ex-Rebel. As soon as Vogel explained his mission Tracy became infuriated, drew his revolver, and killed Vogel on the spot. The soldiers at once stormed the house and captured all but Tracy.

The civic authorities, for the most part ex-Rebels or Rebel Democrats, were incensed because soldiers had dared to invade the sanctity of Boise! Tracy was a Southern gentleman and a gambler and he should not be arrested, etc., etc.! The lawabiding citizens, to the contrary, wanted Tracy punished. Tracy was caught at a late hour, and the lawabiding people were for hanging him; there was talk of a vigilance committee. The following morning, a coroner's jury was impaneled by Squire A. Haas in the capacity of justice of the peace and coroner. The squire asked me to go to the fort and take down the proceedings of the jury. I consented, and when we arrived at the fort we were taken to see the body of Vogel. One of the jurors calmly approached the body, ripped off the sheet, and took a look at Vogel's face; it startled me not a little, but the free-and-easy style of the jurors in such matters was customary in Idaho. We were then taken to a small room where were held in custody those, other than Tracy, who had been found in the house where Vogel was murdered. The mistress of the brothel was a most pitiable object; she was a nervous wreck, for she fully expected to be shot. Testimony was taken from her, and she was discharged under bond for reappearance as a witness. Then two soldiers brought in a man who had been caught in the back room of the house, and I never was more surprised in my life than when I saw the soldiers held a German sausage maker of Boise by the name of Keyser! Poor old Keyser in a predicament like that! I knew him to be an honest hard-working German who never harmed a soul in his life. He was a sight to behold! When he saw me he began to make wild motions with his fingers toward his mouth. The motions were partly directed at me, but I appeared not to notice until Keyser became violent. I approached him and said, "What is it?"

"Vasser! Vasser! Fer der loaf uf Got, gif me Vasser!"

"Water!" I said in astonishment, at the same time handing him a pitcher. Keyser emptied one half of its contents at one draught. "More!" he cried. "More!" I handed him another partially filled pitcher but Post Surgeon Moffett said, "Stop! That man will kill himself." Nevertheless, down went another quart, and Keyser panted:

"*Mein Gott,* dot vos goodt! Say, Judge, I aindt hot a trop of *Vasser* since six o'glock lasdt nide!"

"What!" I cried. "Why didn't you ask for some?"

"Me?" said Keyser. "Me ask fer anydings frum dem guardts? Dey vos all Irish undt ton't like der Dootch! Dey vud have carvedt me! Say, Judge, ledt me go home."

Squire Haas asked Keyser what he knew about the murder, but it seemed that the poor fellow had chanced to stop in the house to sell sausages and chanced, also, to be taken as one of the perpetrators of the murder. Upon being discharged, he fairly galloped home to his shop.

The jury promptly found that Peter Vogel was killed by William Tracy. Vogel was extremely popular with the officers at Fort Boise and with his comrades, and he had a splendid record in the army. Tracy's case was in due time brought before the grand jury but—I regret to write it—powerful influence was brought to bear to prevent the indictment. H. C. Riggs was chairman of the grand jury, if I remember rightly, and from the adjoining room I heard

Riggs asking questions or cross-examining the witnesses in such a way that it was apparent he was trying to prove Tracy had acted in self-defense; trying to prove that Tracy feared Vogel was about to shoot him. The bill of indictment was ignored—but by a close vote. Tracy and Riggs and many of the grand jurors were Masons. Tracy left Boise at once, and it was best that he did. The following year I saw him at Bingham Canyon, Utah, where he was following the profession of gambler.

Now for a curious sequel to the Vogel murder. The Democratic city and county officials filed a formal complaint against Captain Sinclair for invading the city and arresting persons! The complaint was sent to regimental headquarters at Portland, Oregon. It was received by Lieutenant Colonel A. J. Dallas, who was an unusual Democrat and something of a Copperhead. Dallas recommended that Sinclair be dropped from the Army. Strange to say, without a hearing being accorded Sinclair, the War Department dropped him from the Army as of January 1, 1871, doubtlessly for interference with the civic authorities at Boise. We did not hear of this until seven days after the formal dismissal and another man had been appointed in Captain Sinclair's place. Sinclair and all of us were astounded! Sinclair had fought his way in the Civil War from private ranks in a New York regiment to brevet colonel and attracted the attention of President Andrew Johnson, who promoted him through warm friendship. Because he was one of "Johnson's men," in a friendship grown in the hot partisanship of Johnson's administration, it was likely that he had enemies in the War Department. The Union men and national officers at Boise at once made up a series of testimonials for him, and he started East for Washington the same day that he heard the astounding news. His wife and mother remained at Boise.

Mrs. Sinclair was a Miss Rothermel, of Philadelphia, niece of the celebrated artist, Peter F. Rothermel. Her marriage was rather romantic. In 1867 or 1868, during the war against the Snake Indians, Captain Sinclair was associated with a young lieutenant named James A. Rothermel, 8th Cavalry, from Philadelphia. On February 15, 1868, young Rothermel chanced to place his gunstock in a gopher hole, and the gun went off and killed him. It happened a few miles from Boise while the troops were pursuing Indians. A correspondence was necessary with the young man's relatives, and Captain Sinclair became acquainted with his future wife, the lieutenant's sister, through the letters about the dead soldier.

When Captain Sinclair arrived at Washington, in January, 1871, Senator Simon Cameron took him to see President Grant, who did all that was possible to right the injustice done Sinclair. On March 9, 1871, he was appointed to the only vacancy, a second lieutenancy in the 16th Infantry. He was retired as captain, July 1, 1871, and I think he died in April, 1885.

I met Major, or Lieutenant Colonel, Dallas on a Central Pacific train going East in the winter of 1872. He was a jealous, suspicious, narrow-minded individual and he told me with pleasure of his recommendation in the Sinclair case. He boasted of his family connection and told how he entered the Army. I remember that he was very bitter against the recent promotion of General George Crook, who was promoted from lieutenant colonel of the 21st Infantry to brigadier general. The crux of the matter was that Crook had been promoted and Dallas had not! Dallas was the usual man—short in acts of kindness and merit and long in pedigree!

THE TERRITORIAL PENITENTIARY AT BOISE

My old friend Edward Stevenson made some scathing statements while he was governor (1885-89) in reference to the penitentiary at Boise. He proclaimed it a "disgrace

Photo courtesy *Mr. Cunningham, Boise.*
Idaho Territorial Penitentiary, Idaho City, Idaho, in the sixties.

to a great, rich, proud, and human government." I might have taken offense, for he was referring to the penitentiary built under my supervision in 1869. Crime in Idaho must have been on the increase during the eighties, because the governor stated that guards with shotguns were necessary to maintain order in overcrowded cells.

Rome wasn't built in a day; neither was the territorial penitentiary at Boise. We were forced to limit ourselves to funds at hand, but we made sure that the building at least received the benefit of all the appropriations sent us, even if it failed to possess expansible qualities sufficient to meet the influx of prisoners of future years.

I was appointed superintendent of construction by Jacob D. Cox, Secretary of the Interior, on August 12, 1869. A month later bids were called for by notices in the *Statesman*, the *Idaho World*, and the *Tidal Wave*. The bidders were Robie and Rossi, George H. Twitchell, Charles L. Ostner, Charles May, and Lyman B. Munson. May bid $34,745 and was awarded the contract. The bids were opened by Governor Ballard, Judge Lewis, and Thomas Ranney. The first ground was broken by Judge Whitson on April 2, 1870, and the cornerstone was laid July 4 of the same year. My personal supervision was from August, 1869, to April, 1870, and the amount paid me was $1,000. On May 13, 1871, I formally surrendered the building to United States Marshal Joseph Pinkham.

The building (a small addition was erected in 1870) was east of the fort and near the farm of Jerome Walling. If I recollect rightly, its capacity was ninety prisoners. Poor Charley May found a white elephant upon his hands before he had been long at work; the contract practically ruined him. It called for stone laid in cement, and cement in Idaho was worth about twenty-six dollars a barrel. Many months of delay were occasioned in meeting all requirements in the contract. Labor was very high-priced, and the laborers—skilled mechanics—needed more watching than the men who were ultimately to occupy the penitentiary. I obtained considerable amusement—and some annoyance—by spying on them from afar! My wife and I frequently rode out to the building and I carried a pair of field glasses in the buggy. From a distance I could see the men gracefully reclining upon the walls, but when the dust from our tracks caught their eye the walls were suddenly a scene of great activity. O. S. McHenry was for a time foreman of construction.

Forty thousand dollars each was appropriated for penitentiaries in Colorado, Montana, and Idaho. We built ours for less than that, but Colorado and Montana asked for more money to complete their buildings.*

---

* A clipping from the *Idaho Statesman* of July 18, 1871, found among Mr. Donaldson's papers, says: "It seems that the territories of Montana and Colorado got the same amount for a penitentiary as we did—$40,000. Their main building has been constructed and they have run out of money. They are both asking for a further appropriation to build a wall and a keeper's room. Therein we beat them. Mr. Donaldson is entitled to crow a little over his brother superintendents, because he built both and had money left."—T.B.D.

CHAPTER VI

COURTS, JUDGES, AND ATTORNEYS

BY THE powers vested in him under Section 15 of the Organic Act of Idaho Territory, Governor Wallace in 1863 temporarily defined the judicial districts, assigned the judges, and fixed the time for holding court, until the first legislative assembly should take up these matters. The first legislature of the territory, held at Lewiston, December 7, 1863, to February 4, 1864, arranged the judicial districts and assigned judges to them. The judges, being appointees of the President of the United States, were, naturally, Republicans, while the Idaho legislatures were, in the formative period, Democratic. Three judges in 1865 were Democratic, but nearly every other judge, barring judges between 1884 and 1889, was a Republican. Thus, the judges were at the mercy of the legislature, since that body decreed where their courts should be held. Judges who, through honesty or perhaps through want of tact, incurred the dislike of the legislatures—which neither appointed nor paid them—were banished to the backwoods, where life was anything but agreeable. The matter was ended, after years of quarrel and bitterness over judicial assignments, by the act of Congress which authorized the territorial judges to assign themselves to judicial districts. At times this proved a difficult matter to adjust, but the relief from interference by the legislatures was appreciated.

THE COURT BUILDINGS

In the winter of 1869 the supreme court and the district court of Idaho occupied quarters in the Moulton Building, a one-story stone structure situated on the south side of Main Street, next to the "Stone Jug." It was partially occupied by law offices and the office of the secretary of the territory. The building had formerly been a storehouse.

Colonel C. W. Moulton, the United States marshal, came to Idaho from Newburyport, Massachusetts, in 1869 and purchased the structure. Moulton was an appointee of Charles Sumner and he used to recount incessantly, in his vigorous vocabulary, conversations with Sumner, Franklin Pierce, and other dignitaries. He was an intelligent, businesslike man and after purchasing the storehouse, he reconstructed it, making a second-story room in which were held the sittings of both the supreme court and the Ada County district court. The ascent to the second story was by an open stairway on the outside of the building. In the winter, when there was much ice and snow, it was amusing to see people trying to avoid a fall as they gingerly made their way up or down the stairs.

In the rear of the clerk's office on the ground floor were the judges' chambers and a library room. In 1871, by act of Congress, we received a law library of five hundred volumes, costing about twenty-five hundred dollars, for the use of the supreme court. Colonel Moulton made the building very comfortable. He leased the building to himself for a term of years; this was within his province as United States marshal. Moulton left the territory in 1870 for the East, and we heard that he called upon Senator Sumner, presented him with gold, corn, and wheat from Idaho, and related wild adventures in which he had defended Chinamen from frightful persecutions of license-tax collectors—it was quite romantic! He did not return to Idaho after 1870, much to the disappointment of my old friend, Joseph W. Huston, United States district attorney, who took great pleasure in "sticking pins" into Moulton and inveigling him into arguments.

THE SUPREME COURT

The supreme court of Idaho that I knew was a body curiously formed. It consisted of three judges—a chief and two associate justices—who, collectively, comprised the supreme court and who also, individually, presided over the three district courts. The territory was divided into three judicial districts by the territorial legislature, and the district courts tried, or heard, both territorial and United States cases. The judges assigned the districts and, as Boise was the best place for residence in the territory, there was consequently a large amount of breath-burning among the judges on the question of assignment to districts. The judges were appointed to four-year terms by the President of the United States, subject to confirmation by the Senate. Although they were paid by the United States, they were not held to be United States judges, as are United States judges in the states. The National Government paid them $3,000 a year, and they received $3,500 from the territory, making $6,500 in all. Through dislike of Chief Justice David Noggle, the territorial legislature of 1870-71 abolished the territorial allowance of $3,500, leaving the judges with a pittance of $3,000. The money of the territory was then gold coin, so currency was at a discount. For a $500 greenback, or national bank note bill, we received but $375 in gold coin. This discounting continued until 1871.

It was the rule from 1864 to 1869—after the appointment of the first territorial officers—to fill all official vacancies by appointing men from the Pacific Coast. Oregon, Washington, and California contributed governors, judges, and other officers. When Grant was president he filled the vacancies by appointing men from the Eastern states, and the name "carpetbagger" immediately came into play. An appointee from the Pacific Coast was warmly welcomed, but when an Easterner came to assume office he was labeled "carpetbagger."

TERRITORIAL JUDGES

The Idaho judges were few in number, but, with one or two exceptions, men of marked characteristics. Judge

Joseph R. Lewis, of Iowa, though somewhat disposed to be autocratic, was the best trial judge I ever saw on a bench. In my time he was the ablest and most fearless judge on the supreme bench of the territory. He was a most able and levelheaded lawyer, and his common sense usually cropped out on all occasions. Sitting in matter-of-fact cases, he was unsurpassed. In his business habits he was quick and exact. Judge Lewis was particularly fond of children, and I remember how, in a district court session in 1870, the judge's fondness for children resulted in a ludicrous occurrence. Judge Roxborough entered court one day, bringing with him Johnny Boomer, a youngster of seven or eight years who was well liked by everyone. Johnny clambered up on Judge Lewis' knee and watched the court proceedings with interest; we were trying a manslaughter case. Suddenly, Johnny gave a loud yell as if some one had pricked him with a pin. The judge turned to him and said, "Don't do that again, Johnny, or I shall have to send you home." Johnny turned at once on Judge Roxborough and commenced to fight with him; the judge was probably responsible for Johnny's yell because he emitted another in a very short time much to the amusement of the court. When adjournment was called, Judge Lewis said, "Enough for today, Mr. Marshal, adjourn court!" The marshal was absent. "Mr. Sheriff, adjourn court!" The sheriff was also absent. "Well, well," said Judge Lewis, "no marshal, no sheriff, not even a crier in attendance!" At this point, Judge Heed arose and convulsed the crowd by saying, "Your Honor is in error! We have," he said, looking at Johnny Boomer, "one of the best criers in court that I ever heard, and your Honor threatened to put him out!"

JUDGE MADISON E. HOLLISTER

The man who succeeded Judge Lewis on the supreme bench was Judge Madison E. Hollister, of Illinois. How he secured the appointment and the clouded atmosphere attached to the proceeding is a bit of scandal in Idaho's history. Judge Hollister was a pious, God-fearing man of excellent habits, who, presumably, had an ever-present desire to do right. He had begun the practice of law late in life and had been fairly successful. He was a middle-sized man, with florid complexion, and was about sixty years of age when he came to Idaho. He had been United States consul at Buenos Aires and, so it was said, had been a judge at Galesburg, Illinois. He was a cousin of Burton C. Cook, of Chicago, one of the prominent attorneys of the West. It was Mr. Cook who obtained Judge Hollister's appointment from President Grant.

Judge Lewis was very unpopular with the Democrats of Idaho because he was a strong Union man and absolutely fearless and outspoken. The very first thing that we knew of a successor being appointed to Judge Lewis was what we read in a copy of the Sacramento *Union,* which reached us (1871) five days after issue. In the *Union* we read that Judge Madison E. Hollister had been appointed by President Grant as associate justice of Idaho. Of course we thought this an error, as there was no vacancy! In a day or two some of us wrote to Washington on the subject; it took about sixteen days to send East and receive a reply. Judge Lewis wrote to G. C. Bennett, his old Iowa law partner, at that time delegate to Congress from Dakota, asking him to ascertain what Hollister's appointment meant. The answer came back, "He was appointed vice you, J. R. Lewis, resigned." This served to deepen the mystery. Other letters followed and finally came a photographed copy of the resignation duly certified by the attorney general. This copy was used as evidence in court.

It was plain to all of us that Judge Lewis' resignation was a forgery. James H. Hawley, an attorney and Democratic politician of Idaho City, a man of some standing, was arrested for the forgery. He had a hearing before Judge Hollister and was discharged for want of evidence. I felt certain after hearing the evidence and after further investigation that the idea of forging Lewis' resignation originated with a certain woman and that her husband executed it. As I write this, both of the people are residents of Boise City. A curious feature of the resignation was that scarcely anyone in Washington believed the story of the forgery. The thing was most daring and had never before been done in the history of the country—at least, it was not on record. The perpetrators had skillfully concealed every point of rascality. It took a long time to convince the authorities at Washington of the truth of the matter. Judge Lewis wrote his valid resignation in the exact form of the forgery and sent it to Washington; then the forgery was acknowledged. In a letter from Burton C. Cook to Judge Hollister—it was Cook who secured the appointment—I saw this peculiar statement: "Pay no attention to Lewis' talk about not having resigned. Of course he did and now regrets it and wants to recall it. You hold on to the position! Such are hard to get."

Judge Hollister did not appear to hear any suggestions made to him at Boise—suggestions that under the circumstances he should refuse the position. A committee consisting of Judge McBride and J. S. Reynolds waited on him, but to no purpose. After Judge Hollister arrived and qualified at Boise City, Judge Lewis went to Kansas to reside. He was appointed associate justice in Washington Territory. of the supreme court of New Mexico. In the seventies he was apointed associate justice in Washington Territory. While he was living at Seattle the Idaho affair was revived, for someone again forged his resignation and sent it to Washington. Judge Lewis was a man of means and moved from Seattle to San Jose, California, where he now resides, an honored and respected citizen.

JUDGE DAVID NOGGLE

Judge David Noggle, of Wisconsin, by reason of age and a prominent lack of legal knowledge, was the least able and the most unfit of the judges that I knew. He was a man of six feet or more in height, had a large head, a thick chunky body, and thin legs. He had bad teeth and a disagreeable squeaky voice; plenty of gray hair surmounted his head, and his gray eyes, carried lowering, were somewhat like a Chinaman's. He must have been nearly seventy years of age when he came to Idaho in 1869 and he was then suffering from incipient paresis. He was in fact not responsible for his acts, and this was known to the authorities at Washington. In spite of protests from lawyers and statesmen, from the press, and a public which suffered from Noggle's irresponsibility, President Grant, who knew that Noggle was mentally affected and unfit for the bench, retained him in position until 1876, when Judge Noggle had to resign and shortly afterward died in a retreat.

In April, 1872, I saw President Grant in the White House. He said that while he did not believe Noggle to be a bad man, he considered him unfit to be judge and would not reappoint him after the expiration of his term in 1873. But he did reappoint him and gave as his reason that Senator M. H. Carpenter desired it because Noggle was old and had no money; Grant and Carpenter were old friends, and Grant chose to oblige the senator.

Judge Noggle of course fell under the stigma of "carpetbagger" as soon as he arrived. He had lived in a county of Wisconsin where farm products, meats, and groceries were cheap. The price of food and goods in Idaho paralyzed him! He was very free with his disagreeable opinions when purchasing goods in stores, and this did not add to his popularity. He stopped me on Main Street one day to chat, and I saw the stubs of a checkbook protruding from his coat pocket. He detailed the exorbitant price he was forced to pay for things and grumbled about the lack of small coin in the territory.*

Judge Noggle then detailed to me, somewhat in the manner of the lamentations of the prophet Jeremiah, his astonishing purchase of a turkey from a townsman, Bob Wilson. Forgetting that he was in a country where turkeys were prize birds, he incautiously said, "Yes, you may fetch me a turkey on Thursday next." In Rock River Valley, Wisconsin, he could probably have secured a mate for the turkey at an outlay of certainly not more than one dollar. When Wilson carried the turkey to Noggle's house, he politely demanded a five-dollar gold piece! The shock certainly aged the Judge more than did Jim Reynolds' attacks upon him in the *Statesman*. The Judge's wail at Wilson's pull on his wallet was very, very sad! A sigh arose from him, but he was forced to "pan out." I didn't blame him for objecting, although Wilson's price was the usual one. In those days attempts at economy were looked upon by the old Coasters as evidences of personal meanness. Economy, however, was a necessity with all Eastern people who went to the territory at that time. There was a transitory state which kept prices high; there were but few signs of permanent home building. Even the oldest residents expected to remain only until they earned a "home stake"— that is, enough money to escape from Idaho and purchase a house in California or some Eastern state.

Noggle was a disturbing political element from the first day he arrived in Idaho, owing to his mental infirmities. He came with President Grant's batch of appointees, and with the advent of these carpetbaggers, Idaho's public men started on a four or five years' quarrel which has scarcely been equaled in the history of any of our terri-

---

* He was right about the latter. I carried some five-cent pieces with me to Boise in 1869, and they were saved as curios for watch charms, etc. It occurs to me now that I was in the town of Ardmore, Chickasaw Nation, Indian Territory, in 1890, and a copper cent was only seen there when excursionists carried them over the line from Texas. Nothing smaller than a five-cent piece was used, and the standard was the old-style "two bits," or twenty-five cents.

tories. In 1869 Governor D. W. Ballard desired a reappointment to office and certainly deserved it. Noggle at once began a factional fight against Ballard. I have no doubt but that Senator Carpenter, in his personal plea with Grant at Washington against Ballard's reappointment, was instigated to a great extent by sentiments from Noggle against Ballard. Judge Lewis, able and strongly assertive, at once became Noggle's enemy in that gentleman's mind. J. S. Reynolds then went after Noggle in the *Statesman*. Some letters had been received from Noggle's old home in Wisconsin, where he had been a district judge for nine years, and these letters all testified to his judicial unfitness in a manner which aroused the people. This controversy over Federal officers permeated the social life of Boise to an alarming extent. With the exception of James Stout, the receiver of the land office, all officials were embroiled. Around Judge Noggle's home, and elsewhere, there were coteries of gossips who intensified feeling and aided in making bad blood among the citizens.

Judge Noggle's unpopularity did not remove him from the bench but it resulted in his relegation to Lewiston. As before stated, Boise City, the metropolis and capital, was the favorite place for the residence of the judges. A struggle began between Chief Justice Noggle and Associate Justice Lewis, the cause of which was the desire of both men to get possession of the third judicial district, with Boise as the objective point. Associate Justice W. C. Whitson, newly appointed from Oregon, came to Boise in 1870. Whitson was a rather weak man in worldly matters. Judge Lewis joined with him in rearranging the judicial districts, with the result that Noggle was "banished" to the first district, at Lewiston. Judge Whitson complained that Judge Lewis had overreached him in the matter of assignment and he, Whitson, was forced to live in Idaho City, where all that one could see were played-out gravel-bed washings and remnants of a town which once boasted greatness. The truth of the matter was that James S. Reynolds, editor and proprietor of the *Statesman,* had been more instrumental than anyone else in forcing the assignment of Noggle to Lewiston. Reynolds conducted an astounding crusade against Noggle and then worked upon Judge Whitson so that he would join issues with Lewis. Whitson, politically ambitious, probably saw Congress in the dim distance, solely through the help of Reynolds and the *Statesman.* His desire to win the support of Reynolds and his paper gave Boise much-needed relief from Noggle.

ALEXANDER SMITH

Alexander Smith, one of the first appointed associate justices of the territorial supreme court, must have been a decidedly original character. Smith was from Washington Territory and a son-in-law of Dr. A. G. Henry. I never met Judge Smith, but E. J. Curtis, in his inimitable style, detailed to me many of Smith's peculiarities. Judge Smith held one of the first, if not the first, district courts in Ada County.

The courthouse was a remarkable affair in those early days. It was a one-story building, brick or adobe, about twenty feet by forty, situated some paces north of Main Street, on Eighth Street, the thoroughfare running along the east side of the Overland House. It was fitted up with a rostrum for the judge, a table, a few chairs, and many wooden benches. On the south side a small room was reserved for the clerks and recorders. The supreme court used this building, and so did the district court. Judges Noggle and Lewis held their first session of the supreme court there in June, 1869. The building was used as a morgue when accidents occurred or when a body was publicly exposed, and it was also used, to my knowledge, as the polling place of Boise City from 1869 to 1878; the entire city voted en masse in one place. In addition to the many natural and unnatural uses of this courthouse, and in addition to the many bad odors which arose within it, the jail was located directly in its rear. When the weather was warm, the jail was ever self-assertive, and if the wind blew east, the courtrooms caught a double infliction.

Curtis told me that when Judge Smith held his first court, it was a circus. To the grand jury, when it was called, Smith made a lengthy charge, saying, "Gents, it will be part of your duty to examine the jail! I have been prospecting these parts for several days and haven't even found any such shebang! You may find one, however, so look around!"

Judge Smith was not fond of tobacco and took occasion to tell the court so one day. Customs, as is usual in a new country, were loose, and the bar members were wont to enter court carrying lighted cigars. Smith became very indignant one morning and blurted out, "Gents, if you don't stop this tobacco smoking in court, hell will pop!" Then he looked over at Curtis, who was smoking, and said, "Ned, you can smoke if you want to, because you told me that you had a toothache last night."

John Henley told me that he was sitting on the porch of the Overland House one evening when Judge Smith walked along with a variety actress named Belle —— on his arm. An attorney—probably it was Henley, although he did not say so—called from the balcony and told the Judge of the report of the commission filed that day in a divorce suit which gave decision in favor of the plaintiff. Judge Smith stopped his companion, looked up on the porch, and saw the clerk of the court sitting with Henley. Thereupon Smith called out, "Mr. Clerk, enter a decree of divorce for the plaintiff in So-and-So *versus* So-and-So."

"All right, Judge!" answered the clerk.

Smith swung his companion jauntily down the street, remarking, "That's the way to do it, Belle!"

If the Ada County bar was as bright in those early days

as it was from 1869 to 1875, the bar must have had lots of fun with Alexander Smith. Smith was a native of Jacksonville, Illinois, who had gone to Oregon in 1852. He died at Kalama, Washington, May 9, 1875.

JUDGE MILTON KELLY

Judge Milton Kelly left the bench about the time of my advent to the territory. He was an appointee of President Johnson and was removed by Grant in 1869 in a whirl of jugglery to afford a place for another person. He was not removed because of dereliction in office but simply because all Johnson's appointees in the territories were removed by President Grant. Judge Kelly was a man of ordinary mental capacity but he was fairly well read and educated. Reticent by nature, reticent beyond any need, he spread an unfortunate atmosphere of secrecy and cunning. He was a very industrious worker. All sorts of charges and judicial crimes were hurled against him, but, although we were not friends, I never saw any ground for the charges against him. Kelly was vicious toward his enemies, and as he did not always discriminate as to who were really his enemies, he was unpopular personally at Boise. He remained in Boise after leaving the bench and when, in the early seventies, he purchased the *Statesman,* he held a rod of terror over his enemies. Kelly once told me that he was from New York state, if I remember rightly, and that he had read law with ex-Governor Washington Hunt. Judge Kelly had unfortunately joined Judge Noggle in his social crusades, and much of his unpopularity was thus incurred.

JOHN R. MCBRIDE

Judge John R. McBride, with whom I was intimate for many years, played an important role in the early history of the territory. Judge McBride was born in Franklin

Milton Kelly, who retired from the law in order to buy the *Idaho Tri-Weekly Statesman* from its founder, James S. Reynolds.

County, Missouri, August 22, 1833, and from Missouri he went to Oregon in 1846. His education was received in common schools and under private tutors. In 1854 Judge McBride was elected superintendent of common schools for Yamhill County, Oregon. Two years later he was admitted to the Oregon bar and practiced law there.

When in 1858 Oregon was about to be admitted to the Union, the Republican Party but recently organized, nominated Judge McBride for Congress. He was then not twenty-five years of age, and his nomination for Congress gave rise to the statement that he was twenty-six. I have seen biographies of the Judge which have repeated this error. In 1860 he was elected state senator from Yamhill County. Two years later he was elected to Congress on the Republican ticket and served through the Thirty-eighth Congress. At this time Judge McBride became identified with Idaho in her formative period. He was present in Washington during the last sessions of the Thirty-seventh Congress and took an active part in furthering the organization of the territory.

President Lincoln appointed Mr. McBride chief justice of the territory in 1865. He arrived in Boise on June 5, 1865, and served on the bench until the thirtieth day of June, 1868, when he retired to private practice. In June, 1869, he was appointed general agent of the Treasury Department to superintend the building of the United States Assay Office at Boise. This building was completed in 1871, and for one year he filled the position of superintendent of the Assay Office. Then he resigned, went to Salt Lake City, and practiced law there until 1892. While in Utah, Judge McBride was as usual very active in national and territorial affairs. He had been, for four years, a member of the Republican National Committee from Idaho, and he filled a similar position for eight years on the Utah national committee. It is of interest to note that he was the youngest member of the Thirty-eighth Congress and sat next to James G. Blaine. Since 1892 Judge McBride has resided in Spokane, Washington, where he has an extensive clientele in mining regions and devotes himself to mining litigation. From 1892 until 1897 he was the Northern Pacific Railroad's attorney for the section west of the Rockies. Elsewhere I have mentioned some of his valuable efforts on behalf of Idaho interests.

SIDNEY EDGERTON

The first chief justice of Idaho was Sidney Edgerton. He was chief justice in name only. His appointment was made March 10, 1863, and, despite the fact that Edgerton had, ex officio, first choice as to his district, Governor Wallace assigned him to the district east of the Rockies, a country which reached into Montana before that territory was separated from Idaho. In July, 1863, Silas Woodson was appointed chief justice. The fact was, Edgerton did not serve.

Mr. Edgerton was born in Cazenovia, Madison County, New York, the son of Amos Edgerton and Zevirah Graham. After the death of the father—the boy was then but six years of age—the family moved to Ontario County, New York. Edgerton learned the builder's trade, taught school —in fact, did all that an ambitious boy could do to earn a living. About 1840 he went to Akron, Ohio, and read law with Rufus H. P. Spaulding. In 1844 he was graduated from the Cincinnati Law School and went into legal partnership with V. R. Humphrey and William H. Upson.

Edgerton was a man of strong character and won respect and admiration of the honest voters in his district. He was elected on the Republican ticket to the Thirty-seventh Congress, the first session under President Lincoln. Ohio was well represented that year, and Mr. Edgerton, a young man, was in a galaxy of men who won national distinction. John A. Bingham and Samuel Shellabarger,

Valentine B. Horton, and James M. Ashley, S. S. Cox, and George H. Pendleton—all these were Ohio men, Republicans and Democrats.

In 1863 Edgerton's appointment came as chief justice of Idaho. When he arrived in Bannock, there was no one to administer oath of office and no court was held within the district assigned to him. The people of Montana were desirous of breaking away from Idaho and forming a distinct territory. Mr. Edgerton was asked by the residents to assist in the organization of Montana Territory. He interested himself in their behalf, and when Congress passed an act providing for a temporary government for Montana, Edgerton received the appointment of governor. He was commissioned June 22, 1864, and served until late in the summer of 1865. General Thomas Francis Meagher succeeded him. Governor Edgerton was placed in a position which won for him little other than severe criticism. When he left the territory in 1865, he returned to Akron, Ohio.

Judge McBride knew him well and admired him and often spoke to me about Edgerton's manhood and ability. At the time of his appointment he was a man of about forty-five years. Judge McBride said to me in 1870, "Judge Edgerton was a man of more than ordinary ability and yet was the subject of very bitter political attacks in Montana. He was respected because he was deserving of respect. He was honest and in every way was a superior man." It is interesting to note that James M. Ashley, of Ohio, who was in the Thirty-seventh Congress with Edgerton, was governor of Montana from 1869 to 1870.

PURCHASED JUDGES

I never placed much faith in the stories of purchased judges in Idaho. Defeated parties, without a shade of truth or reason for their statements, would sometimes denounce the judge or judges who decided against them and intimate or assert purchase by the other interested parties. There was an indirect assault upon one district court judge, prior to 1870, who decided adversely to the interest of certain mining capitalists. The capitalists were alarmed at the decision, fearing that the supreme court judges would also decide against them on the appeal. The supreme court was constituted of the three district judges, and they sat in judgment on appealed cases: certainly, the one of the three who had heard the case in the district court would not be likely to reverse his own decision. To prevent the possible agreement of the other two district judges with the judge who had already ruled against them, the capitalists raised a sum of money sufficient to pay this judge's salary for the remainder of his term of office; three years remained. Territorial judges were always appointed for four years, but were as a rule turned out at the expiration of the term of the party in power whether the judicial term had reached four years or not. The capitalists opened negotiations, and the judge who had decided against them in the district court resigned, and the money was paid him for his unexpired term. A new judge was then appointed who had the "right faith," and the interests of the mining company, under his watchful eye, were preserved. My friend, George W. Grayson, of Oakland, California, knew the details of this transaction and was my informant.

In the winter of 1871-72, I knew of an attempt to buy one of the associate justices of the supreme court. The associate justices were Joseph R. Lewis and W. C. Whitson. The judge whose purchase was desired was certainly not Judge Lewis. No man in Idaho would have presumed to approach him. Judge Whitson was new to the bench and an untried quantity, and the attack was made upon him. David Noggle was then chief justice. Certain people with a case on appeal from northern Idaho wanted a decision.

Noggle was in sympathy with the case and he eventually decided the case for the appealing parties. To my knowledge, however, there was no attempt made to buy Judge Noggle. Joel B. Oldham, a genial, cunning man of the world, kept a saloon and gambling house on Main Street, Boise, and he was selected by the appellants to approach the associate justices. Oldham was a pleasant fellow; he afterwards became sheriff of Ada County. When about to begin operations, he approached one of the supreme court officers and opened up his project of capturing Whitson or Lewis. He said, "We want a judgment and we have money."

Promptly scenting danger, the court officer replied: "I think that your work in that direction will be entirely futile. Judge Whitson is impecunious and is always telling how poor he is, but I don't believe you can buy him. However, you might try him as you associate with him a great deal. As for Lewis—just mention money to him and he'll knock you down." Oldham decorated the stove of the court officer with tobacco juice and left the house; the affair was never again mentioned.

The truth of the matter may have been that Whitson wanted this court officer's position for another man and had no reason for being publicly adverse to him. Judge Noggle did not hold enmity toward the same officer, and it was patent that if Whitson had a case against this officer, out he would go. Oldham and a coterie of his kind were intimate with Whitson. All were Masons; the court officer was not. Oldham's supposed attempt to bribe the judges was nothing but an attempt to get the court officer to declare against Whitson, and then it would be Whitson's turn to become loudly virtuous and cause the removal and downfall of the official. The official knew the judges of the court and he was not pandering his knowledge for bribery cases.

JOHN C. HENLEY

John C. Henley was one of the brightest, ablest, and most gentlemanly young men I have ever met. He was small and wiry in stature, always wearing glasses, always smoking, and always carrying a cane. His kinky black hair covered as brainy a head as ever entered Idaho. Henley was of German extraction and was born at Zanesville, Ohio. He lived in Iowa until 1862, crossed the plains in 1863, and located at Idaho City before coming to Boise. He had been clerk of the district court of the second judicial district, and was a lawyer of great promise. When Chief Justice McBride resigned from the bench in 1868, Henley became his law partner. He had previously been a partner in the firm of Gilbert and Henley and was also the Idaho member of the Republican National Committee; his position I afterward filled. Henley died in Boise on August 27, 1872, a victim of drink. He died in the rear room of his office in the "Little Stone Jug," Main Street, and while I watched with him many nights before his death, in his delirium he described as no man ever did before the events which he was witnessing in the vagaries of his diseased imagination; his ravings were a marvel of descriptive eloquence. Two nights before he died all the gentle nature of the man came back and burst out. The old sweet manhood asserted itself as he told me of his boyhood and his home. Dissipation had simply exhausted him, so that after days of frightful paroxysms, death came like a gentle sleep. Henley knew that he was dying and courted death as a relief. All who knew him loved him, and every man, woman, and child in Boise mourned his loss, for we realized that a splendid intellect, capable of the highest development and utility, had gone into oblivion from excesses which were, with Henley, beyond control.

OTHER MEMBERS OF THE BAR

In 1869 all the Idaho lawyers were by courtesy called "Judge," a custom which was in vogue on the coast. John R. McBride, ex-chief justice, was the best general practitioner and ablest lawyer at the supreme court bar, in my time. Samuel A. Merritt was the best man before a jury on the facts and was clever and adroit before the supreme court; Joseph Roseborough was the best consulting lawyer. Joseph W. Huston, a man of genius, was a ready lawyer and a most eloquent advocate. He was afterward appointed to the supreme bench of the state. Richard Z. Johnson, of Silver City, knew as much if not more law than any man at the Idaho bar; his pleadings were the best, but he lacked readiness as an advocate. George Ainslie was too much of a politician to be a strong lawyer, but had he stuck to law none could have excelled him. Albert Heed was the best natural lawyer in Idaho. He had no culture, but he had a clearer head for judicial principles than any of his contemporaries.

There were but thirteen practicing attorneys in Boise City in 1869. I recall Jeremiah Brumback as an attorney with the best legal manner and one who presented his cases clearly and logically. Henry E. Prickett was a man of ordinary abilities, but his studious habits and impressive manner won success for him. He afterwards became an associate justice of the supreme court of the territory. Robert H. Nugent, of Silver City, was a well-read and competent lawyer but from living a secluded life he lacked a certain breadth. Frank E. Ensign I remember as a gentleman and a fair lawyer. Frank E. Ganahl was an attorney noted for eloquence rather than legal acquirement. The large southern element in Idaho inoculated the people with the absurd beliefs that oratory was essential at the bar, and that good speakers could never fail to be good lawyers.

The most singular attorney we had was H. L. Preston, a man of erudition and many mannerisms. I never could detect whether he was or was not a lawyer. I heard him often in the lower and supreme courts, and although he was a splendid speaker he seldom seemed to see the point in his case. He was fortunate in having our good old Joe Roseborough for a law partner. A peculiar specimen of the exclusive Southern type was Major R. E. Foote, a son of Henry E. Foote. I never saw his excuse for being a lawyer. Although ever polite, he possessed the rather disagreeable attitude of a man with a chip on his shoulder and was not popular. We had an ex-actor at the bar, Robert H. Lindsay, a fair lawyer and very much a man. He left Idaho in 1869 and went to Nevada, where he achieved a reputation. John S. Gray, "Genial John," was a clever and obliging gentleman who won well-deserved success at the bar.

Lack of space prevents me from mentioning other members of the bar, but there was one curious member decidedly worth describing. The first time I heard him was in the supreme court, in an appealed murder case in 1870. This man was S. S. Fenn. Fenn had a habit, when excited, of getting choked in his speech and blurting out his words as if his mouth were full of a substance. He was a fearful Democrat; there are Democrats and Democrats, but he was of the most pronounced type. The territory's Democrats sent him to Congress for two terms. He had nothing to do in Congress of a public nature and as merely a territorial delegate had no vote, but private matters for his constituents were well watched. He was honest and upright but careless in his manners and dress; he seldom wore a collar and often appeared upon the streets in carpet slippers. I boarded at the same hotel with him in Washington, and the waiters knew him as "Liver and Onions," that dish being his favorite food.

E. J. Curtis, "Old Ned," was general utility man at the bar. He could play any part—none with marks of greatness, but he did all parts well. Nature never intended Curtis for an attorney. He had pronounced ability but lacked application, and his general culture best fitted him for executive functions. He was a master of conversation, and a man of most taking manners. Curtis was a splendid public official, genial, courteous, exact, accommodating, and he made friends everywhere. He had vast experience in public office, and in recognition of his abilities the Idaho Republicans, when the state government was organized in 1890, tendered him the nomination for secretary of state. This Curtis refused to accept. As a conversationalist and yarn-spinner, Curtis was unsurpassed. He had a remarkable memory and a faculty of relating events in a most engaging manner.

OUTGOING ATTORNEYS

Many of the leading attorneys and Democrats left Boise City and Idaho City in 1869. The outgoing chief justice was Thomas J. Bowers, of California. I am under the impression that Mr. Bowers never qualified or sat in the supreme court. He was a genial, able, clever gentleman— one of the best yarn-spinners I ever heard. He had been appointed in July, 1868. David Noggle, his successor, was appointed in April of the following year.

In the late summer and autumn of 1869, a number of farewell receptions were held for departing members of the bar. The chief factotum at all these meetings was I. N. Smith, formerly of Oregon. Smith was tall and thin, a good-natured soul, full of anecdote and gossip, some of it historically valuable, about Oregon and Washington. Smith wore boots so heavy that he could be heard for many blocks when his heels met the board walks.

One of Smith's masterpieces in reminiscence was a description of the part he played, in 1860, electioneering in Oregon for General Joseph A. Lane, vice-presidential candidate. Congress had presented Lane with a sword for gallantries in the Mexican War, and of course the blade had been in the general's possession for many years. The suggestion was made that, to arouse enthusiasm, the general should tour the Oregon backwoods and then this sword could be re-presented on several occasions. I. N. Smith was one of the presenting parties. The form of procedure was, first, for the state Democratic committee to call a meeting. The speaking would commence with General Lane seated on the platform. While the introduction was on there would be a loud cry outside, and a messenger on horseback would gallop up and rush into the meeting carrying an American flag. He would announce to the voters that a committee was approaching bringing with them a sword which the United States had voted to General Joseph A. Lane, the "Marion of the Mexican War." As if unprearranged, the messengers would rush in with a whoop and a hurrah, waving the sword. Speeches of presentation would be made, and General Lane would humbly respond about the modest service he had rendered to his country, the unexpected honor, etc., etc. Then the crowd would cheer. This farce was carried on time after time without discovery.

On the occasion of the departure from Boise of "Judge" Morford, a leading attorney, a testimonial farewell meeting was held, and the affair had one amusing incident and one that terminated fatally. Morford was a big burly fellow but a thorough gentleman. He was unfortunate enough to marry a handsome woman who was very fond of attentions from men other than her husband. At the farewell meeting we had refreshment of the usual liquid sort and, strange to say, lemonade. Lemons were procured at the moderate price of one dollar each. I. N. Smith, the handy man of the occasion, entered the room carrying the lemonade cooled by a lump of ice in a large tin bucket. The crowd, not used to lemonade drinking, set up a shout when they saw Smith. Considering it a duty, we refrained from drinking the lemonade and held it for the end of the meeting. Clad in a long linen duster, he fairly outdid himself as a floor manager and imbibed freely of liquids. Toward the end of the evening I noticed that he had fallen in a doze and as I passed near him, I saw that his duster was wet all the way up the back. Looking closer, I saw that Smith was sitting on the lump of ice in the large tin pail, and capillary attraction had drawn much of the lemonade up his back and wilted his linen duster. The company were outraged at this violation of the amenities! In an instant, a man lifted "I. N." off the pail, set him in a chair, emptied the entire bulk of lemonade over him, and jammed the pail over his head. Everyone at once ran out of the room, leaving I. N. standing on lonely duty with a tin helmet and peacefully unconscious of what had happened.

The incident which had a fatal termination began by the exchange of warm fraternal feeling between Morford and Theodore Burmester, another member of the bar. Burmester fell on Morford's neck and fairly wept tears at the thought of parting from his dear friend. All of us were deeply touched. Within one week after that affectionate and formal farewell, Burmester deliberately murdered Morford, shot him dead on a public highway. It was considered murder, and the wonder of it was that Burmester was not hanged. The influence which freed him had secured the acquittal of many others charged with the crime of murder. Morford's handsome wife seemed to be the provocative figure in this case.

SCANNIKER AND BURMESTER

The law firm of Scanniker and Burmester was noted for charging large fees and for seldom, if ever, losing or lowering its fees. They were very exacting collectors. Scanniker had the dignity of the firm, and Burmester had the push!

Eugene Howard, Hill Beachy's stage agent, was a handsome "quasi" sport with a happy faculty of getting into debt and with nothing in prospect to liquidate save faro probabilities. Life and he played a game of chance. His indebtedness reached an enormous sum on one occasion. Howard went for advice to Scanniker and Burmester. "Bankruptcy, of course!" snorted Scanniker. Howard at once went through the proceedings for discharge in bankruptcy, the two attorneys advancing the costs. Scanniker and Burmester were to receive five hundred dollars for all expenses and fees. When the schedule for discharge was being made, Howard said he would write a list of his debts and he took the form to his office. Scanniker was very emphatic that Howard should write a complete schedule of his debts. Scanniker then hurried to court and prepared the final decree of discharge so as to have it ready for the court's signature when Howard returned with the schedule. The haste was necessary because court was about to adjourn for that term.

Just before adjournment Howard rushed into court and handed the schedule to Scanniker, who made him swear to it before the clerk. Then the judge signed, and it was at once entered, discharging Eugene Howard from all debts to date. This was in accordance with the bankruptcy act of 1867. A certified copy was handed Howard, and the young man shook hands with the judge and with Scanniker and quickly left the room. Scanniker looked over the list of debts and was immensely interested in one item:

> Due Scanniker & Burmester for Legal Services in
> Bankruptcy Proceedings _____$500.00

LEGAL ADVICE FROM A SPIRITUALIST

In 1871 several important cases on appeal from Owyhee County were pending in the supreme court at Boise, and there was also a proceeding in bankruptcy which came before the three supreme bench judges who sat as an United States circuit court in bankruptcy. For a week or ten days before the Owyhee cases were heard, I noticed a fine-looking man of fifty watching proceedings from the rear of the courtroom. He was a stranger, stopping at the Overland Hotel, and, as strangers were always a curiosity, people at once remarked him. I was clerk of the supreme court then, and the stranger approached one afternoon and asked when the Owyhee cases would be heard. These were the bankruptcy cases. I answered him, and he handed me a card which read, "C. W. Coolidge, of Boston, Agent for the Administrators of the Estate of Zenos Wheeler, Deceased."

Zenos Wheeler was the inventor and owner of the "Wheeler Pan," used in gold and silver mills for extracting the precious metals from quartz. Nearly all the Idaho gold and silver mines used the Wheeler pan. The Wheeler estate had moneys due it from the several Owyhee mining companies at Silver City, and Mr. Coolidge was there to receive the estate's share of the moneys in the court from the bankrupt companies. Some $54,000 was in the hands of the court awaiting distribution.

The evening of the day I met Mr. Coolidge, I went to the home of C. W. Moore and found among the guests this same Coolidge. He had a letter of introduction to Mr. Moore but had not, until some days after his arrival, introduced himself. We found him to be a curious but most interesting man and a fluent and easy conversationalist. He combined keen observation with quaint descriptive powers and, toward the end of the evening, after the departure of the other guests, chatted for an hour with Mr. Moore and me on Boise City and particularly the purpose of his visit. His conversation was made all the more remarkable because of the sincerity of his views, and Mr. Moore and I were astounded when he told us that the business transactions of the Wheeler estate were guided by a medium, a woman. Mr. Coolidge said:

"You have queer people here! Some of your lawyers are great rogues or are only waiting for a chance to be rogues. One of your official dignitaries, I see, is a drunkard! He will prove to be a defaulter as well!" He named the man and strangely enough he did eventually prove to be a defaulter! Mr. Coolidge went on. "In all my movements to recover royalties for the Wheeler pan, I am entirely guided by a woman." And then, if I remember rightly, he named a Mrs. William Foy, of San Francisco. "This woman keeps her magic touch upon the interests of our invention. I am going from Boise to Elko and afterwards to White Pine to bring suit against a mining company in Nevada. I have just received a letter from the medium to go to these points. The suits at Silver City, which have been closed here, were begun on her advice, and the data as to the probable money due and the facts stated in the cases, were given us by her. The books of the company show that her statements were correct. In fact, we proved our cases by bringing the company's books into court. There are skeptical people who doubt a medium's ability in business matters, but Alvin [or Alvah] Adams, of Boston, told me that every successful business venture he had ever made had resulted from following the advices of a medium, and he never ventured without consulting one."

Mr. Coolidge then told us of physical demonstrations he had witnessed of the power of mediums. He chatted for an hour but simply confirmed the skepticism of both his listeners.

I finally said, "Mr. Coolidge, if you are guided by the advice of this woman, how do you receive your advice?"

"When I am through at one point," Mr. Coolidge answered, "I write and ask her where I shall go and where I shall bring the next suit. She answers, and off I start."

"Has she ever been mistaken?"

"Not once!"

"Couldn't you find out," I asked again, "where to bring these suits without advice from her?"

"I don't know," said Mr. Coolidge. "I simply place faith in her, and thus far she has not failed to direct me where to go and against whom to bring suit. I firmly believe in the value of a spiritualist medium in business."

The next day Mr. Moore and I compared notes, and Mr. Moore wondered just how long a man could run a bank by lending notes on the advice of a spiritualist. The conclusion at which we arrived was that Mr. Coolidge had been fooled by a shrewd woman. Mrs. Foy probably knew that Coolidge was a spiritualist and, having a list of mining towns—a list was printed and distributed on the coast—and a list of milling companies, and knowing from publications that the Wheeler pans were used almost everywhere, she advised him to bring suit, particularly in those places where no royalties had ever been paid the Wheeler estate. Coolidge could have learned as much as Mrs. Foy had he read widely and been called upon to use his wits as was she. The incident was most interesting, at any rate.

THE BRYON-LINDSAY CONTEST FOR SHERIFF

One of the memorable legal contests in Boise was the Bryon-Lindsay contest for sheriff of Ada County. Lute Lindsay, a livery stable proprietor and a Boise sporting character, was a Missouri Democrat and a very clever man. He was quiet and unpretending and had a host of friends. William Bryon, a man of high character and widely respected, was nominated for sheriff by the Republican Party with the hope that he could defeat Lindsay. The contest was close, and the "sports" were making even bets. Bryon pulled the full Republican vote and also the votes of many Democrats who disliked ex-Rebels and people from Missouri in particular. The polling place was the old courthouse, and there I went on election night while the judges were counting the ballots. I looked through the window, hung with an old holland curtain, and heard one of the judges say, as he strung the ballots on a black thread after puncturing them with a needle: "It's all right! We're only three votes short." This sentence struck me forcibly because during the day I had heard that the ballots of John West, John Seavy, and "Old Bill," three negroes who voted the Republican ticket, had been tampered with by the election judges. There were but four negro voters in Boise, and the Democrats were bitterly prejudiced against them. Universal suffrage had been extended over the territory by act of Congress early in 1870, and these negroes were as much entitled to vote as any white citizen. The election judges really did not know this.

The returns began to come in the next two days from outlying precincts, and it "looked like" Bryon; the third day the returns showed that Lindsay had been elected by one vote. Then it flashed upon me that the cast-out ballots of the three negroes would elect Bryon on the Republican ticket; I hurried over to Judge Prickett and told him my views.

"Judge," I said, "it will be necessary to find out if the three negro votes polled for Bryon were counted or cast out."

"How shall we find that out?" asked Prickett.

"You're a Mason!" said I. "I'm not! Go over to Captain J. W. Griffin, at the Overland House, who holds the ballot boxes. He's a Mason and the right sort and was an election judge yesterday. He probably knows nothing about what I told you. Griffin has all the tally sheets and ballots cast. It may take legal proceedings to open the box, if he has no authority to do so. You go there, however, and perhaps he will open the box for you." Prickett was usually slow, but when aroused he was all action. He hurried over to the Overland, and I waited two hours for him. He came

William Bryon, early-day sheriff of Ada County.

A famous Boise jurist and Speaker of the House, A. W. Flournoy.

Judge H. E. Prickett, Boise jurist.

J. Waldo Huston, who later was on the Idaho Supreme Court.

COURTS, JUDGES, AND ATTORNEYS 213

back and said that he had opened the box, counted the ballots and found, as I expected, three votes short in comparison with the votes registered on the tally sheet. The names of the three negroes were on the tally sheet as having cast votes, but their votes were not counted. Then we swore each other to secrecy. I went after Bryon at midnight, told him what I wanted, and asked his authority to go ahead. I retained Judge Prickett and J. W. Huston and with them acted for Bryon. We filed a petition and began action in contest for the shrievalty before Judge A. G. Flournoy, probate judge of Ada County, the law providing for such cases. He decided against our method. We got a hearing in the district court before Judge Joseph R. Lewis and brought the case full on. Not one human being in Boise, save Judge Prickett, Captain Griffin, and myself knew that the ballot box had been opened, so that when the ballot box was brought before Judge Lewis it was as if it had been untouched since election night.

Several days were consumed in the trial. The three negroes testified as to whom they had voted for, and the election judges themselves stated that, while they had received the ballots, they had thrust them under the table, and, although not registering them for Bryon, neither had they counted them for Lindsay, in whom they were interested. The judges said that they considered the votes of these three negroes a trick on the part of the Republicans, because no negro had dared to vote in Idaho before. Judge Lewis, after counting in the votes of the three negroes, entered a decree confirming the election of William Bryon as sheriff of Ada County by two votes. This election gave Bryon a profitable position and one which he filled admirably. The Democrats, despite their dislike of Judge Lewis, did not appeal to the supreme court from his judgment in this case.

I am sure that this is the first time the explanation of the Bryon-Lindsay contest ever appeared in print.

EMMA COX V. THE NORTHWESTERN STAGE COMPANY

A very famous case in litigation was the suit at Boise in 1870 of Emma Cox, an unmarried woman of twenty-four years, against the Northwestern Stage Company. One day in the spring of 1870, a stage driver—I am under the impression that he was a brother-in-law of Miss Cox—invited the girl to take a free ride with him from one stage station to another. The ride was of course a free one, and Miss Cox's name was not entered upon the waybill of passengers. She was sitting on the box with the driver when the stage upset. How it happened was never explained. Miss Cox rolled down the bank of a grade and hurt her hip. She was at once brought to Boise for medical attendance, and tenders were at the same time made to the stage agent for compensation for her injuries. When the stage agent refused to pay, Miss Cox instituted a suit for damages. Ex-Judge McBride was the chief counsel for Miss Cox, and this should have been warning enough for the stage company that large damages would result; McBride was the best trial attorney in the territory. Henry E. Prickett was the chief counsel for the stage company, assisted by H. L. Preston, an attorney never quite clear on any point he argued. Judge Lewis presided at the trial, and the jury were men of the best character in Ada County. Medical experts were used by both parties. The plaintiff's attorneys had secured the skeleton of a squaw from the foothills back of Boise, and the femur and socket were used to illustrate Miss Cox's dreadful injuries. Dr. Clinton Wagner, ex-Army surgeon and later an eminent specialist in New York, was chief medical expert for Miss Cox. One of the stage company's medical experts practiced medicine and surgery in Idaho for years. He was an excellent citizen with a home-obtained knowledge of his profession. During the trial he was asked if he had or had not received a diploma from a reputable medical school; this was of course asked with the hope that his "No" would weaken his testimony with the jury. He answered promptly, "Well, no! I'm not a diplomatic doctor." As the verdict showed, the jury evidently agreed with him.

Miss Cox did not appear during the trial, but her attorneys read affidavits from physicians stating that she was unable to leave her room at the City Hotel and asked that the jury be taken to the hotel to view her. Attorney Preston, for the defense, resisted this proposition and agreed to admit as evidence what statements Miss Cox might make as to her injuries. The stage company was relying upon proving not only that Miss Cox was a free rider but also that she, by her pleasantries in conversation, had distracted the attention of the stage driver and caused the accident. The stage-company attorneys forgot one important thing; they forgot they were in a new country where the jury, with one exception, were unmarried and the sympathy of the unmarried jurors was decidedly with the young woman who, should she perchance get a large damage award, would become a very marriageable person. Judge McBride intimated that the defendants were afraid to permit the jury to see Miss Cox because she was so badly injured; defendants replied that a person always looked worse in bed, surrounded with the accessories of a sickroom, than when walking on the street or in court.

After several days of trial proceedings, the jury rendered a verdict of $14,000 damages for Miss Cox! The case was appealed to the supreme court, the verdict was sustained, the remittitur was sent to the district court, and execution was ordered. When execution commenced, the stage road was stripped for miles of its horses and coaches. The stage company thought that because it carried United States mail it would be exempted, but this did not save it; in order to resume business, it paid the judgment. The attorneys obtained one half of the sum awarded, and the remainder was fooled away by Miss Cox in the purchase of jewelry and clothes for herself and the women who had become suddenly attached to her. All that Emma Cox really had by which to remember the famous case was a large amount of notoriety and a short leg which lamed her for life. There were many in Boise who saw no justice in the damages awarded her; she was riding on the stagecoach as a free passenger, contrary to the company's orders.

When the end of the case was near, and the attorneys for the company had exhausted all known remedies and resources, they evolved a brilliant scheme destined to get me into trouble, but I knew something of the law and the craftiness of attorneys, so nothing came of it. The scheme of the defendants was to apply to me, as clerk of the third judicial district, Boise, for a notice to plaintiff on filing of a notice or writ of error to the supreme court. This, if issued by me after bond being filed and approved, would, when a certified copy was served on the plaintiff, act as a supersedeas. Of course, the plaintiff would at once apply to a district judge to set aside my writ of error notice, and it would be set aside. Then the defendants would have the right to, and would, appeal at once from the order of the judge vacating my notice of writ of error to the supreme court; meantime, the defendants would compromise with the plaintiffs, and I would have been officially decapitated. Judge Prickett, for the Northwestern Stage Company, was very cunning; he really did not want to see me ousted but, true to his calling, he was willing to try everything to save his clients from such a large verdict. On the evening of March 23, 1871, Prickett came swinging into my office, very busy in manner and carrying a bunch of papers.

"Hello, Donaldson!" he said. "Got a bond here, and I want your approval!"

"All right!" said I. "What is it?"

"Oh," said Prickett carelessly, "It's the defendant's bond in Cox versus the stage company on an application for a writ of error to the supreme court."

"Indeed!" I exclaimed. "Sit down, Judge, and let me read it." The Judge sat down and began to stroke his long red beard and impressively patronized me. The bond was a praecipe bond, and, as I read it, Prickett handed me the statutes of Idaho and pointed out Section 315 of the Civil Practice Act.

"I'm familiar with that clause, Judge," I said. "But you have been to the supreme court and you have been decided against. What are you going up on now?"

"Oh, generally!" he replied. "You see, the law says that any party—it doesn't limit the number of times he may go up."

"Doesn't it?" I asked innocently.

"Ah, no!" said Prickett blandly. And then he came at me in his low and impressive voice. "Mr. Donaldson, I now desire you to consider this matter in a serious light and to consider as well, that you are under solemn oath to do your duty impartially, and you are also acting under your official bond." Prickett and I had always been good friends, and he once favored me in an important personal matter; therefore I waited awhile before answering.

"Thanks, Judge!" I said. "I appreciate the responsibility and know the law. I will not approve this bond, and I will not issue a certified copy of any notice of writ of error. I have no authority to do so and I do not intend to give the judge a chance to lift my official scalp; nor will you get a chance to appeal from the judge's rule setting aside my illegal deed."

"Then, sir," he stormed, "do you refuse to obey the law?"

"Quite to the contrary, Judge!" I retorted. "I simply refused to suspend or break the law! That is all." Prickett arose, gathered up his papers, except the praecipe, which I retained.

There was an odd little twinkle in his eye as he marched out. Judge McBride, chief counsel for Miss Cox, came in almost immediately afterward and looked much flustered and worried.

"What's up?" he asked quickly. "Did you issue the copy of the notice of error?"

"No, Judge, I did not."

"Good!" smiled McBride. "I felt sure you would not because I knew you would observe the law. The act they asked you to do would have been, as you knew, a supersedeas." And out walked McBride looking more pleased than when he came in. I then endorsed the praecipe which Judge Prickett had handed me and filed the following:

DISTRICT COURT
3RD JUDICIAL DISTRICT, I.T.
ADA COUNTY

EMMA S. COX
vs.
THE NORTHWESTERN STAGE COMPANY
} Application for Writ of Error from Supreme Court of I.T., Praecipe for Notice to Plaintiff.

Boise City, March 24, 1871.

I refuse to proceed further in this matter. The case of Emma E. Cox vs. The Northwestern Stage Company has already been to the Supreme Court of Idaho Territory on appeal; been affirmed and the Remittitur received from said court ordering the District Court to proceed as if no appeal had been taken.

I have no authority to issue a supersedeas when the Supreme Court has ordered otherwise.

THOMAS DONALDSON,
Clerk, 3rd Judicial District, I.T.

How the jury decided upon the amount of $14,000 as damages in the Cox case, I was always anxious to hear, and I ascertained the details about a year after the settlement. I met one of the jurors, W. N. Cowen, a handsome, dignified man of forty years, in front of Jacob's store one afternoon, and Cowen gave me the amusing details.

"You see," said Cowan, "all the jury except Mounts

Byrd were single men. You know Byrd, one of our good citizens and proprietor of the City House where Miss Cox boarded after she was injured. All of us were interested in the little Cox girl, but Byrd was working in the interests of the stage company—not for pay, but because he was honestly convinced that Miss Cox deserved no damages. When the jury got together, we discovered that the performance of the 'diplomatic' doctor had cooked the stage company's goose! Again, Preston's hard fight to keep us from seeing the little girl, Miss Cox, when she was injured and in bed convinced most of us that the 'little girl' was deserving. Mounts Byrd had an idea that the damages were already fixed in most of our minds, and we soon saw that he was in favor of a verdict only big enough for Miss Cox to pay medical experts, lawyers, and a large hotel bill due Byrd himself! Bowlby, bighearted Sam, who has a place down the valley, was on the jury, and he proposed that just for fun we take an informal ballot as to what each fellow thought Miss Cox should get for her injuries. I voted $500; Bowlby voted $1,000; Byrd voted $5,000. At any rate, the highest vote was for $5,000. We had to keep it low because Byrd was doubtful. After twelve ballots had been laid on the table, Bowlby spoke up again and said, 'All of us seem to be of one mind as to what the girl should get. Suppose we take another ballot, take the sum of twelve ballots, divide by twelve, and let the average be the verdict!' That sounded reasonable, and we all agreed. Byrd, quick at figures, saw that this would make the the amount about $2,000, and of course he agreed. Then we prepared the second ballot. Old Mounts voted as he did the first time—$5,000; but Bowlby voted $60,000; a man to my right, $80,000, and I voted $100,000. Only three of us knew the secret. Old Mounts went blue in the gills when he began to read the tallies and sat paralyzed when the average came out $14,000. 'Gentlemen,' he said, 'I don't go back on my word. It's an ungodly pile, but I will stand for her.' And he did! Then after some chat and smoking, we took a third ballot, each juror voting a twelfth part of the $14,000. That's how Emma Cox got damages."

I met Sam Bowlby, one of the jurors, in New Mexico in 1879. Bowlby was then living in Coffeyville, Kansas, and making a name for himself. He said to me, "I remember every detail of that Cox case, and you bet your life I wish I had voted for a million dollars damages. I married after the Cox case was settled and have one child and I know that a husband needs all the money his wife might get from a stage company or any other source."

A SIGNAL DIVORCE

A very pretty young woman entered the courtroom one day early in the seventies and stated to me a case for divorce. She left instructions as to procedure and promised me a cow for my fee. Immediately after this I was appointed clerk of the district court and asked my friend Joseph Huston to take charge of the case for me. Huston did so, and the case went along smoothly until the day of the decree. The young woman entered the court the morning the decree was expected, and I told her that she was all right, that I would prepare the decree—being the commissioner in the case—and hand it to Attorney Huston for motion for a decree.

"What time will it be entered?" she asked.

"Can't say," I replied. "But if Major Huston isn't here before noon, I'll ask the judge to enter this decree for divorce."

"Do you think it will be before twelve o'clock?" she persisted.

"Undoubtedly," I replied.

"Well," she said, "I am over at Green's Hotel, across the way, and if the decree is entered at noon, I will look out of the east window above the porch, and if I get no signal to the contrary, I shall consider that I'm divorced. I must hurry back as he's waiting."

"Who is waiting?" I queried.

"The other fellow!" she retorted. "He is very nice, and I don't want to leave him alone! You can't tell what may happen in this country," and her black eyes snapped saucily as she went out. About noon I called Judge Hollister's attention to the case, offered the decree, as if by Huston's authority, and it was entered. At twelve o'clock, I saw the young lady's black head peering out of the hotel window; at two minutes past twelve it was withdrawn. I ascertained that at twelve-thirty o'clock, she and the "other fellow" were married. Whether or not Huston received his cow for a fee, I never learned, but he laughed heartily when I told him of the "signal" divorce.

BISHOP V. RIGGS

The case of *Bishop* v. *Riggs* at Boise City in the district court, 1871, was a laughable affair. Dr. Edward Bishop was a London physician who was from 1866 to 1869 a visitor in Idaho in the interests of certain mining investments. He was a genial and shrewd man and the boon companion of Dr. Clinton Wagner, who lived opposite my home. Dr. Bishop owned the large brick store on the north side of Main Street, opposite the Overland Hotel, which the Wells, Fargo Express Company occupied until it was taken over by William H. Nye and used as a drugstore. Dr. Bishop practiced in Boise and was attending physician to the Riggs family. When his bill was presented it was not paid, and Dr. Bishop sued Mr. Riggs for $250, professional fees. Riggs put in an offset and counterclaim for the use of a scab from the arm of his boy, Boise Riggs, claiming that the scab from his son had been used to vaccinate scores of other people, and Mr. Riggs deemed that the scab had rendered services worth more than $250. Riggs further said that every one of Bishop's patients vaccinated with this scab paid Bishop $5.00.

The case was tried before Judge Lewis and a jury. Mr. Riggs, an immense man and heavily bearded, was wrapped in a muffler. He took the stand and gave evidences of much physical suffering. He was perfectly honest in his belief that Dr. Bishop really owed him money for the use of the scab but during the cross-examination he wriggled and squirmed and perspired profusely. His testimony was an earnest plea to the court against the outrages his family had suffered through Dr. Bishop. He said that there were all sorts and stray ends of people living about Boise, and when Dr. Bishop jabbed vaccine from his boy's arm into people indiscriminately it was very likely that "he might jab a stray nigger and the honor of the Riggs family was at stake when its pure blood was being infused into the arms of niggers and poor white trash!" Riggs was most eloquent as he described his mental anguish and nights of suffering at the fear of this indiscriminate inoculation!

The judge smiled, and so did the jury. The attorneys, it is unnecessary to state, had lots of fun with the argument. The end of the decision was that Dr. Bishop got the verdict but was forced to deduct $50 from the bill for use of the scab from the arm of Boise Riggs. When the verdict was read and the jury discharged, Mr. Riggs solemnly arose, glared daggers at everyone, and stalked toward the door. H. C. Branstetter, the sheriff, was an old friend of Riggs, and, desiring to keep Riggs's wrath bottled, walked with him outside the building. I hurried from the room and reached the stairs in time to hear Riggs say in a melodramatic voice, "Clay [Branstetter], before I die, I shall teach these groundlings [the jury] that the blood of a Riggs is worth a princely ransom, and no English doctor shall go around jabbing the blood of a Riggs into the common herd of mankind with impunity! I protested then; I rebel now! Sir, the verdict is an outrage on a gentleman and a first settler."

CHAPTER VII

IDAHO'S TERRITORIAL GOVERNORS

SECTION 12 of the Organic Act of Idaho Territory empowered the governor to select a temporary capital town. Governor William H. Wallace selected the village of Lewiston, on the Snake River, by his proclamation of September 22, 1863, which organized the new territory for administration. He also called for election of a legislative assembly, defined the judicial districts, and assigned judges. There were assembled at Lewiston that September day, when the first governor signed his organization proclamation, William B. Daniels, of Oregon, secretary; Dolphus S. Payne, United States marshal; Sidney Edgerton, of Ohio, chief justice, and Associate Justices Samuel C. Parks, of Illinois, and Alexander C. Smith, of Washington.

To imaginative people, the organization of a new territory, the shaping of its administrative lines, possibly suggest the dramatic; but the actual process of formation is usually commonplace and businesslike. My old friend, B. F. Lambkin, familiarly dubbed "Ben," who was appointed territorial auditor by Governor Wallace under the laws of the first legislature, was present at Lewiston on the occasion of the first meeting of territorial officers. He told me that the proceedings were attended with but little excitement. When the first legislature assembled at Lewiston on December 3, 1863, the vastness of the new Northwest was at once appreciated. Members-elect from the counties to the east of the Rockies—a region eventually included in Montana's boundaries—had had to make horseback journeys of several hundred miles. It was quickly perceived that fair administration was out of the question; the lack of railroads and telegraph lines placed members from far counties under a great disadvantage both individually and in respect to the wishes of their constituents. It was through a desire to assist the central government in Idaho that the projected plans for the formation of Montana were furthered.

The situation of the capital was, too, a matter for serious thought. The first assembly adjourned in July, 1864, without taking action upon a quietly discussed plan of moving the territory's capital to Boise, but in the next session, December, 1864, a change of location for the capital was voted. December 24, 1864, Acting Governor Daniels signed the bill which made Boise the capital. A great row resulted. The outcome of the matter was that the seal of the territory and the legislature's records were actually stolen by night and transported to Boise. Lewiston was practically wiped out of existence when she lost her proud possession, the seat of the territorial government.

Before and during my residence in the territory, it was customary for the governor or acting governor to read his annual message to the legislature in joint session. The council and house would appoint a joint committee to meet and escort the governor to the House chamber, where, in addition to members, there were present officials and spectators. The president of the council, the upper branch of the legislature, presided, and the governor sat beside him, next to the speaker of the house. Formally, the joint committee arose and reported the governor present; he was then introduced to the assembly by the council's president, and then, standing, the governor read his message. Upon conclusion of the reading the session adjourned, and a public reception was held. This custom emanated from the routine in vogue in the Canadian provinces adjoining Idaho. Many of the Idaho legislators had seen the provincial governors employ this method annually and, naturally, it was copied. It was a relic of royalty.

I recall one session of the legislature which I attended in Boise in 1870. The council members were in stated meeting in a wooden building across from the Boise courthouse. To say that parliamentary methods on this occasion were peculiar would be putting it mildly. The entire proceedings savored so of burlesque that I rapidly withdrew and laughed! The first legislatures of the territory included many rough diamonds, and the governor's veto was the political safety brake. With one exception, Idaho's territorial governors were Republicans: the legislatures were Democratic. However, the weeding out of the rabble and the election of honest Democrats, honest and educated, brought about rapid improvement in the personnel of lawmakers. There were a few instances of bribery, for ferry franchises or toll-road privileges, in the early sessions, but on the whole the Idaho legislators were very honest men; they were particularly free from "spot cash" transactions. On political lines arose most of the dissension between the governors, the legislatures, and the people. Rebels and Secessionists made bold efforts to override the laws of the national Congress, but their plans were always squelched. In discussing Governor David Ballard's administration, I shall offer an instance of a bold attempt by the territorial legislature to thwart the national lawmaking power.

CARPETBAGGERS AND OTHERS

When a nonresident of a territory is appointed governor there is much curiosity and some apprehension aroused within the territory concerning what may be expected from the new governor and his family. Idaho had its periods of apprehension; she experienced the same fears and anxieties about her newly appointed carpetbag governors as did every other territory situated as was she. The Organic Act which made the territory of Florida—all similar acts since have been virtually a re-enactment of the Florida organic act, the slavery clause excepted—created the first political plum of its kind in America, a territorial governorship. The history of Idaho's gubernatorial appointments is the history of our other territories. A few of the appointees were selected in recognition of merit; the majority of them were appointed through political influence or as the personal choice of the national executive. Again, it may have seemed safest to remove from the sphere of Eastern politics men who loomed too prominently in the political arenas—particularly men looking toward the United States Senate. Overambitious men were often foisted upon long-suffering communities in a territory to spend years in genteel banishment. Appointments went to extremes on more than one occasion, for political beats and confidence men had their names connected with territorial governorships.

Our territories really proved to be Botany Bays for political hacks. A review of Idaho's governors, 1863 to 1890, offers a marked example of a territory at the mercy of the appointing power of a distant national government that cared little, if at all, for the opinions of the denizens of the territory. William H. Wallace, the first territorial governor, used his position intentionally for a steppingstone. Caleb Lyon, his successor, was a burlesque. Run the gamut, and more burlesques are found, both in the ranks of those who accepted the gubernatorial appointments and in the ranks of those who were tendered the appointment but who did not accept it. On the other hand, I wish to voice my sincere appreciation of many of the men who served the territory with honesty and efficiency and who, whether they were or were not carpetbaggers, did their best for Idaho while incumbent.

In twenty-seven years of territorial life Idaho cowered prone to the swoop of twenty-odd governors or gubernatorial possibilities. Only two of the men who served were prominent residents of the territory. They were Stevenson and Shoup. Curiously enough, these men were the last two governors of the territory; Shoup was the first governor of Idaho, the state. The instance of Idaho emphasizes the universal truth that the advent of chief executives from outside commonwealths interferes with the inner tranquillity and retards the advancement of a particular territory. It is but fair to state, however, that Idaho was the loser in one or two instances when men of ability and integrity refused to accept the appointment to serve as her governor.

WILLIAM H. WALLACE

William Henson Wallace, Idaho's first territorial governor, was born July 17, 1811, on a farm about halfway between Piqua and Troy, Miami County, Ohio. His father was Andrew Wallace, a personal friend of General William H. Harrison, "Old Tippecanoe," with whom he was engaged in many fights against the red men. His mother's maiden name was Jones; she was a Virginia woman and relative of John Paul Jones of Revolutionary fame. She was a woman of strong and upright character. William H. Wallace's brothers were David Wallace and John Milton Wallace. The former was in Congress at one time and was also governor of Indiana. John Milton Wallace was a prominent attorney; he served as a district court judge in Indiana. David Wallace was the father of the well-known General Lew Wallace, author of *Ben Hur*, so that Idaho's first territorial governor was an uncle of the famous soldier-writer.

William H. Wallace was a man of marked personality and strong influence. Wherever he lived he was a factor in public affairs. In 1837, at the age of twenty-six years, he moved to Iowa, a country then about to organize a territorial government. It is most interesting to note that this young man was chosen speaker of Iowa's first territorial house of representatives which assembled at Burlington in 1838. He was a member of the Iowa legislature for several terms. In 1849 President Taylor appointed him receiver of public moneys at Fairfield, Iowa. Mr. Wallace became acquainted with Abraham Lincoln sometime in the early fifties in Illinois. On one occasion, at a time when Lincoln was practically unknown, he so arranged that the future President of the United States was enabled to speak at a public meeting. It was, so I have been told, one of the very first opportunities given Lincoln to make a public address. He never forgot the kindness, and that fact was proved in after years. Mr. Wallace was intimate with Mr. Lincoln until the time of the latter's death. Mr. Wallace's son informs me:

"Father [Wm. H. Wallace] was rather happy in his introductory speech for Mr. Lincoln at the Illinois meeting, and Mr. Lincoln never forgot it. So far as the affairs of the north Pacific Coast were concerned, father had great influence with Mr. Lincoln, and during his four years in Congress—1861 to 1865—was never refused a single request which he made to the president. Father was almost the last public man to hold an interview with Mr. Lincoln. He called on him late in the afternoon of the day of Lincoln's assassination. Mr. Lincoln told father on that occasion that he would reappoint him governor of Idaho. Andrew Johnson failed to carry out the expressed wish of Mr. Lincoln in this matter of appointment. Father was one of the Congressional committee which escorted Mr. Lincoln's remains to Springfield."

In 1839, at Mt. Pleasant, Henry County, Iowa, William H. Wallace married Luzena Brazelton, daughter of Samuel Brazelton. Mr. Brazelton was born in 1796 near Guilford Courthouse, Guilford County, North Carolina. He removed to Indiana in 1820; thence to Illinois, and finally reached Iowa in 1835. He was a farmer and a sturdy, intelligent old fellow. He was a simon-pure Democrat of the Andrew Jackson stamp and must have been an odd character. He was brigadier general of Iowa's territorial militia but took no hand in politics other than to stump the territory for his personal friends. He was a man of fine presence and personal courage; in fact, a type of sturdy and worthy pioneer.

The qualities of the father were transmitted to the daughter. The wife of William H. Wallace was a splendid woman who was of invaluable help to her husband with advice and encouragement during that stirring period of early days in the West.

In 1853 William H. Wallace moved to the Northwest and at once took an active part in affairs of that section. He practiced law in Washington and achieved a reputation as a counselor. He was elected to the territorial council for several terms and was once president of the House of Representatives. In 1854 Mr. Wallace ran unsuccessfully as Whig candidate for delegate to Congress. In April, 1861, President Lincoln proved his regard for Mr. Wallace then in the East on business by appointing him governor of Washington. When he returned to the territory to assume the governorship, he found that a hot campaign was being waged for delegate to Congress, and he was nominated as the Republican candidate. He defeated Selucius Garfielde, Democratic candidate, and Judge Lander, Independent.

Once back in Washington and on intimate terms with the President and influential members of the House and Senate, Mr. Wallace, with the help of his colleagues, was in a position to scheme further for the formation of Idaho. Just why he was particularly interested in Idaho, or her formation, is difficult to say, but no doubt the main reason was that political possibilities seemed great in the formation of the new territory. The discovery of gold throughout the eastern sections of Washington, Idaho, and Montana Territory—or what is now Idaho and Montana—promised rapid immigration from the Atlantic as well as the Pacific Coast, and a rapid influx of people meant money and political influence. Mr. Wallace, A. G. Henry, and Judge McBride were those most interested in pushing the

Idaho bill through Congress. Mr. Wallace had the individual support of the Pacific Coast delegation, and the scheme to build the new territory was made possible mainly because of his determination and acumen in the matter. He not only formulated the bill but canvassed the House and Senate, and his every wish, even to the naming of the new territory, was heeded. It is again significant that Mr. Lincoln, to assist Mr. Wallace in carrying out to the fullest extent his cherished scheme, appointed him on July 10, 1863, as the first governor of the territory.

In September, 1863, six months after the passage by Congress of the Idaho Organic Act, Governor Wallace issued a proclamation calling an election to choose the delegate to Congress and the members of the legislature for the territory. The election was to be held the following month. A hot political fight had already begun in midsummer. Governor Wallace was nominated for delegate—no doubt as a tribute of confidence from the administration party— and in the October, 1863, election he defeated the Democratic nominee, John M. Cannady, by a comfortable margin. This left Idaho without a governor. W. B. Daniels, of Yamhill County, Oregon, secretary of the territory, assumed the reins of office.

Mr. Wallace was in Congress for two terms, 1861-63 and 1863-65. In 1869 he returned to Steilacoom, Washington Territory, and practiced law until the time of his death. He died at Steilacoom, February 17, 1879.

From conversations with intimates of Mr. Wallace, I find that he was a man of lovable disposition and of splendid executive abilities. He won recognition for his personal integrity as well as for his marked ability. In 1863, at the age of fifty-two years, he was a man of about five feet, nine inches in height and of very dark complexion. His eyes, as black as night, had a merry twinkle hovering in them, indicating a kindly heart and happy disposition. He was an inimitable yarn spinner, and because of his charming manners was at his best when surrounded by company. He was best known throughout the West as a polished and eloquent public speaker. His son, in a recent conversation with me, summed up his father's character by saying: "He took active part in politics with some success but with more defeats. His success he viewed as a matter of course; his defeats he looked upon with smiling indifference."

CALEB LYON

One of the oddest figures in Idaho's history was Caleb Lyon, governor of the territory from 1864 to 1866. Ben Perley Poore claims that Caleb Lyon was born at Greig, Greig County, New York, but other biographies state that Caleb Lyon was born at Lyonsdale, Lewis County, New York, December 7, 1822. Lyonsdale was named after Caleb Lyon, senior, once a member of the New York legislature and an intimate of De Witt Clinton. The grandfather of Idaho's Caleb Lyon is said to have been an officer in the Massachusetts militia and was wounded at Bunker Hill. In 1841 Caleb Lyon was graduated from Norwich University, Vermont, and when he was launched upon the world he promptly overcame the handicap of a college education and asserted himself as a young man determined to accomplish something. President Polk appointed him consul at Shanghai, and Lyon went to the Orient and served four years among the Chinese. It is to be regretted that no facts are available concerning his four years of consular service. In the light of his later life, certainly the Honorable Caleb must have been active in China. He returned home in 1848. He then sailed for San Francisco in 1849 and, child of fortune that he was, inveigled himself into the California Constitutional Convention and served as assistant secretary of that organization during the exciting times incident to the state's formation. More than that, Lyon is credited with being the designer of the California state seal.

He visited South America, Mexico, and Europe, and looked for and found excitement wherever he went. In 1850 he was at Smyrna and stood by Captain Duncan N. Ingraham, U. S. N., of the *St. Louis,* in the international dispute involving Martin Koszta, a naturalized American citizen from whom Austria attempted to claim military service. This was the famous case in which Daniel Webster, Secretary of State under President Fillmore, had a "tilt" with Chevalier Hulsemann, the Austrian minister.

Returning to New York, Lyon was in 1851 elected to the New York assembly, but he resigned. The same year he was elected to the state senate. From 1853 until 1855 Lyon served in the Thirty-third Congress on the Independent ticket from New York, defeating one Mundy, Democrat. His home at Lyonsdale was burned in 1856, and Lyon moved to Staten Island, where he resided until the time of his death. His acquaintance with prominent men of the times was generous, and he availed himself of the influence of men in power.

My first knowledge of Lyon was in the early sixties when he was at Washington on intimate terms with William H. Seward. When Lincoln came into office, Lyon achieved some notoriety, for he it was who went to Arlington, Colonel Lee's house, in May, 1861, and took possession of the contents in the name of the United States. The Washington relics from Arlington were sent by him to the Smithsonian Institution, where they remained many years and were not disturbed until a quasi-Rebel administration, along in the eighties, returned the relics to the Lee family. It is quite likely that Lyon held a Government position in Washington from 1861 to 1864. In the latter year he obtained his appointment as governor of Idaho Territory.

His appointment to succeed Governor Wallace, who was represented by Territorial Secretary William B. Daniels, aroused some public comment. The Idaho people were curiously interested in the name of Lyon and Lyons-

Idaho's second and most fantastic territorial governor, who always signed himself "Caleb Lyon of Lyonsdale." He was called "Old Cale," or "Cale of the Dale" by his political adversaries.

dale. He went to Idaho by way of Portland, Oregon, and arrived at Lewiston in time to make himself unpopular by meddling with the secret theft of the territorial capital from Lewiston to Boise. His advent was preceded by glowing press notices in the *Idaho Statesman* and the Portland *Oregonian*, and the notices recounted marvelous things of Lyon's life. It was recounted that, besides a varied civil service, he had been a go-between in the matter of missionary Jonas King, D.D., versus the Kingdom of Greece in 1852; was with General Winfield Scott in Mexico; participated with great honors at Bull Run with McDowell; was an intimate and fought at the side of Phil Kearny through many campaigns, and, all in all, filled outstanding engagements to the number of eighteen on the Union side during the Rebellion. The glowing accounts in the papers indicated that the Honorable Caleb had personally furnished most of the facts to ensure that there would be neither misunderstandings nor errors. Randolph, of Roanoke, and Carroll, of Carrollton, were familiar names and places to Idahoans; but Lyon, of Lyonsdale, though it rang with alliteration, was open to suspicion.

It is but fair to state that Caleb Lyon arrived in the territory when politics were in bad shape. He came into office in a storm and left it in a cyclone. The removal of the capital from Lewiston to Boise, however, was due not to him, but to the fact that the construction of the transcontinental railroads and the opening of the Boise Basin mines made Idaho people demand that the capital be situated nearer the center of the territory. Lewiston was entirely too far north. Fort Boise, too, had been completed and was well garrisoned, so that the Boise region was safe from Indian attacks. Lyon at once took hold of his office with vigor and toured the country. He arrived in Boise on October 12, 1864. The fact that he had been a Northerner, or antislavery man, made him unpopular with a large portion of the Idaho inhabitants. The first three legislatures of the territory were frightfully Democratic and Rebel in sympathy, and all United States civil officials were looked upon as aliens and enemies. The garrison at Boise was needed for other reasons than the subduing of Indian outbreaks. What the Rebel sympathizers in the territory ever hoped to gain, were they to be attached to Confederate states, I have never been able to see, nor has anyone else. What they could have lost is now patent in a thousand ways. Without the aid of the U. S. Treasury, which kept the military force present to awe the red men, neither Rebels nor Northerners could have remained in the country.

Caleb Lyon, in conversation and reminiscences, was far above the heads of his constituents, and they considered him a cheerful liar. He was a storyteller, a scholarly observer, a traveler with conversational powers of marked degree, and a man who wrote crisp and clean English. The pioneers who told me of Lyon said that he made a mistake in talking of people and places of whom Idahoans knew little and cared less. E. C. Sterling, of Boise, told me that he was present at a dinner in Boise which Lyon, soon after his arrival, tendered to his friends at the Overland Hotel. It was the first attempt to hold a course dinner in Idaho Territory. Governor Lyon presided and did the honors like the king that he was. The company was large, and dear old Captain James W. Griffin, landlord of the Overland, was at his wit's end to meet the occasion gracefully and properly. He was an experienced sea captain and had had the misfortune to be in command of a bark, the *Santos*, which was captured and burned by the Rebel pirate, *Semmes*. After this, Griffin had crossed the plains and settled at Boise City and drifted into the hotel business. Mr. Sterling said that the governor so paralyzed his guests with stories and wit that they were awed into absolute silence. He had the evening to himself. The dinner was lengthy, from seven to eleven o'clock, and chiefly notable for the absence of champagne—for only a few bottles could be found in town. What was there had come around the Horn from New York to San Francisco and had been hauled overland from that point to Boise. What a journey! Whisky was plentiful and of good quality. Lemons, *non est!* No fresh fruit was to be had. Canned goods from New York, via San Francisco or Portland and the Columbia River, made up the staples of the dinner. It was a gorgeous affair and furnished gossip for months afterwards. The guests (all males) tried to "round up" Caleb—to place him —but they soon abandoned the effort as a too difficult task. His reports of chats and associations with great men (and they were true) the guests hardly swallowed. Familiar association with Daniel Webster, Henry Clay, John C. Calhoun, and others? "Oh, no! Caleb, we know you were in California in an early day, but them fellows as your pards? Oh, no!" One of the guests took two or three others into his confidence and whispered, "I think we have dined with Adam."

When I arrived in Idaho the air was still laden with accounts of Governor Lyon. At The Dalles, in 1870, I heard many funny anecdotes of him. In 1890 a barber at Umatilla, Oregon, gave me some odd instances of Governor Lyon's oriental proclivities.

I recall the telegraphic outcry in December, 1866, when Governor Lyon was robbed of $47,000 in a sleeping car en route between New York and Washington. The governor of Idaho was at that time, and until 1870, ex officio superintendent of Indian Affairs and handled large sums of money for that service. The $47,000 which Lyon lost was Indian Bureau money. The Government apparently did not consider the robbery story of sufficient density to investigate it but at once brought suit against Lyon and his bondsmen and forced the bondsmen to refund the sum to the treasury. No Congressional relief bill was ever passed to reimburse them.

Lyon was out of the territory several times while governor. He was East during the summer of 1865, when he was sadly represented by C. DeWitt Smith and Horace C. Gilson. The year 1865 was notable in Idaho's territorial history because the fomenting trouble over the removal of the capital from Lewiston to Boise reached a climax. Lyon escaped most of the responsibility in this matter. While he was East the legislature of 1865-66 cut him off from the territorial compensation originally granted as an addition to the Federal salary. In the late summer of 1865, Lyon returned to Idaho with a grand scheme for money-making. He had decided to resign while East but changed his mind after meeting, in May, 1865, a man named Davis, who claimed to be an Owyhee miner and who showed to Governor Lyon a sample of diamonds, or what were supposed to be diamonds, which he, Davis, had found in the Owyhee Mountains. Davis sold one of these diamonds for $1,000. Under a veil of secrecy Davis and Lyon agreed to form a pool and boom the Owyhee diamond fields. They decided to meet in Idaho and then "discover" these fields—which had already been discovered. Davis started for California by way of the Pacific Mail Steamer Line on the ill-fated *Brother Jonathan*. He was drowned in her when she sank off the Oregon coast, July 30, 1865. Lyon evidently crossed the plains. He arrived in Boise City late in July, where, a few weeks later, he heard that Davis had been lost at sea. Lyon then went to Silver City and in August or September, 1865, met Colonel D. H. Fogus. (What fun we had with Fogus in the seventies, twitting him about his diamonds!) Lyon opened the scheme to Colonel Fogus, showed some of the diamonds to him, and Fogus gave a silver bar to purchase a $500 interest. The partners at once began to prospect for the diamonds. Fogus was known as a prospector and Lyon as a sharper, so the denizens of the district at once spotted the pair and followed them to the

IDAHO'S TERRITORIAL GOVERNORS 237

alleged diamond fields, where they were found digging up the ground. The crowd at once turned in and helped. Of course nothing of value was found, but excitement was rife over the diamonds until the bubble burst. In 1872 John Farnham, a rancher living below Silver City, took me over the ground, and we prospected about the water washes in the foothills. I procured a cigar box full of the famous diamonds. They were quartz pebbles and crystals known as common chalcedony. A few carnelians and a few trashy opals were among them.

Lyon returned to Boise in November, 1865, and convened the legislative assembly on December 3. It lasted forty days. Had it lasted forty more days, the territory would have been disgraced beyond redemption. After creating all havoc possible, Lyon fled the territory in March or April, 1866, and never returned. He died at Rossville, Staten Island, September 7, 1875.

Lyon would have made a rare advertiser at the present day for a patent-medicine firm. He attracted attention wherever he went, and his peculiarities have been recorded more than once. He was a passenger on the clipper ship, *Tarolinta (Floating Rose)*, which sailed from New York on January 13, 1849, and arrived in San Francisco, July 6, 1849. Captain William Cave was in charge, and the passenger list contained notables. Among the 125 passengers were: William O'Brien, afterwards "Flood" O'Brien; Nicholas De Peyster, New York City; Pet S. Halsey, New Jersey; H. L. Pearson, the famous hotel man; John Short, afterwards captain of police of San Francisco; J. Winchester, editor; William C. Hoff; George P. Vail, author, of Troy, N. Y.; and William Coddington, San Francisco. In a little book published in 1895 by William Doxey, San Francisco, with the title of *To the Golden Goal and Other Sketches*, written by Dr. J. C. Tucker, who was a passenger with Caleb Lyon on the *Tarolinta*, there are some interesting revelations of Lyon.

From New York the *Tarolinta* sailed round the Horn and entered the Pacific. The ship was abreast of the south of Chile, writes Dr. Tucker, and "as the days grew longer and the warm sunny atmosphere of the South Pacific thawed us out, the old deck yarns were resumed. The Hon. Caleb Lyon, of Lyonsdale, came up from below with a Turkish rug of diverse colors on his arm and a Turkish smoking cap upon his flowing locks. As he sat cross-legged upon his mat and smoked his pipe, he modestly told us how he was appointed by the United States Government, Minister Plenipotentiary and (Very) Extraordinary to Constantinople. The recital of his interview with the Pashas, the customs of the country, etc., were very entertaining, for the Hon. Caleb [Lyon] was a man of much erudition and an acknowledged elocutionist and poet."

After describing how the ship lay a few days at Valparaiso, Dr. Tucker continues: "A party of half a dozen men from our vessel, including the Hon. Caleb landed, decorated with blue ribbons around their hats and in their button-holes. They registered at the hotel as 'The Hon. Caleb Lyon and his suite,' and inflated immensely. Our fellow passenger, George Vail, heretofore spoken of as a man of big intellect and body, a gentleman in education and manners at all times, proposed to burlesque this aristocratic party. He hired an open barouche, drawn by four gray mules, decorated with blue ribbons and as many of our darky (black) sailors as could sit on the front seat and hang behind. Similarly ribboned, likewise bedecked with blue streamers, Vail sat upon the back seat and was driven around to all the hotels, registering as 'The Hon. George Vail and suite.' "

I was present at the sale in New York City of the Caleb Lyon library which was auctioned by George A. Leavitt & Co., beginning Wednesday, March 22, 1882. The catalogue contained 885 numbers, but many of the numbers embraced several volumes. There were many interesting works on hunting and fishing, many on the drama, and some rare editions of Shakespeare. The dramatic portraits were numerous and valuable. The special features were a copy of *Aesop's Fables* (1694) with George Washington's bookplate and much data in his handwriting. The library was strong in United States Government publications and history and in ancient books. The gems were a half-length contemporaneous portrait in oil of Nell Gwynne (supposedly) by Sir Peter Lily, and a two-volume, 1847 edition of Beranger. This was presented to Mr. Lyon by Lola Montez, the actress, adventuress, and spiritual lecturer. Her autograph to him written on the flyleaf was:

> Marie de Lansfeld, "Lola Montez." Gift of sincere friendship to Caleb Lyon, of Lyondale, with the hope that each time he takes up this book of the true prophet, People's poet of France, he may think of the pleasant hours in memory of the giver. New York, 31 July, 1852.

I think from what I have heard of Caleb that he was quite a connoisseur of the gentler sex. There were some exceedingly rare etchings and engravings by Rembrandt, Turner, and Corot. Governor Lyon knew a good thing when he saw it, in books or in art.

After 1866 and to 1875, the year of his death, Governor Lyon haunted the studios about New York City and was a ghost in the secondhand and bric-a-brac stores. He resided in a house known as "Ross's Folly" on Staten Island, where my friend Julian Scott, and other New York artists, used to visit him. Mr. Scott described Governor Lyon to me as a man slightly above medium height, full bearded, gray, and with a pot belly. He was an agreeable man of much tact, an intelligent conversationalist, and a sharp and cunning trader. At "Ross's Folly" he had several mysterious passages and odd rooms full of curios which he showed with great pleasure to visitors. Governor Lyon dropped out of public sight after 1866.

Robert Sommerville conducted the sale of Lyon's collection of art. He told me that two sisters of Lyon were the owners of the collection. It was rich in ceramics and historical plates and cups, with a profusion of Leeds, Holland, Lowestoft, and Staffordshire ware. He had a series of historical plates from the White House. The administrations of Presidents John Adams, Jefferson, John Quincy Adams, Van Buren, Taylor, and Lincoln all contributed plates—a rare series. The antique furniture, armor, firearms, and swords were superb. There were many theatrical robes and costumes in the collection. What he did with these or from whom he obtained them is merely conjecturable. He was a collector with a mania! The Washingtonia comprised fifty-one numbers, including oil portraits of Washington by Peale and Gilbert Stuart, and a large number of pieces of china from Washington's set; also bits of funiture and locks of hair from the heads of the immediate Washington family. These articles sold very high because they were authentic. Governor Lyon had exceptional advantages in collecting these articles. He was about Washington at the breaking out of the Civil War and acted for the Government in taking possession of Arlington and the property of the Lees. The oil paintings, 108 in number, contained many fine samples and sold at sight. There was Abigail Adams, by Gilbert Stuart; a Mrs. Siddons, by Washington Allston; an Ojibway chief, by Benjamin West; West's "Christ Giving the Keys to Peter"; and a number of good examples by the best contemporaneous artists. The gem of the pictures was an oil of Lola Montez, by Laure(?). It was a superb example of art and showed her as a handsome woman. The head was completed; the bust figure was in outline. A very handsome young woman bought this picture after a spirited contest. She was not an actress but looked like a woman of New York's sporty set who wanted the portrait for the notoriety of it.

It was an interesting sale. The prices were high, and the articles exhibited and sold were a fine tribute to the taste and energy of Governor Lyon. Many in attendance seemed to have known him in the flesh. Now and then, when an article sold low, you would hear, *sotto voce,* "If Caleb were here, how he would groan!" "My, old Caleb must have turned over in his box at that sale!" "Ah, that was a fair price! Caleb, if present, would have said, 'Thanks.' " After the sale I asked Mr. Sommerville if there was a certificate of authenticity with one article just sold. "No," he said with a smile, "I don't think there is, but if Caleb were alive he would write one for you!"

To sum up Lyon's character: he was egotistical and lived for flattery. He was ambitious, a scholar, a poet, and an art lover, but in no wise fitted to govern a territory then rotten in its public morality and politically diseased to the core. He was doubtlessly intimidated by the lawless element of the territory. The frightful murders committed during his occupancy of the gubernatorial chair testified to the disposition of the large element of adventurers, and when crime went unpunished or unchecked, neither the good nor bad citizens had respect for the governor. He seemed to have looked upon Idaho in the light of a curiosity, a piece of bric-a-brac. He found no interesting people or relics in the territory. The loss of the moneys which went astray while under his care was all that could be traced to his mismanagement of public funds. An interesting man was Lyon; without a settled business or calling, he was a drifter, perhaps a daydreamer, and he was born with a gold spoon in his mouth. Toward middle life the spoon turned to silver, and, in his old age, to pewter. He at one time had close and intimate friends with power and influence; he died neglected and unmourned. Had he applied himself to one profession he would have attained eminence, but he vacillated; as a great or useful man he is not on record. He was a conspicuous and dangerous failure as an executive. A son, of the same name, died at Staten Island in 1898.

DAVID W. BALLARD

Idaho's third governor, David W. Ballard, was in office when I arrived in the territory. Mr. Ballard was a native of Indiana, who in 1855 crossed the plains with an ox team. He located in Yamhill County, Oregon, and I think that for a time he followed his profession, that of a medical practitioner. At one time Mr. Ballard served in the Oregon senate. He was appointed governor of Idaho at the instance of Senator George H. Williams, of Oregon. He once told me with great humor of the trials and tribulations incident to his fitting out for his march across the plains in 1855. "Got the wrong kind of oxen, got the worst kind of guides, and had the worst kind of luck!" he laughingly said.

Short and somewhat portly in stature, with blue eyes, sandy hair and whiskers, red cheeks, and good teeth—such was Governor Ballard. He was usually laughing or in agreeable humor. He was honest and fearless and devoted to the interests of Idaho. His strongest characteristic was good old horse sense. His administration was dreadfully stormy. The Secessionists by whom he was surrounded hated and reviled him, but he bore their attacks bravely and did not yield an inch. Governor Ballard knew that he had the sympathy of the respectable element of the territory and the support of the government, and the Army was practically at his command. The excitement following Lincoln's assassination and the political somersaulting of Andrew Johnson encouraged the ex-Rebels in the territory to bold statements and open defiance against the Federal Government. Ballard was, however, equal to most emergencies. His wife, an evenly balanced, cool, motherly woman, played the role of adviser. He had a family of two

Gov. David W. Ballard was a physician by profession and often left his gubernatorial duties in order to administer surgical aid when the few other doctors of Boise were unavailable.

boys, aged about ten and fourteen, and clean, manly youngsters they were. In 1870 he was not reappointed, so he left the territory, much to the regret of the lawabiding and respectable element. There was considerable dissatisfaction with Grant's refusal to reappoint him. The Idaho people forwarded to the President an enormous petition asking that he be reinstated, or retained as governor.

In manner and method Ballard was modest but determined. He was shrewd if not great and, above all things, he understood men. We were close friends, and in our many chats he detailed to me his early struggles with the turbulent elements in Idaho politics. He said to me one night:

"We Republicans, official or otherwise, lived in perpetual danger. When I arrived at Boise in June, 1866, I at once made myself solid with the commandant at Fort Boise so that, in case of need, we would have the United States regulars to aid us. All the officials of Ada County were Rebels. The city officials of Boise were the same, so that in case of political trouble we could expect no aid from them. James S. Reynolds and his paper, the *Statesmen*, was our main stand-by. What a fearless man he is! He published at all times the most vigorous possible Republican paper right here in the midst of the 'new Confederacy.' Of course, the Rebels [Democrats] were emboldened by the fact that President Andrew Johnson was leaning their way and was against the party which elected him. My position was a critical one, personally. I expected to be removed every day after the winter of 1866. I am and always was a radical Republican. I had friends in Washington who advised me of current matters and kept me posted. Mrs. Senator George H. Williams, of Oregon, and President Johnson were good friends. I think that she and Judge Williams kept me in office. The Murphy-Gibbs appointments to the governorship in my place were instigated from here. It would have done your heart good to have seen the Rebels' faces when the news came of the election of General Grant to the Presidency, in 1868. Consternation does not express it! Before the news reached here some of the leaders used to pass me without speaking and say under their breaths, 'Old villain!' 'Old Radical humbug!' 'Somebody ought to do him!' They had been led to think that Horatio Seymour would defeat General Grant and then they would be fully in the ascendancy.

"The day the news of General Grant's election to the Presidency arrived, I walked down Main Street and I felt good! On all sides the old Rebels saluted me! 'Howdy do, Gov.! Why, howdy!' An hour before, they would have cut my throat, had they dared. They were an abject lot, abject but treacherous. My, but I did a sight of secret and inward jollifying that week! I do not doubt but that I and Captain Porter, my secretary, did some boyish things when we were alone, and if there had been a commandment against imbibing, we would both have been guilty. How good the Grant election news did make us feel! The Union men whooped it up in earnest. Old Jim Reynolds grew several inches in one night.

"The humor of the thing began when the Rebels, along in the fall of 1868 and spring of 1869, started to flee the country. They fled in the night on stages, in wagons, or on horseback, and some, I fear, on foot. Men, women, and children were in a mad scramble! Arizona caught some, Nevada more, and Utah, unfortunately for her, caught quite a dump of them. Their departure was a godsend to Idaho.

"A stranger coming here now, in 1870, and seeing how peaceful this city and country is, can form but little idea of the exciting times that we had from 1866 to 1868. You should have seen the legislature of 1866-67 and you should have heard the members talk. A tempest in a teapot! Such coarse mud as some of them were! A few were dangerous men; some were mere bags of wind; some were murderous;

others were ex-Rebel soldiers. They did not have the slightest idea of responsibility—not any more than if you had assembled a mob. The oaths they swore and the barrels of whisky they consumed were amazing! A mere job lot of common and uncommon men! At this distance, recalling it all makes me laugh! The flag of the Boise fort alone held that gang in check."

The details of the above relate to the period from early in 1866 to December, 1868, at which date Grant's election was confirmed in Idaho. All that time the Democrats held high carnival. President Johnson's queer regime encouraged them to assault all national officials in the territory who were known to be Union men. Governor Ballard was at once made a target. The territorial governor was ex officio superintendent of Indian Affairs and custodian of Indian funds, and the sums of money handled for the Indians were large. If there was anything in the world that ex-Rebels or Democratic Rebels in the territory had a penchant for, in addition to whisky, it was Uncle Samuel's money. They denounced Mr. Lincoln, the Yankees, and the Federal Government as usurpers and oppressors, but they speedily reached out for coin or greenbacks dispensed by that same coterie of "usurpers." Governor Ballard was, in a word, too honest for the good of the country, so the ring decided to supplant him. E. D. Holbrook was the delegate to Congress from Idaho at this time, and his efforts to remove Ballard, aided by petitions, were successful. John L. Murphy, of Idaho, was named by the senate in June, 1867, as Governor Ballard's successor. This appointment was the result of a series of fraudulent charges made against Ballard's character. The Indian Office at Washington was prevailed upon to give notice that the office would no longer disburse Indian money in Idaho through the governor, though he was authorized by law to disburse it. At this time, the Indian Office contemplated gathering all Indians upon one reservation in Idaho and, consequently, it seemed that a large amount of money would be forthcoming from the National Treasury.

Who John L. Murphy was, I have not been able to learn. All that I heard of him in Idaho was that he was a Democrat and Rebel sympathizer. At all events, Murphy's name did not meet with the sanction of President Johnson. His name was withdrawn from the Senate and that of Isaac L. Gibbs substituted. Gibbs was confirmed by the Senate late in 1867. In the meantime, Senator Williams received many protests from Union Republicans and loyal people of Idaho, urging that Governor Ballard be retained and praying that Idaho be not again turned over to murder and robbery, and pointing out that the violent elements of the territory were against Governor Ballard, and that continuance of the supremacy of law and decency demanded that these wretches should not succeed in ousting Ballard and putting a man of their kind in to do their vile work in his place. Many of these petitions and protests were placed on file in the Senate. They would probably have been destroyed had they been filed in the Johnsonized departments. A motion to reconsider Gibbs's appointment as governor of Idaho was made the day of the final adjournment of the Senate, and it was reconsidered and the nomination laid on the table within twenty minutes of the Senate's final adjournment. President Johnson, on the adjournment of the Senate, reappointed Isaac L. Gibbs. A fierce legal battle then began. President Johnson insisted on his right to reappoint Gibbs, as he had suspended Ballard during the recess of the Senate on evidence satisfactory to him of Ballard's crimes and misconduct in office. The Tenure of Office Act thus came in question and the president's right thereunder. The question was referred to Attorney General Henry Stanberry, who held that Ballard's removal during the recess of the Senate and the reappointment of Gibbs, after rejection by the Senate, was illegal. When the Senate reconvened in December, 1867, Gibbs was rejected by reason of the numerous protests filed by the people of Idaho against the removal of Ballard. From that time on no further attempt was made to remove Governor Ballard, for it was evident that Senator Williams, of Oregon, a man of great influence in the Senate, could and would prevent the confirmation of a successor. The Senate had been convinced that Governor Ballard was honest and efficient and that the confirmation of a Democrat for his successor meant the turning over of the public funds in Idaho to robbers, and the peace and order of the territory to a disloyal mob, thereby rendering unsafe the lives and property of orderly people. Many of the loyal petitions were on file in the Senate in 1867 and 1868 and, with Senator Williams' influence, were effective.

The so-called "Tempest in a Teapot" incident in the legislature of 1866, mentioned by Governor Ballard, was really a ludicrous affair.* Idaho's territorial secretary at that time was S. R. Howlett, who had been Governor Lyon's private secretary. Howlett was originally from western New York. He was small in build but vigorous and determined, and his anti-Rebel views and vocabulary were marvelously complete and active. I do not think that Howlett was ever afraid of anything, man or beast, in his entire life! Howlett and his brother were proprietors of a commission house on Broad Street, Columbus, Ohio, in my early days, and I knew both men. In Boise, Howlett conducted a commission and storage business on Main Street; how he became secretary to Governor Lyon, I did not ascertain. The defalcation and departure of Horace C. Gilson, after Lyon's withdrawal, left a vacancy, and Howlett was appointed secretary of the territory; he served as acting governor until the arrival of Mr. Ballard in June, 1866. From 1866 to 1869 Mr. Howlett acted as secretary of the territory; in the latter year, E. J. Curtis assumed his

---

* Owen Wister has used the "Tempest in a Teapot" incident for the theme of his short story, "The Second Missouri Compromise."—T.B.D.

position. Howlett was the principal actor in the "Tempest in a Teapot," and his account of the tempest was one of the most delightful reminiscences I ever heard. He fought the entire Democratic legislature and refused to pay them their salaries until they had taken an oath of allegiance to the United States. Against the ex-Rebels from Missouri in the legislature Howlett had ample chance, and availed himself of it, to vent his anti-Rebel spleen. As secretary of the territory, Howlett was empowered to disburse salaries, but when a committee from the Council and House waited upon him and demanded their pay, the irate official mentioned a few matters decidedly personal. Said he: "You won't take the oath of allegiance? No oath, no money! You ought to be shot anyhow, you damned Rebels, for asking money from a government you detest! Not a cent do you get until you subscribe and hand me the ironclad oath."

The offended lawmakers promptly retaliated with threats of personal violence, but Howlett was not worried at all. He was backed up by armed force; a crook of his finger and the Boise garrison and the United States marshal were with him! Howlett roared in delight when describing to me how Ben Anderson, sergeant-at-arms of the House, smashed all the lamps, and how disappointed members carried off all the furniture, from both chambers, in part payment of their salaries.

The most absurd feature in the tangle was that the mob-rule legislature actually passed a bill changing the oath of allegiance to be taken by Idaho officials and legislatures. This was a direct attempt to override the authority of Congress. A territory is a mere body corporate and may be made or unmade at the discretion of Congress. When this extraordinary act to create a new oath of allegiance reached Governor Ballard, he at once vetoed it—possibly before carefully reading it. In the meantime, anticipating a veto, the ex-Rebels communicated with their partisans in Washington, D. C., relating how the secretary of Idaho had withheld the legislators' salaries. To their dismay, Howlett's course was upheld!

Governor Ballard's veto message deserves reprinting because it pertains to a historical incident which was the first of its kind in territorial annals:

Executive Department,
Boise City, I.T., December 24, 1866

Hon. George Ainslie, President of the Council:
Sir:

I regret having to return herewith Council Bill No. 9 with my objection to its becoming a law. Said bill provides an oath of office for the members of the Legislature and all other officers elected or appointed within the Territory, and all attorneys admitted to practice in the courts of this Territory and repeals the oath of office prescribed by the first Legislative Assembly of the Territory of Idaho. Our Organic Act provides that all civil officers shall take an oath or affirmation "to support the Constitution of the United States and faithfully to discharge the duties of their respective offices."

Congress may legislate over a territory within the scope of its constitutional power, and may establish a territorial government, and the form of local government must be regulated by the discretion of Congress.—*(Dred Scott v. Sanford,* 19 How, 395). Congress may also legislate directly for a Territory. (See U. S. Statutes, vol. 12, p. 432, 501).

The Constitution and laws of the United States not locally inapplicable are the laws of our Territory.—(Organic Act, section 13).

Our territorial government was created by Congress, and the oath of office required by the Organic Act, and such other oaths as may be deemed necessary, are legitimately within the province of that body to prescribe.

The passage of the bill now before me cannot do away with the existing laws of Congress. All civil officers, before entering upon their official duties, are required to take an oath or affirmation, not by reason of its being upon the statutes of Idaho, but by reason of its being a law of Congress. Had this bill merely repealed the act of the Legislature passed December 28th, 1893, entitled "An act to regulate official oaths," I should have signed it without hesitation. The difference in the oath provided by this bill and the oath repealed is quite immaterial. The latter oath is stated in both the affirmative and negative form, while the oath proposed is stated only in the affirmative form. The man who swears conscientiously to the oath provided in this bill, swears to all that is contained in that portion of the existing oath, and perjury will lie as far in the one case as in the other, and no further. The bill provides that the oath which is recited shall be the *only* oath required of members of the Legislature, district and county officers, attorneys, etc. Now if Congress prescribes this oath of office for the members of the Legislature, etc., she may at any time alter or change the oath, or prescribe an additional oath, and the Legislature of Idaho cannot limit the power of Congress in such cases. I do not deem it proper that we should say to Congress, while yet a Territory, that we will take such and such oaths and no other shall be imposed. It is doubtless quite proper that we should have upon our statutes some law defining official oaths, but in fixing this law we should be careful to incorporate all that is required by the laws of the United States, and in no case should we say that *only* such an oath should be required. The Organic Act prescribes the oath of office, and in the laws of the United States, July 2d, 1862, we find the oath of allegiance. Every federal officer is required to take both, and I am satisfied that the practice of the government has been to require members of Territorial Legislatures to subscribe to each of these obligations before drawing their per diem, and I know of no rule or law making any change.

Section 4 of the Organic Act says: "The legislative power and authority of said Territory shall be vested in the Governor and Legislative Assembly." No doubts are entertained but that the act of Congress of July 2d, 1862, requires the executive branch of the legislative power to take the oath of allegiance, and it would appear very strange that the other branch should be exempted from taking the oath.

The law which declares that one branch of the legislative power shall take a certain prescribed oath "before entering upon the duties of office, and before being entitled to any of the salary or emoluments thereof," does without doubt extend to the other. As the bill before me prohibits any other oath to be required of any member of the Legislative Assembly, except the one therein named, it is clearly in violation of the law of Congress referred to, as understood and interpreted by the departments, and in opposition to the practice adopted by the government under said law, on which account the bill is returned to your honorable body without my approval.

        (signed) D. W. BALLARD, *Governor.*

The small rebellion was quickly ended. Howlett was guided in his course by the governor, and Judges John R.

McBride and John Cummins, of the supreme bench. His advisers had many a quiet chuckle in after years over the agitation in the riotous legislature of 1866.

GILMAN MARSTON

After Ballard's departure from the territory there was considerable conjecture as to whom the President would appoint to the vacancy in office. We finally heard that Gilman Marston, of New Hampshire, had received the appointment. We anxiously awaited his arrival, but he failed to appear. Secretary E. J. Curtis read the annual message to the legislature of 1870 and, in fact, Curtis served, ably as usual, as acting governor for a year and a half. Marston's arrival was not to be; he did not come to Idaho but resigned without serving.

It is conjectural whether or not Marston would have been a success had he assumed the office of governor of Idaho and taken residence in the territory. Marston was a New Englander of pronounced type—hardly the man to succeed with Westerners. He was a New Hampshire man, born at Oxford, August 20, 1811. He was a graduate of Dartmouth, 1837, and the Harvard Law School. He taught school for a time in Indianapolis, Indiana, and then began the practice of law in Exeter, New Hampshire, under many discouragements. Exceedingly careful in preparation and indomitable in his purposes, sensitive to a high degree, and dreading defeat in anything, Marston soon, by consistent labor, asserted himself at the bar of his state. Mr. Marston died at Exeter, July 3, 1890, after forty-nine years of legal practice. Dartmouth conferred upon him an honorary Doctor of Laws degree in 1882.

Undoubtedly the political positions accorded to Marston were a tribute by the people to his ability and honesty rather than a self-gained award for his astuteness as a politician. In 1845 he was elected to the New Hampshire legislature and served at different periods for a total of twelve terms. In 1857 he was a delegate to Congress and in 1861 and 1865 was again sent to the House of Representatives. Mr. Marston, at the outbreak of the war, was made colonel of the 2nd New Hampshire Volunteer Infantry. At Bull Run he was badly wounded. He served under McClellan, in Virginia, at Cold Harbor, Drewry's Bluff, and Petersburg, and led his command as brigadier general, a promotion accorded him in 1862. It is said that he was one of the "three men of New Hampshire who rose from civil life to wear the stars of a general officer."

In 1869 Mr. Marston was in Washington, where he held, if I remember rightly, a brief appointment in the Senate, accorded him by the governor of New Hampshire. I saw him there several times; his stay was not prolonged. He was a man of quick temper and largely open to flattery. Ambitious to a high degree and bitter under disappointments, he was, I think, the type of man who would have found it difficult to fill satisfactorily the position of governor of Idaho. Why he decided not to serve as governor I never learned.

SAMUEL BARD

On February 9, 1870, we heard rumors of the appointment of Samuel Bard, vice Gilman Marston. We wondered what next was coming our way! Bard did not come. All that we knew of him then or afterward we learned from a few newspaper accounts of him. They led us to believe that Bard was a "screamer." I have been unable to learn anything further of him barring a few bare facts. He resided in Louisiana before the Civil War and was an ardent friend and supporter of Pierre Soulé. He edited a Southern newspaper for some time. President Grant appointed him governor of Idaho in January, 1870, but, as I have said, Bard did not accept. The records of the Post Office Department show that Bard was appointed postmaster for

Atlanta, Georgia, March 2, 1874, and was succeeded by Benjamin Conley, April 27, 1875. I have heard it stated that Marshall Jewell, postmaster general, caused Bard to be removed from office "because he was too damned unanimous!"

THOMAS M. BOWEN

The resignation of Thomas M. Bowen from the governorship of the territory shortly after his appointment lost Idaho a chief executive of ability. His stay in Idaho was of short duration; he arrived in August, 1871, and left a few days after his arrival.

Mr. Bowen was a native of Iowa, born near Burlington, October 26, 1835. He was educated at public schools and admitted to the bar when but eighteen years of age. In 1856 he was a member of the Iowa legislature. Two years later he removed to Kansas. At the outbreak of the Civil War he was commissioned captain, organized the 13th Kansas Volunteer Infantry, and commanded it until the end of the war. He was brevet brigadier general and from 1863 to 1865 commanded a brigade on the frontier with the Seventh Army Corps. In 1864 he represented Kansas in the Republican national convention. After the war Mr. Bowen settled in Arkansas and became very prominent in state political and judicial spheres. He was president of the state constitutional conventions of 1866 and 1868 and from 1867 until 1871 was a justice of the Arkansas supreme court.

Soon after his arrival in Boise, after Grant had appointed him governor of the territory, Mr. Bowen called upon me, and, after a brief conversation, I found that he was a distant relative of mine. Bowen was a tall, thin, wiry man, with dark hair and small eyes, and was then clad, as I always saw him clad, in a frock coat. Both in private and in public he constantly puffed at a cigar.

Mr. Bowen was a man of immense vitality and great

energy coupled with splendid faculties for organization. He arranged his plans and then swooped down like an eagle on his prey. His object in coming to the territory was, as far as I could gather, to find natural resources with which to make a grand coup! But at the time he reached Boise the natural wealth had been cleaned up, for the silver mines in Owyhee were about played out and the placers in Boise Basin were paying poorly, with the exception of some large ditch properties. Mr. Bowen soon saw that there was little chance to amass a fortune either by his personal effort or by interesting Eastern capitalists to invest. He not only saw it at once but made up his mind to "jump" the territory: he forthwith did jump.

He said to me one day in his characteristic manner, "Donaldson, what do you mean by coming here and burying yourself? Great Scott, man, there won't be a senator to elect from Idaho for fifteen years!" And then he gave a hearty, manly laugh. "Of all the countries I ever saw, this gets away with them all! Boise City, a small bunch of houses under the lee of a fort, is the only oasis in 300 miles of desert! Oh, that stage road from Kelton! Every bone in my body aches when I think of it. Oh, that hotel at Kelton! I peered out of the coach window and took a long look at sky, sagebrush, and desert, and formed my resolution right there—a resolution to fly the country. In confidence, Donaldson, as soon as the country north of Salt Lake burst on our gaze, my wife and I determined to return East. I never saw so much land to the acre in all my born days! I counted my subjects as I came in, and there were 130 people in 250 miles. My wife and I will remain here a few days, just for appearances, and then we shall go on to the Columbia, back to Frisco, return to Arkansas, and I'll resign. Dorsey "Pow" Clayton, and the rest of my people in Arkansas procured this appointment for me. They said it was a good thing, that I was the man, and so forth, but I am led to believe that they wanted to get rid of me!" His humorous manner of expressing himself and the laughs he had at the territory were indescribably funny.

Suddenly he said, "Donaldson, in the name of heaven, what are you really doing here?" I told him that I was making money and reading law, and it was good experience for me at twenty-seven years of age, although it seemed bad to him at thirty-six.

"Bosh!" he said, "it's bad anyhow! What do you consider a rich man here in the territory?" I told him that $50,000 meant a comfortable fortune.

Mr. Bowen laughed again and told me that he had seen ten times that amount lost in a jiffy in Wall Street, and he had dropped a fortune there of his own. I remarked that $600,000 would buy everything portable in the territory, and then Bowen said, "I see it all! Out I go! Come along with me, and I'll foot the bills back to the States. Stay here and you are a dead one! This place is a sucked lemon —squeezed dry! Last night I saw some Boise sports playing poker with grains of corn—red, black, and white—which they cashed for two, three, and five cents. Great Scott, such a sporting community! One day-and-night poker session of the Arkansas legislature would clean out this entire territory. This morning I saw a body of men and soldiers walking down Main Street. A patriarch told me that it was a squad of soldiers accompanied by a patrol. The patrol consisted of touters for a gambling house who had in tow the soldiers who had just been paid off at the fort." Then he again laughed.

Chatting about Arkansas, Governor Bowen gave me much interesting personal reminiscence of the *modus operandi* of reconstructing the state, and his personal comment was most entertaining. He said that the object of the Arkansas ring was to get possession of the paying offices and then to fix the terms, under the constitution, for a long number of years. I heard much about General Powell Clayton, and Jack McClure, once a minister and then chief justice, who threatened to thrash Attorney General William or Ackerman, and was only prevented from so doing by the mediation of those on the spot. The doings of the "Minstrels" and "Brindle Tails" of Arkansas politics, Mr. Bowen recounted with gusto. The night before Mr. Bowen left Boise he took me back of the Overland Hotel and impressively said, "My dear boy, seriously now, don't you want to escape? Don't be modest or backward! I'll stake your wife and you with a wad to fly the territory." August 15, 1871, he and Mrs. Bowen, a most intelligent and estimable lady, left Boise, much to our regret.

Mr. Bowen returned to Arkansas and was subsequently defeated in the race for national senator. He then removed to Colorado, where I saw him at Denver in 1878. He now resides at Pueblo. For four years he was district judge in Colorado and a member of the legislature in 1882. The following year he was elected United States senator and served the full term, until 1889. I saw much of him in Washington, and we had agreeable chats about his first impressions of Idaho and her people. When he returned to Colorado, after the expiration of his term, he became identified with large mining interests.

THOMAS W. BENNETT

The successor of Governor Bowen, Thomas W. Bennett, was an Indiana man, born there February 16, 1831. He was prominent in his native state, for at one time he was state senator. In the Civil War he had a splendid record. He enlisted as a private but was soon commissioned captain of the 15th Indiana Volunteers. In 1869 he was elected mayor of Richmond, Indiana.

Bennett was a man of some ability, sharp and cunning and with a glib and interesting tongue. He was jolly and dissipated at times but possessed withal noticeable energy and determination. Mr. Bennett was small in figure, thin, pockmarked, and had weak, nervous eyes. He had a world of good stories at his command and was decidedly companionable. He had many facets, but turn him as you might, "Bennett" showed on all sides.

His appointment was promoted by Senator Oliver P. Morton, of Indiana, and granted by President Grant as a political favor. I first met him at Boise on Christmas Day, 1871.

While Bennett was Idaho's governor, in 1873, he ran against S. S. Fenn, Democrat, for delegate to Congress. There arose some controversy over the election. On a night after the election, he told me that he was determined to get the election, and, when he was determined, he always procured what he wanted. I do not recall just how the quibble was fixed up, but the canvassing board which checked the votes cast for delegate to Congress threw out, without authority of law or otherwise, enough votes to give Bennett a majority, and issued to him the certificate of election. My impression of it then was that the perpetrators should have been severely punished; this was confirmed by the report of the Committee on Elections of the Forty-fourth Congress, which unanimously (it was a Republican body) reported against Bennett's right to the seat and in favor of Fenn's being seated. I was in the gallery of the House of Representatives at Washington the day that the report was taken up and Bennett ousted and Fenn seated. Governor Bennett resigned as governor as soon as Congress met, and Fenn was sworn in. My opinion at the time was (and reflection confirms it) that Governor Bennett, wanting to get away from Idaho Territory, took this means to escape. His administration was in no wise remarkable and reflected no particular credit on him or the people. He added nothing to the standing of the territory with the outside world, and, inside of Idaho, obtained the reputation chiefly of being "one of the boys." The territory did not progress under his administration: it rather declined. From the fact of being merely a temporary resident, he took no particular interest in the territory's future. Much of the respect shown him was due to the influence of his accomplished and lovely wife. He served from 1871 to 1875 and was succeeded by D. P. Thompson.*

DAVID P. THOMPSON

D. P. Thompson, governor from 1875 to 1876, represented the active type of self-made man who had battled in many spheres of life and had invariably won his way. He was born in Cadiz, Ohio, November 8, 1834, and after an education at local public schools, learned the trade of blacksmith. He crossed the plains to Oregon in 1853 and by hard work and determination rose to eminence in the state. He took up surveying and bridge building as his vocation and was the builder of the railroad around the Willamette Falls at Oregon City. Sometime in the fifties he was appointed deputy surveyor of public lands of Oregon and Washington. In 1872 he had charge of the surveys and allotments of the Indian reservations in Washington and Oregon. For many years he also controlled all the contracts for the surveys of public lands in Idaho and retained in office my friend L. F. Cartee as surveyor general of Idaho Territory. The contracts were owned by D. P. Thompson, but were sublet to his brother, Allan, associated with Mr. Meldrum. From 1872 to 1878 he held many mail contracts.

Mr. Thompson had been active in Oregon politics, for he had served in the state senate from 1866 to 1872. He was appointed governor of Idaho at the suggestion of Senator Mitchell, of Oregon. When he came to Idaho he was in the prime of life. He was tall and bony in physique,

---

* If I remember rightly, it was after Bennett's departure that we heard the name of A. H. Connor, of Indiana, mentioned as our next governor. Mr. Connor has been sometime chairman of the Indiana Republican State Committee and was voiced by Senator Morton. However, Mr. Connor was not seen in Idaho.—T.B.D.

and awkward and as sly as a fox. He was a money-maker and loved wealth because he knew its power. As governor of the territory he contributed little or nothing toward the country's progress, for he doubtlessly took the position merely as a steppingstone toward a higher political position.

Mr. Thompson was by no means popular as Idaho's chief executive, but this resulted from no other thing than a want of tact. He was a frontiersman, rugged and bluntly straightforward, and he could not appeal to people through the brusqueness of his manners. Particularly correct in habits and morals, he yet had little weaknesses which opened him to attacks. He never had a home of his own in Idaho and he lived cheaply at all times. A man's domestic habits should be his own business; nevertheless, when a chief executive lacks conventionalities in home life, he is likely to be slurred by his constituents.

I knew Mr. Thompson personally and by reputation, and I knew far more good than evil of him. His money-making proclivities (he was rich but not liberal) turned public opinion against him. After he left Idaho in 1876 he moved to Portland, Oregon, and subsequently served two terms as mayor. He was also sent to the legislature for three terms, 1878, 1882, and 1889. In 1890 he ran for governor on the Republican ticket. He was defeated, and I learned from good authority that his defeat resulted from the fact that many people looked upon him as a money grabber and exacter of high rates of interest.

Undisputably, Mr. Thompson did much later on for the advancement of the Northwest, and in leading public enterprises he assisted many others to obtain wealth. Most of the Oregon Railroad and Navigation Company's line was built by him, and as director or president of many financial institutions he was active. He was keen and shrewd and practical; just the sort of man needed in a new community to inaugurate business enterprises. In latter-day Oregon he proved valuable in connection with public schools of the state; in fact, he accomplished exceptionally good results in behalf of public education.*

MASON BRAYMAN

Brayman's record looks well in print. He was born at Buffalo, New York, May 23, 1813. He was brought up on a farm but became interested in printing and served his time in a printing shop. In 1834-35 he edited a modest sheet, the Buffalo *Bulletin*. Mr. Brayman was of industrious nature and certainly was ambitious. He read law after business hours, when the opportunity came, and persevered in the study so that in 1836 he was admitted to the bar. That same year he moved to Monroe, Michigan. In 1838 he served as a city attorney in Monroe, but in 1841 he was again at work editing a newspaper. The following year he established a law practice as Springfield, Illinois. In 1843, Mr. Brayman won much notoriety because he was identified with a matter which claimed national attention. He was detailed as special Government commissioner to adjust difficulties with the Mormons at Nauvoo, Illinois. He was employed as a special counselor in prosecuting the offending Latter-day Saints. He worked with great zeal, and most of the negotiations which resulted in the withdrawal of the Mormons from Illinois were conducted by him. In 1844-45 Mr. Brayman revised the statutes of Illinois. In 1851 he was attorney for the Illinois Central Railroad and from that time afterward was identified with railroad interests. He was a promoter of railroad enterprises throughout Arkansas, Missouri, and the Southwest.

At the outbreak of the Civil War, Mr. Brayman entered service as major of the 29th Illinois; he was appointed colonel the following year. He was at Shiloh and Fort

---

* Mr. Thompson was in 1892 appointed U. S. Minister to Turkey by President Harrison. He served for one year and held a firm hand in the trouble arising from the Armenian uprising in which American property and life were destroyed.—T.B.D.

Donelson and for gallantry in action was promoted a brigadier general. He commanded at Bolivar, Tennessee, when Van Dorn's attack was repulsed. He was then detailed to Camp Dennison, Ohio, to reorganize the returning regiments. From July, 1864, to May, 1865, General Brayman commanded at Natchez. He was also appointed presiding officer of the commission to examine into the cotton claims. In 1872 and 1873 General Brayman edited the *Illinois State Journal*. He moved to Ripon, Wisconsin, in the latter year and there practiced law. After serving four years as governor of Idaho Territory he returned to Ripon. He died there February 27, 1895.

My first impression of Mason Brayman, an unfavorable impression, never left me. I saw him when I was but a youngster, and he acted the part of a snob. In the summer of 1864, May or June, I was at Cairo, Illinois, at the International Hotel. The other chief hostelry was a pile of bricks on the riverbank called the St. Charles; it was all name. One Briggs, landlord of the International—red-headed and clever was Briggs—seated me at a table at which sat General Mason Brayman, in command of the Union forces at Cairo. I recalled him then as the man who had employed Abraham Lincoln as attorney in a suit against the Illinois Central. The road refused to pay Brayman a fee which seemed exorbitant. He sued and recovered. Well, I sat down at the table, and the minute I did so this gray-bearded, stiff old martinet looked at me with great contempt of manner, then arose, sniffed, and stalked away to another table to eat his dinner there. I was a youngster, but I was clean, and I was dressed neatly. The insult in his manner cut me to the quick. I remembered him as I never remembered another man. His subsequent career proved that he was a mediocre soldier—a man who served as a "filler-in." He was mortar and not brick.

When President Grant appointed Brayman governor of Idaho, in 1876, he did a rather unfortunate thing for a territory that held toward Grant no enmity. From the records filed at Washington, it seems that Brayman was engaged in a continuous and violent row while he was Idaho's governor. He was the storm center in a typhoon of religion, women, and politics. Criticism was so bitter and so violent that Idaho people even accused Brayman of furnishing Indians with arms and ammunition and thereby stirring up the Nez Perces and Bannacks. Whatever else he did, Brayman did nothing so reprehensible as "chumming" with Idaho Indians. The Idaho people went to every extreme to get rid of Brayman. From 1878 to 1880 Idahoans filed petition after petition at Washington asking for Brayman's removal. The authorities were convinced that a successor must be chosen, and no doubt several men were considered. One of the petitions asked that I be appointed Brayman's successor. The Interior Department tried to influence one or two others to accept.

JOHN P. HOYT

It is not often in public affairs that honest personal connections prompt a man to "turn down" an appointment. Idaho was deprived of the services of a capable governor by the refusal of John P. Hoyt, now of Washington, to accept the governorship to replace Governor Brayman.

Mr. Hoyt was an Ohio man, born at Austinburg, October 6, 1841. He was a graduate of the Ohio State University, Columbus, and the Union Law School, at Cleveland, 1867. Mr. Hoyt served in the Army from 1862 to 1866. He moved to Tuscola County, Michigan, in 1867, where he was prosecuting attorney in 1868 and served in the legislature, 1872-74. The following year he was elected speaker of the lower house. In 1876 Mr. Hoyt was appointed secretary of Arizona Territory; the following year he was appointed governor. He was a man of ability and of much experience in public affairs and was well liked by the administration at Washington. When the Indian trouble of the Bannacks and Utes (1878) came so closely upon the heels of Joseph's Nez Perce raid, the Interior Department was in search of a man who could assume the gubernatorial chair of Idaho and perhaps effect order from the chaotic condition of affairs which could not be met by Governor Mason Brayman. Mr. Hoyt was offered the position to succeed Brayman, but refused, because he was honestly convinced that Brayman was unfairly treated, or would have been, had he taken his place. The following facts in the case are authentic as well as interesting and should be recorded.

In June, 1878, Mr. Hoyt was serving as governor of Arizona. At Prescott he received a telegram from Carl Schurz, Secretary of the Interior, to the following effect: "The President has nominated you to be Governor of the Territory of Idaho, a man known to the department to be energetic and capable being required by the conditions now existing in that territory." At this time what was known as the Bannack and Piute war was in progress. Mr. Hoyt wired the department that if he could be relieved of duties in Arizona at once he would accept the position in Idaho. In view of this acceptance of the new position, General John C. Frémont, who for some reason did not desire to go to Idaho, but was willing and anxious to go to Arizona, was nominated to be governor of Arizona. At the time these nominations were sent to the Senate it was about ready to adjourn, and an objection by a single senator was sufficient to prevent the consideration of the nomination at that session. Senator Oglesby, of Illinois, was a warm personal friend of General Mason Brayman, then governor of Idaho, and, not being satisfied that General Brayman had been treated fairly, objected to the consideration of the nomination to take his place. Whereupon Senator Ferry, of Michigan, asked Mr. Hoyt if he desired to have the nomination of General Frémont go over with his nomination. In response, Mr. Hoyt requested in the strongest terms that no objection to the confirmation of General Frémont should be urged on his behalf, stating to Senator Ferry that if his nomination to Idaho was not finally confirmed he cared but little. The result was that General Frémont's nomination was confirmed, and the President, almost immediately upon the adjournment of the Senate, suspended General Brayman, and designated Mr. Hoyt to fill his place until the next session of the Senate. Mr. Hoyt wired the department that if he could be relieved at once he would accept the designation and suggested that he should turn over the government of the territory of Arizona to the secretary. The department refused to allow this, stating that it was desired that Hoyt should remain until General Frémont arrived, assuring him at the time that they would hasten Frémont's departure from the East so that Hoyt would not be long detained in Arizona. One cause after another arose to prevent General Frémont's departure for the territory, and, pending his arrival, Mr. Hoyt had, through Senator Christianson, of Michigan, who was a warm personal friend of his and likewise of Brayman, entered into correspondence with the latter. As a result, he became satisfied that grave injustice had been done General Brayman in suspending or removing him on the flimsy pretext that he had been guilty of disloyal conduct in his dealing with the Indian tribes. On account of this and of the high standing of General Brayman as an officer during the War of the Rebellion, Mr. Hoyt finally concluded not to accept the designation to succeed Brayman and wrote the President his views in that regard. He supposed his connection with public office under the United States, at least while President Hayes was in office, would be terminated by reason of this letter. He was obliged, under business complications, to proceed to Washington, where, as a matter of courtesy, he called upon Secretary Schurz, who stated that the President wanted to see him in regard to the subject matter of his letter. Mr. Schurz immediately took Mr. Hoyt to the White House for an interview with the President. At this interview he found that President Hayes had accepted his letter in the spirit in which he had written it and was in no manner offended by its tone. Secretary Schurz insisted that the reasons assigned in the public press for the removal of General Brayman were not those which had influenced him (Schurz) in recommending the same, but he did not believe Brayman could ever be a success in the position which he occupied. The President and secretary urged Mr. Hoyt's acceptance of the place and went so far as to prepare his appointment for transmission to the Senate for confirmation. After a further interview with Senator Christianson and Senator Oglesby, who stated that they feared a disastrous effect upon General Brayman's health if he were subjected to the indignity of a removal, Mr. Hoyt persisted in his refusal, but presented the matter in such a light that President Hayes assured him that he would be given an official position equal to a territorial governorship if the opportunity arose. Law was Mr. Hoyt's vocation, so the result was that, in 1879, he was appointed an associate justice of Washington Territory's supreme court.

Mr. Hoyt has held many positions of honor and is today one of the best-known men in the Northwest. In 1883 he was reappointed to the associate justiceship. He was a member and President of the constitutional convention of 1889. From the same date to 1897 he was justice of the Washington supreme court. At present he lives in Seattle and is a member of the law firm of Hoyt and Haight.

In 1879 Mr. Frank Porter, of Idaho, came to Philadelphia as a special messenger and asked me to consider the matter of accepting the appointment of governor of the territory. I had left Idaho in 1875 and had since resided in Philadelphia, but my work with the Smithsonian Institution—and my various official connections from 1875 to 1879 with Idaho—kept me in constant touch with the territory. Moreover, I had traveled extensively through the Northwest during 1878 and 1879. President Hayes, with whom I was on intimate terms at that time, urged me to accept the appointment and finally wrote me as follows:

> Executive Mansion,
> Washington
> 16 June, 1880
>
> Hon. Thos. Donaldson,
> Philadelphia, Penna.
>
> My Dear Sir:
>
> A vacancy is to occur in the Governorship of Idaho by the expiration of the term of Gov. Brayman. It gives me sincere pleasure to offer you the position. I am satisfied that your appointment will be acceptable to the people of the Territory, and that you will fill the place creditably to yourself and to the administration.
>
> Please reply at your earliest convenience and oblige.
>
> Sincerely,
> (Signed) R. B. HAYES

The above was entirely in the autograph of President Hayes. I did not accept. General Brayman probably knew me about as well as he knew most of his Idaho constituents —which was not at all—but I must confess that my temptation to accept the honor was very strong. One of the most alluring reasons was the visionary gratification to be mine when I should succeed Brayman and then have the pleasure of telling him that I was the young soldier with whom he had refused to dine at Cairo, Illinois, many years before. I laugh now when I think of that phase of the question. Heroics of the kind do not affect me much. Brayman had forgotten the incident probably for the reason that bad manners were habitual with him. All in all, I do not wonder that he was a failure as a governor. He was too old to affiliate with the Westerners, and he lacked ordinary tact and manners.

JOHN B. NEIL

John Baldwin Neil, Mason Brayman's successor, was a schoolmate of mine at Columbus, Ohio. He was a son of Robert E. Neil, a rich man and one of Columbus' early settlers. He was born at Columbus, Ohio, July 28, 1842. John attended school at the military institute at Frankfort, Kentucky, the school where General Charles C. Walcutt, of Columbus, was also educated. William Dennison, governor of Ohio in 1860, married John Neil's first cousin. Neil served in Company B, 2nd Ohio Volunteer Infantry in the three months' service in 1861. This corps was the old Columbus Videttes, under Captain Thrall.

When Neil returned to Ohio he wanted a commission. Governor Dennison hesitated to grant it because charges had been made that the governor had put all his relatives in office or commission. I went with Neil to interview the governor at his office in the statehouse, one day in October, 1861. The governor was courteous but promised nothing. At Worthington, a town nine miles above Columbus, a regiment of infantry was being organized by Colonel Thomas Worthington, an odd and noted Ohio character. He was an old man whom I had known for years and for whom I had often done favors. It occurred to me that my friend Neil would make a good adjutant for Worthington. Neil was good-looking, gentlemanly in the extreme, had a good voice, and had been thoroughly educated in military tactics at Frankfort. I saw Colonel Worthington at once. He listened to me and said, "Send Neil up to camp, and if he can handle a dress parade, I'll take him." So, to camp went Neil, and he was tried and accepted. The Worthington regiment became the 46th Ohio Infantry. Neil remained with the command until the regiment was mustered out of service and, by courage and capacity, he reached the rank of lieutenant colonel.

Two days after the battle of Shiloh I was at Savannah,

Tennessee, a few miles below Pittsburg Landing on the Tennessee River, looking for a wounded man of my regiment, the 19th Ohio. I did not find my man, but as I passed a little group of buildings, I saw John Neil and Captain T. C. Platt, of the 46th Ohio, basking in the sun beside one of the frame houses. Both had been wounded in the first day's fight at Shiloh. Neil was shot in the neck; both men were so badly used up that they were helpless. After the war both Neil and I were again in Ohio. He became private secretary to Governor R. B. Hayes. In 1869 I went to Idaho, and a short time afterwards Neil went to Utah, originally on a mining venture. He was appointed at Salt Lake to the position of receiver of the land office. I met him and his charming wife at Salt Lake in 1879. Mrs. Neil was Marion Jones, daughter of Captain E. Penrose Jones, U. S. A.

In the summer of 1880 Neil became ambitious and wanted to be made governor of one of the territories, especially Idaho. Mason Brayman, it was generally understood, would be retired at the end of his term. When I declined the offer from President Hayes to appoint me governor, I at once thought of Neil. I was temporarily in Washington. Neil came East, we visited the President, and shortly afterward Neil was appointed governor of Idaho. As governor of the territory he did nothing remarkable, but he served with honesty and candor. He was removed simply because someone else wanted the position. President Arthur's appointment of a successor was in the regular line of many of Mr. Arthur's other acts by which his friends were placed in positions created for them. The removal, under the circumstances, reflected credit upon Mr. Neil. He returned to Ohio and now resides there. He was not a man of marked ability, but he was a valuable citizen and a worthy soldier.*

---

* Governor Neil died at Columbus, Ohio, October 6, 1902.—T.B.D.

JOHN N. IRWIN

John Nichol Irwin, Idaho's governor from 1883 to 1884, was another of the "short-term" appointees. Mr. Irwin was born in Ohio in 1847, and when he was quite young his family moved to Iowa, where Mr. Irwin has since resided. He was educated at public schools in Keokuk and for a time attended Miami University, Ohio. In 1867 he was graduated from Dartmouth College. Mr. Irwin engaged in the dry-goods trade at Keokuk, Iowa, and soon forged ahead in business. He was looked upon as one of the prominent men in the state and, in 1875, was elected to the legislature; in 1882 he was again elected. From 1876 to 1879 he was mayor of Keokuk; in 1887 he was again elected mayor. During the Civil War he served as private in the 45th Iowa Infantry.

Mr. Irwin was appointed governor of Idaho in the winter of 1882 and visited the territory in the following spring. He remained but a short time because of business complications at his home in Keokuk. His resignation was tendered the following year. While he resided in the territory he won the respect of the people because he showed capability and intelligence, but was, withal, unassuming and tactful. In 1890 he was appointed governor of Arizona but resigned two years later. He later engaged in business with a prominent business firm of Keokuk. Mr. Irwin would have undoubtedly proved a capable governor had he filled out his term in Idaho.*

WILLIAM M. BUNN

William Malcolm Bunn, governor of Idaho in 1884 and 1885, was born in Philadelphia, January 1, 1842. He was raised in the 16th ward of the city and received his early education in local grammar schools. For a short time he attended his uncle's school at Havana, New York. Mr.

---
* Mr. Irwin served as United States Minister to Portugal from 1899 to 1901.—T.B.D.

Bunn learned the trade of wood carving and started in business with his brother.

At the outbreak of the Civil War he enlisted as a private in the 72nd Pennsylvania Volunteer Infantry, Company E. This organization was known as "Baxter's Philadelphia Fire Zouaves." On June 29, 1862, Mr. Bunn was severely wounded at Savage Station, Virginia. He was captured by the Rebel forces and taken to Richmond and held prisoner. He was sent home later in the same year and honorably discharged.

At the end of the war Bunn and his brother continued in business. The future governor of Idaho at once began to interest himself in local politics. He began modestly but in a very few years was sent to the Pennsylvania legislature after contesting an election first accorded to his opponent. In the early seventies Bunn was elected register of wills in Philadelphia. He waged a splendid campaign against fearful political odds. In 1878 he purchased the Philadelphia *Transcript,* a Sunday newspaper which was conducted on lines political and personal. The "personal" element in the paper comprised several columns of local scandal which outclassed anything printed between the two oceans! Naturally the *Transcript* made money.

In 1883 a movement was furthered to place Mr. Bunn in the gubernatorial chair of Arizona Territory. This came to naught despite Bunn's capable backing. That is, it came to nothing at the time. However, on March 26, 1884, President Arthur accorded him the governorship of Idaho Territory. Mr. Bunn served less than two years, but we in Philadelphia thereafter invariably dubbed him "Governor."

I have known Mr. Bunn personally for many years. At the time of his appointment he was considered one of the best-dressed men in Philadelphia. Neat in figure and clothes, rather daring at times in style and colors, he might be taken for an ordinary club man, but Bunn possessed splendid ability and was straightforward in his dealings. He was a wit, speaker, and writer. One of his poems, "My Ships," is widely quoted. Bunn did almost everything and did everything well—decidedly an exception to the proverb about versatility. Moreover, he was always a money-maker. On a few occasions he dropped his dignity, and you then felt sorry for him—just as you feel sorry for clever people who stoop to bathos.

Governor Bunn's administration in Idaho was reputable in every way, but during his time factions in the Republican Party became more and more pronounced because of the assured dawn of statehood which, consequently, meant a future contest for governor and senators. The laws locating and building a capitol building at Boise and locating and erecting the insane asylum at Blackfoot were passed during his administration; Bunn commended both bills. C. W. Moore, of Boise, told me that four thousand dollars was expended upon the legislature and officials to secure the passage of the Blackfoot Asylum bill. Bingham County, in southeast Idaho, was organized during Bunn's reign, and he induced the legislature to name the County Bingham, in honor of the man who secured his (Bunn's) appointment as governor of the territory. General Henry H. Bingham was a well-known Philadelphian.

Bunn arrived in the territory on June 26, 1884, and was invited to deliver the Fourth of July oration. Bunn acquiesced and, when the holiday came, he, with acumen, plunged tooth and tail into the Mormon question and made a speech against Mormonism that attracted much attention. Needless to state, it "fixed" his popularity with most of his constituents. The Mormons chanced at that time to be the best-behaved citizens in the territory, but they were Mormons! Bunn resigned from office July 15, 1885, and "fled" the country just before the coming of Idaho's era of progress, about to be occasioned by the completion of the Oregon Short Line and the influx of Denver capital to

Boise. His resignation was not accepted until September, 1885.

Bunn's ability did not receive the credit due it from the Idahoans. He is remembered as an entertaining and humorous man who did no harm and did some good.

Bunn was remembered markedly for his social sway as Idaho's executive. He was known as the "Dude Governor!" For many years Bunn had been vice-president of the famous Clover Club, of Philadelphia, and his wit and repartee were features of Clover Club dinners. As a diner-out and expert in cuisine, Bunn had no superior. In January, 1885, he presided over the Sagebrush Club, in Boise, and the dinner served on the occasion is memorable in the annals of Idaho. Mary Hallock Foote, authoress, who then lived near Boise, painted the menu cards. A favorite song of the Clover Club begins: "Gather your families around you Sunday morning." This phrase Bunn incorporated in a Thanksgiving proclamation for Idaho (he printed it in brackets). Bunn always claimed (and it must be conceded) that he at least taught Idaho people how to hang meat and game before cooking. He said to me a few years later, "When I went to Idaho there wasn't a soul in the territory who knew how to prepare meat and game. When I left there you could see many roasts of beef and game galore hanging from windows." Socially, Bunn was a shining light. He set a pace that none before had had experience or wealth to maintain.

In 1884 Bunn was petitioned for pardon of one "Johnny-behind-the-Rocks," a murderer who was subsequently hanged at Hailey, Idaho. Bunn refused to pardon and he was right. The man had committed two murders. While "Johnny" was on the scaffold ready to hang he asked for a cigarette and, as he methodically struck the match upon his knee and puffed idly, he said, "Remember, gents! Me, an old-timer, wuz hung by a dude governor!"

EDWARD A. STEVENSON

A sturdy pioneer was well rewarded when Edward A. Stevenson received the appointment of governor, September 29, 1885. He was next to the last of the territory's governors. His successor, Colonel Shoup, ended the list, and also took office as the first state governor of Idaho. Stevenson retained office, with E. J. Curtis as secretary of state, until March, 1889.

The last time I saw Governor Stevenson was a few years before his death. In 1890 I visited Boise and, as my son and I walked down Main Street, a buggy came rattling around a corner, and the driver had to pull sharply to avoid running into us. I glanced at the driver and was delighted to see the grizzled but kindly face and the sharp, bright eyes of Stevenson peering at me from beneath a peaked brown hat. His greeting was characteristic. He dropped the reins, stared fixedly for a breath, and snorted, "Cuss me, Tom, how in hell are you?" There was no mistaking the greeting or the man.

Stevenson was a Pennsylvanian by birth. He joined the ranks of forty-niners and resided in California from 1850 until 1863. He was a member of the California assembly in 1854 and 1855 from El Dorado County. E. J. Curtis, of Idaho, was also in the assembly of 1855 (and 1856) representing Siskiyou County. Stevenson was an excellent parliamentarian and a ready debater. He went to Idaho about 1863 and settled in Boise County, where he was always progressive in business and active in politics. Near the place where Grimes was murdered by Indians, in 1862, Stevenson and Dr. Noble owned extensive placer mines. About 1882 Colonel Stevenson moved over to the Payette region in Ada County. He served many terms in Idaho's council, the first time from Boise County in 1866, and was frequently chosen speaker of the council. He was probably the strongest leader of his party in the territory. His executive abilities and forceful manner accorded him a large following. At the expiration of his four years as governor—the position had been accorded him by President Grover Cleveland—he settled in Boise and took the contract for carrying mails between Boise and Quartzburg. In the later years of his life he suffered many bitter disappointments and afflictions. Fortune treated him severely.

Stevenson was a man of decided ability. As a friend he was warm-hearted, genial, and true. Strict partisan though he was, his bitterest political foes were often his warmest personal friends. He did much for the territory; he understood its needs and labored toward its betterment during his early and late years. His memory is well respected by Idaho people.

Colonel George Laird Shoup* succeeded him in March, 1899, as governor and held office until Idaho was admitted to statehood, July 3, 1890. On October 1, 1890, he was chosen governor of the new state.

E. J. CURTIS

A chapter might well be headed "Idaho without a Governor." E. J. Curtis, to whom I have referred in the chapter on members of Idaho's bar, did not at any time hold the official title of governor but for many years he was acting governor and chief executive in all but formal title.

Curtis was particularly well versed in formalities and intimate with Idaho history and people. When Gilman Marston failed to qualify as governor, Curtis delivered the

---

* It is to be regretted that Mr. Donaldson did not write of his acquaintance with George L. Shoup, the last territorial governor. Mr. Donaldson knew Colonel Shoup well for many years and was associated with him officially in Idaho's behalf. He has often expressed his appreciation of Colonel Shoup's able services for the territory at home and abroad. When Mr. Donaldson revisited Idaho in 1890, Colonel Shoup had served for two months as governor of the new state. Under date of November 26, 1890, Governor Shoup commissioned Mr. Donaldson colonel and aide-de-camp in the National Guard of Idaho. The commission is in his family's possession and is prized for the compliment it implies. As Colonel Shoup's record is so well known, data is omitted.—T.B.D.

Photo courtesy J. J. Curtis, son of Edward J. Curtis.
Edward J. Curtis during his long tenure of office as Territorial Secretary saw many governors come and go.

annual message to the 1870 legislature and for nearly two years was acting governor. Curtis was afterwards at the helm in all periods when the governor's office was vacant by reason of nonappointments or the failure of the appointees to qualify. He did much to effect system in the management of the territory's affairs and was well liked by the citizens. He was territorial secretary of state for a long term of years and in that capacity could quickly, as he was so often compelled to do, assume the role of governor. He was secretary of state at the end of Idaho's territorial history, in 1890, and was proffered the position of secretary for the new commonwealth. Knowing Curtis as I did, I am able to attest to the value of his public services and the amount of efficient work he did for Idaho. He deserves a prominent place in Idaho history.

CHAPTER VIII

IDAHO INDIANS

BY THE census of 1870 the Indians in Idaho were enumerated as follows: Nez Perces, 3,200; Pend d'Oreilles, 700; Bannacks, 600; Kootenais, 400; Spokanes, 400; Coeur d'Alenes, 300; Boise Shoshonis, 200; Western Shoshonis, 200; Bruneau Shoshonis, 100; Weiser (River) Shoshonis, 68.

The most numerous were the Nez Perces, of the Shahaptian tribe proper. Lewis and Clark wintered with these red men in their tour of 1804-06 and knew them as "Chopunnish." In the early part of the century they numbered 8,000. In 1836, when a mission was established among them, they numbered 4,000. In personal appearance, intelligence, and ability, they were, in their prime, surpassed not even by the clever Sioux.

The sachems of the early Nez Perces were seekers after knowledge, but the latter-day tribesmen have been the victim of the white men and their own inability to adjust themselves to changed environment. No more impressive story is chronicled in our annals than that story of the four Nez Perces, who, having heard of the white man's God from William Clark in 1805, journeyed to St. Louis in 1832, sought Clark, then superintendent of Indian Affairs in the Northwest, and asked him about the white man's Great Spirit and about "the Book." The two elder Indians who made the pilgrimage died in St. Louis; the two younger men journeyed up the Yellowstone River in 1832 aboard a steamer which carried George Catlin, the artist. Neither of the red men mentioned their quest or its failure, but it was reported to Catlin, and he confirmed it by interviewing Captain William Clark. In 1833 Mr. Catlin wrote for the New Y *Commercial Advertiser* a complete story of the Nez Perces and their quest. The result was that the Methodist Board of Missions and the American Board of Commissioners for Foreign Missions took steps to enlighten the Northwest Indians on the subject of our Bible. Jason and Daniel Lee and others were sent out by the Methodists in 1835; the famous Rev. Marcus Whitman and Dr. Samuel Parker followed the next year. In 1836 Mr. Catlin met, at Pittsburgh, the Rev. H. H. Spalding and wife, en route to Oregon as Indian missionaries. It is quite true that Lewis and Clark found the Black Gowns (Jesuits) among the Indians, but their presence did not hinder the four Nez Perces from traveling overland to have audience with Captain Clark in a further search for the white man's God. Dr. Spalding founded the mission at Lapwai and for many years was in charge among the Nez Perces. He is buried there. In 1847, Marcus Whitman, his wife, and thirteen associates were murdered by the red men; Cayuse Indians, not Nez Perces, were the perpetrators.

During my residence in Idaho most of the Nez Perces were known as nontreaty Indians; that is, Indians who considered themselves not territorially bound by signing treaties with the Government. They were free to roam and hunt wherever they wished. They were peaceful and friendly in spite of oppression by white men. The downfall of the Nez Perces, the series of events which led up to Chief Joseph's fight in 1877 and the subsequent banishment of the tribe to Indian Territory, was, as in almost all Indian troubles, the fault of white men. In 1855 I. I. Stevens, governor of Washington, saw that a crisis was imminent because of the influx of gold seekers who encroached upon Indian lands. A first treaty with the Nez Perces was signed in 1855 and another in 1859, and trouble was averted until 1863, when the increasing presence of white miners and whisky necessitated more formal action between the Indians and the Government. Lapwai Reservation was laid out by the treaty of 1863 for the Upper

Nez Perces, of whom Big Thunder was chief. Old Joseph, who died in 1871, was chief of the Lower Nez Perces, and his tribe refused to accept the conditions of the treaty of 1863. I saw Old Joseph a few times and vastly admired him, even though he was an Indian. He was a man of brains, honesty, and foresight. His son, Young Joseph (Thunder traveling over the mountains) was an able successor as chief. Six feet in height was Young Joseph, superb in bearing, keen, and shrewd. He and his father were quite the diplomatic equals of all the commissioners representing the Indian Department with whom they came in contact. Both of them saw further than the rest of their followers; they realized that the white man made one-sided treaties whenever he could, and that treaties were violated by the whites whenever the latter found it expedient to do so. That the Nez Perces were ultimately to become mere baggage in Uncle Sam's depot, the two Josephs clearly foresaw. I saw young Joseph on many occasions and always regretted that indignity had been done him and his people in 1877. His raid wasn't a murdering affair; had not he directed it, it would have been far worse for the whites.

In 1873 the Interior Department set off the Wallowa country for a reservation for the Lower Nez Perces, but two years later, although the Indians under Joseph were quite content to abide there, the Government refused to sanction the purchase of the land there for them. During all this time white men persisted in invading Indian country, and several conflicts took place between hotheaded young bucks and roustabout whites. Naturally, the appellation "murderer" was applied to every Indian who dared protect his stock and resist aggressions. There were, however, fair-minded men in the Northwest who endeavored to influence the Interior Department to treat Joseph's people honorably. General O. O. Howard, in command of the Department of the Columbia, wrote a report in 1876 on the status of Joseph and his band and gave it as his opinion that the Lower Nez Perces were not bound by the treaties from 1855 to 1863 because the United States Government had conformed to none of its obligations of those treaties. In spite of General Howard's protest, the Government, actuated by the mystic "pulls" of the inside ring, moved along in its regular rut. Joseph and his band were given thirty days to gather up their possessions and move from the lands they considered theirs—the land they owned and loved. There was a rapid and violent reaction, and yet a reaction that was most natural. Unable to restrain his followers, Joseph and his tribe took the warpath, June 14, 1877, and were out until October 5. During that short time he worsted General Howard on two distinct occasions and still behaved humanely. For cleverness in warfare he ranked with the best generals of the Apaches or Sioux. General Miles finally surrounded him, and with 87 warriors, 184 squaws, and 147 children, Joseph surrendered, a brokenhearted man. Despite the conditions of surrender, the subsequent treatment accorded Joseph and his people was as inhuman as anything in military history. After years of enforced residence in an unhealthful part of Indian Territory, the Nez Perces were returned to Idaho in 1886, depleted in numbers and weakened in health.

The Shoshonis, or Snakes, including the Utes and Bannacks, were most numerous in southern Idaho. They roamed through south central Idaho to hunt and fish. The Bannacks were very frequent visitors at Boise. A Bannack squaw, Jane, did a few chores about our home, and her husband Jim helped her spend her hard-earned cash. In 1868 the Bannacks and several straggling tribes in the southern portion of the territory were placed on the Fort Hall Reservation, nine miles from Ross Fork, but with or without permits the red men roamed over much of the territory. In physical appearance and intelligence they were very good types of Indians.

In the winter of 1890, my son and I visited the Fort Hall Indian encampment and saw the festive bucks daubed with war paint. Throughout the Northwest the Messiah craze of the Dreamer cult was inciting all tribesmen, and the Bannacks were dancing every night and recounting the wrongs done them by white men. Agent Fisher, a very clever and efficient man, drove us to the campgrounds, and we were at once besieged by the bucks, who asked if we were soldiers. Suspicion was present in gesture and action, but the presence of the agent made it safe for us. I was much surprised to see our old acquaintances, Jane and Jim, apparently in good health and not a whit more aged than when I had last seen them sixteen years before. After some persuasion, Jim deigned to recognize me; he rather feared to be familiar with a white man when the camp was in an excitable state of mind. I heard afterwards that a bunch of the Bannacks slipped over to Wounded Knee and joined the Sioux in their rampage of December, 1890.

The Utes were mainly in Utah and Nevada, but at times a few wanderers traveled through Idaho. A stray Coeur d'Alene from northern Idaho chanced our way infrequently, and sometimes we saw visitors from the Shoshoni reservations at Duck Valley, Malheur, and Wind River. Once in a while came red men from Grand Ronde, Klamath, Umatilla, or Warm Springs reservations.

INDIANS' LACK OF INDIVIDUALITY

The Anglo-Saxon follows no set rules of individual or race progress. He may be started at birth with a rule of order or of action, but he is disposed to make rules for himself. His thoughts open, through mental suggestion, into new fields of action, and therefrom result laborsaving inventions for mankind in general. Is there on record an invention designed by an Indian? No! The Indian lives in the day, in the hour, and invents or utilizes for the moment; he never provides for a rainy day unless under the most pronounced stress of circumstances. Give him a sheep on Tuesday and he will try to eat it all before Wednesday. He will gorge himself into insensibility; I have seen an Indian do it. He has no forethought, no individuality other than that of pre-eminence in the hunt or on the warpath; the latter is for his vainglorious boasting. Whatever spark of individuality the present Indian generations may have had has been blighted by the attempt at Government control. He prefers to do things in the manner in which they were, by fable or demonstration, inculcated in him by buck or crooning squaw. He cares not to disturb his thinking powers to open a new avenue of approach. Time to him is nothing.

A few of Chief Tendoy's Shoshonis and Sheepeater Bannacks stopped at my house one August day in 1872. Tendoy was a very sociable Indian, a very good talker, and he usually stopped at my place when he came down from Lemhi. On this occasion he had with him a dude Shoshoni named George. Without doubt he was the best-dressed buck in the tribe; handsome in appearance, he rode a magnificent black horse, gaily caparisoned with ribbons, bells, bone rings, and silver ornaments. His face was streaked with vermilion, and around his neck was a cruel white collar, a very high one of the "choker" brand. While Tendoy chatted with me, George reclined in the saddle with arms resting upon the pommel, and with a hand mirror, busily inspected his smooth chin for indications of a growing beard. It was a very warm day, and dust was plentiful; the restless horses kicked it up in clouds. George wore a sugar-loaf army hat with orange cord twined about it; he had obtained the apparel brand-new by swapping with a cavalryman. It sat jauntily upon his head, topping him off nicely, and the dude was happy. Suddenly, the mirror showed him that dust had collected on the brim of the hat. With an "Ugh," he grabbed the hat from his head, rolled over and slid from his horse, and plunged the entire hat into an irrigating ditch. The water soaked in, and then George thumbed it, soused it again with greasy hands, slapped it on his head, and mounted his charger with a satisfied grunt. Of course, the luster of the felt was ruined, and the cord was tinged. What would a white man have done? He would either have blown the dust off or flicked it with his finger. I repeat that an Indian doesn't think! Had I space, I could retail a hundred incidents just as foolish.

I recall that Tendoy was always accompanied by a squaw named Maggie, who acted as his interpreter. She was a pleasant Indian, a Shoshoni about thirty years of age, who had been raised among Mormons. Her English was very good. Maggie was unconventional, particularly in two things; she wasn't married and she rode man-fashion on a horse. Rather curious to learn of the sort of undergarment which permitted Maggie to ride split-leg fashion, my wife gave her a trinket one day and watched carefully to see how Maggie disposed of it. Maggie yanked up an overskirt and displayed a pair of buckskin trousers, neatly embroidered with beads. She placed the trinket in a trouser pocket, meanwhile laughing at our comments.*

WHY TENDOY REMAINED AT LEMHI

In 1878 George Ainslie succeeded S. S. Fenn as Idaho's delegate to Congress, and served two terms. During his service at Washington I saw much of him and always respected him despite his bitter political views; he was on the opposite side of politics, the Democratic side. But while he was in Congress he managed to get everything within the range of a territorial delegate, either in laws or appropria-

---

* The North American Indian holds inborn contempt for the female sex in human beings or animals. I have seen it evinced in twenty different tribes. When it happens that you see a buck Indian riding a mare, you may wager that he is "stony broke." In fact, he is quite an object for derision from his own people, especially from women and children. Just the minute he gets money he will buy a horse, discard the mare, and again move in good society.

tions, for Idaho, and he won the good will of the Republicans as well as the Democrats.

After Chief Joseph led his Nez Perces on their raid of 1877, there was a renewal of a former attempt to remove Chief Tendoy and his band from Lemhi, where he had lived since 1869, to the Fort Hall Reservation. An attempt was made in 1874; it was revived in 1878, and Ainslie and I played a part in frustrating the scheme. It should be explained here that the Interior Department, under President Hayes, seemed determined to concentrate all Indian tribes of each state or territory on one reservation. Tendoy was very much averse to this plan and, strange to say, he was supported by the citizens of Salmon City, who did not want to see him abused. The reason for the friendship of the whites was that during Joseph's raid the hostiles passed near Salmon City on their way to Montana. Had the Nez Perces chosen to attack the town, they would doubtlessly have done, or could have done, much damage. But when Tendoy's scouts apprised him of Joseph's approach he joined his forces with the whites, who were preparing to defend their town. He sent out messengers to notify Chief Joseph that he, Tendoy, was prepared to fight against him. Whether this actually deterred Joseph or not, I do not know, but at any rate the marauders skirted toward the south. George Ainslie was communicated with when the removal of Tendoy from Lemhi was planned. Ainslie called upon me and asked me to aid him in revoking the order for Tendoy's removal. The order, so Ainslie said, was about to be enforced.

I called upon President Hayes and requested a private interview for Mr. Ainslie, of Idaho, and perhaps another man who desired to speak on Indian matters. President Hayes said that he would be glad to be at Mr. Ainslie's service and requested us to call at the White House late that night in order to avoid interruption. When Ainslie and I left our hotel we were joined by John G. Campbell, of

Arizona, who, knowing that we were bound for the White House, asked if he might be one of the party. It was then about eleven o'clock. We entered the White House, and Mr. Allen directed us to the library where President Hayes expected us. We sat for ten minutes without hearing anyone. Finally Ainslie became nervous and said, "If a watchman walks this way, he'll think that we are burglars."

I laughed and answered, "Well, you and Campbell are Democrats, and he might be disposed to look at matters in that light." Ainslie didn't argue the question.

Another ten minutes passed, and then Mr. Hayes entered. He greeted us cordially and chatted with Mr. Campbell, who finished his plea and was about to depart when Mr. Hayes told him to remain.

"Wait a moment," said he. "I want to hear what Mr. Ainslie has to say about an Indian matter." Thereupon, Ainslie opened up on the Tendoy matter in a most suave and adroit manner. It was cleverly done in a very few words. President Hayes sat and watched him narrowly from the corners of his eyes, and, when Ainslie finished he asked him a few questions which Ainslie answered readily.

"Mr. Ainslie," said Mr. Hayes, "I am convinced that you are right. You have won your case, if I may put it that way. Tendoy shall remain at Lemhi. Please keep this in confidence. The order for his removal to Fort Hall will be revoked in the morning and the Lemhi Reservation will remain intact. I am very much obliged to you for coming to me and explaining the facts in the matter." We said good night and walked out.

Once in the open air, Ainslie leaned up against a fence and said, "Well, that is a man—even if he is a Republican! My, isn't he all business! He nearly took my breath, the way he decided that Tendoy matter! P-h-e-w!"

Promptly next morning the order was revoked, and Tendoy and his people continued to reside peacefully at Lemhi. A few months afterward an official of the Interior

Department complained to me that someone with influence had been meddling with inside Indian affairs. He cited the instance of the revocation of the Tendoy order and also complained of the President's action in forbidding the sending of any more wild Indians to Indian Territory, now Oklahoma. With the latter affair I was also quite familiar, because President Hayes sent for me and asked for information in the matter; I was fortunate enough to be on the "inside." The official received no information from me. What little influence I have ever had I have carefully refrained from boasting of. If any man has influence and wants to keep it, he had better refrain from mentioning it. Should a man have none, and should he desire it, let him incidentally mention the matter to newspapers. It may result favorably—at least, in politics.

INDIAN AMBASSADOR EXTRAORDINARY

"Behave yourself, and no questions will be asked!" That was our rule in Idaho, a rule which encouraged many who had been under a cloud in another country but who lived correct lives on the frontier. But we were frail humans; many, many times did we bite our tongues to keep back the involuntary queries which arose.

Sometime in 1871 there drifted into Boise a man as peculiar in habits and appearances as any who ever rambled through our Northwest. This man was Clitus Barbour. Barbour was once heard to say that he had come down from Salmon City after settling a lawsuit there, on which he had been retained in his former home, Montana. At the time I first saw Barbour he was a man of thirty years and a fraction less than five feet two inches in height. Surmounting his chubby figure was the largest head I have ever seen on a sane and healthy man. Black hair, restless black eyes, and short side whiskers completed a curious and astounding figure. Barbour's home was

Galesburg, Illinois; General George McKee, member of Congress from Jackson, Mississippi, told me in 1873 that he had been at school with Barbour, and he was known as "Stub and Twist," but also as a very bright boy. Barbour was a mental mystery and a natural agitator. For a time he assisted Jim Reynolds in the editing of the *Statesman* and then he tried his hand at law practice and also made political speeches. He was popular and had as few vices as he apparently had dollars. He never borrowed but he sported once in a while, and rumor had it that Clitus always won. Bright in his address, clear and forcible in voice, and endowed with superhuman conceit which begot personal courage, he was a conspicuous man in Boise. In one connection—I shall remember it until memory leaves me—I have a constant picture of Barbour before me.

In the summer of 1872 we had an Indian scare occasioned by a number of Bannacks and Shoshonis who had strayed from the Fort Hall Reservation into Camas Prairie; they were reported to have begun hostilities against the whites. Very few children strayed in Boise after dark when that rumor reached us, and we looked to bolts and wondered just how long the soldiers would be in arriving! Acting Governor Curtis called a meeting of Boise citizens, and a consultation on the whys, wherefores, and what's-to-be-dones was held in his office. After a lengthy debate, it was decided that we should send a messenger to Camas Prairie to interview Chief Collins and ascertain whether or not the red men were hostile. I confess that we held our breath; it was easy to suggest a messenger, but whom could we select? In an instant Clitus Barbour arose. Said he, very impressively, "I'll go!" The assembly unanimously proclaimed him, "Barbour, the very man." I hope that he was flattered; I trust that he looked upon the selection as our selection and not as his own. I am forced to say that the "very" man was *any* man! To be frank, most of us had families, and as Clitus had none depending upon him, we accepted his proposition with joy. Doubtlessly a few in the room felt their scalps tingle when they thought of big Chief Collins and what he might do. Well, we raised a purse for Barbour's trip and chipped in the equipment. One of us gave a horse, another a gun, another a saddle, until Clitus was a fair sample of job-lot ambassador. The following morning, when he passed my house, importantly starting forward on his errand of peace with admiring Boise waving tearful farewells, I confess that I dared not speak. Laughter was choking me. He rode a white horse at least seventeen hands and an ax handle in height! Little Barbour, a long horse—well! Courageously he rode northward, deigning not to look back.

For days we waited with much anxiety; we feared that the raid might have caught Clitus before he reached the prairie. But, no, everything went smoothly on, and the sixth day brought the jaunty Clitus back to us. He reported at once, in private, to Governor Curtis that the Indians were out on a permit from the Fort Hall agent, and that they were peacefully engaged in digging camas roots and holding their annual horse races. This was soon afterward confirmed. But what surprised us was Barbour's entire reticence to explain the results of his audience with the Indians; all he talked about was the variety of country through which he passed, the weather, dust, etc. He mentioned that he had eaten vast quantities of dirt at various places along the road and expressed the fear that it would take some "ground sluicing" to clear his stomach. His reticence aroused our curiosity; we felt that Barbour desired to hide something!

With the Shoshonis were the Kelly brothers, two white men who had married Indian women. One of these "squawmen" I knew quite well, and when he rode into Boise a month after Barbour's trip, I asked him if he had been present on the occasion of Barbour's conference. Kelly roared with laughter and then let the cat out of the bag. He said that when Barbour galloped into the red men's camp, the Indians were astonished; such a little man, such a big horse! Barbour sat like a statue and demanded to see Chief Collins. Collins was hastily summoned and stalked over to the squat-figured Barbour on the gawky horse.

"What's wanted?" queried Collins, who spoke English well.

"I am a messenger from the governor and commander in chief at Boise!" said Barbour pompously. Whereupon, Collins sized up the horse and then the rider and said, "Ugh."

"I want to know," demanded Clitus, "whether you Indians are for peace or war?" Collins sniffed and said, "Can't you see that we are peaceful? Women and children are with us. We dig camas and race ponies. Agent he give permit."

But Barbour was not satisfied. Said he, "Let me see the agent's permit!"

Collins made no move to produce the permit but stood looking at Barbour. Then he said, "If my people wanted war, would you send that old-man sergeant and eight soldiers here from your fort? [The Boise garrison, for a month past, had numbered just that many soldiers.] You can't send no big guns down here, for I saw the wheels of your big gun wagons sold by talk [auction] last moon for Lemp's place [brewery]. Lemp, he haul beer on those wheels [which was quite true]." Unnoticed by Barbour, Collins tipped a signal to his braves, who instantly formed a double line with space enough between to admit Barbour and his horse. An improvised gauntlet was about to start! Said Collins, "Get off your pony and eat with us."

"No, sir!" said Barbour shortly. "I want an answer to take back to my people. Our squaws and papooses are alarmed because so many braves are off the reservation. Are you, Collins, for peace or war?"

"I say," said Collins irately, "that we be peace Indians. You say you come from white chief, governor at Boise. I don't believe you. You—" at this, Collins placed his outstretched hand about three feet from the ground— "you are no messenger. You a boy, a papoose! The governor would send man to us!" At the same instant Collins' Shoshonis whirled the white horse about, slapped him on the haunches and gave a wild whoop. Down through the double line of Indians swept Barbour, his horse crazed with fear and excitement from the slaps and yells of the Indians. Kelly said that Barbour sat like a centaur and showed not the slightest fear. On a bit of rising ground, half a mile away, he succeeded in checking his alarmed horse and then turned and looked back as his persecutors. The entire band of red men were standing like statues, each in the same posture, hands rigidly extended about three feet from the ground, indicating, as Collins had, "Boy!" Kelly said that twenty minutes covered the entire conference and gauntlet and that the affair would have "made a cow laugh." Barbour disappeared from Boise in 1873 as suddenly and as unannounced as he had come. When we next heard of him, he was in San Francisco, a leading sand-lot orator in the Dennis Kearney movement. He and his colleagues became terrors to lawabiding citizens. In 1878 Barbour ran for Congress on the Kearney ticket and he was politically pulverized. Since that time I have heard nothing about him.

LIVING BUT SCALPED

While Captain J. W. Porter, Governor Ballard's private secretary, was ill I frequently sat with him and enjoyed hearing him tell of his life in the East and West and his participation in public affairs. Captain Porter was dying of consumption; most of his time he spent in bed. The captain wore a wig and he was in the habit of removing it, placing it on one of the bedposts, and donning a skullcap of velvet. At that time there was among the Bannacks a headman named Bannack Jim, well known because he spoke English fluently and was always willing to make himself disagreeable to white men. As the governor of the territory was ex officio superintendent of Indian Affairs, Captain Porter's room was often visited by tribesmen. I was with Porter one afternoon when Bannack Jim (his own people called him "Bannackee Jim") came in and asked for Porter. "Forter," he called the captain, for an Indian can not usually pronounce the letter "p." He entered the sick man's room and seated himself; his deceitful black eyes roamed everywhere and sized up things of interest. Finally, his gaze fell upon Porter's wig surmounting a bedpost.

"What's that?" queried Jim.

"Oh, that's a scalp!" said Porter unconcernedly. Jim asked some more questions concerning business on which he had come, but his attention was still hovering about Porter's wig.

"You say scalp?" he again queried. "Where you get 'im?"

For an answer, Porter took off his velvet skullcap, idly rubbed his hand over his entirely bald head and sighed, "Sioux, he take him!" At the sight of the bald head Jim gave a shriek, jumped out of the door, and rode away like mad. He was disappearing for his camp like a mounted maniac when I reached the street. A scalped man and alive! It was "bad medicine"—too much for a Bannack!

Coming down Main Street one day, I saw Bannack Jim boldly stalking along with a carbine under his blanket. He stopped me and said angrily, "I hear that all Indians who come to Boise will be shot. I come to buy sugar and clothes. I hunt and earn my money. I come here if I want. Nobody will shoot me for nothing."

I asked him where he had heard such nonsense.

"Over on Weiser River," he replied.

I told him that if he didn't want to be knocked down and put in jail he'd better throw his carbine away. With a snort, he stalked into the governor's office, and I followed. Judge Madison Hollister was standing in the anteroom. As he had much sympathy for red men who behaved themselves, he smiled affably at Jim as he entered. Jim seated himself on a table and asked for the governor.

"He is out," said Judge Hollister.

"I wait!" snorted Jim. He pulled two half dollars from his pocket and began to click them. One of the half dollars chanced to fall from his hand and rattled along the floor. Jim watched it roll under a chair.

"Pick it up!" said he to Judge Hollister, with the air of an emperor. To my amazement, the judge stooped and handed the coin to the Indian.

I expostulated and then turned to Jim and told him who Judge Hollister was. Jim stood upright, looked the judge all over, sniffed at him, and airly stalked out of the office. In clean-cut impudence and majestic insolence, it was sublime!

A NEW SORT OF CANNON

A small band of Nez Perces under Chief Eagle from the Light refused to live at Lapwai and chose to roam in the strip northwest of Boise about the headwaters of the Payette and the Weiser. They committed no depredations, but the settlers did not want stray Indians near them, and the Indian agent needed a few more red men on the reservation—it gave him a chance to make a little more money. Eagle from the Light and his band were well armed, and the Indian had a strong dislike for white men and an intimate knowledge of everything which was going on in the white man's military camps at Boise and Lapwai.

D. P. Thompson, of Portland, Oregon, afterward governor of Idaho, had charge of the surveying of Idaho public lands in 1870. His brother Allan, and a Mr. Meldrum did the actual work; probably the contracts were sublet to them. Allan Thompson and his party were surveying along the Weiser River in the summer of 1869 and of course had their field equipment with them. Their theodolite had a telescope that was of large size, and the brass glittering in the sun's rays was noticeable from a far distance. One day at noon, while the men were running a survey, a terrific war whoop sounded, and in a trice Thompson's party was the vortex of an encircling band of mounted, yelling Indians, led by Eagle from the Light. They were ready for battle, and Thompson and his party, not knowing the sign language for "peace," held one hand on their scalps while raking their outfit for a white flag. There wasn't a white shirt or a white handkerchief in the gang! The cook, in a moment of inspiration, handed out a white flour bag and it was waved violently. Old Eagle at once rode in with his party but kept the white men covered and demanded to know whether the palefaces meant fight or peace. He said that his braves had watched the party for days, and they thought that Indians were being hunted. Thompson lost no time telling Eagle that he and his men were looking not for Indians but for peace; all that they wanted was peace and plenty of it!

"So," snorted Eagle, "you white men for peace? So, you go roun' from sunup with brass cannon on stick and point at my people?"

When Thompson and his men stopped laughing, they told him that the telescope was not a howitzer. Eagle took a peep through it and when he saw its remarkable powers he gave a surprised "Woof!" and grinned like a boy. Old Eagle and the survey gang had a small potlatch together and departed good friends.

In connection with the Thompson incident, I recall a bit of philosophy expounded under aggravating circumstance by my good friend Orlando ("Rube") Robbins, one morning in 1870, while Rube was Boise's city marshal or United States deputy marshal. He was an entire success with lawbreakers; he had a very persuasive way with him. I was riding past May's brickyard, when ahead of me I saw a knot of men scuffling in the road. Although not looking for trouble, I went nearer and saw Robbins in altercation with Indians. A group of Umatillas, en route from the game country east of the divide, had overindulged in firewater. Two or three were making hostile advances. Robbins was deeply interested in a hostile buck; when the buck resisted, I saw Robbins knock him down. The buck staggered to his feet, grasping at a murderous knife, and Robbins promptly "swatted" him again. He staggered to his feet and went down again, covered with blood, and badly mauled. I called from my wagon, "Let him alone, Robbins. If you crack his skull and he dies, there will be music here!"

Rube yelled energetically, "Talk's cheap! Get out of that cart and hold him till I handcuff him. If I let him up, he'll knife me, and you bet I'm worth more to myself than he is to me!"

With an alacrity far from cheerful, I alighted and assisted. The buck's companions gathered about him and advised him to surrender, and then Robbins lugged his charge off to Boise. Mr. Indian was fined, with costs, for getting drunk on whisky sold to him under United States license, the tax on which helped pay Congressmen and others in reputable positions!

INDIAN PAPERS

When a buck left the reservation to come into town or visit other tribes, the agent customarily gave him a written permit, and this the red man used both for identification and safeguard. There were many white men in my day in Idaho who took no chances; they shot first and sought information afterward! At different times I've met Indians who carried with them not agency letters but testimonials from white acquaintances. Some of the testimonials were absolutely libelous, and it was almost pathetic to see a red man offer the letter for inspection with great pride and an accepted assurance of the good things the letter must tell about him. Along the Boise River, one day in 1869, I met a superb specimen, a Shoshoni buck named Taytober. Taytober presented the following complimentary letter:

Ross Fork, Idaho, July 4, 1868

This Indian's name is Taytober. He is a thoroughbred. He goes without the bell tapping. He is also a gentleman and you can bet your life he will do what he agrees to do. Make him your friend for he is a good one. Do the square thing by him, and he is a honey-cooler. Do anything mean to him, and he is a johan, and will get even. Brace him up with food when he hands you this, as he is always hungry; no rum, but beef, and plenty of it.

(signed) WILLIAM TROTTER AND UNCLE

Taytober had fallen into good hands; but, ah, how cruelly was poor Lo treated in this testimonial which was turned over to me by a Western man, who had met the original:

Bridger, Utah, June 1, 1867

This will be presented to you by Moss Rose, or "Dirty Pete," a Washakie Shoshone. Keep him away about five feet when he presents it; also lock your valuables up in your fireproof when you see him coming, for he is a great beggar. In the meantime, if you have any jerked meat, turn him loose at it. He don't care whether it's cooked or not. Ten to twelve pounds of good meat, bear, elk, deer, or buffalo, lunches him. He don't want any trimmings with the meat, and you needn't hand him a napkin either. He is not a bad Indian, but he is so dirty. He counts in dirt for two Indians when the agent rounds up the band for issue. Treat him well; his faults are few, and vices small ones. His word's good.

(signed) JAMES BRIDGER

If the average Indian, under Government control, was ever sized up better than by Bridger, I'd like to see the digest. A beggar and dirty! The reservation red men have become the most constant and persistent beggars to be found anywhere. The average Pullman porter measures his services by the amount he is able to extort: the reservation Indian's devotion comes in exactly the same way, except that the Indian expects everything for nothing, and he will gladly accept things entirely useless to him. Absolutely devoid of shame, he positively stares a prospective donor out of countenance; fronts him boldly until the white man, if he be new to the country, "shells out" and feels as if he should apologize for not giving more. And as for dirt, he wears his clothes until they rot away and fall from him. Vermin simply run riot over him! It must be said though, that the average reservation red man is not the dirtiest human being in the world. The scum of Europe possibly outrival him. When a squad of Indian youths just off a reservation arrive at an industrial or training school, a large garden hose is generally applied before these first Americans are permitted to enter the halls of learning. I have known cases where the coach drivers who hauled the Indians from the railroad to the industrial school invariably chose to ride a lead horse, permitting the guests to occupy the entire vehicle. It was not inhospitality; it was personal safety!

MAJOR GENERAL GEORGE CROOK

General Crook's name was as familiar to Idaho Indians as it was to the white people of the territory. "Crook can handle the thing if an outbreak comes," was the white man's firm belief. The red men rather agreed in this view of Crook's ability; they had learned to their sorrow that when the "Gray Fox" took the field against them, death, capture, or far retreat was the inevitable outcome.

General Crook came to Boise on the evening of June 10, 1870, and paid a visit to Captain Sinclair. He was a great favorite throughout the Northwest and every town received him with honors. On this occasion, Dr. Wagner held a reception for Crook, and later in the evening Wagner brought Crook to my home. I recall that the General was suffering from an excruciating headache, but he chatted pleasantly for an hour and gave no sign of weariness. Crook was at that time just forty-one years of age and was lieutenant colonel of the 23rd Infantry, in charge of the Department of the Columbia. Directly after the Civil War, after having commanded the Army of West Virginia, Crook was mustered out and then re-enlisted as a captain; in the Army reorganization he was commissioned lieutenant colonel of the 23rd. In 1866 Crook was placed in command of the Boise district; that is, he was pitted against all hostile Indians of southern Idaho and Nevada. Prior to the Civil War he had rendered splendid service against the Rogue River, Pitt, and Yakima Indians.

While he sat with us that evening in Boise, I confess that I never felt for any man more respect than I did for General Crook. He did not noticeably suggest the soldier, but he impressed one with a sense of hidden force and quiet determination and shrewdness. Bright, sharp eyes and rather unkempt whiskers were the prominent features in his physical make-up. His talk was on various topics, in no way remarkable, but his views abounded in that rare quality—common sense. Common sense was the dominant strain in his life; some might have called it brains, but it was common sense, the ability to recognize and do the right thing at the right time. He was beyond question the greatest Indian fighter our Army has known, and when one reads the story of his campaigns the common sense traits are predominant. Crook set a thief to catch a thief; he aligned Indians against Indians! When he trailed Apaches, he used Apache guides who knew not only the country but also knew the methods of warfare of their people. Crook was a generous conqueror. The tribes which he subdued were never badly treated; Crook believed that red men could be taught to earn a living, and he labored always to put the subjugated at employment. He had no use for murderous renegades, and sooner or later they wended their way to the "Happy Hunting Grounds."

By the Indians whom he conquered, or those who avoided him, he was looked upon with the greatest respect. The wild man knew that his warfare was the right kind—shrewd and effective. Those who had fought as scouts under his command would pilgrimage hundreds of miles just to say "How!" to him. Men of our Army who were on field campaigns with Crook told me that when he took the field, he was the most disreputable-looking soldier in the command. "All rawhide boots and dust," one of them said.

After Crook left Idaho he was detailed to wipe out red marauders in Arizona, and when, in 1871, the little general swooped down upon the deserts of the vast territory, his was the most decisive campaign ever waged against American Indians. Two years afterward, in 1873, he was made brigadier general, and when, in 1888, he was made major general, he had earned the confidence of every man in the regular establishment, not to mention thousands of civilians who had always a warm spot in their hearts for the modest fighter. As major general he was the same man that he was in 1852 with the humble title of brevet second lieutenant. His mode of dealing with Indians should serve as an example for our Indian Bureau. Crook was known to the red men as a man who never lied! Shoshone, Arapahoe, Crow, Sioux, Apache, Piute, Klamath, Rogue River, Modoc, Navaho, Pawnee—with all these tribes he battled, and these tribes he treated fairly, as worthy foes, and his bravery and noble nature were as much appreciated by the dusky opponents as they were appreciated by the men who fought side by side with Crook in the fight for the West.

AN INDIAN'S PATIENCE

An Indian's reticence when with white men is equaled by his patience. His patience, ancestrally developed to a remarkable degree, results from his mode of life. He doesn't need to hurry; tomorrow is just as good as today—work is distasteful, anyhow. The ordinary Indian is particularly reticent with white men because of his inborn suspicion of them. Cash and tobacco or whisky usually arouse a fairly good response.

When I was on my Oregon trip, told of in a later chapter, we were en route on one occasion to the ranch of T. Maupin, an old frontiersman who had a well-known location on the main road, halfway between The Dalles and Canyon City. We were traveling ahead of an ambulance in which was General Crook and one or two of his staff. We reached the brow of the hill which overlooked Maupin's and saw at the right-hand side of the road an Indian perched upon a rock. He glanced at us briefly and then resumed his attitude of apparent indifference to his surroundings. An agency blouse, a pair of blue breeches, and a slouch hat marked him as a reservation Indian.

When we rattled up Maupin came to the door and gave us a cordial welcome. After greetings had been exchanged, Maupin said, "See that Indian on the rock, as you came by? His name is George; he's a Snake from Warm Springs. A couple of years ago he was one of Crook's scouts and, like every other redskin who ever scouted under Crook, he's stuck on the old man. He's been sitting on that rock three days and two nights. Yesterday I sent food out to him although he didn't come and ask for it. Somehow or other, he heard Crook was going to pass by here. He'll be there if Crook doesn't come until Christmas!"

Much interested in the solitary figure, we watched in order to see what would happen when Crook's ambulance came over the hill. When the "hack" approached the rock, General Crook (then Colonel) saw the Indian and called out to him.

"Hello, George!" But George didn't move. "Come and sit on the box with the driver, George!" called Crook again, and George obeyed with much alacrity. When the ambulance reached us, Crook asked Maupin to give George a bunk in the barn.

Directly after dinner, Crook interviewed George and a meaty, reminiscent interview it must have been. Sign language was mostly employed; Crook asked about the Indians who had served with him when the campaigns were being waged, and George gave him all the information he had. Then Crook told him where he was about to travel, and George was in silent raptures over the attention shown him; at times he vouchsafed an animated "Ugh" or "Woof." Crook presented him with a blouse, a pair of shoes, and tobacco.

Next morning the Indian, from his stand on a meal sack, witnessed his chief's departure, and as the soldier called "Good-by, George," the Indian solenmly raised his hand and grunted "Ugh." Then he began his solitary foot journey across country more than one hundred miles.

I think that George's patience is a very fair sample of ordinary Indian patience. His reward for his long tramp and wait was his audience with Crook; it appealed to his vanity and gave him splendid opportunity to blossom forth as a liar when he returned to his people. Once back at the reservation, George would gather his clan about him and detail everything he had seen. He would remember— what he failed to remember he could easily invent—and tell just what Crook wore, how he talked, how he looked, how the officers with him were dressed, where we were going— in fact, George would serve in the capacity of a newspaper and exaggerate as much as many of them do.

COLONEL DE LANCEY FLOYD-JONES

Governor Ballard was relieved as ex officio superintendent of Indian Affairs in Idaho Territory in August, 1869, by Colonel De Lancey Floyd-Jones. The decrease in the regular Army force and the disbandment or consolidation of regiments resulted in a large number of supernumeraries being given commissions. Under President Grant many officers were dropped from the lists by acts of Congress; others were retained with a year's pay and allowances. Many officers were assigned to the Indian Service, particularly to take over superintendencies previously held ex officio by territorial governors.

Colonel Floyd-Jones, an officer of the regular establishment, had seen much service and had rendered valuable aid to the nation during the Mexican and Civil wars. He was born in Queens County, New York, January 20, 1826, and was graduated from West Point in 1846. At Vera Cruz, Cerro Gordo, and the capture of the City of Mexico, he was present, and he was brevetted for gallant and meritorious conduct at Molino del Rey. From 1861 to 1865 he served as major of the 11th Infantry and was conspicuous at Manassas, Malvern Hill, Antietam, Chancellorsville, and Gettysburg; for gallant conduct during the peninsular campaign he was brevetted lieutenant colonel.

Colonel Floyd-Jones was a man of much culture and refinement. He was just a trifle too particular in early days, and much criticism was heaped upon him. One of the officers who had been at Fort Steilacoom with him in 1853 told me that the Colonel, then a lieutenant, was known as "the only man in the Northwest who changed his shirt every day." He was looked upon as "too blue-bloody," but in spite of the criticisms, which were caused by actions entirely proper and made conspicuous only because of the rough-and-ready life at Steilacoom, the Colonel was considered a very efficient officer.

For about a year he remained in Idaho; on December 31, 1870 he was assigned to the 3rd Infantry, although he had left us prior to that time. Colonel Floyd-Jones was a bachelor; he resided with Dr. Clinton Wagner while in Boise. Exact in methods and correct in every phase of life, he was popular with our people. I was under the impression that he was a Democrat; most of the regular Army officers, prior to 1861, were of that political complexion. When he arrived in Boise and formally talked with Governor Ballard, preparatory to assuming duties as Indian superintendent, I was present and heard the conversation.

"Governor," he said, "it will be necessary for us to start on an exact understanding. I will receipt to you for only those things which I see."

Ballard was abashed and colored in an instant. He construed that the Colonel did not trust him; that he had been "primed" by the frequent innuendoes which had been hurled against Ballard's character by his Democratic opponents. He felt that the Colonel was about to renew the accusations of the Democrats on the score of misappropriation by him, Ballard, of Indian moneys. But Floyd-Jones meant nothing of the kind; he was simply actuated by his military training, a quartermaster's principle which said, "See that a thing is there and then sign for it." Colonel Jones offered me the position of assistant to join him as Indian Affairs superintendent, but I was forced to decline, much to my regret.

Jones toured all the territory's reservations and minutely inspected them. He and the governor concluded official relations amicably, but personally Ballard felt a strong dislike toward him because he looked upon him as a Democrat. Ballard failed to understand how an Army officer could be a Democrat; he did not appreciate the fact that Colonel Jones was a different make of man from the Oregon and Idaho Democrats and that politics, at any rate, were not paramount with him.

One Sunday morning while Ballard and Jones were chatting in my office the Civil War was mentioned. Ballard became heated in a moment and said something to the effect that all Democrats were Rebels or Rebel sympathizers. Thereupon Colonel Jones mildly said, "Oh, surely, Governor Ballard, some Democrats were loyal during the war and some aided the Union cause."

Ballard snapped, "No, sir. I repeat what I said. All Democrats were and are Rebels." To make the sentence emphatic, he whipped out a huge jackknife and clicked open its blade. Upon my soul, I was alarmed; Ballard was rage personified. He no doubt awaited a "teaser" from Jones.

But the Colonel spoke calmly. "Well, perhaps they are in this latitude. Donaldson, what did you think of the sermon this morning at church?"

It was so gently done that Ballard was discomfited and offered his apologies. Poor Ballard was so badly worked up over the Democratic attacks against him that he was ready to "carve" someone. Not that I feared, however, a jackknife duel in my office.

In 1879 Colonel Jones retired from the Army, and in the eighties I saw him at times in the East. He was always the consistent, modest gentleman. Sometime in the eighties Colonel Jones toured Europe, and he afterwards published a readable little volume entitled *Letters from the Far East*. He was a wealthy man, a fact which rather stunted the growth of his inherent talents.*

DR. CLINTON WAGNER

One of the most able and charitable men who ever resided in Idaho was Dr. Clinton Wagner. He was the leading medical man in Boise and was certainly the equal, if not the superior, of any medical man in the entire North-

---

* Colonel Floyd-Jones died in New York City, in January, 1902.—T.B.D.

west. He was an accomplished surgeon and a thorough gentleman. Dr. Wagner was born in Baltimore in 1837, prepared for postgraduate work at St. James College, Maryland, and was graduated doctor of medicine from the University of Maryland. In 1860 he entered the Union Army as assistant surgeon and served in Texas during 1860 and 1861. Throughout the entire war he did most capable work in the Army's medical staff; he was conspicuous in hospital duty and established several branch hospitals. Dr. Wagner was medical director of the second division of the 5th Army Corps in the Army of the Potomac, and at Chancellorsville, Gettysburg, Mine Run, and other important engagements, his services were noticeable. In 1863 he was medical inspector of the 5th Corps and in 1864 he was brevetted major and lieutenant colonel; in 1866 he was promoted surgeon with the rank of major. After leaving Idaho, Dr. Wagner resided in New York City, where he achieved a reputation as specialist in nose and throat diseases.

No one in central Idaho was better known than he. He once told me that a fee of $2,500 in gold had been paid him for amputating the arm of a man injured in the "Marion More War," at Silver City, for possession of the Golden Chariot mine. The size of the fee, if nothing else, should have made the doctor well-known! While in the Army and at Fort Boise, Dr. Wagner cared for Bannack and Shoshoni Indians who were camped about Boise. In the summer of 1869 and 1870 Dr. Wagner occupied, with Colonel Floyd-Jones, the Slater residence in Boise. Many Indians were at that time living on the island below Boise, engaged in fishing. Although Wagner had resigned from the Army in 1869, the Indians remembered him as the post surgeon of former years and invariably sought him when they were ill. In the kindness of his heart, the doctor attended them free of charge and did all that he was able to relieve the misery of the red men. On many days of the week one could see eight or ten Indians lined up at daybreak along the irrigating ditch running west past Wagner's house. They were not in need of medical attendance but were calmly and silently waiting. After a time, Dr. Wagner's servant would appear and dispense food, and the noble red men would carry off their booty. The doctor explained to me that these were Indians whom he had treated and cured. They considered that a man who cured them was under obligations for the privilege allowed and must be interested in their welfare, and they and their relatives were free to ask his food or medical aid always afterward!

An old man on the island, a Shoshoni, was too ill to drag himself to see Dr. Wagner, so one evening Dr. Bishop, Dr. Wagner, and I started for the Indian encampment. The sick man was fearfully afflicted with rheumatism. Dr. Wagner left a pint bottle of aconite with an attendant and explicitly instructed him to rub the lotion upon the sufferer's legs. On the following day the sick man's attendant called at Wagner's and saw the doctor.

"How is Pete, the sick man?" queried Wagner.

"Oh, he happy!" grinned the Indian. "He much happy!"

"Ah," smiled Wagner, "I'm glad to hear it."

"Yep!" smiled the Indian. "He dead."

"What? Dead?" gasped the doctor.

"Dead, heap dead! All happy. He swallow all bottle." The invalid had gulped down a pint of aconite.

GENERAL P. E. CONNOR

The noted Indian fighter, General P. E. Connor, I knew quite well for many years, from 1872 until his death in Salt Lake City in 1895. At the time I first met him he was a man of fifty years, an Irishman straight in build and nervous in actions. He had kindly blue eyes and wore side whiskers which were ruddy in hue. Sometime in 1862 he went to Salt Lake City from Sacramento, California, where he worked at his trade, that of a house painter. Prior to the Civil War he was captain of a volunteer California troop called the "Saarsfield Guards." Promptly at the outbreak of the Civil War he enlisted and was commissioned a captain of volunteers. Upon his arrival at Salt Lake City he assumed command of a military district and located at Fort Douglas with his California men.

Connor was a fine type of volunteer soldier, brave and able, modest and determined. He frequently entertained me with chats about early Indian campaigns, and I was fortunate enough to hear from him his account of the famous battle of Bear River, Idaho, January 27, 1863. The fight really took place on Bear Creek, a tributary of Bear River, eleven miles from what is now Franklin, Idaho. The fight, according to statistics, is one of the severest ever recorded. Of the 267 Indians in the fight, fewer than 15 escaped. Of a total of 250 men General Connor's losses were: 15 killed, 53 wounded, and 75 fearfully frozen. Depredations had been so vicious, so many settlers on the Oregon Trail—from Omaha, through Cheyenne, Wyoming, across North Pass, along Green River, and to Hampton's, on Bear River, and then along the Snake to Oregon—had been killed by Indians that Connor determined to clean up the entire band of offenders. The culprits were not to to be classed with average Indians; they were a renegade, murdering band, primarily thieves, of Bannacks, Shoshonis, and Utes, who lived like typical wild men, hunting and fishing through the country. General Connor was soldier enough to bide his time; he wanted to strike when winter was severe, appreciating the fact that Indians can not fight when lack of grass prevents them from moving their pony herds. Small military detachments had pursued the offenders many times, but they had invariably been beaten. The settlers in the vicinity of Franklin—the town nearest the Indian camp—said that the Indians were becoming bolder and bolder because of their success against the soldiers. Many of the miscreants were free to come and go in the Mormon settlements; not being known directly as hostile, they were well able to act as spies, return to camp, and report all that was being done by the palefaces. In Bear Creek ravine they were snugly entrenched for the winter. That they did not fear attack was well proved by the result of the fight; women and children were encamped with the bucks. Indians invariably place the squaws and papooses some distance from the fighting ground, or from the place where an attack is expected. Bear Hunter, Sag Witch, and Sand Pitch were three of the rabid leaders of the redskins.

The first month of 1863 opened fearfully cold and severe. Ice was everywhere; in fact, the marching possibilities were so bad that when the Indians were told that Connor's men were going to attack, they laughed and said, "No! Too cold for soldiers."

Camp Douglas was two hundred miles from the Indian stronghold; food, ammunition, and other supplies had to be transported all that distance. On the twentieth of January General Connor started the expedition; his vidette, or advance, consisted of forty men of Company K, California volunteers, under Captain Samuel N. Hoyt, with two light howitzers. On the sixth day after leaving Camp Douglas, Captain Hoyt leisurely entered Franklin, having invited inspection by his approach. Franklin was then but a settlement, protected by a quadrangular stockade with gates at the angles. As a singular fact, when Hoyt's vidette entered Franklin, Bear Hunter, one of the renegades, rode out of the north gate as Hoyt entered the south. When a settler called to Bear Hunter that Hoyt's men were after his tribe and would "clean 'em up," the Indian insolently answered, "Maybe so!" and rode to his people, secretly laughing up his sleeve at the small force under Hoyt.

Hoyt went into camp as if prepared to remain a week,

but secret orders were given his men to be prepared to move at daybreak. The entire affair was, from Fort Douglas to the final engagement, planned and executed with wonderful secrecy. Just at midnight of the day of Hoyt's coming to Franklin, General Connor pulled in with the 2nd California, under Major McGarry. All told, Connor's force numbered nearly two hundred and fifty men, comprised of companies A, H, K, and M, cavalry, and Hoyt's videttes, company K, of the infantry. The cavalry, with Connor and McGarry, did not leave Douglas until two days after the advance; their march was forced through snow and ice, and the troopers and animals arrived at Franklin in bad condition. It is worthy of mention, here that infantry far outclass cavalry when forced marches or long campaigns are waged. The escape of Indians from reservations is almost always on horseback, but their ability to elude pursuers is due to the fact that they have several changes of ponies; in rough ground and hard service, one infantryman is worth two horsemen.

Connor allowed his men a brief breathing spell at Franklin, and then, with the greatest stealth, the troopers and infantry turned north about one o'clock in the morning. Several Franklin settlers, familiar with the ground, acted as guides. Bear Hunter's people expected a fight; the headman had reported to his people that forty men were coming sometime soon to fight. Joy was widespread through the Indian camp. Forty men? Ah, that meant an easy victory, forty scalps, all the wagon stores, mules, and guns. Hoyt's men marched in advance to break a footing in the snow for the cavalry horses. A little before daybreak the cavalry forged ahead and drew up on the banks of Bear Creek. They were at once seen, and the ravine echoed with war whoops.

McGarry's men plunged into the stream, filled as it was with floating ice, and, benumbed and suffering, drew out on the other shore. Before the command had entirely crossed, the companies of Lieutenant Chase and Captain Price were in the fight. General Connor, still at the south bank and out of the fight, was awaiting the arrival of Hoyt's detachment, but when firing commenced the doughty Irishman forded, leaving word that Hoyt was to ford as soon as he arrived. The fight was on in earnest; Bear Hunter's people had already dropped a few of the cavalrymen. McGarry swung his men to the north, Connor deployed his men to the east, protecting themselves from murderous shots and seeking a point of vantage. With a whoop and cheer, Hoyt's men reached the south bank and quickly forded on the cavalry horses awaiting them. The plucky soldiers, many of them already badly frozen, spread to the west of the ravine, opening fire as they ran. The red men, just as Connor planned, were caught in a trap. Down into the cozy little ravine, wherein the tribesmen had built their wickiups and windbreaks, deadly flames spat from the north, east, and west; at the south the creek stopped any who tried to escape and gave the soldiers time to drop them at long range. In just four hours' time, the rout was complete; the entire tribe, with the exception of fifteen, was wiped out of existence! The tribesmen of the Northwest were taught a lesson which they never forgot, and General Connor removed a most serious obstacle in the way of emigration to Oregon. The general won the admiration of every man under him; throughout the long four hours he was constantly exposed, oftentimes far more so than his men.

The 143 of his command killed, wounded, or frozen were brought back in wagons to Franklin. Many were cared for in the settlers' homes, others in the Franklin schoolhouse, and when transportation was secured, all of them were carried to Salt Lake City. The sufferings of the men and officers were terrible; barely a man came out of the fight without being permanently disabled. Those who were not hit by bullets lost feet and arms by freezing.

An incident of the fight is worthy of special mention. Sag Witch, one of the headmen, was shot through both legs. The intense cold, hovering below zero, congealed the blood and prevented him from bleeding to death. Under fire from the soldiers, Sag Witch dragged himself down to Bear Creek, jumped into the water, and swam for an eighth of a mile almost entirely submerged. Then he dragged his frozen body ashore and traveled by crawling and sliding, twenty miles across the snow to a friendly lodge, that of Chief Pocatello. Sag Witch remained on the Fort Hall Reservation until the day of his death, a badly crippled and deeply dejected red man.

RED-HAIRED INDIANS

The only red-haired Indians I ever saw were two of the Idaho Nez Perces. I have neither seen red hair in any other tribes nor have I heard of any. Certainly, the two Nez Perces were uncommon sights.

In this connection a comical bit of scandal has arisen. The Lewis and Clark expedition was intimately associated with the Nez Perces in 1805; indeed, the two explorers and their associates were warmly welcomed by almost all the Northwest tribesmen with whom they came in contact. The red men were lavish in their attentions, and temporary loans of Indian maidens to the explorers were made. If the Gass narrative of the Lewis and Clark expedition be true, some of the bold, bad explorers took prompt advantage of the Indian courtesy and accepted several Indian maidens to their bosom. Captain William Clark had red hair! He was known to the Indians as "Redhead," and St. Louis, where Clark resided from 1807 until his death, was known to the Nez Perces as "Redhead's Village."

One day in 1879 I was at the Ponca Indian Reservation, Indian Territory, with U. S. Indian Inspector General John McNeil. Here were Chief Joseph and his band, who had been transported from Idaho, contrary to the terms upon which Joseph surrendered to General Miles in 1877. General McNeil called my attention to a tall old Nez Perce, weather-beaten and worn, with a fine crop of bright red hair.

"See that fellow, Tom?" said McNeil to me. "He is named Clark. Named after William Clark, so they tell me. At any rate, Clark had red hair and two of the Nez Perces have red hair. They are the only red-haired Indians I ever saw."

SPOTTED TAIL'S REPLY

Although this is not on the subject of Idaho Indians, nevertheless an incident occurs to me because it was told me by General McNeil. In 1887 he was at my home in Philadelphia, and we chanced to mention Spotted Tail, the able Sioux chief who had that year passed over the Great Divide. General McNeil vouched for the truth of an amusing reminiscence which showed Spotted Tail's view of Christianity.

The Rev. Alfred Riggs, of the Episcopal Church, was missionary agent among the Sioux at the Rosebud Agency. Riggs spoke Siouan languages; he was ambitious and with an eye to a bishopric, endeavored to convert Spotted Tail to the true faith. Riggs was worldly enough to know that a well-fed Indian offers a far better chance for conversion than an Indian unfed. Through old Spot's stomach, the churchman waged a campaign. Spot was invited to the Riggs's home, and solid food was placed before him in large quantities. The wily Indian was quite well aware that Mr. Riggs had an ax to grind, but he did not anticipate; he was quite polite and very careful to put edibles where they belonged. Mr. Riggs had opportunity to become closely acquainted with the proportions of an Indian's appetite, and in a month's time he became alarmed! Old Spot's conversation was mostly about the big game in Canada and the heavy snows of recent date.

Old Spot wandered to Riggs's one day at mealtime and was ushered in. There was no odor of cooking in the air, and the chief began to feel the approach of a crisis. In fact, old Spot was clever enough to know that his meals in that house were things of the past—and he silently mourned like a true red man whose innards are about to be denied their portion. Riggs's manner confirmed Spot's suspicions. The reverend began impressively:

"Spotted Tail, I have known you long. I have fed you and treated you as my brother. I know that you are a great chief, a wise man. I know that you believe in a hereafter, that you have great say with your people. I have not yet talked to you about the white man's God but I want to do so now. Our church is no stranger to you; you must already know something about us and our God."

The chief sat calmly listening.

"I am prepared to discuss our faith fully with you. Now, I want to know what you think of our religion. I want you sometime soon to join our church, accept our God, and then all your braves and women and children will do so."

Spot saw that the time had come for a definite answer and he gave it.

"Look here!" said he. "The religion you want to teach me, the points of it, the creed, are not new. I heard them all from the Black Gowns [Jesuits] many years ago. Now, my people have a good God and we feel proud of him. We are not such a scurvy set as you white men! By your own story, when your God sent his only son to you as a mark of his love and confidence, what did your people do? You took him out and nailed him on a cross, put iron through his body. Would one of my people, or any Indian, be that mean? Not much! If our God sent his only son to us, if he sent any of his people, we would be very proud and happy. What would we do, nail him to a cross? Not much! We would make a fine tepee for him, shoot a fat deer for him every day, give him our finest ponies, and give him our prettiest young woman for a squaw. Mr. Riggs, I guess I'll stick to my religion. I'm an Indian but my religion won't kill the son of its God!"

AN INDIAN COUNCIL AT BOISE

One of the very last volunteer Indian councils held with Idaho Indians by the governor, or acting governor, in his ex officio capacity of superintendent of Indian Affairs, was held in June, 1870 (Colonel Floyd-Jones had left the territory at this time) in front of the "Stone Jug," the governor's office, on Main Street in Boise. The council was an impromptu affair brought on by Jim Collins' Shoshonis, who, in their wanderings about the southern part of the territory, had aroused the fears of the settlers.

The barrenness of many sections of southern Idaho did not make the country generally attractive to Indians, for game and fish were scarce. Salmon were not found higher than the junction of the Malad with the Snake; the red men, if they wanted fish, were forced to go westward to King Hill or the mouth of the Malad. Crickets, grasshoppers, rabbits, and a few elk and antelope made up a scanty diet, but neither game nor grass was abundant, and living was poor. When in 1868 the southern Idaho Indians were placed on the various reservations, they were much disgruntled. They did not want to be confined by land lines, nor did they choose to ask permission from an agent every time they wanted to travel to the game country. The Indian agencies, then as now, were places of deposit for men who had worn out their usefulness and who, in the main, were political wrecks, decayed politicians of the East, or selfish beasts who sniffed a chance to obtain returns far above their salaries by a clever manipulation of agency funds. The majority of the Indian agents prior to 1870 were the cause of intense dissatisfaction; some of them were even contributing factors in our Indian outbreaks. When the red man, confined to his land limit and dealt with unfairly by his agent, wanted to go hunting or fishing he was only asking for that which had always been his to do. And, moreover, if the Indians were denied the privilege of absenting themselves from the reservation, they naturally wanted to know why white hunters were allowed to roam at will. Hundreds of sportsmen from the East annually visited the Northwest game ranges, on ground forbidden to the Indians, and killed for the fun of killing, not for food. The Government wards had to be content with agency shoes and trousers and agency pork and beef when they were only too willing to kill wild game for food and make their own clothes from the skin. In 1869 and 1870 many small bands of Fort Hall Indians quietly left the reservation, some with permits and some without, and in their hunting expeditions molested neither white men nor their crops.

A large party of Bannacks and Shoshonis came into Boise Valley in June of 1870. Most of them pitched their tepees at Middleton, twenty miles from Boise. A few of the band camped on the island below Boise, others camped near the hot springs, and a few were in the gulch near the Boise penitentiary. They brought with them pelts which they exchanged for sugar and flour. Our people became very uneasy because of the presence of so many Indians, and the result was that Secretary E. J. Curtis, then acting governor, summoned the headmen and chiefs for a council.

The headman of the Shoshonis was Jim Collins, the man who later dubbed Clitus Barbour "boy" when Clitus acted as our ambassador. Jim Collins was an Indian of six feet in height and weighed more than two hundred pounds. He spoke English well, was shrewd, and was Indian all over; females, white or red, he thoroughly despised. Jim came to my home one day and, although my wife had prepared the dinner to which I had invited him, he refused to sit at the table with her. Jim didn't eat with me that day; he ate alone in the kitchen! My wife served him, and Jim grunted with satisfaction when the food tickled his palate. Stewed tomatoes he dumped into his tea and when I grinned, Collins grinned and said, "Same thing when it's down." I recall that the tablecloth was a flaring red, an ordinary kitchen cloth. The brilliancy of it caught Collins' eye. He wanted half of it for a saddle blanket. To explain his meaning, he whipped out a huge knife and sliced at the cloth in the line which he wanted cut. Mrs. Donaldson involuntarily grabbed her hair and adjourned to a neighbor's house. Collins laughed and seemed to understand the reason for her panic. The Indian was very, very shrewd; he was popular among his own people, for they knew that as a diplomat he was about the best man among them. Collins' faculties of observation, not only in woodcraft but in judging men and conditions, were particularly keen. Felix Brunot, chairman of the Indian Peace Commission, visited Fort Hall in 1869 to investigate charges which had been made against the Fort Hall agent by the Indians there. Collins was there and heard all that took place before the commission. Said he to me, two years later:

"Heap strange that when Brunot come to Fort Hall and take an Injun to Washington to tell heap trouble, the agent he pick out Injun who can not speak 'Merican. The interpreter he go along but interpreter he friend of agent. When Injun tell his troubles, interpreter don't say what Injun say but what this agent ask him to say. White man at Washington no finds what red man wants. He finds out what agent wants." Which was quite well sized up, I thought!

To return to the Indian council. Collins was the first to arrive at the the governor's office. He galloped up on his cayuse pony from the direction of the fort; I ascertained afterward that he had gone to interview Captain George M. Downey, of the post, in order to assure the latter that the Indians were at Boise with no intention of harming anyone. Following Collins came Little Jim, another Shoshoni; then a Bannack chief, and two headmen. There were ten Indians in all, standing beside their horses, holding to bridles, and ranged in a semicircle. Truly, they were a motley, ill-dressed gang! Collins wore a gray wool shirt, a pair of drab trousers, and a straw hat; a revolver and sheath knife hung from his belt. One of the Bannacks wore a tall beaver hat with the top cut out, the rim missing, and gores slit into the sides. That he was a mighty hunter was proved by the trophies about his neck; a bearskin necklace was made up of claws each practically the same size which meant that each pair of claws (perhaps each claw) represented a bear killed. About the Bannack's waist was a massive buffalo robe—and the thermometer stood at ninety degrees!

Mr. Curtis was surrounded by a group of Federal officials, of which group I chanced to be one. Curtis opened the council with a flowery speech; he was very clever in efforts of the kind. In a dignified way he demanded to know the reason for this incursion by red men and whether or not the visit was peaceful. What did they want? Why did the red men not stay at home on the Government reservation and refrain from annoying white women and children, who feared their wandering about Boise?

"You Indians," Curtis said, "are consumers; you are not producers. Some one has to care for you. You are wards of our Great Father at Washington and you must continue to reside where our wise Great Father places you. It may be that agency food and limits do not suit you, but that isn't the question—you must stay away from here. We want none of you."

After Curtis had finished, the interpreters sailed in,

and it took them many minutes to give the bucks (except Collins) an idea of what Curtis had said. It was curious to see the several branches of the same tribe could not understand the same dialect; the sign language was the interpreter's last resort. When one of the interpreters mentioned the possibility that the Army would be employed to keep the Indians on the reservation, Collins grinned audibly. One of the white men in the circle had been overindulging in a brand of liquid pyrotechnics known as "Jacob's Rest." The effect of the whisky was plainly apparent both in the official's attitude and in his breath! The Indians noticed it at once. A queer expression crossed their countenances—perhaps a wave of regret that samples of the same poison were not passed around; Collins was sponsor for his people.

"Governor," he began dramatically, "all my people come here for peace and pleasure. Collins was born in this valley, long and many snows, long 'fore white man he come here. In rocks by warm springs here, Collins bury his father and mother. I come here, I, Collins, all years to these graves. These braves all the same as me [indicating his companions]. They have ol' people, all buried same as Collins, and all sleep in this valley. We know we be Injuns but we have dead people and we like our dead people. So, we come each twelve moons [year]."

At this he jumped upon his horse, and his retinue followed suit. Once mounted, he raised his hat to Curtis and said, "Governor, I sorry that no white man like it. I say good-by. I go home now, Fort Hall. Next twelve moon, when grass he grows good, all come 'gain to see our dead. Not you, not Great Father, can stop us, not soldiers can!"

The little cavalcade formed into line, and then Collins turned and pointed his finger at the drunken white man. Said the chief, "Injun, he get whisky and drink um. He become big fool. White man [indicating his victim] he get whisky and he drink um. He worse as Injun. Injun only fool. White man, he damn fool!" With a thunder of hoofs and a cloud of dust the red men vanished.

INDIANS IN GENERAL

The origin of our Indians, those now within the United States, has been the subject of more speculation than the origin of any other race. Soon after the white people settled in America the origin of the North American Indian engrossed attention at home and abroad. Throughout many succeeding generations has the issue been fought. Early-day speculators had neither culture nor experience in fabrication to employ in their conclusions: now, advanced science and art are factors in creating and perpetuating monstrous fallacies in the white man's version of the red man's origin. More absolute rot in the guise of truth has been given, and is now given, to the world as Indian fable or tribal history than can ever be atoned for.

The United States Government has cordially assisted in disseminating ignorance and foolish invention, for the Government's many publications upon the North American Indian's origin and legends are eagerly grasped and too often swallowed. The fact that Government publications are free may have much to do with the popularity of its books. One branch of our Government, noted for the numerous publications annually distributed, is at present engaged in rethreshing old straw and publishing in a new guise that which is already well-known to the humblest investigator. Few as they are, facts concerning the aboriginal character of the North American Indian have been long since noted; invention now supplies a collection, not of facts, but of stuff! Honest investigators learn to their sorrow that the Indian abandons aboriginal habits and methods just as soon as he comes in contact with the white man. He is not educated, in the white man's sense. His people never carried, nor do they carry now, a coherent history of the tribe carved in stone or cut in bone or wood or molded in iron. The Indian has never shown, collectively, any evidence of progress, attainment, labor, or research. His relics which come to us are implements of the chase, or of war, or of most humble domestic furnishings. Not one thing indicates imagination, breadth, or development! His model was nature, the habit and method of animals. Indian art is only a utility, just above barbarism and close to real savagery.

Since our tribes have been well known, since the great West has been well opened, efforts have been made to varnish the North American Indian by giving him a mysterious past; to prove him to be the relic of a once-great prehistoric people who covered North America and ranked with ancient Babylonia in arts, sciences, and culture; who owned a history with a civilization creative, erective, and comprehensive. What has been the result? Seekers for notoriety, cranks, and designers upon the public treasury have written or compiled hundreds of treatises which are the vaporings of a fanciful brain. When the Indian first saw the white man a change for the worse began—for the Indian. He at once copied the white man's laborsaving devices and grabbed for castoff clothing. In but one thing has the Indian improved; he is, if it is possible to conceive of it, a more lavish and picturesque liar about his own origin than is the white man who attempts to write it.

The modern ethnologist who understands possibly three words of Indian dialect pursues investigations, interviews his red brother, and obtains in a short time the red man's tribal history for a thousand years past. But does he obtain it? There is no history of the North American Indian. What is known to us exists in books written by white men; they are white men's histories of that which did *not* happen. In the matter of research—historical or otherwise—one fact is worth a million fancies. The greatest fact about the North American Indian is that his history holds no fact worthy of record. The last statement is to me one of the truest and most pathetic things in the entire Indian problem. It is not astounding, this statement, when we reason from what we actually know of our Indians. The red man furthers no civilization of his own to vie with the white man! He not only fails to try to keep pace with his white brother, when it is quite plain that the white man is a creature whose habits and methods are come to stay, but he fails even to keep pace with the tail end of the white man's vast procession!

When the first ships came, bearing white faces and huge white wings of canvas, as if a monster bird were floating in from the sea, the Indian looked with awe and thought that a great deity was dropping from the clouds. The red man envied the strangers their visible chattel, their clothes, armor, guns, and swords, and made deep obeisance to their magic firewater. The white man sized up the red man's land possessions. The Indian owned no chattel; save for a few pelts, all he could claim was land. But land was what the strangers wanted! Firewater and a few trinkets, when force failed, purchased thousands of acres. Firewater made such a different man of the Indian!

And then came the aggression of the whites. Poor Lo soon found that he was deadwood in the load and could not dwell in peace with his white brother unless, like the lamb in the fable, he lay calmly at rest and disputed not for his own. The result? The Indian, under stress of differences with the white man on basic lines of varying modes of life, took to the "hoof," and when he failed to hoof it of his own accord, the boot of the white man urged him.

As a class, the North American Indians had no civilization, in the Anglo-Saxon sense of the word, when the foreigners first met him. Since the white man has taken hold of him, since the Government, through agents or otherwise, has seen fit to make a ward of him—in order to grab all his land—the Indian has had, relatively speaking, even less civilization than when he roamed untrammeled in the wilds of his virgin forest.

To prove my statement that there is no Indian history which has stability or coherence, uniformity or universality, consider the possibilities that lay open for history making by the very topography of our country, formerly occupied solely by our Indians. There were—unless in the very remote period of thousands of years past—no natural barriers from the Atlantic to the Pacific to tribal intercourse or confirmation of legends or mythologies. But has it been recorded in stone, iron, or wood that the wise men of the various tribes ever met in council to adopt a general religion or tradition? No such council, or even a suggestion of it, is on record. The very existence of countless tribal legends shows that a continuity is lacking and truth and fact have gone helter-skelter. The Indian, as we know him, hasn't stability enough to write his true history; he leaves it to the vain efforts of white men.

TRIBAL LIARS AS HISTORY MAKERS

Tribal liars are a necessity for the North American Indians as well as for other illiterate tribes who have not a written history. Indian women are not permitted to display in public their art of untruth; the old men, the bucks, are the soothsayers. The Indian has no books or newspapers. He conveys, when his valor may be recounted, the story of his battles and conquests by drawing pictures on a robe or tent canvas, or on a rock—if the manual labor isn't too much. He may paint a few arrows, dye feathers in a certain way, proclaiming them to be the survival of custom years and years old. His sign language, universally understood, is primarily for convenience; writing is hard work, and, communicating by gestures always saves breath.

The world of the ordinary tribe is an indefinite space filled with day and night and a search for food and water. After that, no mental labor; all the physical labor which savors of anything but recreation, the buck Indian relinquishes to his squaw. As a consequence, memory is the entertainer, the newspaper, and we know that memory is often the thing with which a person forgets!

About the campfires, in the wigwams, the Indian myth peddlers and makers of tradition squat and chat—provided that they are fed. Kelly, a squawman, once said to me: "They lie fer their mush!" The audience laugh and applaud the story as it is told time and time again. To illustrate: the Moqui-Pueblo Indians of New Mexico and Arizona, more isolated by customs and opinions than any Indians in this country, are rich in storymongers who, in the estufas, entertain men and boys by the week with invented traditions and romances of Pueblo people. The more ingenious and impossible the yarns told by a patriarch, the higher his social position. In fact, "banters" are sent out from pueblo to pueblo, challenging the prize liar of one place to compete with the prize liar of the other. The myths do not die with the originator; on the contrary, they are handed down for a generation or two, constantly changing their identity. The astounding part of all this is the credence accorded the nonsensical myths by our so-called experts and ethnologists who publish the stuff as they hear it and circulate it as history.

One of my special agents in the Indian census of 1890 was Julian Scott, the well-known artist. He laughingly recounted to me an incident which gives a splendid example of the origin of a Pueblo, or Moqui, fable. In the summer of 1893, two English brothers named Sykes had a bunch of cattle or sheep at Turkey Tanks, the water holes near Fort Wingate, Arizona. These water holes were often visited by the Moquis, who refreshed their stock while on trading trips. The Sykes brothers were well marked; they owned the reddest crops of hair in the entire territory. On a very warm afternoon the elder of the brothers stripped entirely naked for a plunge in the tanks, but before entering the water he stood for shelter from the sun behind a large rock which hid him from view. Just then four Moquis, with a string of burros loaded with pottery, drove down to water the animals. Sykes waited behind the rock. Some minutes went past, and then the Indians decided to take a smoke. Seeing no prospect of their departure, Sykes, in a moment of boyishness, jumped on the rock, gave a wild yell, and plunged into the water. Puffing and spurting, he came to the surface and was surprised to see Indians and burros galloping southward like mad. Pottery was distributed in large pieces for two miles. The Moquis reached Fort Wingate, fagged and frightened, and right then and there was told a marvelous story of the appearance of their water god. Oh, yes, had they not seen him? He had a red hat on, and he was snow white and naked! When they reached their people that same night, I warrant that a fable was planted which took root and grew to vast proportions in a night. There was, certainly, fine opportunity for the ancient yarn spinners, who vied with each other raking up all fables extant of gods of sea and land. I am awaiting a report of the Bureau of Ethnology, John Wesley Powell, director, that will give full and accurate account of the size, shape, and date of appearance of the water god of Turkey Tanks. It should be distributed very soon.

THE CREATION OF MYTHOLOGY

At the expense of my friend, Frank Hamilton Cushing, I offer the following incident. Mr. Cushing has achieved much renown for his explorations of modern Zuñi and for his general work among the Pueblos, a peaceable people who have been conderably exploited in recent years by railroad guidebooks and New Mexico merchants who have reaped quite a harvest selling Moqui, or Pueblo, pottery and baskets.

In September, 1879, I was at Tesuque, a pueblo nine miles from Santa Fe, New Mexico, chatting with the pueblo's governor. A sudden disturbance on the housetops of the adobe village, a signal that a stranger was coming, caused the governor to glance down the Santa Fe Trail and exclaim, "My, my, what is that coming?" In the distance I saw a man on horseback. The housetops were now very much alive; even the lazy dogs were alert. When the newcomer rode in, Brown, of our party, said, "That's Frank Cushing. James Stevenson, executive officer of Powell's survey, is at Santa Fe, and Cushing is with him making collections. This is his first visit to the pueblo, but I guess they are on to him!"

Cushing rode in, and we were introduced. He was then a man of about twenty-four years, homely in appearance, particularly marked by a large sunburned nose. A glaring red shirt, blue trousers, white neckerchief, a white horse, surmounted by a blanket roll as glaring as his shirt, all served to make him a rather conspicuous figure. The governor and his constituents were very much impressed by his appearance; the color scheme completely paralyzed them with its giddiness. With much dignity, Mr. Cushing announced that he was in the service of the United States, was studying the Indians, and wanted to remain at Tesuque. At this, the Indians looked toward his pockets, endeavoring to locate money. The governor politely told him that he was welcome and that there would be a room at his disposal. At once the governor called me aside and queried whether or not Mr. Cushing had money to liquidate, asking if the "outfit" (blankets, etc.,), belonged entirely to Mr. Cushing. He stated—very wise governor was he—that previous visitors had come to the pueblo since the railroad's completion, announced themselves just as Mr. Cushing had, and after accepting the pueblo's hospitality had departed unceremoniously—taking with them, by mere oversight, a burro. "In fact," said the governor solemnly, "we have to be very, very careful of white visitors!" Being apprehensive that Mr. Cushing might be despoiled of his outfit and cast adrift to hoof it for Santa Fe, I cautioned the governor that any violence done Mr. Cushing would call down the Government's wrath. The governor wasn't awed; to the contrary, he seemed deeply interested in Mr. Cushing's financial status! To this I replied that Mr. Cushing was a history hunter, that he wanted tales of the Pueblo people, and that he would pay for them—pay well.

The governor's eyes sparkled and he said, "Heigh ho! He wants our history? We haven't any that I know about except that which is remembered by our oldest man. But if I find Pedro Sanchez, he can give Mr. Cushing all the history he wants."

We had with us a smart Indian named Kentuck, who had worked with the railroad squad. The governor called Kentuck to him, whispered a few words in his ear, which caused Kentuck to grin knowingly. Then Kentuck winked at me.

"He's another one of them history fellers, is he?" he said. "Wants to know where we come from, eh? All about Montezuma an' his gang, I suppose? Why, say, Mr. Donaldson, all our pueblos have old men who tell the story of our people to the young men in the estufas. But nothing is wrote down. Our old men say as they heard these things, when they were boys, from old men. Our old men is not writers—none of us write down—an' what they not remember, they make up an' talk, talk. You want history from our old men, you get him started on one line an' pay him an' pay him more, an' our old men talk all night! Mr. Cushing must know what he want. Tell him to tell Pedro what he want—an' Pedro will push right along. Sanchez —that ain't he right name—was born people say way down on the Pecos River, hundred years ago. Others say he born hundred an' ten years in a cave. No tales 'like! Our people sit an' listen, an' Pedro blow hisself all night—all our people got to do at night is to is to sit an' listen. Pedro, he want money; he will talk, talk if Chief Cushing pay him!"

The governor sent for Pedro, and he ambled forward, very ancient, all rags and hair, a few sores, and doubtless much vermin. I passed him a half dollar—by way of political introduction—and Pedro grinned and at once squatted, nodding as much as to say, "Here I am! Pump away! I'm your man, ancient or modern yarns! History by the hour." His English was limited to about ten words; nine of them were profanity, the other was "money." He of course spoke through an interpreter, although a man knowing Spanish could do fairly well in all the Moqui country.

The governor introduced Pedro to Mr. Cushing, and as I was due at Santa Fe within two hours I said good-by. Pedro had been, needless to state, "primed" by the governor concerning Mr. Cushing's wants. The governor followed me and said that he would charge Cushing one hundred dollars a day for his room. Seeing that, Indian-like, he couldn't deal in real values—one hundred and one were almost alike in his mind—I ventured to suggest one dollar a day, and the governor acquiesced. I looked back when well down the trail and saw Cushing and Pedro busily chatting.

The above is an instance of what I mean by the fallacy of Indian mythology or history. Mr. Cushing certainly did not speak the Moqui tongue at that time; I doubt if he was conversant with Spanish. He talked through an interpreter who could do shortcutting in repeating the ancient Pedro's statements. Worst of all, Pedro was an out-and-out liar, a Baron Munchausen of the pueblo. Even had he, Pedro, been accurate in retailing what was told him by his father, his father might have been just as big a liar as the son. How in the name of common sense could

Cushing or any other man as weakly equipped obtain facts, vital truths, by talking secondhand through an Indian who didn't speak English and who talked legends in proportion to the pay!

There has just reached me a volume called *Lo-To-Kah*, by Verner L. Reed (1897), which contains a collection of Indian legends which are a fair example of an Indian's ramblings when duly fed and led. The stories are impossible. The proper names given to the towns in Mr. Reed's fables are the Spanish or American names and are not, as a rule, known to the Indians of the country he describes. The illustrations add to the unconscious humor of the book.

The George Catlin Indian Gallery, a work which I compiled for the National Museum, containing the life of Catlin and reproductions of paintings made by him during his early tours among our Indians, includes (Plate 49), a portrait of Naw-Kaw, a Winnebago chief. Mr. Reed, or his publisher, has taken the same portrait and described it as that of an Apache! The Winnebagos and Apaches are as different in customs and equipment as are Chinese and Japanese! His Indians have, in the illustrations, superb muscles, wonderfully developed. I confess that I've yet to see an Indian with muscles of prodigious size. The red men are supple and wiry; they do but little manual labor—if they can avoid it; all they have is an inherent strength of sinews. The legs of plains Indians are usually undeveloped in the calf and are bowed from gripping horses. Of course, Apaches, being mountain climbers, are better developed in the legs. Some of the reviews of Reed's book state that the stories are Ute legends. They are not; the author has simply repeated some imaginings told him. He would hardly claim that they were distinctly Ute legends.

Whether or not I'll be forgiven for this I do not know, but my good friend Otis T. Mason, of the National Museum, has been imposed upon and has made, as a result, a curious technical error. In his book *Woman's Share in Primitive Culture* (1896), he faces page 207 with a photograph of a Pueblo girl entitled, "Fig. 51. A Maiden in Savagery. This maiden in savagery was posed for her photograph and "fixed up" before posing. The probabilities are that one half of the articles on her body were borrowed for the occasion. With an adobe wall and pine pole to lean against, she is of course picturesque. The two water jars at her feet bear evidence of non-Indian origin; the decorations thereon are of European and Spanish origin. The silver necklace about her neck was made by Navaho Indians from either American or Mexican silver currency. The patterned blanket about her neck isn't Pueblo; it is Navaho, made from wool clipped from the Navaho sheep (their herds are remarkable in size) and shipped to Roxborough, near Philadelphia, dyed, and returned for weaving. Her leggings, made of cowskin and wrapped with hide strips ending in moccasins, are imitations of the Spanish boot. In fact, almost all her adornment shows European design, copy, or work. The cotton shirt under her blanket is probably a purchase made from a trader. She is a nominal Catholic, prays, lives in a covered house, eats cooked food, and makes and sells pottery for a good fat sum. And yet she is called "A Maiden in Savagery"!

INDIANS HAVE NO FAMILY NAME

Indians have no family name. When pupils of either sex are taken into schools—Government schools, or those conducted by private endowment—they are usually named by the person in charge. It will be found that the pupils, upon arriving, have names of the most indefinite kind— "Lazy Bear," or "Dog on the Floor," or something similar. Like horses and mules they come into the world minus a name, and their parents have no family title to confer upon them. The statement that the Indian lacks a history is made all the more emphatic when we know that experts have failed in the attempt to trace family connections. One Indian may have several names, and the white man, in search, fails to obtain his proper one. In my work of taking the census of Indians in 1890 almost every attempt made by my agents to trace Indian names and relationship in the tribes was a failure. One of the best of my special agents was James A. Cooper, in charge of the Tongue Agency, in Montana. He wrote to me on August 30, 1890, and forwarded a letter, reprinted below, which is an admirable summary of the situation, particularly as it comes from a man thoroughly qualified to assert his opinion. Said Cooper:

> I have the honor to transmit to you general schedule of Indians of this reservation and beg to state that it is filled out as correctly as can be done in accordance with the best information obtainable. I hope that the same will be satisfactory to the Department, as I understand the Indians' names, of this tribe, have never been procured before this. If they have, this office has no record of it, and I can assure you that it has proved a very tedious undertaking. I take the liberty to enclose herewith a letter received from the Reverend A. Vander Velden, a Catholic priest, in charge of the St. Labres Indian Mission School, located on Tongue River, about twenty-five miles from this agency. The contents of the same will give you his experience in trying to obtain certain information relative to this tribe of Indians [Northern Cheyennes].

Father Vander Velden's letter is:

St Labres Mission,
Ashland, Montana.
July 16, 1890

James A. Cooper, Esq.,
    Special U. S. Indian Agent

Dear Sir:

> In answer to your question in regard to the tracing of the relationship of these Indians [Northern Cheyennes], I tell you that it is an impossibility. I am now with this tribe five years and have several times tried to make out a correct list of separate families and with the same result every time; namely, a failure! I will give you the reasons

why it is so. A child adopted by a family, although a perfect stranger, will, from the moment of adoption, be their own child and if the Indian who adopts the child has two or three wives, each wife will call herself the mother of that child. The sisters of each of these squaws call themselves, in many cases, the mother of the child. An aunt calls herself the mother of her nieces and nephews. A man has two wives, each one is the mother of all his children. If he marries a woman who has already several children he is considered the father of these children. Again, parents will give a child to a near relative. Those to whom the child is given are from that time the father and mother of the child. Some squaws, who are thrown off by their husbands, will take another; be thrown off again, take another, and so on until some make three and four changes, having borne children to each husband. In this case if you try to trace relationship you will find yourself in a labyrinth from which you will be heartily glad to escape. Again, others will be married to Indians of other tribes and will refuse to give the names of their husbands. Others have borne children without there being any marriage, even according to Indian law. They will not tell that to a stranger! So it goes. There are many reasons why the task is a hopeless one. A person will try it to-day and congratulate himself upon his wonderful success. He will go over the same ground eight days afterward and he will be surprised to find many things changed. So, one cannot rely too much upon his work. I speak from bitter experience.

THE OTHER SIDE

The Indian's side of the Indian problem will never be overargued; the Indian has too few friends. But there must be, there is, a plea for our red man. Some years before the death of Sitting Bull, the wily Sioux headman, he said to the commandant of Fort Buford: "The Indian that says he likes a white man is a liar, and the white man who thinks an Indian likes him is a fool." To General Nelson A. Miles, Sitting Bull also said: "God Almighty made me an Indian, and he did not make me an agency Indian, and I do not intend to be one." There is the situation in a nutshell!

The Indian question is now one of common right and common justice, and the equity of the case lies beneath a load of useless treaties, laws, and obsolete customs. When Sitting Bull said that God Almighty had made him an Indian, it was not the statement of a truism; it meant rather, that his ancestors were the original holders of this country, and he, the descendant, and his people, saw no right or justice in the aggressive policy of the white man. For that white man's policy was not only a policy of "grab all" but its worst result was a strenuous attempt to mold the red man to the white's mode of living and thinking. Despite what I have said regarding an Indian's shiftlessness and lack of initiative, it must not be assumed that I have failed to appreciate the red man's good qualities. In the first place, the white man confronted a most formidable opponent in the American Indian. He met a wild man, it is true, but he met a most peculiar wild man, one endowed with inherent intelligence capable of being educated, although not in a day. He met a red man who extended the hand of welcome—until it was singed—but who showed not the slightest inclination to adopt the white man's mode of life, even if he did avail himself of white man's clothing. In fact, the North American Indian has always held an inborn contempt for his white opponent; that is, for his civilization, not for his military prowess. We know that the white man taught the Indian how to use firearms; we are fairly certain that he introduced him to whisky; it is a safe thing to say that he taught the Indian how to lie! When the Indian first began to realize that the white man's treaty was a one-sided affair, that promises made in 1750 would possibly be broken in 1760, he absorbed the new method. Casting aside war clubs, he prepared himself for "diplomatic digressions." But there is not a case on record where an Indian was first to violate the obligations of a treaty: it has ever been the white man who first overstepped the boundaries.

While it is sorrowfully true that the intelligence of the vast majority of red men has ever fallen within and not beyond the limits exhibited by the earliest of his ancestors, yet the advent of the whites has somewhat stimulated his weakest point—his reasoning powers. Secretly scorning the white man's religion, openly he saw that the pretense of accepting the teachings of the paleface would avail him much in worldly goods. His inner man could be fed, his outer man clad—very foolishly was he often clad in beaver hat, old military clothing, and hideous-colored castoffs—if he would but profess much interest in the white man's teachings. Uneducated as he has always been, a rover depending upon the land for food, not in its yield through tilling of the soil, but in its yield of game, fish, wild fruits, and cereals, he has ever shown an inborn trait of ferocity and cruelty. Suffering appeals to him; it appeals more to the Indian woman, the squaw, for she it is who has covered the field after battle and mutilated the dead opponents. Cruelty and egotism go together and the Indian has both. The study of mob destruction, the study of criminals, shows that the uneducated, those whose minds have never been subjected to routine or discipline, are ever the first to fly off at a tangent and turn vicious under small excitement. The United States Army officers have appreciated this in the Indian outbreaks; when Mr. Indian goes on the warpath and tastes blood, the one way to quell him is to kill him! And the Army has very wisely wiped out bucks, squaws, and boys together. *

With the egotism of the red man stalks pride. It hovers about him, an invisible but ever-present wall in his intercourse with the whites. It is reflected in the dignified ceremonials of the ancient council chamber, and it will stick to him until the Indian language is forgotten and the customs and deeds of his ancestors have fallen into oblivion.

By the census of 1890 we have a total of 248,000 In-

---

* For fear of being misunderstood here, I wish to state emphatically that the very best friend—perhaps the only friend—our Indian has had, has been the Army, the force paid to keep him subjected. I feel quite sure that had the recommendations of our officers been followed by the Indian Service, there would have been fewer millions spent, thousands of lives saved, and more peace on the frontier.

dians within the United States; of these approximately 134,000 spread throughout twenty states and territories, are untaxed. The estimated cost of each Indian to the Government is $28 annually; the cost of each soldier, $1,000 annually. So, under our recent policy we have hired a man at $1,000 to watch a $28 man! Until 1869 the Indian Service of our Government was the worst of any of the Government's branches. To say that it was weak would not be sufficient; it was almost criminal in its weakness. Mainly through the influence of brainy and sincere churchmen, the national executives were prevailed upon to effect a better system; a system which, although far from satisfactory now, has at least proved superior to the various plans projected since the time when our Government entered upon its first Indian policy—that of treating with the red men as distant nations. Our present-day system is an educational and allotment policy, with emphasis upon the educational training of the red men. In other words, the purpose is to educate the Indian youths and maidens by schools directly upon reservations assisted by industrial schools like those at Carlisle, Pennsylvania, Genoa, Nebraska, and the school near Salem, Oregon.

The allotment principle is very old in its origin. Governor Cadillac, at Detroit, put it into effect as early as 1710, and his sensible plan has been rigorously adhered to at the present day throughout Canada, in the Dominion's Indian policy. And I must say that the Canadian system is so far ahead of America's that comparisons fall flat. In the first place, Canada set aside for her red men land of fertility and land pleasing to the future occupants. The United States has dumped the red man wherever it chose and in most cases upon a tract offering no chance for agriculture unless irrigation was to be employed. Irrigation ditch construction and maintenance is very costly. The Rosebud and Pine Ridge Sioux agencies would not even attract a hungry crow to their borders. Added to the obstacle of unfertility of the soil, the ration system has worked, as usual, its bad result. Frequently, the red men drive a hundred miles, at times more than that, to obtain their pittance. It frequently happens that the tribesmen exhaust their food supply on the way to and from the agency. It is unfair for our Indian Bureau to expect its wards to care for themselves, to learn farming and home building, when the natural surroundings would thoroughly dishearten a white man of enlightened views. Take the Sioux, or the San Carlos Apaches, or any tribesmen as badly situated, place them in a country like that occupied by the eastern Cherokees, in North Carolina, or the Sioux Nations, of New York, or the Cherokee strip of Indian Territory, give them instruction in farming and building, and refrain from meddling with them—and the hopelessness of the situation would disappear like fog before a bright sun.

The greatest weakness of our Indian policy may be characterized by saying that the reservation Indian of today is a corralled ox! The Government has crushed from him all semblance of independence. He sits and broods and expects to be fed. He is told that the land is his, but knowing what he knows of the fickleness of the Great White Father's mind, he probably awaits another despoilment. It would be an easy matter—it has been an easy matter—for a white man to absorb Indian methods of life, but it is a very difficult matter for an Indian to absorb a white man's mode of life. Yet patience, kindness, honesty, and instruction have evolved tangible results with the red men; they are not entirely unable to work, nor entirely unwilling. The ordinary reservation Indian does not, however, see his share to come from exertions. Here again lies the crime of ration issue. If, instead of dealing out food and clothes to the tribesmen on the reservations, the Government were to give cash, a money equivalent, I am sure that the benefit to be derived would be inestimable. After all, our red man is like his white brother; he likes money for the advantages it may bring him, and the trading instincts are latent in him. Were he the possessor of money, a tender receivable both off and on the reservation, certain traits of independence would be revived, and the red man would be more like his white "boss."

The Canadian Indian policy has not only been constant; it has been effective and economical. Undoubtedly the salient principle has been that the Dominion government tolerated no violation of compact, and above all it treated its Indians as if they were men. The Canadian reservations are not for "corralled oxen" but for red men who try, under capable teachings, to eke out their own existence and who are not feathers in the winds of an erratic central administration. To rehearse the instances recorded in our annals involving unfair treatment to the red men by the white would require a very lengthy chapter; in fact, a very full volume which would go back centuries into the past and would not be fully finished even with today's chapter.

The red man is now, and will continue to be, the buffet for the American people. Fair-minded Western men, even those who have no liking for the Indian, are free to acknowledge that he has been far more sinned against than sinning. In the early days of the Indian Service, when agents were appointed solely through politics, the individual agents had plenty of opportunity—and many of them grasped the opportunity—to be dishonest. At the present time, through change in internal mechanism of the service, the Indian agent could not be dishonest without detection. The cry of "dishonest agent" in the present day is a cry born of ignorance. The fifty-odd agents officiating are, all in all, a capable set of men, interested in their wards and too often handicapped in their endeavors to serve with fidelity and discretion, by the distant administration at Washington. Our treaty commissioners, not our agents, have been the source of dissension. The President, under authority, appoints a commission of men, presumably God-fearing and respectable, to meet representatives of a tribe or tribes in dignified council. Too often have our commissions included shack-nasty politicians or crooked legal minds who solemnly ratified an agreement—which they had written—contained either a loophole of escape for the white man or a concealed proviso that Mr. Indian could be further relegated when the necessity arose in the future. The record of the work and results of our Indian commissions disprove the beautiful theory that a benevolent and special providence protects the poor and inefficient from the iron hand of the powerful. Providence seemed to have gone on a long vacation during the celebrated contest of America versus her own Indians! Through threat or misrepresentation—we had better not term it lying—our Government has subjected tribe after tribe to the acceptance of treaties, the obligations of which were never lived up to by our own people and the provisions of which were doubtless drawn up with a design no other than that of ultimate abrogation. Brainy and pious senators of our august Congress have sagely nodded and approved.

I have a brass button from the uniform of one of the mounted Indian police, that splendid body of men who have rendered our frontier army such valuable aid in recent years. The button was given me at Fort Hall in 1890 by a Bannack policeman. It has a motto, *"God Helps Those Who Help Themselves,"* evidently the motto of the organization. Sarcasm, yes, irony, seems to me to stand between the letters! It must be assumed that our administrations have had God with them; for they have helped themselves freely to that which belonged originally to the very Indians who have fought for Uncle Sam even against their own flesh and blood.

CHAPTER IX

A CHAPTER OF WESTERN MISCELLANY

IN MAY of 1870, I left Boise to stump through eastern Oregon on behalf of my friend, George H. Williams, who was desirous of returning to the National Senate. At La Grande, Oregon, I joined with a stumping party consisting of General Joel Palmer, Republican candidate for Oregon's governor, Major Joseph Magone, and George L. Wood, then governor of the state. The three were Republicans, but with them were Democratic gubernatorial candidate La Fayette Grover, and another Democrat, Judge Reed, of Portland. The representatives of the opposing parties debated jointly on their tour. Palmer, the embodiment of personal integrity and popularity, with a short, stubby figure and a genial face, was an indifferent speaker, so Governor Wood was his mouthpiece. Grover was also a poor speaker, so Judge Reed represented him.

I traveled six days with the party, six days that were delightful in every respect. Early in May, we were traveling through the snow line on the summit of the Blue Mountains. Much of the time we were forced to walk, for Crouder, the stage driver, made us "hoof it" on heavy grades to ease the horses.

As we reached the timber line with its growth of tamaracks, Palmer made conversation by contrasting the foliage of the Coast and Blue Mountain ranges. Our walks uphill did not please Grover; he was distinctly on his dignity and did not heed either Palmer's interesting chat or Crouder's comment on points along the line. Crouder would call to us from the stage, "See that scratch on the pine tree? Dutch John hung up [overturned his coach] there and busted things. Last week, the snow was deeper.

A CHAPTER OF WESTERN MISCELLANY   337

John left a lamp hanging on that tree." All of which made us feel sorry for Dutch John's passengers.

When the snow falls heavily on the mountains it is the custom for stage drivers to blaze trees at the snow's surface so that when thaw comes the extreme height of the winter's snow may be recorded. On the Rocky Bar trail to Atlanta, Idaho, in the Alturas Range, I have seen thirty-two feet blazed: that was in the winter of 1870. Snow rarely reaches that depth in the Blue Mountains because of the warm breath of the chinook winds.

About seven o'clock in the evening, we rattled up to the Meacham house. What memories the name Meacham awakens! This house was known as "Mountain Home" and had been built by A. B. and Harvey Meacham on the site of the Jason Lee encampment of 1838, the spot where Lee parted with his friends and traveled across eastern Oregon, through the Snake River Valley to the States. The Meachams, both enterprising men, opened up many miles of roads and trails across the mountains and considerably aided travelers and traffic. Much of Oregon's early history hovers about this Meacham house and the trails from it to the East. Marcus Whitman, Jason Lee, and all the early missionaries were there. So was Joe Meek. J. W. Stanley, the Indian painter, was there at the time of the Whitman Massacre. The leading men of early Oregon, many of them, passed with emigrant trains near the Meacham house en route from the East.

The house was a two-story, undressed log structure ornamented with a front porch. From our coach we saw a spacious reception room glowing with a huge wood fire. When we rattled up to the porch a tall, handsome man of thirty-five years, with red hair and whiskers, came down to greet us. He was accorded a hearty "Hello, Harve!" Except myself, all of the party knew him. He was Harvey Meacham, brother of A. B. Meacham, who as Indian Affairs superintendent, was so treacherously dealt with by

Captain Jack's red men. The Meachams were Indiana boys who crossed the plains to California in 1850 with their own ox train. They went to Oregon in 1863 and, after the discovery of the Florence, Idaho, mines, opened a toll road at Mountain Home. Their house was a trapper's paradise, for over the doors hung superb antlers, on the floors were pelts and rugs of all kinds, about the walls hung guns, pistols, knives, tomahawks, and arrows. There was everything in the Meacham house except whisky: the Meachams knew its dangers.

A short time after our arrival we were seated at the hospitable table of the Meachams, and the excellence of the food was no more pronounced than was our appetite. After dinner we adjourned to the big room, and before the massive fire resorted to pipes and cigars and conversation. General Palmer fairly overflowed with reminiscences; he told of early days on the Coast and of characteristics of the Army officers. Sheridan was Palmer's favorite officer. Palmer had been superintendent of Indian Affairs in Oregon for many years and he was conversant with the ins and outs of the state's history. Major Magone was also chatty and interesting, but Grover was chillingly dignified. He maintained strict silence; only at infrequent intervals did he vouchsafe a remark or essay a forced grin. I ventured into the conversation and soon found that Grover was a brother of Cuvier Grover, West Point, 1850, who served with distinction during the Civil War and particularly at Cedar Creek.

An apparently indifferent stranger, who had arrived on horseback a short time after we pulled into Meachams, reclined on a sack of corn near the fireplace, and during the long round of conversation by Palmer and Magone placidly smoked; he was apparently miles and miles away. About midnight, when the fun was crackling in rivalry to the fire, the stranger "begged pardon" and asked, "May I chip in a little wind?" Without waiting for an affirmative he "chipped," and for two hours I was entertained as I had never before been entertained. The stranger told the funniest string of stories men ever heard. Abraham Lincoln and Tom Corwin paled into insignificance; they were mere second-raters in comparison! Our sides ached, and our eyes ran tears; we yelled and shouted and cried "More," and finally ended with passing cigars to him and installing him in a buffalo-robed chair, as grand master of the lodge of liars, the Munchausen of the backwoods!

Funnier than all to us was Grover's dignified silence. Despite the stranger's flow of wit, Grover never cracked a smile. The stranger eyed him narrowly for an hour or more and suddenly shifted the conversation to the Democratic Party in Oregon. In all my days I've never heard the equal. The man knew every Democrat, leader or layman, everyone who had been in Oregon, passed through, or thought of staying there, and he tore planks out of the Democratic platform and ripped the party up the back until it hadn't a man left worthy of public gaze. Grover sat as if paralyzed and then, without a word to any of us, he quietly withdrew and went to bed. The rest of us retired about three in the morning, charmed and soothed by the stranger's conversation. Who he was, we never learned; when we came down for breakfast, he had departed. While we were at table, Mr. Grover cautiously peered into the room. We saw him and yelled, "Come in. Don't be alarmed! The oracle has departed!" And thereupon Grover laughed loud and immoderately—as if relieved. As a Republican, I regret to say that Mr. Grover defeated General Palmer in the June election for governor, 1870. He served until 1870 and was that year elected United States senator.

The next morning we started for Portland and journeyed down the western side of the Blue Mountains to the valley, crossing the Umatilla Indian Reservation. Scores of Indians were lying about in the grass watching their thousands of ponies for fear that some would be stolen by emigrants passing through their territory. Harvey Meacham followed us in a spring wagon and escorted us to Pendleton, where he bade us adieu. In retrospect, I see his manly figure and healthy, florid countenance. He was the embodiment of generosity and kindliness. In 1872 Harvey was killed near his own home by a falling tree. The Indian burial service accorded him was a most touching thing.

Meacham was the friend of every man, woman, or child, red or white, that he met. The Indians knew him as the "Man of the Glad Heart." When Harvey's death was made known, his brother received hundreds of letters of condolence. The tribute that affected him most was that paid by Smohalla, the Indian chief who dwelt with his Nez Perces across the Columbia from Wallula, the village on the site of old Fort Walla Walla.

Smohalla was a deformed Indian, a sorcerer, or religious fanatic, but withal a bright man, who had inculcated the mystic faith of the "Drummer Dreamers." His followers believed that a new messiah would come from out of the east and deliver the red men from the white man's devil— the church. Smohalla sent a delegation of his people on a three-hundred-mile tramp to Mountain Home. When they reached the place and called on Colonel A. B. Meacham, the spokesman said:

"We hear that Man of the Glad Heart is dead and that Man of the Strong Heart [A. B. Meacham] is grieving for him. So we come from the great Chief, Man of the Four Mountains [Smohalla] to comfort Man of the Strong Heart."

Then they entered the house and saw the evidences of great grief there. Continued the spokesman: "Your religion is not good or you would cease to grieve for your brother. His spirit is here; it cannot go away and be happy if you weep and make his children weep by being sad. Man of the Glad Heart fears no Great Spirit."

The delegation then prayed to the Great Spirit to comfort the mourners and make them understand that Man of the Glad Heart was in a better world than this, and that, by and by, they, his brother and children, would go to him and be happy with him. The Indians then silently withdrew and made their long march homeward. The tribute was natural and graceful for him whose memory lingers with all who knew him.

In writing of the Meacham case, another instance of memorial tribute by Indians occurs to me. The Stuart brothers, Thomas, Granville, and James, were Montana pioneers who stood high in the list of prominent men of the Northwest. Granville Stuart, a dignified and pleasant man, I met frequently in Helena in 1879. His brother, James, died at Sun River, Montana, September 30, 1873, and his death was widely mourned. James was a man of much the same character as Harvey Meacham. The Indians admired him for his honesty, and in honor of his long, flowing beard named his "Po-te-has-ka," or "Long Beard." Stuart's body was transported five hundred miles from Fort Peck to Deer Lodge. Seven days of the overland journey were on the trail leading through Sioux country. On the eighth day, as the cortege bearing the casket pulled into a little ravine, a large party of Sioux made their appearance. The procession halted, and the leader of the band asked Agent Simmons what the procession meant. Simmons said that Po-te-has-ka's body was being taken to Deer Lodge. Thereupon, the Indians drew up in line, and as the procession filed past them, the warriors bowed their heads, clasped hands, and then pressed them over mouths. It meant, "Our friend, Po-te-has-ka, is dead. He was a good man."

HOLDING THE MARE'S TAIL

Later in the month, after leaving General Palmer and his party, I was with a companion, Church, traveling on the snow line of the Little Powder Mountains en route to Winters Station; this placer mine, forty miles from Baker City, was a stage stop on the road from Umatilla to Boise. We arrived at Winter's on the afternoon of May 21, 1870. Mr. Winter was the brother of Mrs. Ben Anderson, of Boise; he was a quaintly interesting man of forty-five years, a pioneer who had tramped Oregon and California from end to end. His settlement consisted of a blacksmith shop and a dozen rough-hewn cabins chinked with mud. We were cordially received and provided with a generous, well-cooked meal. The dinner table was a ten-foot pine log dressed flat, and the stools were made of pine tops cut squarely, with the legs inserted in the same manner as table legs. The cloth was patterned calico, and the dishes were the frontier ironstone ware. Winter's outfit was a good sample of Oregon backwoods environment.

I was slated to speak at a place named Parker's, a camp of miners just a jaunt from Winter's. After dinner Mr. Eph Day, a gentleman who had volunteered to conduct me to Parker's, came in and, after a brief chat and smoke, we started for Parker's. The view of the country about Winter's place was extremely interesting. We were in the timber line, midst pine and tamarack towering a hundred feet and more and drawn up in long files like a woodland army. Although June was coming apace, snow lay everywhere; the sun's days had not yet been able to banish the snow heaps. In fact, snow stays all summer at that altitude. In daytime it slowly melts, and the waters run down the valleys and feed the ditches built by the placer miners. When night falls the water again freezes on the surface and checks the flow of water until next day. Nature thus constructs her own reservoir. Lower in the valleys, where snow has but little chance to remain, the miners construct reservoirs to hold the snow water from upper gorges. About Winter's, pine cones were strewed as thick as grass in the valleys. Grass is scant in the timber line, for the sun and rain are deflected by the tree foliage, and the tree roots have, as a result, a barren circle about them. Wind and gravity carry the pine cones hither and thither, "willy-nilly blowing," and so the seed is propagated. The food that we ate at Winter's, save venison, wild fowl, and bear meat, was imported, for at mining camps of high elevation few if any vegetables are raised, or can be raised.

When Eph Day and I left camp we had been preceded by Church and a small party. Church bestrode a dun mare from the team in which we had driven to Winter's. Day had, as I supposed, an intimate knowledge of the trail by daylight or dark. He steered me along a mining ditch, and in the course of half an hour—it was then near sundown—we reached the ridge of a mountain clear of the timber line and on a narrow foot trail across the snow. Mr. Day remarked that the journey was two and a half miles. I believed him then but not afterward. Although my boots were soaked from the clingy-wet snow, the invigorating air and the color display in the sky from a superb sunset made the walk enjoyable.

Eph Day was clerk of Grant County, within the limits of which county we were traveling. Eph seemed particularly well informed on national and local affairs, and I soon ascertained that he had served as purser for many years on the Columbia River boats of the Oregon Steam Navigation Company. As purser he had met and mingled with many leading men and he was a walking encyclopedia of Oregon's foremost citizens. When Eph cut loose on steamboat history he staggered me, for he told me the mishaps and adventures of every steamer in the Northwest. He told how the *Lot Whitcomb*, the first steamer built in Oregon, was launched at Milwaukee, Oregon, December

26, 1850, and how, after long service on the Columbia and Willamette, she was run on the Sacramento as the *Annie Abernethy*.

Eph gave a few choice anecdotes concerning Sim Reed. "He now owns his millions. I knew him when he kept a saloon at Portland. And Captain J. C. Ainsworth? Why he ran a river boat about two feet long in early days."

All in all, Eph told so much about men and boats, particularly boats, that I had prepared myself for a detailed description of the assistance he rendered boss builder Noah, in placing the keel of the Ark! After events proved that Eph was better versed in water navigation than he was in trailing.

The mountain air suddenly grew chill as we walked, and the blue mist peculiar to mountain regions at sundown gradually enveloped us. Night was all too near. It occurred to me that we were walking the longest two and a half miles on record. Said I to Mr. Day, "Excuse me, but where is Parker's station?"

"Jest ahead," said Day, a trifle anxiously.

We plodded another mile without conversing further about Oregon or her steamboats. In twenty minutes the sun left us in fast-increasing darkness. We turned the summit of a ridge, and then Day stopped and faced me. The conviction was strong that I was about to be highwayed, but Day had other thoughts.

"I'm damned," said he. "I'm damned if we ain't lost."

I was staggered but managed to growl, "I thought so half an hour ago! Well, we're lost and just you find us again. I have no matches, I'm not built for sleeping in the open, and I'm wet and hungry!" Eph rubbed his head and peered through the gloom.

"Oh, if I was down on the Columbia," he said, "I'd be all right. I know every river bend, tree, rock——" My interrupting speech consigned Eph to a place where, had he gone, he would have been far beyond timber and snow lines. Mad all over, I jumped to the lead and put the Columbia pilot to the rear. We hustled along through the gloom, thinking of unpleasant things until Day said, "Stop at the bend, Judge. Some of the boys will come for us from Parker's."

On we jogged toward the bend when suddenly from the woods to the right rang out a weird sound, a wail, or howl, deep within the forest. Years before I had heard that same sound in Licking County, Ohio, and I recognized it as a panther.

"It's a painter!" said Eph very cheerfully. "Listen to that! H-o-o, h-o-o, h-o-o! Say, the woods are full of 'em. However, they never fight two men. If they're real hungry they'll sometimes go for a single feller." This was quite comforting! On we traveled, and the wails from the forest were louder and more frequent.

When we reached the big bend in the road there stood a man from Parker's. He led us another mile down a steep trail, and, tired and sulky, we pulled into the settlement about nine o'clock.

In anticipation of my coming, about two hundred miners had gathered there, journeying in from the hills to hear me. At eight o'clock they departed in disgust, believing that Day and I would be out until morning. A few of them remained about the settlement. When they saw us, Day was tendered a forcible if not polite reception, and they ventured personal remarks about his ability to guide, which were unchaste allusions, to say the least, upon the legitimacy of Day's ancestors. We bade them good night and an hour after arrival started the return to Winter's on what proved to be a ludicrous trip.

Because Church's dun mare would follow the trail better than a guide, Church was placed at the head of our procession. Then Mr. Winter grabbed the mare's tail, and I, at post of honor, held Winter's coattail. There were eight of us strung along Indian file. Eph Day, by way of punishment, was the end man. We dragged along at the mare's pace for half an hour, soothed by the sweet music of the panthers—the woodsmen called them "coovers," a corruption of the word "cougar"—and as the wails reveberated, the mountaineers cheered me with remarks like, "Them varments sure is hungry" and "Gosh, I wonders, will they jump us!"

At half-past ten something happened, happened suddenly! Winter lost his hold on the mare's tail, for the animal started suddenly. Church yelled, "Stay with me boys!" and then we heard him crashing down the hillside, the mare running wild. It was done in a second, and I thought we were out for the evening this time, certainly.

Mr. Winter laughed and said, "That mare saw a light, I suppose, down the mountain. We'll keep on home and get a rescue gang together and find Church. He may have been hurt, although it isn't likely."

Half a mile farther and we reached Winter's settlement. Without urgings or commands being given, a squad of men at once left to retrace our trail; others jumped on the roof of a cabin and fired guns at minute intervals, while others blazed two pine trees. That was interesting. A fat pine was lighted at the base, and with a roar and crackle a wonderful pillar of flame shot into the air and glared in the sky; it could be seen for miles. The mountaineers held the belief that Church had stumbled upon a miner's cabin and that he would return safely in the morning.

For my own part, my anxiety about Church was overcome by my weariness. Winter insisted that I go to bed, so with a roaring fire in the room I tucked away under covers made of calico. I awakened after copious perspiration and found that the heat of my body had so acted upon the calico that I was a human mimeograph: I acquired impressions by absorption! Weird things had been transferred to my body. On my right hip were, in hazy outlines and flaring colors, two unicorns and a lion rampant.

Church came in at five in the morning full of fun about the mishap. He said that when the mare bolted, he lay flat on her neck to escape overhanging trees. The mare, as Winter supposed, had seen a cabin light and had galloped pell-mell against a log building. Out rushed a brawny miner, flourishing a gun and yelling, "A bear, b'God!" But it wasn't a bear, and Church called out, "Don't shoot! It's a lost man on a fool mare!" From the cabin came a yell, "The lost mon will come in ond bring th' phul mare wid him." Nothing could have been more Irish.

Four Irish brothers named Kelley were the proprietors, and a jovial night of it they made for Church. Hospitality, whisky, and yarns were swapped, and then the men cooked breakfast and set Church on the home trail. They told him to call again on horse or on foot. Church was delighted with them and their hospitality.

JOAQUIN MILLER, POET IN EMBRYO

While Mr. Church and I were associated in the stumping tour, he took me to Canyon City, Grant County, Oregon, on May 17, 1870. As we walked along the main street of the town, Church asked me what I thought of poets. I replied by saying that there were poets and poets, but Church interrupted by saying, "I mean the wild-eyed, dreamy poet! We have one here who is a thing of picturesqueness if not beauty. He wears long hair, writes verses, and prowls about the country day and night afoot or horseback. Some time ago, he published a pamphlet of verse. Most of it is pretty bad. The man's name is Miller; he floated in here from the upper country, and we elected him judge of the county—principally to keep him from starving to death. He's about thirty years of age, and his verse is like the country—all rough and rugged."

"I'd like to take a peep at him," I said.

"Easy enough," said Church, "so come along and we'll visit him."

In the south end of town, a squalid settlement, we came to a hut built on stilts. Under the flooring was room enough for a horse or stray pigs—or a flood. We climbed a flight of rickety stairs and read a penciled note, "Off for a week." When Church read it he said, "I guess he's off all the time. He is a great dodger. Miller tucks away in odd places and devours books or reads verses. More than likely, he is inside there now, lying flat on his back reading or writing. We don't bother him much."

"What's his vocation?" I queried.

"He's a sort of lawyer, but outside of his judicial duties he has a hand-to-mouth existence. Existence and subsistence don't bother him; he's a poet and just lives! His room in there is a sight! The bed is ax-hewed pine, the stove is sheet iron, but he has a pile of books that would delight you. It doesn't look like a poet's cozy corner, does it?"

I was compelled to say that it didn't.

Church continued, "He's a good man and probably has sense but despite his own belief in his future greatness, I can't tell whether sense or tomfoolery will predominate. He has smooth manners and is rational on all things save Indians. He chums with the red men and that's enough. What any man can see in those lousy beggars, I can't understand. Miller has been a pack freighter and messenger. Says he is destined for great things. Most of our people think he's a three-decked idiot! Most of us were afraid that if he lay about idle he'd get a gun and kill something, so we put him in as a judge. It's cheaper to keep him busy. But say, Donaldson, you should see his politeness. When he meets a woman, it's superb to see him sweep off his hat and bow to the ground. He's effeminate at times but no slouch in a fight."

When we reached the foot of the steps, I saw a tin sign, slightly battered, which read, "C. Heine Miller." That stood for Cincinnatus Heine Miller, the Western writer who has achieved reputation under the name Joaquin Miller—the "poet of the Sierras," so called.

THE TOWNSITE OF BOISE

Hermann L. Judell, a German youth of thirteen years, was touring the world for his health when, at Christmas, 1859, he landed in San Francisco. Mr. Judell remained there until the war broke out. He overcame technicalities of age limit, and in February, 1862, was mustered into service with the 1st Washington Infantry, Company D, half of which company was recruited from California. The young man's qualities soon won him recognition, for he was sent to Sacramento and Folsom on recruiting duty. When his regiment was ordered to Vancouver in the fall of 1862, he accompanied it and at Yaquina Bay, the Siletz Indian Reservation, was detailed to assist in maintaining order among the Siletz, who were confined there after their participation in the Rogue River war. Frederick Seidenstricker, captain of Judell's company, commanded.

Because of Indian depredations, the National Government had deemed it advisable to found a central inland post for the distribution of military stores. The present site of Boise City was selected. Judell's company was detailed to guard a column sent there with supplies. The expedition was under command of Major Pinkney Lugenbeel, West Point, 1840, a gallant officer who was rewarded for services at Contreras, Churubusco, and Chapultepec in the Mexican War. In 1867 he was made lieutenant colonel; he died in 1886.

Mr. Judell was with the advance guard of Lugenbeel's expedition, and the advance covered one thousand miles through the Northwest country and afforded much protection to travelers and settlers. In March, 1863, the advance entered Boise Valley with a hundred wagons and many head of cattle. Mr. Judell wrote to me recently:

> The day I entered Boise valley, at the mouth of Boise river where it meets the Snake, is still very vivid in my memory. There were then but three white men in the valley; two old Canadian trappers and a venerable Yankee. The site of that which later became Boise City, looked just like the balance of the valley, a flat sage-brush country with a shelf-like bluff at the foot of the hills to the north and the Boise river, with its belt of cottonwoods, to the south. The original map of the Boise townsite, I drew.

Lugenbeel's main force left Fort Walla Walla and crossed the Snake River in May, 1863, two months after the advance guard. The force included four companies of Oregon cavalry and six of California infantry. The establishing of the post and preservation of peace in the country offered no small difficulties. The Indians, principally Shoshonis, with some Blackfeet, Diggers, and Bannacks, attacked settlers at frequent intervals. Mr. Judell wrote to me:

> We were out on Indian hunts week after week and I can assure you that our men suffered much through privation and lack of necessities. Toward the summer of 1864, four companies left Boise and the remainder were distributed as far as Salt Lake for the protection of travelers. My command was sent to Fort Douglas and when a party of immigrants collected at Salt Lake we would escort them either as far as Boise or until another detachment was met en route. We had skirmishes with Indians almost daily, surely weekly. At one time the Indians swooped down and massacred several teamsters; again, they killed Stage-driver Billy Yonker, two companions and an army sergeant's wife. We escorted immigrants, government officials, supply trains and, on one occasion, Major Thomas C. English, inspector-general. The worst fight we had was at War Eagle mountain where our command, under Lieutenant Woods, corralled about six hundred Indians. This band had a short time before murdered ninety Chinamen near Jordan Valley on the road from Winnemucca to Silver City.

In April, 1865, Mr. Judell was honorably discharged from service and went into business at Boise to work with

Dan Roth in a merchandise store. In 1867 he worked for the Hawkins brothers, delivering grain along the stage routes. Mr. Judell had a business of his own along the Leviathan Ledge, at Silver City, in 1869, and also assisted Colonel T'Vault, who was editing the *Owyhee Index*. He returned to San Francisco in 1870 and there engaged in the tobacco business. A fire destroyed his entire collection of notes and relics. His part in the early history of the territory is interesting and worthy of record. There is no reason to doubt the statement that he drew the original townsite map of Boise.

CAPTAIN HOWARD STANSBURY

Captain Howard Stansbury, U. S. A. topographical engineer, was one of the officers sent to Columbus, Ohio, in May, 1861, to muster Ohio volunteers into the Union Army. The captain was noticeable for his physical characteristics. He was about sixty-five years of age, short, stout, and vigorous, with highly colored cheeks, and a very red nose. He walked with quick, nervous motions which at once attracted attention, and his gold-rimmed eyeglasses swung pendulum-like before him on a long chain. He was exceedingly amiable, courteous, and cultured. By the dignity and severity of his dress—top hat, stock, and all—his relation to the old school of gentlemen was made clear. Stansbury would have done well in the role of one of Dickens' Cheeryble brothers. He was earnest and determined in everything he tried. Patriotic to a high degree, Stansbury was all enthusiasm for the North; Rebels he detested. I recall the excitement in which he was plunged the day we received, at Columbus, the news of the capture of the Atlantic Coast forts.

Captain Stansbury, a native of New York, was graduated from West Point in 1838. He was in charge of the noted expedition which crossed the plains in 1849 and surveyed Utah and the Great Salt Lake. His party of eighteen men and equipment left Fort Leavenworth, Kansas, on May 31, 1849. His survey was published under his name by the Government, and the volume contains much interesting and valuable matter. The captain often told me of his trip and related his Army-life experiences. He was cordially welcomed by the Salt Lake Mormons, and his book accords to the Mormons a character for hard work and thrift. He told me that they were earnest people, no matter what the light in which civilization viewed their religion.

Stansbury knew well the Shoshoni Indians and their great chief, Washakie. He described Washakie as a friendly and intelligent Indian. Of the Shoshonis and Utes in general, Stansbury said, "Poor souls, they are a mass of vermin—the victims of white man and insects!"

It was a source of regret to him that the Civil War found him too old for active service. He had served in the Mexican War and was anxious to serve again. He built Fort Snelling, Minnesota, and if I remember rightly had been stationed there prior to coming to Columbus. His captaincy was given him in 1840; in August, 1861, after twenty-three years of service, he was commissioned major. In September of the same year he was retired.

Stansbury was a "young-old" man; quick of speech and with a merry twinkle in his eye, he won friends everywhere. His chats filled me with a determination to see the West of which he spoke, and often did I think of the good captain when I repeatedly traversed the country which he had surveyed in its wilderness state and through which I was carried by the product of civilization—the railroad. His many friends throughout the country were deeply shocked when the merry little man dropped dead of apoplexy, April 17, 1863. The Civil War brought him one boon—a chance for promotion. It was, in fact, his sole chance.

THE GREAT BONANZA MINES

C. W. Moore, of Boise, and George W. Grayson, of Oakland, accompanied me in 1875 on a tour of the Virginia City, Nevada, mines. I was then engaged in making a collection of minerals for the Smithsonian Institution's exhibit at the Centennial. We had inspected the Belcher mine, and then Mr. Moore suggested that we enter the Consolidated Virginia. In that year, 1875, the Consolidated Virginia had mined 169,000 tons of ore, milling more than $16,000,000.

John W. Mackay was in the office, and we applied for the customary permit to enter the mine. Word came back to us that as Mr. Grayson and Mr. Donaldson had often been down the mine he saw no reason for another trip. Mr. Mackay was Irish and choleric. Had we applied the next day, the chances were that Mr. Mackay would have personally escorted us. Mr. Moore wasn't deeply impressed with the Bonanza king's courtesy.

We then visited the Ophir mine, which lay in the Bonanza lode and which, like all adjacent mines, was at that time experiencing a boom. In January, 1875, the Ophir was valued at $31,000,000. This mine had proved of frightful expense to its owners because of claim litigation. From 1860 to 1865, the Ophir was involved in thirty-seven suits, and she was plaintiff in twenty-eight of them. At the mouth of the mine, we were cordially greeted by Captain Sam Curtis, the superintendent. Glorious old boy that he was, Heaven never encased a better heart in human frame! Sam took us down the shaft, and we inspected it and secured a few specimens. After returning to the surface, we bathed and dressed, and then Sam told us of interesting matters in connection with the diagram on the wall, of the Ophir claim and patent.

"About this place," he said, "there are scores of prospectors roaming in search, possibly, of unclaimed mining stakes. The other day at noon I came up the shaft and saw two men driving stakes at the north end of our claim." He indicated the place on the map. "One man had a bundle of stakes, and the other had a map. When I accosted them and asked what they were doing, the larger of the two drew a gun, cocked it, and replied, 'Locatin' a claim. Got any objections?' At the same time he lazily brought his gun on a line with my heart. Said I, 'Have I any objections? None at all. I'm tickled to death to meet you. Come with me to the Ophir mine office and we'll take a finger or two. It's a trifle warm out here.' Down went the gun and both men followed me. As the big one emptied his glass, he said, 'Sah, youah licker does yuh proud.' Next, I passed cigars and asked them to be seated. I showed them the Ophir map and then placed both men at the window. 'Look, gentlemen! See that white stone post out there, just this side of your stakes? You do? Well, that's the initial corner of the Ophir claim, or ground. Now, run your eye over this map. See, there is the stone. Now, you have staked fifty feet inside our ground; the ground for which we have our United States patent. There it is!' The big man stood up, scrutinized the map, and said to his companion, 'Bob, that's keerect, an' Uncle Samuel has given them his ground, an' that there's his John Hancock [the President's signature on the patent]. Say, Cap, a man down to Gold Hill told us that this here was vacant claim an' if it wuz held, it wuz held by a pack of Frisco skinners. But since we've saw you we've had light! Cap, excuse us—we're off! The document's agin us. When I sees Uncle Samuel's John Hancock, I gits up an' skits. Cap, I bucked agin Uncle Samuel fer four years in the late war, on the Johnny Rebel side, an' I come out with nothin' but a pair of breeches. So long, Cap, we're off!'—and off they went."

We stepped to the window at Curtis' request to see the ground where the stakes had been driven, when suddenly

Curtis yelled, "My God, gentlemen, look there!" We looked across the gulch and saw a party of men driving stakes on the south side of the hill. "So help me," cried Curtis, "if they aren't jumping the Jewish graveyard!" Curtis spoke the truth, for a party of prospectors, finding a rich cropping in the Hebrew graveyard, had struck stakes. The local newspaper next day chronicled the event.

Curtis laughingly told us of the visit of Hank Smith to General Grant, in 1873. Hank Smith, whom I knew well, was a clever, hard-working fellow, superintendent of the Belcher mine at Virginia City and one of the famous men of the Comstock. Colonel Harry Beckwith also told me the same yarn.

It seems that Smith was an intimate of John P. Jones, of Nevada, and when Jones went East in 1873, he took Hank Smith with him, and the two called upon President Grant at his Long Branch, New Jersey, home. Smith was well entertained and duly appreciative. The story went the rounds that Hank wired back to Gold Hill: "Long Branch, New Jersey. All well. I, Grant and Jones are here having a good time."

CLARENCE KING, THE GEOLOGIST

At Major J. W. Powell's house in Washington, February, 1879, I first met Clarence King. For many years afterward I was associated with him, especially in the completion of my work, *The Public Domain*. King was then thirty-seven years of age, having been born in Newport, R. I., January 6, 1842. In 1862 he was graduated from the Sheffield School, Yale, and the following year he joined the California Geological Survey, having crossed the continent on horseback to do so. He remained West until 1866, doing valuable work and equipping himself with practical knowledge for the future work that he planned. He was the originator of the plan for the fortieth parallel, 1867 to

1872, and was in command of the expedition under the auspices of the Army Engineer Corps. It was King who, in 1872, exposed the Arizona diamond scheme and pronounced it a robbery.

In 1879, King was an applicant for a position about to be created—that of geologist in charge of United States surveys. The department came as a result of King's suggestion, and its present state of excellence is due to his careful work and capable administration. He approached James G. Blaine, when applying for the position of chief geologist, and his plea was characteristic. Said King, "Mr. Blaine, I want that position! It is a case of a man seeking the office; not the office seeking the man."

King was frank and admirable in every way and was one of the most charming conversationalists I ever met. In his travels he came in contact with prominent men, and many and interesting were his personal chats. He told me the most astounding things in connection with Francis Bret Harte, novelist. King had been on intimate terms with Harte sometime in the sixties, when Harte was on the staff of either the *Overland* or the *Californian*. On one occasion, Harte told King that he desired a technical article and that the magazine would pay King a good sum for writing it. Accordingly, King wrote the article at much labor and expense. The pay never reached him; King ascertained that Harte had deftly "fobbed," or stolen, his pay for the article. Several years afterward, when King went to New York, he met Harte and casually reminded him that the promised pay had never been forthcoming. When Harte searched his memory apparently in vain, King made the direct statement:

"Now, Harte, you know very well that you fobbed my money!"

"Bless me," said Harte reflectively, "did I really do that, old boy? Well, we shall soon settle that! Come with me and lunch at Delmonico's."

To Delmonico's both went, and a fine luncheon was ordered; far finer than King would have ordered had he known the outcome. When the bill was presented, Harte thrust his hands in pockets searchingly, and then with an eloquent burst of feigned astonishment, cried, " 'Pon my soul, King, I changed my trousers before coming out and left my purse at home! Just pay this check for me, will you, and give me enough cab fare to get home!"

King said that Harte was a literary highwayman of the first rank: he never paid a debt that he could possibly dodge; he was the most successful borrower on record. At theaters, parties, luncheons, entertainments, he would corral acquaintances in corners and extort loans. The royalties on his books must have been enormous, but Harte snapped his fingers in the faces of men to whom he owed money, because he never permitted creditors to come within reach. King said that whenever Harte succeeded in "landing" a man for a large loan, or whenever he outwitted a creditor, he would hurl himself on the floor and yell in paroxysms of delight. On one occasion Harte had been invited to New England to read a new and original poem to a large university, during its alumni-day exercises. En route, a constable attached his valise for debt, and in the valise was the poem. Harte promptly read an old poem. Despite the fact that the students and newspapers discovered the imposition and scored him in print, Harte retailed the incident with great gusto.

When Harte thought that he would like to live in Newport, King suggested that he procure new clothes. The novelist ordered sixteen pair of trousers without either coats or vests. In an unfortunate moment, King gave Harte a note to one of his (King's) rich relatives in Newport, stating that Mr. Harte was a stranger and desired entertainment for a few weeks until he could procure a suitable cottage. King's relative extended every courtesy, and Harte searched for a "modest little cottage." To everyone's astonishment, he rented a place for $4,000 for the summer, entertained lavishly, used the name of King's relative with outfitters and tradesmen, and staved off all creditors. Foreseeing imminent trouble, King went to Newport, arranged for the payment of Harte's bills for a month, and left him to shift for himself.

To give an instance of his ability, Harte, while in New York, was in the habit of arising at daybreak and wandering about in quest of a cocktail. He met odd characters during the early hours, and at King's suggestion wrote about fifteen hundred words describing some of them. The New York *Sun* paid Harte one hundred dollars for the article. Soon after this Harte became the victim of absurd fancies which drove him into excesses as ridiculous as they were costly. He became firm in the belief that gas lights in rooms were poisonous; accordingly, he purchased fourteen French lamps at twenty-four dollars each—and presented them to the landlord in lieu of rent when he departed. Whenever he moved his apartments, about all that the respective landlords had to show was a collection of furniture installed by Harte; installed, but infrequently paid for. King's estimate of Harte was that he was a selfish financial brigand who mercilessly preyed upon friends or acquaintances.

MARY HALLOCK FOOTE

King and I were in Leadville, Colorado, late in the summer of 1879, when one morning King asked me to accompany him: he wanted to make a call upon James D. Hague's relative, Arthur D. Foote. We left the main street of Leadville and trailed cross-lots to a cabin half a mile north of our hotel. A short distance beyond the town limits, we saw a group of men standing on a hillside, apparently expecting someone. We came abreast of them and a voice called, "I have two ready, a little above the average size! Twenty-five dollars each and free from water."

Close by was the graveyard, and these men had jumped a portion of it. They kept a supply of opened graves on hand and called to us on the assumption that King and I wanted to bury a man. "A man for breakfast" was the rule then.

King and I forged along through a forest, crossed a mining ditch, and in a little clearing espied a cozy log cabin. As we approached, we discerned a rustic porch made comfortable by armchairs built of barrels sawed in half and stuffed with straw and covered by gunny-sacks. To the right a hammock swung lazily, suggesting that an eastern woman, and a cultivated one, lived at the house. When we pounded on the porch, a clear voice called, "Is that you, Arthur?" We regretted that we weren't "Arthur," but hastened to say who we were. The voice from within called, "Please be seated; I'll be out presently"; so we sat down on the porch. Then Mrs. Foote came out.

King had known her, but it was the first time I had met Mary Hallock Foote, afterwards well-known through her literary works. She was dressed in white and she rounded out a pleasing picture in contrast to rugged nature all about her home. Mrs. Foote put us at ease with her sweet manners, and King fell into a conversation interesting and bright. We went inside the house and saw every evidence of artistic taste and culture. The main room, which served for parlor, bedroom, and reception room, was skillfully decorated in brown and gray—as neat an arrangement as I had seen, despite the fact that because of my bulk a table was thrust to one side in order to make room for me in an armchair.

Mrs. Foote settled herself for a chat until her husband returned, and my, my, how she did talk! She was well read on everything and ripped out an intellectual go-as-you-please backed up by good looks and brightness. She told us of their hopes, hers and Arthur's, in Mr. Foote's engineering schemes. What was more interesting, she showed us some of her black-and-white illustrations for the work of other authors. She spoke of her early education at the Cooper Union Art School and of her childhood on the Hudson, with her father, Nathaniel Hallock. Love of nature was her dominant theme, and there was an evident contentment with her life, arduous as it must have been at times because of the lack of comforts and dearth of suitable female companions in Leadville. Mrs. Foote said that because of household duties, the mountains, and her husband, she had little time to be idle. As we chatted, many people passed by, and from Mrs. Foote's conversation we could understand that she was jotting down the characters for future use in literary work; at that time, however, she was known by her art work and not by her literary efforts.

Mr. Foote came in, and his wife introduced me as one whom she had known through Governor and Mrs. Joseph R. Hawley and Miss Kate Foote, our mutual friends. Mr. Foote, a handsome, intelligent, healthy man of thirty or thirty-five years, said that Leadville pleased him in all but the isolation forced upon his wife. Mrs. Foote laughed and said, "Never mind about me! You see, afterwhile Arthur will be rich and then what a life and home we shall have! Hurry up, Arthur!" she said to him. "Stick your pick in the magic 'Foote' ledge and let our silver run out."

She broke off suddenly, peered from the window, and turned and called to us, "Quick! The cow is in the well." We, the male visitors, started for the door with visions of three men with ropes tugging a fat cow out of a deep well, but we saw in a shallow ditch which ran past the cabin, a contented, lazy cow calmly chewing her cud and returning our stare. When Mr. Foote yelled, the animal switched her tail and lumbered off to the north.

"There," said Mrs. Foote, "she'll be safe for another hour. That ditch is our well, our water supply from the hills. That wretched cow sneaks in there ten times a day and seems to enjoy herself when we chase her."

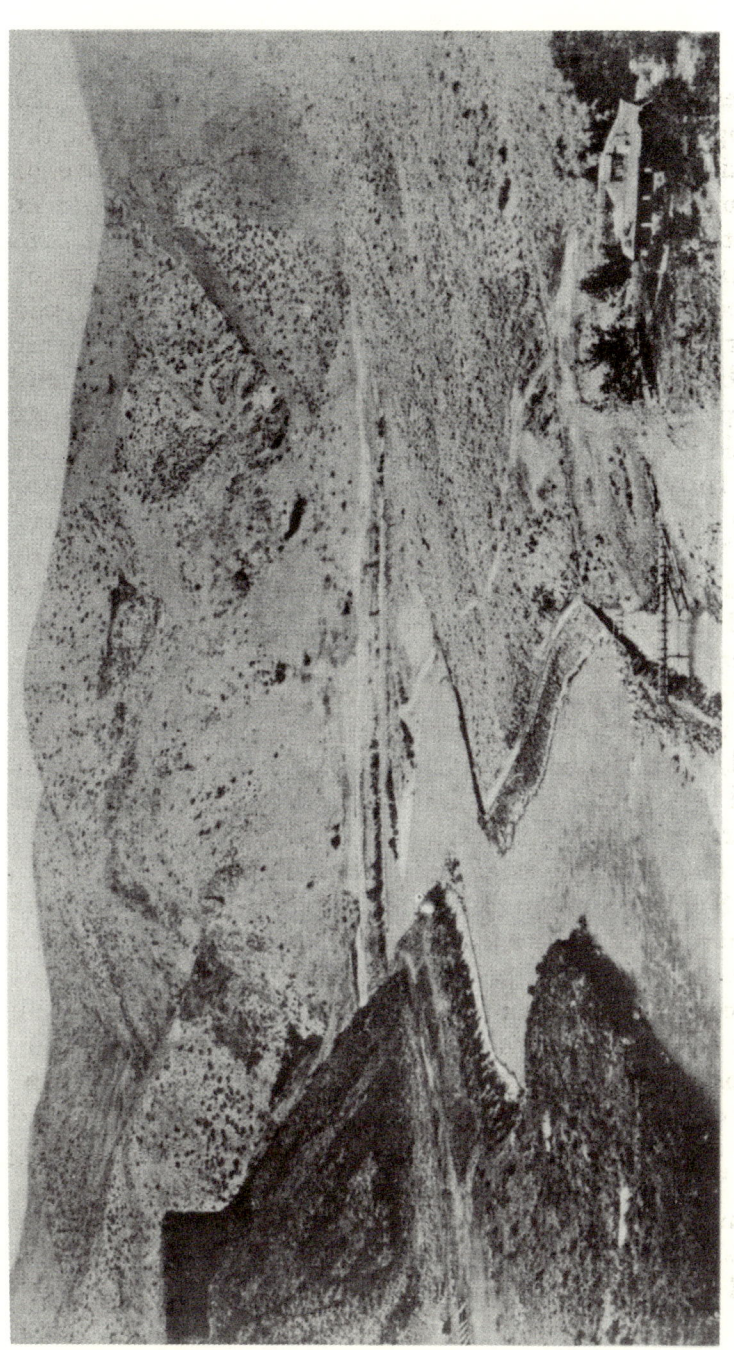

Mary Hallock Foote's cottage on the Boise River. In this primitive but beautiful solitude she wrote some of her best-known novels. A portion of her husband's irrigation project may be seen to the right of the river.

Christopher W. Moore, prominent businessman of Idaho Territory, 1869.

A CHAPTER OF WESTERN MISCELLANY 361

After a short stay, King and I departed for Leadville, much pleased with our visit.

In November of 1890, my son and I were visiting friends at Boise—C. W. Moore and family—and in the years which had elapsed since my last sight of Idaho, I found wonderful progress made in the town. Denver capitalists had arrived and boomed the land, and speculation was rife. The city was well lighted with electricity, a trolley road ran through town, and a fine natatorium was being built.

One afternoon Mr. Moore drove me to the "bench," the south side of Boise, to see the new engineering scheme, the great water ditch. As we rattled through the sagebrush, dust settled over us in clouds. Idaho dust is abundant and something to be sneezed at! Abruptly from the plain rose a mammoth line of earth, a leviathan ditch twenty-five feet wide and, strangely enough, entirely dry.

"This is the New York Canal Company's ditch," said Mr. Moore. "It's a fine piece of engineering, no doubt, and the idea of it sounds well on paper, but where the water for it is to come from is beyond my comprehension."

He broke off suddenly and called my attention to several men plowing in a field south of the ditch; they were planting wheat.

"If sufficient rain comes to fill that great ditch, there will be water here enough to irrigate those fields. But if the rain doesn't come, and other water supplies fail, this ditch will be a failure of enormous cost."

We headed for a bluff about four miles from Boise on which stood a dainty little cottage overlooking the landscape. When I asked who lived there, Mr. Moore said, "Oh, one of the ditch men."

We drove to the cottage, and I alighted and knocked on the cottage door. A breath of air might have floored me when Mary Hallock Foote walked from within.

"Well, Mr. Donaldson," she cried, "where shall we next

meet?" I laughed and said that I couldn't tell. Mr. Moore was decidedly amused and reminded me that he had not been presented. We sat upon the porch and from there looked upon a superb panorama stretching north and west. I of course referred to our meeting at Leadville, eleven years before, and regretted that I had lost track of Mrs. Foote and her husband.

"Why, you haven't lost track of us!" she said. "You helped Arthur get the position which brought him to this country." So I had, but it had slipped my memory. Continued Mrs. Foote: "Arthur finished the engineering work which first brought him here and then became engineer for the New York and Idaho Ditch Company. He is now in Boise, at the office. This house and dry farm are his and also the experiment in crop planting below here. If we get water, we get a crop; if not, we lose. Oh, Mr. Foote is the one to plan! I sometimes wish we were back in Leadville at that dear old cabin, where we could hear the mountain stream purling past us at all times. And I think that I would even be willing to drive that blessed old cow out of the well! Just a trifle of that water from Leadville running out here would make us millionaires. Well, we haven't lost faith, nor hope. Both of us have good health, and I've done well in my writings and illustrations. The canyon of the Boise, above here, is a superb spectacle. I am able to reconcile myself to farming when surrounded with all this natural beauty, beauty to be had without much seeking."

When we left her I told Mr. Moore of her reputation. I recalled that she was well known in literary fields through *The Led Horse Claim* (1883), *John Bodewin's Testimony* (1886), and *The Last Assembly Ball* (1889). *Century Magazine* had published much of her brush and pen work. Mrs. Foote deserved considerable credit for her devotion to her family. She was just as hopeful and buoyant at Boise in 1890 as she had been at Leadville in 1879, and the then apparently near promise of riches. She might have lived East in free access to the educated circles of the day. But she chose rather to devote herself to her family and stood with her husband in all the difficulties with which he was surrounded. I am under the impression that Mr. Foote's schemes were schemes and nothing more. They seemed to be thwarted by natural and financial obstacles.

WITH THE MORMONS

Alexander T. Britton, Clarence King, and I, the three of us public land commissioners, were in Salt Lake City in September, 1879. With us was George L. Converse, member of Congress. At the invitation of Bishop John Sharp and accompanied by other bishops, we were placed on a private car to tour the great irrigating ditches constructed at Lehi to transport water from the river Jordan. We comprised an assembly of forty Mormon saints and many foreign "sinners."

George Q. Cannon, the well-known Mormon, was in our party, and he explained to us the economic basis of Mormonism. Cannon stated that one man in full health was equal in vigor to four women and if he cared for this number of females, he was doing his duty to God, for when men kept women at home, public morals were preserved. Cannon said that the Old Testament pastoral life demanded that man be made the head of a herd; that was the aim of Mormonism. In addition to that, said Cannon, an excess of women in Utah compelled polygamy. He asked King whether or not he had noticed the exquisite beauty of the Mormon women. King, an authority on female beauty, was startled, but he grumbled a noncommital answer. The question was somewhat disconcerting, because experts usually classed Mormon women with the plainest types on earth. Cannon extolled their charms and said that Utah's climate made the women beautiful.

Daniel H. Wells, one of the Twelve Apostles of Utah, was in our party. Wells, then seventy years of age, and tall and gaunt, was an impressive figure. He was general of the Mormon army and had fought valiantly in more than one Indian campaign. Wells was at that time on the eve of arrest by United States authorities on the charge of polygamy, and during the ride he discussed with me the probability of punishment being meted to all Mormons for having plural wives. I noticed that Mormons always said "plural" wives. Wells was a very much married man. His home, opposite the Mormon Temple grounds, in Salt Lake City, contained many women. I saw them frequently and am of the opinion that neither Wells with his many, nor Cannon with his four, could have chosen the women out of real desire; in appearance they were plain and unattractive women. Brother Wells—always the title "Brother," when addressing Mormons—had a glass eye on his left, and this fact led the Gentile paper, the Salt Lake *Tribune*, to dub Wells the "One-eyed Pirate of the Wasatch." Wells had taken up a large tract of Government land in the Wasatch Mountains and deftly stolen the timber from it.

Bishop Snow, of St. George, a most interesting man and a fluent talker, told me how the Mormons about St. George planted and raised cotton. In 1863, they shipped the crop by team hauls to St. Joseph, Missouri, and then by rail to New York. The teams traveled two thousand miles each haul; the cotton sold in New York for one dollar a pound.

With us was the well-known John T. Caine, editor of the *News*, the Mormon newspaper. Caine was agreeable and chatty personally, but his sheet breathed fire and brimstone upon the Gentiles. He was a tall, red-haired man, an Englishman by birth.

When our car reached the station above Nephi we alighted and climbed the hills overlooking the canals. The canal building was a stupendous enterprise, and the enormous activity, the moving forces in the desert below us, was an impressive spectacle. We went down to Nephi and the lake, but a dense fog obscured a view usually interesting. We inspected thoroughly and returned to Salt Lake City at six o'clock.

In the evening, Mr. Cannon called and escorted us to the home of William Jennings, a leading Mormon and merchant. He was most hospitable, and in his intelligent conversation recounted incidents of Brigham Young and the history of Mormonism in Utah. Jennings owned a palatial residence and grounds; he had but one wife, a successor to one who had died recently. Like all Mormons, Mr. Jennings entertained great respect for Brigham Young. He held the view, the same held by every Mormon to whom I have spoken in the past twenty-five years, that if the United States decreed the abolition of plural wives, he would submit to the law. All in all, omitting the question of plural wives, I have never seen any difference between Mormons and other men.

During our call at Mr. Jennings' house, his five sons came in; each one was six feet in height and the picture of health.

"I have," said Mr. Jennings, "thirty feet of sons."

He introduced them all by their formal names, "Thomas," or "James," for Mormons do not give nicknames. The sons were farmers and merchants.

During the evening, champagne was opened. It was wine which Mr. Jennings had doubtless obtained in some business deal, and from indications it was very bad wine. King and Britton glanced stealthily at each other when they drained their first glass. When the second glass was served, King fairly turned blue as he gulped it down. I saw the difficulty, so pressing back a smile, I insisted that I did not drink, but that Mr. King and Mr. Britton were very fond, oh, very fond, of wine. Mr. Jennings promptly opened another bottle and, behind his back, Britton choked with rage and shook fists at me; King made faces. I asked

Mr. Cannon why it was that Brigham Young had publicly requested a plain funeral—why he had ordered a plain pine coffin and woolen pillow.

"For economical reasons," replied Cannon. "Some time ago we were in Brother Young's office discussing the present extravagance, the growing extravagance, in funerals. Each man then wrote out instructions for his burial. Brother George Smith ordered a plain white-pine coffin, but when the undertaker measured him for it he said that it should be stained black; the plain wood made it ugly. President Young then gave his directions for a plain coffin and a woolen pillow."

Later on in his chat, Cannon said that his conviction was that Young's power came through his marvelous logic and his art of mimicry. He would have made, thought Cannon, a great actor.

I chanced to mention the interesting fact that I had seen myriads of sea gulls flying everywhere about Salt Lake City. Mr. Cannon said that Mormons had a love for them since 1849, when matters had looked calamitous for the people. In that year, crickets appeared by the thousands and millions, overran the entire country, and threatened to wipe out all crops and bring on famine. Sea gulls by the thousands flew over the land, swallowed the crickets, flew to the lake, and disgorged, returning again and again to destroy the pests. This miracle saved the crops.

About ten o'clock, Britton and King seemed very anxious to withdraw, so we said good night. Mr. Cannon's brother Thomas drove us to our hotel. We were in a three-seated wagon, and the Cannons sat on the front seat. I was in the middle, and King and Britton had me at their mercy. From the back seat they punched me in the ribs, meanwhile assailing me with sundry threats, "You villain! Wait till we get you in the hotel." King cried out once. "My God, I'm poisoned by that wine!"

When we reached the Walker Hotel, I bade a quick

farewell to the Cannons and scurried around by the side entrance. King and Britton saw the ruse and met me in the main hall; King had a poker and Britton had an umbrella, and my life was in danger. King made me vow never to insist on a second bottle of champagne. Seriously speaking, both men felt the effects of the wine for five days. It was probably a rancid product from a cheap American house.

CHAPTER X

HOW IDAHO RECEIVED HER NAME

HOW AND WHY was Idaho Territory so named? I have been so deeply interested in this problem that I may be pardoned for venturing into a field of events which occurred years before I knew Idaho or her people. Considering the dearth of historical facts upon the subject, any man, in a reminiscence or a history, has the right to attempt the solution, and irrespective of whether his conclusions do or do not convince, at least the facts gleaned may be of use to the successful man who may come after.

There are two distinct phases in the problem of how and why Idaho was named. One phase is the question of the origin of the word; the other is the question of why the name Idaho was inserted at the eleventh hour in the bill which was almost passed by Congress as the "Montana" bill. All in all, these two phases represent events in a period of years as interesting as any in our American history.

Unfortunately, the origin of the word Idaho I have found to be too deeply hidden for solving, and I therefore only touch upon the matter briefly by repeating a reminiscence on the subject by the poet Joaquin Miller. As for the other half of the question—how Idaho directly received her name when she was created a territory—to that I have devoted myself. Personally, I am convinced that the territory was named Idaho because of the expressed wish of a woman—and for a reason truly feminine.

The natural and widely held assumption has been that the word Idaho is of North American Indian origin. *Perhaps* it is, but no one has been bold enough to state so positively. That the word was familiar to Pacific Coast Indians prior to 1860 is a well-established fact, but that it is distinctly of Shoshoni, Modoc, Klamath, Nez Perce, or

HOW IDAHO RECEIVED HER NAME

other origin, none dares authoritatively state. Our Western pioneers always have an abundant flow of picturesque reminiscences on tap whenever the cloudy origin of their country's name is mentioned—especially since the character of word suggests that it is of Indian derivation. On the Idaho subject, several of our Western patriarchs—some claiming personal participation and others claiming to be eyewitnesses on the great occasion—have "cut loose," and as years have passed, their individual versions have become to them, by the retelling, positive facts. Again, their descendants have retold and garnished that which was told them. The Arabian Nights were dreamed a few centuries before Idaho was born, but our first-settler romancers have done fairly well!

JOAQUIN MILLER'S VERSION

The word Idaho came into public notice throughout the East and West when the Organic Act was passed, March 3, 1863, and its universal interpretation has been "Gem of the Mountains." I have at hand a letter from Mayor A. E. Barker, of Idaho Springs, Colorado, dated March 10, 1898, in which Mr. Barker states that the Ute Indians named the place Idaho (Idahoe) Springs, prior to 1859, and the white residents presumed the word to mean "Gem of the Mountains." We also know that about 1860 the Oregon Steam Navigation Company ran a steamer on the upper Columbia with the name—*Idaho*. Moreover, the district now included within Idaho's state boundaries was known as Idaho County before the discovery of gold in 1860, which brought gold seekers into the new country in vast numbers during 1861 and 1862.

Some time ago, a Westerner said to me, "Joaquin Miller tells how Idaho was named. No doubt you've read his version of the incident." I had read it; and I was not, and am not, impressed by the reminiscence, for such it is.

Miller's version I repeat here, briefly, as a matter of reference. In his book, *Memorie and Rime,** Miller devotes a chapter to the subject, wherein he states that Colonel Craig, of Craig's Mountain, Idaho, first suggested the name "I-dah'-ho"—the accent being on the second syllable. Says Miller: "Craig is the man who found and named Idaho."

In the early sixties, Joaquin Miller led a wandering life and during one of his pilgrimages he visited Lewiston, then a modest settlement in its tent days. Early in 1860, rumors were spread that gold had been found in the region toward Camas Prairie, and the rumors traveled rapidly to the Pacific Coast. Mr. Miller writes:

Farther up the Shoshonee [Snake], and beyond the great black-white mountain, a party of miners who had attempted to cross this ugly range, and got lost, had found gold in deposits that even exceeded the palmy days of '49. Colonel Craig, an old pioneer, who had married an Indian woman and raised a family here, proposed to set out for

---

* Joaquin Miller wrote a somewhat different account from that in *Memorie and Rime*, a few years later, concerning the naming of Idaho. His statement, in the form of a letter to an Idaho editor, is as follows:

Guelph, Ontario, Canada, July 30, 1880.

Dear Sir:

The distinction of naming "Idaho," certainly belongs to my old friend, Colonel Craig [since deceased], of Craig's Mountain, Nez Perce County. As for some fellows naming it in Congress, bah! The name was familiar in 5,000 men's mouths as they wallowed through the snow in '61, on their way to the Oro Fino Mines—long before Congress, or any man of Congress, had even heard of the new discovery.

The facts are these: I was riding pony express at the time rumors reached us, through the Nez Perce Indians, that gold was to be found on the head-waters and tributaries of the Salmon River. I had lived with the Indians; and Colonel Craig, who had spent most of his life with them, often talked with me about possible discoveries in the mountains to the right as we rode to Oro Fino, and of what the Indians said of the then unknown region. Gallop your horse, as I have done a hundred times, against the rising sun. As you climb the Sweetwater Mountains, far away to your right you will see the name of "Idaho" written on the mountain-top—at least you will see a peculiar and beautiful light at sunrise, a sort of diadem on two grand clusters of mountains that bear away under the clouds fifty miles distant. I called Colonel Craig's attention to this peculiar and beautifully arched light. "That," said he, "is what the Indians call E-dah-hoe, which means the light or diadem on the line of the mountains." This was the first time I ever heard the name. Later, in September, '61, when I rode into the newly discovered camp to establish an express office, I took with me an Indian from Lapwai. We followed an Indian trail, crossed Craig's Mountain, then Camas Prairie, and had, all the time, E-dah-hoe Mount for our objective point.

On my return to Lewiston I wrote a letter containing a brief account of our trip and of the mines, and it was published in one of the Oregon papers, which one I have now forgotten. In that account I often mentioned E-dah-hoe, but spelt it I-da-ho, leaving the pronunciation unmarked by any diacritical signs. So that, perhaps, I may have been the first to give it its present spelling, but certainly I did not originate the word.

Yours sincerely,
JOAQUIN MILLER.

Colonel Craig, or "Bill" Craig, as he was best known, had gone West in the employ of the St. Louis Fur Company, and when the company went out of existence, Craig settled in Idaho, or in what is now Idaho, married a Nez Perce squaw, and was adopted by the tribe. He was a trapper and scout of the Jim Bridger and Joe Meek school.—T.B.D.

the new mine. Craig was an intelligent man, a rover, and he desired my company because I was familiar with the latest news from the outside world from which he, Craig, had been cut off for months.

I gladly accepted Craig's offer of a fresh horse, and the privilege of making one of his party. For reasons sufficient to the old mountaineer, we set out at night, and climbed and crossed Craig's Mountain, sparsely set with pines and covered with rich brown grass, by moonlight. As we approached the edge of Camas Prairie, then a land almost unknown, but now made famous by the battlefields of Chief Joseph, we could see through the open pines a faint far light on the great black and white mountain beyond the valley. "Idah'ho!" shouted our Indian guide in the lead, as he looked back and pointed to the break of dawn on the mountain before us. "That shall be the name of the new mines," said Colonel Craig quietly, as he rode by his side. . . . I do not know whether this guide was Nez Perce, Shoshonee, Cayuse, or from one of the many other tribes that had met and melted into this half-civilized people first named. Neither can I say certainly at this remote day whether he applied the name "Idah'ho" to the mountain as a permanent and established name, or used the word to point the approach of dawn.

Miller says that Idah'ho means, literally, "sunrise mountains." He made a glossary of eleven Indian dialects in which the word was found. "I note," he says, "that the root of the exclamation is 'dah!' The Shasta word is 'Pou-dah-ho!' The Klamath is 'Num-dah-ho!' The Modoc is 'Lo-dah,' and so on. Strangely like, 'Look, there' or 'Lo, light,' is this exclamation, and with precisely the same meaning." Miller states emphatically that the word refers to dawn or light and he treats at length upon the constantly recurring reference, by Indian tribes, to sunlight, entering as it does into their daily domestic life, their pursuits, and their religion.

Unfamiliarity with actual conditions has caused many of Miller's readers to accept this version as authoritative. For my part, I do not see that anything is proved; Miller is, by his own words, uncertain. He does not know, nor does any other person, whether Idaho is or is not of Indian derivation. He does not know whether Craig's Indian guide uttered "Idahho" as a name for the locality, or as an exclamation. What he does state is, "Craig is the man who found and named I-dah'-ho." Knowing, as we do, that Idaho was a familiar name prior to Craig's trip to the country, and that it was applied to that vast and indefinite land now within the state boundary, I confess my inability to accept Miller's statement. It is quite true that the word came into prominence soon after the opening of the Salmon River mines, and the establishing of the town of Florence, but that was a matter of circumstance. Thousands of gold seekers visited the mines in 1861 and 1862 and returned to the coast, telling of Idaho. But the name was revived, rather than created; the gold discoveries merely gave it emphasis.

THE ORO FINO CONFERENCE OF 1862

The first concerted effort to secure territorial organization for Idaho took place in the autumn or late summer of 1862 at Oro Fino, the mining town due east of Lewiston, within the shadow of the Rockies, and the site of the first mines opened in the Idaho wilderness. A small group of men, including Selucius Garfielde, George B. Walker, Dr. A. G. Henry, and William H. Wallace met there. Needless to state, these were the active men in the movement: two of them, Wallace and Henry, were identified with the scheme both in the East and West. The others' efforts were limited mainly to home influence and persuasion; that is, in the Northwest.

Garfielde's history is well known on the coast, known much better than that of the others, for he was Washington's delegate to Congress and active in all political spheres. I knew him well for several years; we saw him frequently at Boise in the seventies where he came on stumping tours. Garfielde was a gifted orator, a shrewd politician, a man of tact and general ability. He was valuable in his assistance, if not in personal participation in Washington, in the passing of the Idaho Act.

George B. Walker we knew in Idaho as "Growler" Walker. He was a self-made man, vigorous and obstinate, a native of New York state. Walker had resided for a time in Iowa, but in a mining venture he crossed the plains and settled at Silver City. By occupation he was a carpenter and wheelwright. Persevering and honest in his methods, he exerted much influence in his community and was well known throughout the territory. Late in life he married a splendid woman, an Iowan, who had artistic training and temperament. I recall seeing her at Silver City in 1874, where she had a studio and painted capably in oils. To my knowledge, she was the first woman artist in Idaho. Walker left the territory in 1877, and the last I heard of him was that he had settled in Arizona.

Of William H. Wallace, I have written in detail under the chapter devoted to Idaho's governors and have told of his work, of his efforts, in the early history of Idaho. Ever since beginning my search into the records of the formulators of the Idaho Organic Act, I have been impressed by the similarity of aims, abilities, and achievements of Governor Wallace and his associate, Dr. Anson G. Henry, of the Oro Fino conclave. Wallace and Henry were the types of useful men found in every community, men far above the average, but men who, either through inherent modesty or force of immediate circumstance, just missed the attainment of greatness. Whatever they did, however, they did well, and they died blessed with a clean record and mourned by thousands of friends.

Anson Gordon Henry was born at Richfield, Otsego County, New York, October 3, 1804. His family moved West when he was young, settled at Louisville, Kentucky, where he was educated and received the degree of doctor of medicine from the Louisville Medical College about 1825. Dr. Henry practiced at Louisville for some years and married there, March 12, 1832, Miss Eliza Dunlap Bradstreet. Late in September of 1832, he moved to Springfield,

Illinois, and practiced his profession there for many years. Directly after moving to Springfield, he met Abraham Lincoln, then known because of quaintness and not because of greatness, and until 1865 the friendship of the two was unbroken through any change of circumstance or environment. Dr. Henry's son recently told me that when Lincoln called upon Judge Stuart, of Springfield, to borrow his first batch of lawbooks, Dr. Henry accompanied the future President. Henry was well known to everyone in that section of the country, especially to Judge Stuart, so when Lincoln had procured his books and departed, Stuart turned to Dr. Henry and asked, "Doctor, what do you expect to make of that country jake?"

"That man," replied Dr. Henry, "will prove to be a singed cat or I lose my guess."

It is fitting to mention here that both Dr. Henry and William H. Wallace, Idaho's future governor, who then lived in Springfield, were equally close in friendship with Lincoln. At the outbreak of the Mexican War, Colonel E. D. Baker's regiment, the 4th Illinois, lacked a regimental surgeon. Dr. Henry offered his services and served for a year before being relieved by the appointment of a regular Army surgeon. Returning to Springfield, he took active part in the campaign for President Taylor and, in 1850, in recognition of his services, he was accorded the position of general Indian agent for Oregon. This appointment, for pecuniary reasons, Dr. Henry could not accept. In the fall of the same year he broke down in health while serving as company surgeon with Baker's regiment. He then engaged in the construction of the Isthmus of Panama Railroad. Two years later, he decided to cast his fortune in the lands of our new West, and he "ox-trailed" across the plains from Independence, Missouri, to Yamhill County, Oregon, where he settled upon a donation grant of 320 acres. Not hesitating to grasp lucrative opportunities, Dr. Henry combined the occupation of Government land surveying with the practice of medicine. He eventually made surveying his vocation. Dr. Henry became well known, and, quite conformably, he was elected in 1853, to the Oregon legislature.

At the outbreak of the Indian war of 1855, he served creditably as surgeon with the Oregon volunteers, under Colonel Ross, and was present at the notable engagement of Graves Creek. In 1857, Dr. Henry was elected city surveyor of Portland; the following year, he surveyed the route for the first steam railway in Washington, that of the Oregon Navigation Line, along the cascades of the Columbia.

Oregon was, in 1860, passing through the period of political excitement felt in every state of the Union, and Dr. Henry took the stump and waged a vigorous crusade for his friend Lincoln. Later, he campaigned zealously for Colonel E. D. Baker and J. W. Nesmith, who were elected to the National Senate. When Mr. Lincoln assumed office, one of his very first acts was to appoint Dr. Henry United States surveyor for Washington Territory. The long years that had elapsed since Dr. Henry left Springfield severed none of the friendship between him and the "singed cat" of early times. Both Dr. Henry and Mr. Wallace were recognized, or remembered, in the same manner by President Lincoln. One of the very first telegrams sent by Mr. Lincoln after his second election was a message to Dr. Henry apprising him of the result and at the same time inviting him to attend the inaugural exercises of 1865. Dr. Henry attended, with a result almost as tragic as that of the death of Mr. Lincoln. While returning to the West, he was drowned in the unfortunate *Brother Jonathan,* which sank off the Oregon coast, July 30, 1865.

Dr. Henry's popularity was so pronounced in the Northwest that the entire coast delegation in Congress voiced his name for a position in Lincoln's second cabinet. Of course, Mr. Lincoln's death changed the aspect of affairs, but—strange to say—Andrew Johnson did not entirely disregard Mr. Lincoln's expressed interest in Dr. Henry. President Johnson offered Dr. Henry the appointment of governor of Washington Territory. Dr. Henry, for personal reasons, requested reappointment as surveyor general, and his request was complied with, although his untimely death prevented him from entering upon duties for the second term. From Dr. Henry's intimates I have heard splendid tributes to the man's character and ability. His entire life was spent in advancing the efforts of his friends, in contributing to their progress, perhaps more than to his own. As a result, he lived and died in very moderate circumstances, but his associates, the few that are now living, are always ready to speak with reverence of the doctor. He played a conspicuous part in the organization of Idaho Territory and for purely unselfish reasons.

It is regrettable that the men active in the Oro Fino meeting passed away without leaving a written record of what occurred when the Idaho plan was projected. Of course, Idaho's early history grew in rapid and wide jumps; men were too much occupied with rapid changes, too much involved in the next day's work, in the battle for subsistence and existence, to make record of that which at the time of happening seemed commonplace. That the Oro Fino workers were determined to create a territory is a safe conclusion, but beyond that the records show nothing until the final adoption by Congress of the Idaho Organic Act, March 3, 1863. A line of action was determined upon at Oro Fino, having for its basis the needs of the settlers in the new country and, surely, with a view of some reward for at least one of the promoters. Wallace and Henry were especially in favor with President Lincoln, and both held positions of moment so that it was natural the two men should canvass, as they did, for the bill at Washington. The details of the canvass, in the winter of 1862-63, interesting as they must have been, are not recorded. The proceedings of Congress alone give, historically, a faint suggestion of the "hustling" that was done to secure legislation. It is quite likely that the men at Oro Fino talked of the details of organization, planned perhaps for the details of territorial appointment. That is, with their political acumen, it is fair to conclude that a "slate" was prepared in the hoped-for event of territorial organization. Whether they did or not, the chances are that later considerations and emergencies disturbed the prearrangement.

The one person to whom I had recourse was Judge John R. McBride, who had been fairly intimate with Idaho history at all times, and who was on the ground floor when the territory was organized. He was not at Oro Fino, but from Garfielde, Wallace, and Henry he soon afterward heard of the projected plan and, heartily agreeing with the movement, was hand in hand with Wallace and Henry when the canvass of Congress was begun in December, 1862, at Washington. I was particularly anxious to learn from Judge McBride about the possible "slate" for the new territory—whether or not Mr. Wallace was then and there suggested for governor; who were to be the territorial judges—in fact, something definite of this earliest movement.

Said Judge McBride to me, "I was not present at Oro Fino, and many of the details of the transactions there were not told me; neither were they told or known to any others outside the small circle directly interested. However, I was soon made acquainted with the general result, and in Washington I had much to do with the final slate which was drawn up for territorial officers and district judges. If Mr. Wallace was chosen, or named, for governor at Oro Fino, I never heard of it. I really believe that Wallace's selection was the result, not of the Oro Fino agreement, but because he was the creature of circumstance in after months—at the time the territory was formally organized. Dr. Henry and I had several conferences with

President Lincoln in the matter of appointments for Idaho; in fact, I may say that we were almost the only ones consulted, representing, as we did, Idaho interests in Washington. That is, we were, with the exception of Wallace, more solicitous than any others in the Idaho Organic Act, or that which ultimately passed as such. Dolphus S. Payne we named as a territorial judge, but President Lincoln substituted the name of S. C. Parks, of Illinois. In all other respects the slate we selected was ratified. Most of our chats with the President occurred in January and February, 1863. When Mr. Wallace was appointed governor, he said that if the prospects justified his success he might run for Congress that fall (1863). He did so, as you know. Time moved so quickly in those days that calculations were too often upset by changes in the near future. There was conjecture in everything, to a pronounced degree."

It has been stated that Selucius Garfielde was in Washington, early in 1863, in the interests of the new territory, but I am assured by at least one of the promoters that Mr. Garfielde was in Washington neither before nor after the period of activity in passing the act. Garfielde's influence was always present, but he was not, personally, upon the battleground. Dr. Henry, William H. Wallace, and John R. McBride, then representative-elect from Oregon to the Thirty-eighth Congress, were the three who fought in Washington for the cause. These three men worked zealously and indomitably for many weary and costly weeks, pled, coaxed, suffered disappointments and reverses, but withal hung on and succeeded. They were fighting not only Western opposition but also Eastern ignorance. It is too true that scores of members of the House and many in the Senate knew no more of the location or character of the Idaho country than did the Puritans who landed on New England shores two and a half centuries before.

IDAHO REACHES THE EAST

I am frank to confess my inability to discover the true origin of the word Idaho or the date of the first naming of the country, in spite of my criticism of Joaquin Miller's reminiscence. What I really desire to show is how and why the Idaho Organic Act was adopted as such; how and why the already well-known name "Idaho" was given to the created territory. The records of Congress show that Idaho Territory might today be known as Shoshone, or Montana, or Mazaska. Idaho was the first and last name ventured and the one chosen. Had Congress alone had the choice, the result would have been different; but outside influence was brought to bear at the crucial moment by the little group of men interested in furthering their pet scheme. The original bill, as reported by James M. Ashley, of Ohio, chairman of the House committee on territories, was the Idaho, then the Shoshone, and finally the Montana bill. As will be hereafter explained, "Montana" was stricken out in the Senate, March 3, 1863, and the name "Idaho" inserted. The East and West allied to perpetuate the name. Senator Henry Wilson, of Massachusetts, was the prime mover, and Senator Benjamin F. Harding, of Oregon, was an able second, in the successful effort to amend Ashley's bill, as to the proposed name. Harding explained the meaning of the word "Idaho" to his colleagues and insisted upon its adoption. In the House of Representatives, Aaron A. Sargent, of California, and Speaker Galusha A. Grow, of Pennsylvania, and of course the delegates directly interested, were the active spirits in passing the bill as amended.

One January morning, in 1876, I chanced to be in the rooms of the House committee on appropriations, at Washington, and there met General E. O. Babcock and T. W. Bennett, former governor of Idaho, and at that time Congressional delegate. Bennett and I began to chat about

Idaho and her representation in the coming Centennial Exhibition. Bennett suddenly said:

"By the way, Donaldson, in connection with Idaho, I met General Frederick T. Dent the other day, and he told me an interesting reminiscence of how Idaho, the name, came to be inserted in Ashley's Montana bill and what he, Dent, had done to popularize the name. You are always hunting historical data, so go see Dent. He was instrumental in naming the territory."

"Yes, that's true. I know about it," General Babcock at once said.

Shortly afterward, I met General Dent and chatted with him. He was the brother-in-law of President Grant and was then on duty at the White House. Dent told me of his participation in the Idaho matter.

At the outbreak of the Rebellion, Dent, then a captain, was stationed at or near Fort Vancouver, with the 9th Infantry. If I am not mistaken, although I did not ask General Dent, he was the same Dent who, in partnership with A. H. Reynolds and one Simms, owned the flour mill at Walla Walla in 1860 which "flour-staked" Captain E. D. Pierce's prospecting party, the party which found gold near Oro Fino and which, under "Sergeant" Smith, of Walla Walla, spread the news in March, 1861, of the rich lode. The result was the influx of gold seekers which populated Idaho. In the early winter of 1862, Dent made an overland journey from Vancouver to the East, by way of The Dalles, Olds Ferry, the emigrant road on the Snake River's south bank, Tom Hampton's on Bear River, and Salt Lake. The quartermaster's department in those early days instructed all touring officers to note the resources and physical features of all regions through which they chanced to pass. The reports of the Army quartermaster's department prior to 1860 are mines of historical data. From Vancouver to Salt Lake meant a journey of eight hundred miles through a vast country which possessed no civil government and where journeying emigrants reported many murders by Indians and desperado whites. Of course, the finding of gold in the region north of the Snake River necessitated Army protection for the ingoing prospectors and settlers. In January, 1863, Dent reached Washington and that same month was summoned before the House Committee on Territories. He was questioned about the resources of the country northwest of Salt Lake and the Blue Mountains, for at that time the committee was considering Ashley's proposed bill to create a new territory out of Nebraska, western Dakota, and eastern Washington. Dent gave much general information and made a suggestion concerning the new Montana bill. He said that in place of Montana, he would offer a more musical and typical name, Indian, perhaps Chinook, in origin.

"I mean the word 'Idaho'!" said Dent. "It is familiar in that country and expresses the meaning, 'Gem of the Mountains.' On my journey eastward, the country from Grand Ronde to Bear River was a mass of beautiful snow-tipped mountains in the gulches of which were many Indian villages. The Indians called the country 'Idaho'!"

Dent said that the name of the steamer *Idaho*, which plied the Columbia while he was at Vancouver, was generally supposed to be a Chinook word, and that her name translated meant "Gem of the Mountains." In spite of General Dent's suggestion, the name Idaho was not reported in the bill. Dent told me that he called upon several members of the House and the Senate and pled for the adoption of the name. It was after his participation in the matter that the name was formally chosen.

General Dent may not be credited with the naming of Idaho, in spite of what Governor Bennett said, but it is fair to state that he was the first man, not excepting the actual promoters of the bill in 1862 and 1863, who impressed upon the House and Senate the advisability of adopting the name Idaho.

THE LONGFELLOW CORRESPONDENCE

Henry W. Longfellow, the poet, deserves mention in connection with Idaho, because at the time of the furthering of the Idaho Organic Act he corresponded with his friend Senator Charles Sumner on the subject. He did not, however, suggest the name "Idaho"; he suggested the word "Mazaska," a corruption of the Dakota word, "Mazaskasimaka," meaning "money."

The Rev. Samuel Longfellow, Henry's brother, edited a volume of the poet's letters, published at Boston, 1887. Through a technical error, the Rev. Longfellow gives the impression that his brother was suggesting a name for Dakota Territory, which was organized in 1861 as the climax of agitation begun in 1860. On page 66 of the memoirs, the Rev. Longfellow comments: "Mr. [Senator] Sumner had apparently written to his friend [Longfellow] asking him to propose a name for the new territory about to be established, and suggesting a name equivalent to 'Eldorado.'" Above the note are two letters from Longfellow to Sumner, at Washington. Notice that the first is dated May 1, 1860, and the second is dated May 3, no year given.

May 1, 1860

"Eldorado," in the Dakotah tongue would be Mazaskasimaka— as musical as Massachusetts, and not to be thought of for a moment. Decidedly, that will not do! Let us try again! Omaha, Ottawa, names of tribes, both good. Either would do very well, but neither is characteristic. Up to present date I find nothing better than Mazaska, which means, in English, "money"—the mighty dollar even! and is the first part of Mazaskasimaka. Unfortunately the true Indian accent is on the first syllable. I have transposed it for ease of parlance.

The second letter says:

May 3

Too late! I see by last evening's paper that the Territory is already called Idaho—said to mean, "Gem of the Mountains." It certainly does not in Dakotah or what is the use of having a Dakotah dictionary?

The explanation perhaps lies in the fact that the Rev. Samuel Longfellow found the dates of the two notes illegible, or undecipherable, and jumped to the conclusion that the two letters were written in 1860. In the first place, Senator Sumner was in Europe during May of 1860; that fact is suggested in a letter from Longfellow to Sumner, which directly precedes the two letters reprinted above. Moreover, Senator Sumner was in the Senate and voted favorably when Senator Wilson moved to strike out "Montana" and substitute "Idaho." Unquestionably, Longfellow and Sumner corresponded on the subject of a name for the new territory, but the date of the two letters must have been March 1, 1863, and March 5, 1863. It is possible that the poet jotted on the notes, "M—1—1863" and "M—5," no year. His brother assumed the "M" to mean May and the date 1860, instead of 1863. A lack of knowledge of history of the territories would easily cause this mistake. As I have said, the new territory talked of in 1860 was Dakota; it was always known by that name, there was no "juggling," and it retained its name until 1889, when the two states, North and South Dakota, were admitted to the Union.

THE SEAL OF IDAHO TERRITORY*

The history of the seal of Idaho Territory, like the history of the name of the territory, is open to conjecture. Among Mr. Donaldson's papers was found a reproduction of the first seal of the territory and a note as follows: "Silas Cochrane told me in 1870 that he designed the original seal of the territory. Verify this and add data."

I have endeavored to fulfill Mr. Donaldson's wishes in the matter but with little if any success. No one else, so far as I can discover, has ever claimed the honor of designing the seal, nor has anyone denied Cochrane's claims.

* This article on the Seal of Idaho Territory has been supplied by T. B. Donaldson.

Cochrane became acting secretary of Idaho Territory in May, 1864, although he never received an appointment from Washington, D. C. He was energetic, intelligent, resourceful, and well liked. He left Idaho in 1875, and I have been unable to trace him or his family. In the first edition of the Idaho laws, printed at Lewiston in 1864, by James Glascock, territorial printer, the certificate of validity stating that the laws in the volume are true and literal copies of the enrolled laws passed by the first legislative assembly, December, 1863, and January and February, 1864, at Lewiston, contains a reproduction of the first seal of the territory—thus: "Witness my hand and the seal of the Territory hereunto annexed this first day of July, A.D., eighteen hundred and sixty four.—William B. Daniels, Secretary of the Territory."

This volume contains many typographical errors and a sad mixture of names of people and places. The reproduction of the territorial seal is a crude wood cut, a background of black, with relief in white. Briefly described, the details of the original seal were: escutcheon, a shield supported by thirty stars; the crest, an American eagle with outspread wings and arrows in talons. The shield has two compartments divided by an ordinary with the legend, "The Union." The lower compartment holds a sheaf of wheat in foreground and a plow in the rear. The upper compartment has in the foreground an emigrant train, four oxen drawing a covered wagon, a horseman riding ahead and, in the rear, a man on foot evidently saluting the sun as it rises over hills and mountains in the background. The outer circles of the seal contain the words: "Seal of the Territory of Idaho" and the date "1863" with a single star to right and left. The date is at the lower center. The woodcut in the first laws is very crudely executed; a clean engraving of the escutcheon may be seen on the back of the banknotes first issued by the First National Bank, of Boise, in 1867.

LAWS

OF THE

TERRITORY OF IDAHO,

FIRST SESSION;

CONVENED THE 7TH DAY OF DECEMBER, 1863, AND ADJOURNED
ON THE 4TH DAY OF FEBRUARY, 1864, AT

LEWISTON.

ALSO, CONTAINING THE

TERRITORIAL ORGANIC ACT,

DECLARATION OF INDEPENDENCE, THE FEDERAL
CONSTITUTION, THE PRE-EMPTION, AND
NATURALIZATION LAWS, ETC., ETC.

LEWISTON:
JAMES A. GLASCOCK, TERRITORIAL PRINTER.
1864.

Title page from *Laws of the Territory of Idaho* issued in Lewiston, Idaho Territory, in 1864.

HOW IDAHO RECEIVED HER NAME

This seal continued in use until 1871, when a new design was adopted by the legislature. The change was made because several patriotic legislators, or their friends, considered that "Idaho's seal was too much like Oregon's." In an attempt to glean a few facts concerning the seals of 1863 and 1871, I wrote to many pioneers. Receiving no assistance, I wrote to the territorial secretary. His reply is given:

Boise, Idaho, September 26, 1903

Dear Sir:

Replying to your favor of August 27th, permit me to say that I have delayed answering your communication, relative to information bearing upon the adoption of the Territorial Seal of 1871, in the hope of finding some record relative thereto. After considerable research, I am unable to find anything bearing upon this subject, as our records of that date are in a very unsatisfactory condition.

Yours very truly,
(Signed) WILL H. GIBSON,
Secretary of State.

The original seal of Idaho was very much like the seal commonly known or accepted in 1870 as the official seal of Oregon, in general appearance. Of course, the details varied, although in the two compartments of the shield of Oregon's seal were, similarly, an eagle at the crest, an ordinary with "The Union" as a motto, an emigrant wagon, and a plow and sheaf. Close inspection of the Oregon seal showed many distinctive features such as two steamers on the sea, an elk, and a varying number of supporting stars. In this connection it is proper to mention an article by Mr. F. H. Saylor, in the *Oregon Native Son,* May, 1899, Portland, Oregon, entitled "Oregon without a Seal of State." Mr. Saylor's interesting historical bit shows the disastrous— perhaps amusing—effect of legislative juggling with an official seal. To return to the consideration of Idaho's seal, the seal adopted in 1871 (by whom it was designed I am unable to learn) was much different in detail from the original seal. The eagle at the crest was supplanted by an elk head with branching horns and a scroll. The shield contained but one compartment and in that was a river winding through the mountains, with a steamboat in the foreground and a crescent moon in the background. The motto "The Union" on the original, in ordinary, was supplanted by the word "Salve," in ordinary at the lower support of the shield. Two figures are most prominent; the dexter support is exidently, Ceres, the goddess of harvest, and the sinister support is evidently Liberty, for the figure wears a pileus and carries fasces in the left hand and a sword in the right. In the outer circle is "Seal of the Territory of Idaho," and a single star is at the base. This seal was in vogue until Idaho became a state; then a radically different design was offered by Miss Emma Edwards, of Boise, and accepted. The descriptions of the seals of 1863 and 1871, the only seals ever used by Idaho Territory, are written from impressions of the originals.*

HOW THE IDAHO ORGANIC ACT PASSED CONGRESS

The second discovery of gold in Idaho, the opening of the Boise Basin mines by George Grimes and his party, produced an excitement all over America that rivaled the excitement attending the discovery of gold in California in 1848. There was a consequent influx of miners—perhaps some settlers— and naturally the politicians of the Northwest saw opportunity for the apportionment and organization of a territorial government in the newly opened strip. In addition to that, the central government appreciated the fact that protection was necessary for settlers and miners because of the prevalence of roving bands of Indians. An era of "land juggling" began, and when we consider with what freedom thousands of square miles were cut off here

---

* These were very kindly forwarded to me by Mr. W. A. Goulder, of the Idaho Pioneer Society. If any mistakes, or omissions, have occurred, in the description above, they are entirely due to imperfections in the impressions at hand.—T.B.D.

HOW IDAHO RECEIVED HER NAME

and there, comparisons between the vastness of the Northwest and the meager extent of our Eastern states are astounding.

The first changes made in Idaho's boundaries—Idaho that was to be—was made by the Washington legislature on February 12, 1863, when Boise County was narrowed. Of course, Boise County was then a part of Washington Territory, and it comprised that enormous land area which lay south of Idaho County, with Snake River on its western boundary, Utah, as then constituted, on the south, and the main line of the Rockies on the east. Since 1862 eight distinct counties have been cut from the original Boise County.

Late in 1862, demands grew incessant for a separate territorial government for the new gold mining area east of Walla Walla, Washington. In the autumn of 1862, the upper body of the Washington Territory legislature passed a bill providing that the people in this eastern section of Washington should decide by vote on the question of adopting or not adopting a constitution for a new state. It is worthy of note that the name first suggested was, "State of Idaho." The lower branch of the legislature defeated the bill by striking out the word Idaho and substituting Washington, so that the bill, as amended, read, "State of Washington."

Following directly on this came the first attempt* to

---

* In perusing the records of Congress to trace the first appearance of the name Idaho, I was considerably surprised to find that the word appeared in the House in December of 1860. In the report of the transactions of the second session of the Thirty-sixth Congress, part one, there was introduced, December 18, 1860, and ordered to be printed: "A bill [H. B. No. 887] to provide a temporary government for the Territory of Idaho." At the same time, bills were introduced for the organization of temporary governments for the territories of Nevada, Arizona, and Dakota. The Idaho bill was introduced by Galusha A. Grow, then chairman of the committee on territories. Much interested in the early appearance of the name Idaho, I wrote to Mr. Grow and asked for information, for his recollection of the bill and its introducers, or its sponsors. Mr. Grow replied briefly to the effect that he recalled the incident but did not recollect the person or persons who had suggested the name Idaho. "I do remember," he writes, "that the interpretation of the word—for I asked it—was 'Gem of the Mountains.'" To search further was useless. It would be most interesting to read, at the present day, the provisions of the bill of 1860 for comparison with the Organic Act of 1863. Barring the name Idaho, what the bill was, is conjectural. The most interesting point in the above is the early appearance of the adopted name of the territory, although no particular significance was attached to the name at the time; and, moreover, it had no bearing upon the final adoption of the name.
—T.B.D.

obtain an organic act from Congress. On December 22, 1862, James M. Ashley, chairman of the House Committee on Territories, "introduced a bill to provide a temporary form of government for the Territory of Idaho; which was read a first and second time, and referred to the Committee on Territories." (p. 166, "Congressional Globe" for December 24, 1862). It is interesting to note that Mr. Ashley introduced at the same time bills to bring Utah, Nevada, Nebraska, and Colorado into the Union as states. No doubt the name Idaho was suggested to Mr. Ashley by one or more of the Westerners in Congress who knew of the recent action by the Washington Territory legislature. But the name at this juncture was not especially significant; the bill changed its name soon afterward, and no protests were made. The reason for this was that Mr. Ashley was personally desirous of organizing two territories in the new country.

On January 20, 1863, Mr. Ashley introduced practically the same bill under a different name. The record states: "Mr. Ashley asked unanimous consent of the House to report from the Committee on Territories, a bill to provide a temporary form of government for the Territory of Shoshone, in order that it might be printed and recommitted." At this point, W. S. Holman, of Indiana, raised objection. The speaker called for the regular order of business, and the bill was not ordered printed.

The session was now well on toward the end, and it seemed as if the bill creating the new territory, whether it was to be named Montana, Shoshone, or Idaho, was doomed to be held over. However, Congressman Ashley renewed the attack on February 11, 1863, by introducing in the House the Montana Territory bill. Says the record: "Mr. Ashley reported back House Bill No. 626, to provide a temporary form of government for the Territory of Montana; which was ordered to be printed, and recommitted to the same committee." The following day, February 12, the

HOW IDAHO RECEIVED HER NAME

fight for the bill was on in earnest, but a very mild fight it was. Mr. Ashley reported back House Bill No. 738 providing for the Territory of Montana with the recommendation that it pass. The bill was read through, and thereupon Carey A. Trimble, of Ohio, and John B. S. Todd, Dakota's delegate, moved amendments of a technical nature: these amendments referred to Indian affairs, to suffrage, to clerks and attachés for the territorial legislature, and to the probate court clerk and fees.

The instant the amendments were out of the way, Samuel S. Cox, of Ohio, on behalf of the Democrats, opened the attack against the Wilmot proviso in the bill. Said Mr. Cox:

"I move to strike out the proviso to the sixth section, commonly called the Wilmot proviso; and on that motion I demand the previous question."

The proviso as printed read: "Provided, That whereas slavery is prohibited in said Territory by act of Congress of June 19, 1862, nothing herein contained shall be construed to authorize or permit its existence therein."

The yeas and nays were ordered, and on this attempt by the Democrats to strike out the freedom clause from the bill, the Republicans, voting solidly, polled 96 nays. The ayes were a solid 38. The Montana (Idaho) bill was, as amended, ordered engrossed and read a third time. Ashley demanded the previous question, and when William Allen, of Ohio, demanded the yeas and nays, the Republicans voted aye 85 and the Democrats a solid 39 nay.

No bill of similar purport ever passed a Congress with as little discussion as did the Montana (Idaho) bill. The opposition of the Democrats, headed by Mr. Cox, was due entirely to the party's attitude on slavery and the expectation that in the near future the end of the Rebellion would unite the southern Democrats with the northern disciples of the party. When that occurred, the result would be, so thought Cox and his colleagues, the taking of the control of the nation's policy from the Republicans. Idaho being in the "free belt," her creation as a territory, ultimately a state, would injure slavery's cause by placing in the National Senate two members opposed to slavery and at least one antislavery man in the House. The Democrats also knew well that the area to be included in the new territory was the home and refuge of thousands of Democrats who— many of them opposed to war—fled the Army draft. And they knew that the new Northwest also held thousands of deserters from the Union army and hundreds of Southerners who could, and did, defy the National Government. The latter, the turbulent element, preferred to live in a free zone untrammeled by law and beyond the control of a government which they cordially hated. Petitions from these men to their Democratic friends in Congress had aroused the opposition. When the squelching occurred in the House, the Democratic senators wisely refrained from debating the Montana (Idaho) bill on party lines in the Senate for they would have met exactly the same fate as had their colleagues in the lower body.

The bill reached the Senate one day later, February 13, 1863, and was reported back to the territorial committee by the chairman, Benjamin F. Wade, of Ohio. The final consideration did not come before the Senate until almost the last few hours of the session, and the Idaho adherents were on pins and needles with anxiety. On the last day of the session, March 3, 1863, the bill was taken up and, on motion of Morton S. Wilkinson, of Minnesota, was put on its passage by a vote of 22 to 13. The debate that followed was not on party lines, as it had been in the House.

Mr. Wilkinson said, "I move to lay aside the pending bill and all other orders, and take up House Bill No. 738, providing for a temporary form of government for the Territory of Montana."

"I hope not," protested Senator Ira Harris, who was interested in the pending bill—a bill to establish provisional governments in certain cases. Mr. Harris considered, as do most senators, that his bill was more important than any other bill. A lengthy debate took place on the whys and wherefores. Senators Wilkinson and Charles Sumner voiced the opinion that the particular bill furthered by Senator Harris could not pass the House, at all events.

Senator James R. Doolittle, of Wisconsin, then arose and made a strong plea for the prompt consideration of the Montana (Idaho) bill. Said he, in part, "We can take it up and pass it. It is important that it should be passed. The territory of Montana is an important territory, with great gold mines in it, and with a large population in it already."

At this juncture, Senator James W. Grimes, of Iowa, voiced, without doubt, the geographical ignorance of more than one senator by calling out, "Where is it?" referring to Montana's location.

Thereupon, Senator Doolittle explained in full, much to the advantage of the bill. Debate, or discussion, then took place upon the question first raised by Mr. Wilkinson: to postpone, or not, the pending bill and all prior orders to consider the Montana bill. Senators Davis, Wade, Ten Eyck, Harris, Howe, and Nesmith participated in a verbal outburst of some duration.

Benjamin F. Harding, who had been elected from Oregon to succeed Senator Edward D. Baker, deceased, then arose and said,

Mr. President, the territory proposed to be organized under a territorial government by the bill referred to by the senator from Minnesota has not at this time a population exceeding probably five thousand. During last summer, in the mining district known as the Salmon River mines, there were propably ten thousand persons. The usual severity of the winter in that country has induced most of those miners to leave there and go to the lower country for the winter. Since last August other mines have been discovered on the Boise River, where there are now probably from two to three thousand miners at work, according to the best information we can get. In the Salmon River mines there are now probably one, two, or three thousand miners altogether.

The territory included in the boundaries fixed in the bill contains but little agricultural country, and there are, probably, not today more than a few dozen families residing within that territory; but all the accounts we receive from there show that the mines are very rich, and that large numbers of people intend to go there early this spring. I suppose the prospects of the territory are as good today as the prospects of Nevada were the day its territorial organization was completed. I understand that at the time the bill for the organization of Nevada was passed there were only a few hundred people in that territory; but the bill was passed upon the knowledge which Congress had that a very large number of persons intended emigrating to and settling in that territory in the next spring, and that large amounts of capital had been invested there.

As the bill now stands I cannot vote for it, because it does not include the population east of the Cascade Mountains who desire a territorial organization; but by a proper amendment I think the bill can be made a good one. I hope it will be taken up and amended, and then passed.

"The senator from Oregon, in his estimate of the population," rejoined Lane, of Kansas, "does not count the people on the eastern slope of the mountains."

"That is so," replied Mr. Harding. "I know nothing of the eastern slope of the Rocky Mountains on this side. I only speak of the western side."

Mr. Lane continued: "The delegate from Dakota [Mr. Todd] estimates the number of miners on the eastern slope of the mountains as equal to the number given by the senator from Oregon, which would make a population of from eight to ten thousand persons. I do hope that the Montana bill will be passed; and that then we shall take up the bill to enable Nevada and Colorado to form state governments, and pass them."

The question was then taken by yeas and nays, and the result was, yeas 22, nays 13. The motion was accordingly

HOW IDAHO RECEIVED HER NAME

agreed to, and the Montana (Idaho) bill was considered as in committee of the whole.

When the boundaries were read, Senator Wilson arose and said: "I move to strike out the name of the territory and insert 'Idaho.' "

"I hope not," immediately broke in Senator Doolittle. "I hope there will be no amendment at all. Montana sounds just as well as Idaho."

"It has no meaning. The other [Idaho] has," quickly interjected Senator Wilson.

"It [Montana] has a meaning," said Mr. Doolittle; "it refers to the mountainous character of the country."

The amendment was rejected, but the movers did not despair. Wilson and the Western senators did some tall hustling, during Senator Hardin's introduction of an amendment to the original boundaries expressed in the Montana bill.

Senator Harding arose and said: "I move to strike out of the first section all after the words 'to wit' in the fourth line, to the word 'the' in the twenty-sixth line, being the boundaries of the proposed territory, and, in lieu of the words stricken out, to insert:

Beginning at a point in the middle channel of the Snake river, where the northern boundary of Oregon intersects the same; then following down said channel of Snake river to a point opposite the mouth of the Kooskooskia or Clearwater river; thence due north to the forty-ninth parallel of latitude; thence east along said parallel to the twenty-seventh degree of longitude west of Washington; thence south along said degree of longitude to the northern boundary of Colorado territory; thence west along said boundary to the thirty-third degree of longitude west of Washington; thence north along said degree to the forty-second parallel of latitude; thence west along said parallel to the eastern boundary of the state of Oregon; thence north along said boundary to the place of beginning.*

---

* The details of Congressional legislation on the Idaho Organic Act will be found in the *Congressional Globe, Debates and Proceedings of the 3rd Session, 37th Congress.* The proceedings in the House are indexed under Idaho, pp. 166, 884, 914, 1542, 1547, and under Shoshone, p. 403. In the Senate, the references to Idaho are indexed, pp.

The amendment was at once agreed to, the bill was reported to the Senate as amended and concurred in. Senator Wilson then arose, determined and vigorously obstinate in his plea.

"I renew," said he, "the amendment to change the name from Montana to Idaho." Mr. Doolittle arose and settled the question in history.

"As the bill has already been amended," said he, "and will have to go back to the House of Representatives, I do not much care about the name; and if it pleases my honorable friend from Massachusetts to call it Idaho instead of Montana, I am willing to yield to his suggestion." Senator Harding arose for a parting shot.

"I think the name of Idaho is preferable to Montana," said Mr. Harding. "Montana, to my mind, signifies nothing at all. Idaho, in English, signifies 'gem of the mountains.' This is a mountainous country, and the name Idaho is well understood in signification and orthography in all that country; and I prefer it to the present name."

The amendment was concurred in and the newly named bill was put on its passage. John S. Carlile, of Virginia, called for the yeas and nays on the passage of the bill.

Those who voted for the creation of the new territory were twenty-five in all: Senators Anthony; Chandler; Clark; Cowan; Davis; Doolittle; Foot; Foster; Harding; Harlan; Harris; Henderson; Howe; Henry S. Lane, of

---
905, 924, 951, 1509, 1513,. 1525, 1530. The Idaho Organic Act is printed in full in pp. 233-35 of the Appendix.

The boundaries of Idaho territory in the bill as originally reported were as follows: "Commencing at a point formed by the intersection of the 45th degree of north latitude with the 27th degree of longitude west from Washington, thence due west, on the 45th degree of north latitude, to a point formed by its intersection with the 33rd degree of longitude west from Washington; thence due north, along the 33rd degree of longitude, to its intersection with the 46th degree of latitude west from Washington; thence along the 46th degree of latitude to a point formed by its intersection with the eastern boundary of the State of Oregon, in the channel of the Snake river; thence south, along the boundary of Oregon, till it intersects with the 42nd degree of north latitude; thence east, along the 42nd degree of north latitude, to a point formed by its intersection with the 33rd degree of longitude west from Washington; thence due south, along the 33rd degree of longitude, to a point formed by its intersection with the 41st degree of north latitude; thence due east, along the 41st degree of north latitude to a point formed by its intersection with the 27th degree of longitude west from Washington; thence due north, along the 27th degree of west longitude, to the place of beginning." *Cong. Globe, 37th Cong., 3rd Sess., Part II*, p. 1509, and Appendix.—T.B.D.

Indiana; James H. Lane, of Kansas; Morrill; Nesmith; Pomeroy; Rice; Sumner; Ten Eyck; Wade; Wilkinson; Willey; and Henry Wilson, of Massachusetts.

The opponents of the bill were twelve in number: Senators Carlile; Dixon; Grimes; Howard; King; Powell; Richardson; Saulsbury; Trumbull; Turpie; Wilmot; and Robert Wilson, of Missouri. At this date of writing, 1897, just one senator, Lot M. Morrill, of Maine, is alive of all those who voted either for or against the Idaho Organic Act.

On the evening of March 3, between ten and eleven o'clock, the Idaho bill, as amended, was returned to the House of Representatives, and a struggle, a brief one, commenced on the final issue. The title of the bill, "To provide a temporary government for the Territory of Montana, returned from the Senate with amendments," was read. James M. Ashley at once arose, considerably annoyed at the revision.

"I move," said Mr. Ashley, "that the House nonconcur in the Senate amendments and ask a committee of conference." Thereupon, Aaron A. Sargent, of California, took up the fight for the Idaho adherents.

"I hope that will not be done," said Mr. Sargent. "I should somewhat hesitate to try the experiment of the gentleman from Ohio, a friend of this bill, at this very late hour of the session, thereby sending it back to the Senate, and hence to a committee on conference. I am as desirous of the passage of this bill as he, but at the same time it is better to concur in the Senate amendments as they now stand, rather than to risk the loss of the bill entirely."

"I am very much obliged to the gentleman from California for his advice," sarcastically responded Mr. Ashley. "The committee on territories have had this matter in charge, and I ask this House to nonconcur in the Senate amendments, and ask a committee on conference."

Matters began to assume a doubtful aspect. Mr. Sargent, equal to the emergency and anxious to appease Mr. Ashley, who was evidently nettled, said, "I was not offering advice to the gentleman from Ohio. I do not presume to give him information on this or any subject; but as the bill relates to the erection of a territory upon the Pacific, and as I am as anxious for the passage of the bill, as I believe the gentleman himself is, I suggest to the House—not to the gentleman—that it might be well not to hazard the passage of the bill by nonconcurring in the amendments of the Senate at this late hour of the session. That seems to me to be good policy. I made the suggestion to the House, and the gentleman is under no obligation to me. I call the previous question."

The previous question was seconded and the main question ordered, when William H. Wadsworth, of Kentucky, asked, "Is this a mere contest between the two names of Montana and Idaho?"

"Oh, no!" retorted Mr. Ashley. "There is a change in the boundaries as well as in the name. I call for tellers on concurring in the amendments of the Senate."

Tellers were not ordered, and the vote was then taken. The House stood, and Speaker Grow counted the members standing in their places. The amendments were concurred in, ayes 65, nays 33. Although to all intent and purpose, this made the Idaho Organic Act an accomplished fact, William S. Holman, of Indiana, asked, "Is it in order to move to lay the bill on the table?"

Speaker Grow replied, "The Chair thinks not, at this time. The House has agreed to the amendments of the Senate, which was all that the House could do." Thereupon, Mr. Sargent moved, and it was agreed to, to lay the motion to reconsider upon the table.

Brief as was the actual time consumed in passing the bill through both houses of Congress, the promoters present

HOW IDAHO RECEIVED HER NAME

were looking back upon the long months of work spent in projecting the bill, and now that it was passed their exhiliration may be appreciated by us, at this late day. Judge McBride wrote to me recently:

"I have a very distinct recollection of the passage of the Idaho bill. It was among the last acts of the busy final session, March 3, of the Thirty-seventh Congress and the final vote was taken just before midnight. James M. Ashley, chairman of the House territorial committee, had insisted upon the organization of two territories instead of one. The Senate territorial committee were opposed to organizing more than one and when the bill came to the House, Mr. Ashley objected to the amendments, desiring the bill referred to his committee in order that his plan for the organization of two territories should be substituted. The friends of the Idaho bill, realizing the danger of such reference, which would have necessitated sending the bill back to the Senate, were very active in insisting that it should be accepted as it came from the Senate. The result was that Mr. Ashley's motion suffered defeat. The bill passed in the same form in which it came from the Senate. Mr. Ashley was very indignant and thought that a great discourtesy had been shown him by the refusal of the House to refer the bill back to his committee.

"During the evening, William H. Wallace, Dr. A. G. Henry, and I were working hard to push the bill through. We were indebted to the California delegation, especially Aaron A. Sargent, to members of the Pennsylvania delegation, and especially to Speaker Grow, for the ultimate passage of the bill. Within half an hour after it had been enrolled, it was placed in President Lincoln's hands. It was, of course, closing night of the session, and President Lincoln was at his chambers in the Capitol.

"I remember very distinctly that Wallace, Henry and I had a dinner of rejoicing at Hammark's restaurant, on

Pennsylvania avenue, where good eating and champagne were prominent."

The Idaho bill did not actually become a law until March 4, 1863, for the records of Congress show that the House took a recess from 12:50 to 1:50 A. M., the morning of the fourth. Soon after the House reassembled, Bradley F. Granger, chairman of the committee on enrolled bills, reported the Idaho act enrolled, and Speaker Grow signed it. It was then sent back to the Senate, which had adjourned, at 4:15 A. M. A message from Chief Clerk Morris, of the House, was read, saying that the speaker of the House had signed, among other bills, the Idaho bill. Thereupon, the president pro tempore of the Senate also signed the enrolled bill, and it was at once sent to President Lincoln. It was not, as Judge McBride says, within an hour after the passage that Mr. Lincoln signed and made the bill a law: it was about four hours later. The Idaho Organic Act was returned to the Senate at ten o'clock the morning of March 4, at which time the Senate met after a recess.

HOW IDAHO WAS NAMED

Although someone may yet arise to claim the honor of naming Idaho, and although several may have already claimed the honor, for my own part I am convinced that the name Idaho was perpetuated because of the expressed wish of a woman; and that woman was Luzena Brazelton Wallace, the wife of Idaho's first territorial governor. Nothing could be more picturesquely historical—save, perhaps, another reminiscence by gentlemen versed (?) in Indian lore—but picturesque or not, the statement is fair and reasonable when the reason for it is considered.

Frequently, during the last ten years, I have seen articles in Western papers which stated that Mrs. William H. Wallace, the wife of Idaho's first governor, was re-

HOW IDAHO RECEIVED HER NAME

sponsible for the insertion of the name Idaho in the territorial organic act. Strange to say, the various articles told the bit of reminiscence in exactly the same way; that is, as to facts in the case. I had been disposed at first to consider the story as the creation of zealous newspapermen, writing for space. However, the coherency of the story determined me to seek the facts; and my search into the records of Congress convinced me that a person, or persons, must have brought strong influence to bear in order to effect the substitution of the word "Idaho" for "Montana" in the crucial moment, when the bill came up for consideration at the final session of the Congress of 1863.

I was fortunate enough to meet W. W. Wallace, son of William H. Wallace, in Washington, where he has been for many years in the auditing service of the War Department. Mr. Wallace was most emphatic in his claim that his mother was responsible for the final amending of the Montana bill. His recollection of the incident in the case clears up, at least as far as I am concerned, all doubt in the matter. Mr. Wallace was well on in his teens when the Idaho bill was passed, and he was quite well able to remember the events of the period. Said he, in part:

"You of course know that my father, William H. Wallace, was present at Oro Fino in 1862, when the initial steps to form Idaho Territory were taken. Now, the name Idaho was familiar to him and his associates, but it was not familiar to many in either branch of Congress. As soon as father returned to Washington, he and Dr. Henry and one or two members of Congress began active work in the winter of 1862 to canvass for the Idaho bill. Of Dr. Henry we saw a great deal at our home, and naturally we heard of little else but the plans and progress of the canvass for the territorial bill. You see, the promoters had much to cope with in Congress, and the name for the new territory was a matter of unimportance until near the close of the session. An Idaho bill was presented in the House sometime in December of 1862, but there was nothing of importance attached to the name at that time; the bill was changed later to the Montana bill.

"It was probably two weeks before the third of March, 1863—I am not certain about the exact time; it may have been a longer time than that—when a committee of three came to our home one evening. The men were Westerners; Dr. A. G. Henry was one of them. They discussed at length the hoped-for passage of the bill before Congress, and finally someone said, 'How about fixing up a good name for the territory?' If I remember rightly, there was some dissatisfaction expressed with the name Montana, and I know that there was some apprehension felt that Congress, especially the House, would try to juggle with the matter. That is, there was talk of the creation of two new territories. My mother and I were of course present, and when the names were reviewed, Montana, Idaho, and Lafayette had been suggested—Mother said:

" 'I hope you will conclude to name it Idaho.'

" 'Idaho the name shall be,' Dr. Henry at once said.

"My mother desired that name for personal reasons and, as it happened, the fact that the name was Western and well known to the men present, gave her expressed wish especial emphasis. In the summer of 1862, Mother had visited in Iowa and while there met a married sister who lived in Colorado; in fact, under the shadow of Pikes Peak. Her sister had a charming little daughter whose first name was Idaho, and Mother thought her the most wonderful baby in the world. When she returned to Washington she talked of nothing but 'Idaho,' 'Idaho,' until Father and I took it as a byword and twitted her continually. It was very natural for her to request the name Idaho for the new territory and, as the map shows, the territory was eventually named that. The niece's name was Idaho Jackson. The name Idaho meant 'gem of the mountains,' and Mother felt that for the baby or the new territory the name was particularly appropriate. Dr. Henry and my father did all they could to have the name adopted, and I know that their zeal arose at Mother's suggestion."*

---

* Mrs. Wallace died at Steilacoom, Washington, October 31, 1900, aged eighty years. For verification of several things, I saw W. W. Wallace, in Washington, and he wrote to me the following, which is not as detailed but practically the same as the conversation recounted above:

"February 12, 1902, Washington, D. C.

"I wish to make the following statement which may be of some historical value. When the bill was being prepared for the organization of the territory [Idaho], a committee of three from the Pacific coast, met at my father's rooms in this city, and among other things considered was the name the territory should bear. My mother was present during this conversation. The names Lafayette, Montana and Idaho were mentioned. My mother became immediately interested in the proceedings and said, 'I hope you will conclude to name it Idaho.' One of the committee, a Doctor Henry, spoke up and said, 'Idaho it shall be.'

"I will give you the reason why mother selected Idaho as the name of the territory. The year before, in the summer of 1862, my mother was visiting in Iowa and met a sister of hers whose home was in Colorado, near Pike's Peak. She had a little daughter about one year old with her, whose name was Idaho Jackson. Mother thought that there never was just quite as sweet and pretty a little creature in all the world and was talking about her all the time, to the amusement of father and myself. So that when the names mentioned were being canvassed, you can readily understand why mother selected Idaho. The name, an Indian one signifying, 'Gem of the Mountains,' was always used by mother in singing her little niece's praises.

Yours very truly,
W. W. WALLACE."

Mr. Wallace also gave to me the photograph of his father which I had restored and which is the frontispiece of this book. It is, as far as Mr. Wallace knows, the one picture extant of William H. Wallace. It was taken in March, 1863, by Charles D. Fredericks, of New York City.—T.B.D.

INDEX

Adams, Jimmy, 91
Agnew, James D., 113, 115, 116, 117, 118, 149
Ah Kee, 158-60
Ainsley, George, 203, 282, 283, 284
Ainsworth, Captain J. C., 24, 344
Allen, Charles, 175
Allen, Henry, 46
Allen, Joe, 112
Amalgam, 35, 36
Ames, Oakes, 97, 98, 99
Anderson, Ben, 248
Anderson, Judge Stamps Volney, 134-39
Arthur, President Chester A., 268
Ayres, Tubman, 146

Babcock, General E. O., 379, 380
Bacon, Joe, 176, 177
Baker City, Oregon, 97, 101, 163, 342
Ballard, Governor David W., 64, 175, 176, 183, 193, 225, 242-51, 289, 300, 301, 302
Bannock Jim, 290, 291
Barbour, Clitus, 285-89, 313, 314
Bard, Samuel, 252-53
Bartholomew, George, 103
Beachy, Hill, 73, 74, 76, 162, 208
Beadle, J. H., 56
Bear Lake, 53, 54
Benjamin, Thomas Thomas, 53
Benjamin, W. H., 53
Bennett, Thomas W., 256-58, 379, 380, 381
Bishop, Dr. Edward, 221, 222, 304
Blaine, Hon. James G., 97, 98, 150, 198, 356
Blanchet, Rev. F. N., 58
Boise Assay Office, 38
Boise buildings, 32, 202
Boise Fire Department, 32, 33
Boise News, 160
Boomer, Alexander H., 75, 76, 94
Bowers, Thomas J., 205
Bowlby, Sam, 219
Boutwell, George S., 38
Bowan, Thomas M., 253-56
Bowman, I. H., 160
Boyakin, Judson A., 129
Branstetter, H. C., 222
Brayman, Governor Mason, 260-62, 263, 267
Britton, Alexander T., 363, 365, 366, 367
Broadbent, John G., 142, 143
Brouillet, Rev. John B., 59
Brown, L. N., 46
Brown, L. P., 23
Brumback, Jeremiah, 203
Bruneau River, 25
Brunot, Felix, 314
Bryon, William, 169, 211, 212, 213
Bunn, William M., 57, 269-72
Burmester, Theodore, 163, 207, 208
Butler, J. S., 160
Butler, Thomas J., 160-61
Byrd, Mounts, 219

Cache Valley, Idaho, 22
Caine, John T., 364
Camas Prairie, 286, 370
Cannady, John M., 230
Cannon, George Q., 54, 363, 365, 366, 367
Carroll, John C., 145
Cartee, L. F., 36, 45, 96, 99, 115, 116, 156, 258

Carter, Mr. and Mrs. J. C., 105, 113
Catherine Creek, 28
Catholic Church, 57-61, 65
Catlin, George, 276, 277, 326
Catlow, John, 99, 100, 101, 153-55
Centerville, Idaho, 46
Central Pacific Railroad, 79, 84, 94
Chapman, Mason, 110
Chapman, W. W., 95, 96
Chief Collins, 286, 287, 288, 289, 313, 314, 315, 316
Chief Joseph, 277, 278, 279, 283, 309, 310, 371
Chief Smohalla, 340
Chief Tendoy, 281, 282, 283, 284
Chinese in Idaho, 20, 30, 35, 39, 48-53, 89, 136
City Hotel, 128, 215, 219
City of Rocks, 88, 89, 90, 95
Clark, John C., 167, 168
Cleveland, President Grover, 274
Coeur d'Alene, Idaho, 72
Columbia River, 19, 24, 25, 26, 72, 74, 84, 97, 342
Connelly, S. B., 46
Connor, General P. E., 304-09
Converse, George L., 363
Coolidge, C. W., 209, 210, 211
Corinne, Utah, 57, 94, 95, 96, 97
Corwin, Tom, 339
Cowen, W. N., 218
Cox, Emma, 30, 214-20
Crook, General George, 182, 295-97, 298, 299
Cummins, John, 251
Curtis, E. J., 33, 122, 176, 194, 195, 204, 205, 247, 251, 273, 274-75, 287, 313, 315, 316
Cushing, Frank Hamilton, 322, 323, 324, 325

Dallas, Colonel A. J., 181, 182
Daniels, William B., 223, 224, 230, 232
Davis, Thomas, 69
Day, Eph, 342, 343, 344, 345
De Lacy, General William, 76
Dent, Frederick T., 380, 381
Dibble, Judge Henry C., 130
Dixon, James, 162, 164, 166, 167
Doctors in Idaho Territory, 39, 155
Douglass, Charles, 146, 163
Downey, Captain George M., 315

Early, John, 73, 80
Eastman Hotel, 68
Edgerton, Sidney, 198-99, 223
Edmund's Confiscation Act, 57
Eldredge, Horace, 54
Elkins, Stephen B., 98
Englehard, George, 113, 118, 120
Ensign, Frank E., 103, 203

Fackler, Rev. St. Michael, 64
Falk's, 40
Farnum, John, 154, 237
Fenn, S. S., 204, 257, 282
First National Bank of Idaho, 37, 41, 92, 96, 384
Flannigan, Billy, 62, 113, 118
Florence, Idaho, 40, 69, 135, 338, 372
Flournoy, Judge A. G., 213

Floyd-Jones, Colonel De Lancey, 300-02, 312, 313
Fogus, Colonel D. H., 236
Foote, Arthur D., 358, 359, 360
Foote, Henry E., 204
Foote, Mary Hallock, 272, 358-63
Foote, Major R. F., 204
Fort Boise, 24, 39, 65, 166, 233, 245
Fort Douglas, 305, 306, 307, 350
Fort Hall, 279, 280, 283, 284, 286, 287, 313, 314, 316
Francis, James and William, 79
Franklin, Idaho, 22, 57, 80, 305, 307, 308
Frémont, General John C., 263, 264
Frisbie, General John F., 130
Fry, John D., 100

Gamble, James, 100, 101
Gamblers and gambling, 41, 42, 43, 44
Ganahl, Frank E., 203
Gardner's Station, 82
Garfielde, Selucius, 372, 377, 378
Gaulter, Lewis, 53
Gentle Annie, 30
Gibbs, Isaac L., 246, 247
Gilson, Horace C., 236, 247
Gold, coinage of, 36, 37
Gold, used as legal tender, 34, 35
Goose Creek Station, 90
Granger, Wyoming, 22, 98
Grant, President Ulysses S., 127, 153, 182, 187, 189, 191, 192, 196, 243, 244, 245, 252, 253, 257, 261, 355, 380
Grasshoppers and crickets, 70-71
Gray, John S., 64, 204
Grayson, George W., 82, 353
Great Salt Lake, 25, 94
Green, John Henry Thomas, 118, 119, 139-43
Griffin, Captain James W., 122, 164, 212, 213, 234
Grimes, George, 386
Grover, La Fayette, 336, 338, 339
Grow, Galusha A., 379, 387, 396, 398
Gwinn, Rev. Robert M., 64

Haas, Squire A., 34, 179, 180
Hague, James D., 358
Hailey, John, 65, 74-75, 76, 92, 94, 96, 99, 107
Hall, J. H., 103
Hardin, J. L., 132
Harte, Francis Bret, 356, 357, 358
Hawley, James H., 189
Hawley, Joseph R., 360
Hayes, President Rutherford B., 150, 264, 266, 268, 283, 284, 285
Hays Ferry, 152
Hays, Gilmore, 151-53
Hebrews in Idaho, 33, 41
Heed, Judge A., 126, 127, 203
Henley, John C., 195, 202
Henry Dr. A. G., 194, 229, 372, 373, 374, 375, 376, 377, 378, 397, 399, 400, 401
Higbee, Judge L. F., 165
Hill, William J., 125, 131-34
Hoar, Attorney General E. R., 127, 128
Holbrook, E. D., 143-47, 163, 245
Holladay, Ben, 73, 80, 84, 89
Hollister, Judge Madison E., 114, 142, 188, 189, 190, 291
Houghton, Captain H., 112
Howard, Eugene, 208
Howard, General O. O., 278, 279
Howlett, S. R., 247, 248, 250
Hoyt, Governor John P., 262-66
Hoyt, Captain Samuel N., 306, 307, 308
Hubble, H. C., 46

Hudson's Bay Company, 24
Huff, John, 95
Hunter, Colonel George, 46
Huntington, C. P., 98
Huntley, C. C., 75
Huntley, C. W., 76, 78
Huntley, Silas, 76
Huntoon, John, 168
Huston, Joseph W., 203, 213, 220
Hyde, D. N., 168

Idaho City, Idaho, 22, 29, 33, 46, 48, 49, 52, 58, 60, 61, 64, 120, 144, 170, 175, 176, 178, 189, 193
Idaho Organic Act, 230, 250, 369, 372, 373, 376, 379, 382, 386-98
Idaho Statesman, 31, 125-31, 132, 133, 160, 183, 192, 193, 194, 196, 233, 243
Idaho World, 160, 183
Irwin, Governor John N., 269
Isaac, H. P., and J. C., 27, 28
Isaacs, David, 45

Jennings, William, 54, 365
Johnson, Richard Z., 203
Judell, Hermann L., 349, 350, 351

Kaufman, William, 45
Kelley, Barney, 29
Kelly, Judge Milton, 133, 196
Kelton House, 85
Kelton, Utah, 22, 65, 74, 77, 79, 84-85, 88, 254
Keyser, 180
King, Clarence, 355-58, 359, 361, 363, 365, 366, 367
King Hill, Idaho, 89, 90, 95, 96, 312
Kingsley, Rev. G. S., 170, 171

Lambkin, B. F., 223
Lane, General Joseph A., 205, 206
Lapwai, Idaho, 57, 58, 277, 291
Lawrence, Henry W., 54
Lawyer, 23
Lee, Jason, 277, 337
Lewis and Clark, 23, 24, 276, 277, 309
Lewis, Judge J. R., 53, 56, 136, 137, 169, 183, 188, 189, 190, 193, 194, 200, 213, 222
Lewiston, 22, 23, 24, 68, 78, 152, 176, 193, 223, 224, 233, 236, 370
Lincoln, Abraham, 150, 197, 198, 228, 229, 230, 232, 240, 242, 245, 261, 339, 374, 375, 376, 378, 397, 398
Lindsay, Lute, 211, 213
Lindsay, Robert H., 204
Livingston, Joseph, 45
Longfellow, Henry W., 382, 383
Loon Creek, 29, 30
Lootens, Rev., Louis, 57
Lugenbeel, Major, 24, 39, 349
Luna Hotel, 68
Lyman, Amasa M., 54
Lyon, Governor Caleb, 226, 231-42, 247
Lyon, Mose, 111, 112

McBride, Judge John R., 8, 38, 170, 171, 190, 196-98, 199, 202, 203, 214, 217, 229, 251, 377, 378
McConnell, Governor W. J., 8, 171
McCormick, Michael, 46
McGarry, Major, 307, 308
McGonigle, John, 132
McHenry, O. S., 184
Mackay, John W., 353
McNeil, General John, 309, 310
Magone, Major Joseph, 336, 338
Magruder, Lloyd, 73, 162, 175
Malad, Idaho, 55, 56, 57
Marcus, Charley, 165

INDEX

Marshall, Edward C., 130
Marston, Gilman, 251-52
Masons, 45, 103, 164, 165, 181, 212
Maupin, T., 298, 299
May, Charles, 183
Meacham, A. B., 95, 96, 337, 338, 340
Meacham, Harvey, 337, 338, 340
Meek, Joe, 337
Merrill, John, 46
Merritt, Samuel A., 203
Mesplie, Father Toussaint, 58, 59, 60, 65, 176
Methodist Church, 64, 170
Miles, General Nelson A., 279, 310, 329
Millard, H. W., 132
Miller, Rev. G. D. B., 61
Miller, Joaquin, 347-49, 369, 370, 371, 372
Minear, A. P., 42, 99, 100
Missouri House, 118, 139, 220
Montana, 37
Moore, Crawford, 94
Moore, Christopher W., 37, 42, 94, 96, 99, 209, 271, 353, 361, 362
Moravian Church, 63
Mores Creek, 33, 120
Morford, Judge Russell B., 163, 206, 207
Mormons, 22, 52-57, 260, 271, 352, 363-67
Morris, William B., 76
Moulton Building, 185
Moulton, Colonel C. W., 186
Mount Idaho, 23
Munday, Perry, 42
Mundays Ferry, 25, 42
Mullan, John, 72-73
Munson, Captain, 40
Munson, Lyman B., 183
Murphy, Governor John L., 245, 246

Negroes in Idaho, 20, 112, 113, 212
Neil, Governor John B., 267-68
Nesmith, J. W., 375
Newell, Robert, 45
Newspapers, 30, 31, 93, 125-34
Nez Perce County, 45
Nez Perce Indians, 23, 57, 276, 262, 277, 278, 279, 283, 291, 309, 340
Noggle, Judge David, 127, 128, 146, 191-94, 196, 200, 201, 205
North Idaho, 23, 24
Northern Pacific Railroad, 22, 72, 198
Northwest Company, 24
Northwestern Stage Company, 75, 77, 100, 214-20
Nye, William H., 221

Oldham, Joel B., 43, 46, 201
Olds Ferry, 24, 25, 158, 159, 380
Oregon, 36, 37, 69, 205
Oregon Indian wars, 36
Oregon Short Line, 22, 84, 98, 99
Oregon Steam Navigation Company, 24, 343, 369
Oro Fino Conference, 372-78, 399
Ostner, Charles L., 183
Overland Hotel, 21, 65, 68, 122, 123, 148, 164, 194, 195, 209, 212, 221, 234
Overland Stages, 89, 95
Owyhee Avalanche, 31, 77, 131-34, 152

Palmer, General Joel, 336, 338, 339, 342
Parker, Dr. Samuel, 77
Parks, Samuel C., 223, 370
Parks, James, 163-65, 166
Patterson, Ferdinand S., 170
Pauncefoot, George, 107-09
Payette Vigilance, 165, 166, 171
Payne, Dolphus, 223, 378
Paynes Ferry, 89

Peck, Henry, 53
Pierce, Captain E. D., 380
Pinkham, Joseph, 183
Pinkham, Sumner, 170
Pioneerville, Idaho, 46
Pixley, Minnie and Annie, 104
Plummer, Henry, 169
Plummer, Professor, 110
Pomeroy, Mark M., 31
Pony Express, 93
Population of Idaho, 20, 276
Porter, Captain J. W., 289, 290
Portland, Oregon, 37, 95, 101, 135, 181, 233, 259
Poulin, Father A. Z., 58
Powell, Major J. W., 355
Preston, H. L., 204, 214, 215, 219
Prices in Idaho Territory, 38, 39, 40, 79
Prickett, Judge Henry E., 137, 148, 203, 212, 213, 214, 216, 217, 218
Public Land Office of Boise, 20, 28

Ranney, Thomas, 183
Raymond, J. A., 46
Raymond, Reuben, 166, 168
Reed, Sam, 24
Reed, Thomas M., 45
Resumption Act, 1879, 34
Reynolds, A. H., 380
Reynolds, James S., 31, 125-31, 160, 168, 190, 192, 193, 194, 243, 244
Rich, General C. C., 53, 54, 55
Riggs, Rev. Alfred, 310, 311
Riggs, Boise, 221, 222
Riggs, H. C., 180, 181
Roatman, N. C., 46
Robie, A. H., 25
Robbins, Orlando, 292, 293
Rocky Bar, Idaho, 82, 134, 171, 337
Rodgers, Jimmy, 92
Roseborough, Joseph, 203, 204
Ross, Colonel, 375
Rossi, A., 45, 183
Roth, Dan, 351
Rousseau, Rev. Louis, 59

Sacramento News, 31
Sag Witch, 306, 309
St. Michael's Church, 51, 61, 62, 64, 65
Salmon City, 22
Salt Lake City, 42, 78, 308
Salt Lake *Tribune*, 31
San Francisco, 26, 34, 37, 38, 50, 74, 92, 100, 130
San Francisco *Chronicle*, 31
Savage, Austin, 147-51
Scott, General Winfield, 66
Schofield, Major General John M., 122
Schurz, Carl, 263, 264, 265
Schwatka, Frederick, 45
Shafer, Judge J. K., 144
Sharp, John, 363
Shea, John G., 59
Sheridan, General Philip Henry, 153
Sherman, General W. T., 60, 122, 123, 124
Shoshone, 25, 26
Shoshone Falls, 20
Shoshone Lake, 24
Shoup, Governor George L., 7, 226, 274
Sickles, Theophilis, 97, 98, 99
Silver City, Idaho, 27, 38, 42, 49, 52, 58, 61, 68, 73, 80, 82, 83, 96, 99, 100, 103, 120, 121, 131, 151, 152, 153, 154, 165, 203, 209, 210, 236, 237, 303, 373
Simmons, Frederick H., 45
Sinclair, Captain James, 178, 181, 182, 295
Slade, William, 46
Slocum Hall, 102, 104

Smith, Alexander C., 194-96, 223
Smith, C. DeWitt, 236
Smith, George A., 54
Smith, I. N., 205, 206, 207
Smithsonian Institution, 232, 265, 353
Snake River, 24, 25, 95, 97, 135, 151, 152, 223, 350, 380, 381, 387
Soda Springs, Idaho, 53
Sonna, Peter, 50, 136, 138
South Mountain, 154
Spadling, Rev. H. H., 277
Springer, Rube, 52
Stanberry, Henry, 246
Stanley, J. W., 337
Stansbury, Captain Howard, 351-52
Sterling, E. C., 234
Stevens, Isaac Ingalls, 72, 277
Stevenson, Governor Edward A., 182, 226, 273-74
Stilts, George, 113, 114, 115, 116, 117, 118, 119, 120
Stout, James, 155-58, 193
Street, Henry C., 160
Stuart, Granville, 341

Taxes, 40, 41
Tevis, Lloyd, 73
The Dalles, Oregon, 25, 26, 37, 59, 77, 126, 235, 380
Thompson, Allan, 258, 292
Thompson, David P., 258-60, 291
Thompson, W. P., 36, 37
Tidal Wave, 132, 183
Tilden, Samuel J., 99
Timothy, 23
Tracy, William, 179, 180, 181
Trotter, Charles, 89
Trotter, William, 89
Tuttle, Joe, 82, 162
Tuttle, Bishop Daniel Sylvester, 61, 62
Tutwiler, James, 95
Twitchell, George H., 183

Umatilla, Oregon, 24, 74, 79, 84, 94, 97, 235

Union Pacific Railroad, 38, 94, 96, 97, 98, 99
Updyke, David, 162, 164, 165, 166, 167, 171
Utah Northern Railway, 19

Van Slyf, W. H., 103
Vogel, Peter, 179, 180, 181

Wages in Idaho Territory, 38, 39
Wagner, Dr. Clinton, 214, 221, 296, 301, 302-04
Walker, George B., 372, 373
Wallace, Governor William H., 185, 198, 223, 226, 227-31, 232, 372, 373, 374, 375, 376, 377, 378, 397, 398, 399, 401
Walters, Sim, 175, 176, 177, 178
Wasson, Joseph, 132
Weaver, Rev., 63, 64
Wells, Daniel H., 364
Wells, Fargo, 37, 80, 93, 152
West, John, 112
Western Union Telegraph Company, 100, 101
Wheeler, Zenos, 209
White Pine mines, 9
Whitman, Rev. Marcus, 57, 277, 337
Whitson, Judge W. C., 193, 194, 200, 201
Wickizer, Colonel John H., 78
Wilkerson, Billy, 104-07
Willamette Transportation Company, 26
Williams, George H., 242, 243, 246, 247, 336
Winnemucca, Nevada, 22, 73, 77, 79, 82, 96, 99, 132
Winters Station, 342-46
Wood, George L., 336
Wood, James W., 176
Woodson, Silas, 198

Young, Brigham, 54, 55, 148, 365, 366
Young, John, 120

Zion's Co-operative Mercantile Institution, 54

38334 ST. MARY'S COLLEGE OF MARYLAND
ST. MARY'S CITY, MARYLAND